CHARLOTTENGRAD

Charlottengrad

Russian Culture in Weimar Berlin

Roman Utkin

THE UNIVERSITY OF WISCONSIN PRESS

Publication of this book was made possible, in part, by a grant from
the First Book Subvention Program of the Association for Slavic,
East European, and Eurasian Studies.

The University of Wisconsin Press
728 State Street, Suite 443
Madison, Wisconsin 53706
uwpress.wisc.edu

Copyright © 2023
The Board of Regents of the University of Wisconsin System
All rights reserved. Except in the case of brief quotations embedded in critical
articles and reviews, no part of this publication may be reproduced, stored in a
retrieval system, transmitted in any format or by any means—digital, electronic,
mechanical, photocopying, recording, or otherwise—or conveyed via the Internet or
a website without written permission of the University of Wisconsin Press.
Rights inquiries should be directed to rights@uwpress.wisc.edu.

Printed in the United States of America
This book may be available in a digital edition.

Library of Congress Cataloging-in-Publication Data
Names: Utkin, Roman, author.
Title: Charlottengrad : Russian culture in Weimar Berlin / Roman Utkin.
Description: Madison, Wisconsin : The University of Wisconsin Press, [2023] |
Includes bibliographical references and index.
Identifiers: LCCN 2022049612 | ISBN 9780299344405 (hardcover)
Subjects: LCSH: Russians—Germany—Berlin—History—20th century. |
Charlottenburg (Berlin, Germany)—History.
Classification: LCC DD867.5.R87 U85 2023 |
DDC 305.8917/109431550904—dc23/eng/20230126
LC record available at https://lccn.loc.gov/2022049612

ISBN 9780299344443 (pbk.)

For Charlie

CONTENTS

List of Illustrations	ix
Acknowledgments	xi
Note on Transliteration and Translation	xvii
Introduction	3
1 Unsentimental Journeys: Berlin as Trial Emigration	23
2 Guides to Berlin: Exiles, Émigrés, and the Left	63
3 Performing Exile: *The Golden Cockerel* at the Berlin State Opera	91
4 Nabokov, Berlin, and the Future of Russian Literature	116
5 Queering the Russian Diaspora	148
Conclusion	176
Appendix: *The Russian Poets Club Meeting Minutes, Berlin, 1928*	181
Notes	195
Bibliography	241
Index	265

ILLUSTRATIONS

Figure 1. Russian Artists' Ball in Berlin, ca. 1924 — 10

Figure 2. "Russian Berlin," 1923 — 16

Figure 3. Cover of *Veshch'/Gegenstand/Objet*, no. 1–2 (1922) — 24

Figure 4. Cover of *Zhar-Ptitsa*, no. 7 (1922) — 25

Figure 5. A view of the Gleisdreieck station in 1902 — 40

Figure 6. Mayakovsky's poem "And Could You?" with Lissitzky's typographical design in *For the Voice* (1923) — 61

Figure 7. Cover of Andrei Bely's *One of the Mansions of the Kingdom of Shades* (1924) — 76

Figure 8. A fragment of a page from *Berliner Illustrirte Zeitung* (1923) picturing Tchelitchew's costume design for *Savonarola* — 103

Figure 9. Pavel Tchelitchew, set design for *The Boyar's Wedding Feast*, Berlin, 1922 — 104

Figure 10. Pavel Tchelitchew, set design for *The Golden Cockerel*, Act Three, 1923 — 107

Figure 11. Pavel Tchelitchew, set design for *The Golden Cockerel*, Act One, 1923 — 109

Figure 12. Pavel Tchelitchew, set design for *The Golden Cockerel*, Act Two, 1923 — 110

Figure 13. Pavel Tchelitchew, costume design for the Tsarina of Shemakha, 1923 — 111

Figure 14. Ivan Bilibin, "Sic transit . . . ," published in *Zhupel*, no. 2 (1905)   114

Figure 15. A fragment of a manuscript showing Evgenia Zalkind's 1928 poem "My zateiali pirushku" with a caricature of Sirin (Nabokov)   121

Figure 16. Aerial view of Berlin from around 1928   126

Figure 17. A courtyard map of the Hakesche Höfe residential buildings in Berlin Mitte   127

Figure 18. A crossword puzzle published in *Rul'* on May 10, 1925   128

Figure 19. Sergey Eisenstein, "Cosy Corner Berlin" (recto verso), ca. 1930   152

Figure 20. Roman Vishniac, *Recalcitrance*, ca. 1929   155

Figure 21. Photograph of Vladimir and Sergey Nabokov with their siblings in 1918   161

Figure 22. Sergey Nabokov's censored letter of November 20, 1925, to Dmitry Shakhovskoy   168

ACKNOWLEDGMENTS

It took a village to complete this book about a city. I am grateful to many friends, colleagues, and scholars who have helped me in myriad ways over the years that it took to conceptualize, research, and write *Charlottengrad*. The first steps toward this project were taken during my first semester of graduate study at Yale. I took concurrently two seminars: one on the leftist avant-gardes in Moscow and Berlin in the interwar period, team-taught by Katerina Clark and Katie Trumpener, and the other on the poetry of Boris Pasternak, taught by Tomas Venclova. Having grown up at the end of the twentieth century in Russia, accustomed to the notion that the word "Soviet" was synonymous with misery, I was stunned to discover for myself the revolutionary avant-gardists' audacious reimagining of the world earlier in the century. In the Pasternak seminar, I rediscovered an admired poet whom I thought I already knew. Following Pasternak's traces in Weimar Berlin, I kept trying to reconcile the distinct traditions of thinking about Russian modernist poetry and the practice of the interwar artistic left with the fact of exile. Although I did not understand it at the time, this effort eventually led me to this book.

My first thanks are to my advisors, mentors, and teachers at Yale. Katerina Clark taught me the importance of letting go of assumptions and offered numerous practical suggestions for improving an earlier version of the manuscript. Her ability to spot a promising argument in the messiest of drafts reassured me that this project was worth pursuing. Katie Trumpener, whose polymathic range alone is a source of inspiration, modeled a comparative approach to Berlin's many legacies. The intellectual rigor and exacting standards of Vladimir Alexandrov, Marijeta Bozovic, Bella Grigoryan,

Harvey Goldblatt, John MacKay, Constantine Muravnik, and Tomas Venclova profoundly influenced my thinking about Slavic languages, literatures, and cultures. I owe the greatest debt to Molly Brunson. This book exists thanks in large part to her editorial precision, professional guidance, distaste for excuses, and scholarly prowess.

The friends I made in graduate school are among my most prized interlocutors and demanding readers. I thank especially Yasha Klots, Maria Hristova, Raisa Sidenova, Dasha Ezerova, Megan Race, Rossen Djagalov, Jamie Gabbarelli, Greg Bryda, Hugh Baran, Viktoria Paranyuk, Carlotta Chenoweth, and Ksenia Sidorenko. Crucially, I had the good fortune to land in a cohort together with Vadim Shneyder and Fabrizio Fenghi, treasured friends and formidable scholars.

After I graduated, I found a warm and supportive atmosphere for advancing this project at Davidson College. Amanda Ewington tirelessly championed my work and guided my entry into the profession. Scott Denham shared his voluminous knowledge of Berlin both on campus and in situ. I cherish the memories of exploring Berlin with our students and colleagues. For their collegiality and all manner of support, professional and personal, I thank especially Laura Sockol, Florin Beschea, Caroline Fache, Alison Bory, Melissa González, Rebecca Joubin, Van Hillard, Katie Horowitz, Kyra Kietrys, Zoran Kuzmanovich, Lia Newman, Maggie McCarthy, Alan Michael Parker, Mark Sample, and Alice Wiemers.

I reconceived and finished this book at Wesleyan University. I owe many thanks to my extraordinary colleagues in the Department of Russian, East European, and Eurasian Studies. Susanne Fusso read the entire manuscript more than once, each time making generous suggestions for improving narrative flow, argumentation, and style. Her expert stewardship of our department and belief in this project ensured its successful completion. Victoria Smolkin read and commented on countless drafts and was readily available to talk candidly through the process of writing and trying to write. The ability to ask Priscilla Meyer any question about Nabokov and receive a prompt and detailed answer is one of the gifts of being at Wesleyan. Her notes on chapter 4 as well as other parts of the book made the project stronger. Irina Aleshkovsky, Natasha Karageorgos, Sergei Bunaev, Peter Rutland, Justine Quijada, Saida Daukeyeva, Sasha Rudensky, Katja Kolcio, and Duffield White have provided valuable insights, directly and indirectly, along the way. An honorary member of our department, the incomparable Yuz Aleshkovsky (1929–2022), took me under his mighty wing the moment I arrived in Middletown and supported me with hearty homecooked meals, profound chats in the banya, and his spicy wit.

I benefited greatly from Joe Siry's talent for discerning and skillfully transcribing one's not-always-coherent attempts to articulate the stakes of one's project. My colleagues in German studies assisted me with multiple translation queries, especially Martin Baeumel and Krishna Winston, who also painstakingly copyedited parts of the manuscript. Iris Bork-Goldfield connected me with key archivists in Berlin. I am also grateful to my colleagues in feminist, gender, and sexuality studies, Victoria Pitts-Taylor, Jennifer Tucker, Lisa Cohen, Natasha Korda, and Margot Weiss, for their intellectual inspiration and generosity of spirit. I am similarly grateful to my co-coordinators of the Queer Studies Research Collective, Michael Meere and Mitali Thakor. On campus and off, I am continuously buoyed by the wisdom and comradeship of Joe Ackley, Marco Aresu, Talia Andrei, Garry Bertholf, Abbie Boggs, Roger Grant, Claire Grace, Anuja Jain, Ren Ellis Neyra, Jesse Nasta, Gabrielle Ponce-Hegenauer, Yaya Simakov, Anya Shatilova, and Avner Shavit. I am a better scholar thanks to the brilliance of Marina Bilbija.

A faculty fellowship at Wesleyan's Center for the Humanities under Natasha Korda's directorship was essential for finishing the book's final chapter. Natasha's expert steerage of our cohort of fellows through the spring semester of 2020, when the COVID-19 pandemic derailed life as we knew it, enabled me to continue working. For that unforgettable intellectual experience, I thank her and my fabulous fellow fellows, Mitali Thakor, Valeria López Fadul, Sally Bachner, Ryan Fics, and Julia Simon-Kerr, as well as the exceptional undergraduate fellows, Maya Bernstein-Schalet, Jessica Brandon, Tara Mitra, and Maggie Rothberg. I am grateful to my student assistants Anne Kiely and Sam Hilton.

Thanks are also due to Ioanna Emy Matesan for organizing a year-long Exile Reading Group. Reading and discussing a set of recent books on exile and diasporas with Emy and Elizabeth Nugent provided much-needed intellectual stimulation during the many months of pandemic-induced uncertainty. Both Emy and Liz also helped me a great deal with framing the introduction. And our conversation with Hisham Matar about his deeply moving memoir rekindled my belief in the value of writing.

I owe a special debt of gratitude to Michael Kunichika, whose boundless generosity helped me push this manuscript across the finish line. In addition to reading each chapter and sharing his expertise, Michael organized a book manuscript review workshop at the Amherst Center for Russian Culture and assembled a remarkable group of scholars to engage with this project. Harsha Ram, Michael Wachtel, Ilya Kalinin, Serguei Oushakine, Dale E. Peterson, Luke Parker, Colleen McQuillen, Daria Khitrova, Evgenii Bershtein, and Irina Paperno read and responded to various parts of the manuscript with rigor and grace. I only wish I could have incorporated all their feedback. Needless to say, all inaccuracies and errors that remain are my own.

These pages were much improved thanks to conversations during, before, and after ASEEES and other more and less academic gatherings with Iaroslava Ananko, Stephen Blackwell, Eliot Borenstein, Julie Cassiday, Vitaly Chernetsky, Ben Dhooge, Robin Ellis, Jennifer Evans, Nila Friedberg, Philip Gleissner, Bradley Gorski, Anna Hájková, Sara Karpukhin, Ostap Kin, Britta Korkowsky, Mark Lipovetsky, Laurie Marhoeffer, Olga Matich, Kevin Moss, Stephen Norris, Stanley Rabinowitz, Kat Reischl, Tom Roberts, Maria Rubins, Jane Sharp, Svetlana Sirotinina, Maria Taroutina, Zara Torlone, José Vergara, Meghan Vicks, Lisa Ryoko Wakamiya, Lizzie Wolf, and Boris Wolfson. Lilya Kaganovsky, Kerry Wallach, Amy Kohout, Jane Taubman, Vasily Rudich, Barbara Harshav, and the late Benjamin Harshav read parts of the manuscript and provided wise counsel at pivotal junctures. Mark Slobin graciously shared the late Greta Slobin's personal library with me; many of the quotes from the primary and secondary sources come from Greta's books.

Words alone cannot describe my gratitude to Polina Barskova, whose compassion, friendship, and encouragement as well as her own writing about cities kept me working on this project in the most challenging of times. I would also like to express my admiration and gratitude to the late Nonna Barskova, who always found the right words.

Parts of this book were presented to audiences at Reed College, Princeton University, the College of William and Mary, the College of Wooster, Hobart and William Smith Colleges, and the Havighurst Center for Russian and Post-Soviet Studies at Miami University—and I thank them for their attention, questions, and interest in my work. Before I could ever contemplate a book project like this, my mentors in Elabuga and Kazan, Svetlana Konradovna Balobanova, Lyudmila Alekseevna Meshchikhina, Astrid Vilfridovna Sharipova, Olga Olegovna Nesmelova, and Natalia Gennadievna Nikolaeva, were instrumental in setting my intellectual trajectory.

It would have been much more difficult, if not impossible, to conduct research without the helpful assistance of librarians and archivists at the

Amherst Center for Russian Culture; Olin Library at Wesleyan; Yale's Beinecke Rare Book and Manuscript Library, the Slavic Reading Room, and Manuscript and Archives at Sterling Memorial Library; E. H. Little Library at Davidson; Bancroft Library at UC Berkeley; Berlin State Library; Berlin Art Library; Robert Havemann Gesellschaft; the Russian State Archive of Literature and Art; and the Slavonic Library of the National Library of Finland. I would like to thank especially Nadezhda Spivak, Tatjana Lorkovic, Anna Arays, Moira Fitzgerald, Ingrid Lennon-Pressey, Christoph Stamm, and Irina Lukka. Edward Kasinec, Robert Davis, and Tanya Chebotarev shared helpful advice at an early stage of this project, and Doris Liebermann did the same at the final stage.

At the University of Wisconsin Press, Gwen Walker showed an early and enthusiastic interest in *Charlottengrad*. I am grateful to acquisitions editor Amber Cederström for her patient guidance and impeccable professionalism. I extend thanks to the editorial and production teams, most especially Judith Robey, Sheila McMahon, and Jennifer Conn. I was very lucky with my anonymous readers, who revealed their names after the process was complete—my deepest thanks to Catherine Ciepiela and Kevin M. F. Platt for reading the manuscript with great care and offering detailed insights for improvement, both practical and conceptual.

I gratefully acknowledge the material support in the form of grants and fellowships that I received to research and write this book. Early research was supported by the Beinecke Rare Book and Manuscript Library Research Fellowship, the Nina Berberova Fellowship, the Keggi-Berzins Fellowship for Baltic Studies, and the Yale University Dissertation Fellowship. The Faculty Study and Research Grants at Davidson enabled several research trips to Germany. A summer residency at the Jordan Center for the Advanced Study of Russia at New York University allowed for weeks of uninterrupted writing. The Hess Faculty Seminar at the United States Holocaust Memorial Museum was instrumental in completing the final chapter. I am not sure what I would have done without the ongoing support extended to me at the Amherst Center for Russian Culture. Finally, at Wesleyan, I received generous research funds and a semester-long sabbatical leave. At the very final stage, Roger Grant and Demetrius Eudell contributed generously toward book production from their coffers as Deans of Division I and II, respectively. I would like to thank Debbie Pozzetti, Joy Vodak, Vanessa Victor, and Meg Sawicki for their help with administering funds and processing countless reimbursement receipts.

For their help in securing copyright permissions or with finding copyright holders, I thank Petr Pasternak, Alexander Kuznetsov, Pavel Melyakov, and Molly Thomasy Blasing as well as the staff at Landesarchiv Berlin, the Wiley Agency LLC, the Magnes Collection of Jewish Art and Life at UC Berkeley, and Actes Sud Publishing. An earlier version of chapter 3 appeared in the *Slavic and East European Journal*, and I thank editorial assistant Dane Reighard for his swift permission to reproduce that material here.

My family on both sides of the Atlantic reminded me of the virtues of life beyond the confines of academia, while loving and supporting me unconditionally. Spasibo, Mama, Artyom, and Artur. Thank you, Jeff and Prue. A special word of thanks is due to Aunt Di, whose opinion of scholarly prose kept me on my toes. How I wish I could show this book to my late father, who would have been proud beyond compare. But there would be no book at all without Charles Gershman.

~

This book was finished before Russia's full-scale invasion of Ukraine in February 2022. It goes into production as a once-unthinkable war is still raging. Berlin is once again a major center for Russian and Russophone culture in exile. I leave it to future readers to determine whether there are analogies and historical rhymes between Berlin's émigré communities of 2023 and those of 1923.

NOTE ON TRANSLITERATION AND TRANSLATION

I have used a modified Library of Congress system of transliterating Cyrillic when spelling Russian names in the main text and notes (with standard transliteration in the citations and bibliographic entries). First and last names normally transliterated with the ending -yi/-ii are given the ending -y (e.g., Anatoly Lunacharsky). The ending -oi is rendered -oy (Dmitry Shakhovskoy, Alexey Tolstoy). For names such as Fedor, Nikolai, Sergei, and Semen, I use the spellings Fyodor, Nikolay, Sergey, and Semyon. I render the names Aleksandr, Aleksandra, Aleksei, and Maksim as Alexander, Alexandra, Alexey, and Maxim. Names ending in -iia are simplified to -ia (Evgenia), and soft signs are dropped. In some cases, though, I have used established spellings or modified transliterations (e.g., Ilya Ehrenburg, Andrei Bely, Marc Chagall, Vera Lourié, Véra Nabokov, El Lissitzky, Yuri Tynianov, and Pavel Tchelitchew). All translations are my own unless noted otherwise.

CHARLOTTENGRAD

Introduction

Жди: резкий ветер дунет в окарино
По скважинам громоздкого Берлина—

И грубый день взойдет из-за домов
Над мачехой российских городов.

Wait: the brisk wind will blow into an ocarina,
through the keyholes of heavy Berlin—

and a rude day will rise from behind the houses
above the stepmother of Russian cities.

—Vladislav Khodasevich, "All is made of stone..."

"A Visit to Berlin for Everyone!"—*Jeder einmal in Berlin!*—declared an advertisement slogan promoted by Berlin's municipal tourist agency in the 1920s. For hundreds of thousands of Russian-speaking travelers, this catchy phrase became a lived reality, though they rarely arrived in Berlin as tourists. Most of them found refuge in Berlin in the aftermath of the 1917 revolutions and the civil war in what had been the Russian Empire. Historians estimate that the total number of these individuals in Berlin ranged from 100,000 to 500,000 between 1921 and 1925, at one time accounting for one tenth of Berlin's entire population.[1] Situated primarily in the borough of Charlottenburg, this expatriate colony was sometimes dubbed Charlottengrad.[2]

Over a million Russian subjects found themselves abroad in the years following the events of 1917. Some fled for their lives; others were exiled. Some were former prisoners of war, vacationers stranded in foreign countries by imperial breakdowns all over Europe, diplomats of the old and new regimes, foreign correspondents, students, and entrepreneurs of all sorts. Some returned to now-Soviet Russia, but the majority did not and came to be known collectively as Russia-out-of-Russia or Russia Abroad.[3] Charlottengrad, or Russian Berlin, was one of its early and key centers.

The historian Marc Raeff has defined Russia Abroad as a "'society' exiled from its homeland in another 'country' without physical or legal borders."[4] A core assumption about this imagined nation is that its members stood in opposition to communism as both a bastion of social conservatism and an arena of artistic freedom unavailable in Russia proper. It is generally understood that these émigrés "cultivated a rather idealized image of prerevolutionary Russia, remained strongly opposed to the Bolshevik regime, and saw their main mission as working towards its collapse (for some this went as far as supporting Hitler against Stalin during World War II)."[5] When we consider the legacy of Russia Abroad in relationship to its major cities, however, we discover a more complicated, dramatic, and rewarding story, not captured by the familiar communist/anticommunist and exile/homeland dichotomies.[6] The collapse of empire, the rise of large-scale statelessness, and the frequency of international encounters and clashes spurred a wealth of artistic responses that represent a variety of political agendas, national allegiances, and artistic experiments. The primary conduit for these responses was the experience of metropolitan life.

This book tells the story of Charlottengrad by examining the Russian cultural presence in Weimar-era Berlin, the "stepmother of Russian cities," as the poet Vladislav Khodasevich nicknamed it in the 1923 poem quoted in the epigraph at the beginning of this chapter.[7] The metaphor is a twist on the medieval description of Kyiv as the "mother of Russian cities."[8] This famous twelfth-century phrase translates more accurately as "the mother of the towns of Rus,'" but the linguistic ambiguity inherent in the word "Rus'" and related nouns in Russian works to modern Russia's historiographic advantage, allowing for the Moscow-centric view of Kyiv as the cradle of Russian civilization. Khodasevich's comparison of Berlin to Kyiv thus serves to highlight the extraordinary importance of Berlin for Russian postrevolutionary culture.

As if recognizing the tension in historical translation, though, Khodasevich implicitly probes the term "Russian" in his poem. He calls Berlin the stepmother of "rossiiskikh," not "russkikh" cities. The nuance disappears in English, as both adjectives translate as "Russian," but "rossiiskikh" emphasizes the Russian state, while "russkikh" denotes ethnicity. By using the former qualifier, Khodasevich subtly underscores that in its role as a stepmother, Berlin shelters (former) Russian imperial subjects, but not all of them are necessarily ethnically Russian. The son of a Polish father and Jewish mother, Khodasevich elaborated the idea of his own cultural identity as a Russian through the notions of orphanhood and adoption in his other poems from this period. In Berlin exile, Russia itself becomes a stepmother.⁹

To quote Viktor Shklovsky, there were "three hundred thousand Russians of various nationalities" roaming Berlin's streets.¹⁰ Another Russian Berliner, Vadim Andreev, described in his memoirs boarding-house communal meals at which "everyone spoke Russian but with the most diverse accents—Jewish, Caucasian, German, Ukrainian, and God knows what others."¹¹ Indeed, Berlin's larger expatriate community represented a colorful patchwork of ethnic groups large and small with ties to the collapsed Russian Empire, as is demonstrated especially well in the vibrant scholarship on the intersection of ethnic and national identities in Yiddish and Hebrew modernisms.¹² Recognizing the diversity of this community and without implying a causal link between language and national identity, in my account of "Russian culture in Weimar Berlin," "Russian" stands primarily for Russophone.

The fraught complexity of defining the meanings of "Russian" in Charlottengrad at once captures and problematizes the concepts of kinship, modernity, and nationhood. How do poets, writers, and artists maintain a sense of (national) belonging while displaced in Berlin, the capital of a country that had just waged a war—the first world war—against their homeland? What does it mean to be Russian—culturally, politically, institutionally—when the Russia of old no longer exists? Crucially, Khodasevich's metaphor of Berlin as a stepmother captures the spatiotemporal conditions under which twentieth-century Russian culture was undergoing a split—a divorce—into distinct cultural modalities. From the contemporary vantage point, two of those modalities appeared to be developing, one in the Soviet Union and the other in Russia Abroad. Yet such a teleology, tied as it is to national and ideological mythmaking, obscures the view of Berlin in its geographical, political, and cultural position as the most in-between and liminal space for Russians in the interwar period, wherein multiple possibilities of cultural development lay, and the very idea of Russianness was pried open and constantly renegotiated.

The separation of Russian culture into "Soviet" and "émigré" branches has become a foundational premise for characterizations of the Russophone world in the twentieth century. But this separation was by no means instantaneous, tidy, or definitive. Any such binary holds true only insofar as it offers a convenient shorthand for acknowledging that the Bolshevik takeover in October 1917 had brought irreparable changes to Russian culture and society. While the year 1917 indubitably marks a crucial turning point, its status as an epochal divider of mythic proportions developed as a tool for advancing competing ideological worldviews, as Leonid Livak has shown in his study of Russian modernism.[13] Both the Bolsheviks and their opponents utilized the narrative that 1917 occasioned a clean break with the past; the difference lay in how positively or negatively they interpreted the events of that year. Until at least the mid-1920s, it was unclear whether and for how long the Soviet experiment would last, and many Russians abroad harbored hopes of returning home. As time went on, however, the Soviet Union and Russia Abroad became increasingly defined as distinct and mutually exclusive spaces of Russophone culture.[14]

In his pioneering 1956 study, *Russian Literature in Exile*, the literary scholar and émigré Gleb Struve observed that Russian Berlin represented "the juncture of two literatures."[15] A product of the Cold War polarization, Struve's book assumes a certain degree of coherence in Russian cultures on both sides of the Iron Curtain. But before the Iron Curtain became a geopolitical phenomenon, the radical opposition of the Soviet Union and Russia Abroad was but one possible historical scenario. The Russian religious philosopher Nikolay Berdyaev, for example, announced in 1924 the end of modern history and the arrival of a new Middle Ages in his best-selling book *The New Middle Ages*. "The road just ahead will be dark and weary: mankind must pass through a period of difficulty before the new day dawns," Berdyaev wrote.[16] The shape of the future new day remained unknown.

Although Struve reduces the kaleidoscopic intricacy of postrevolutionary Russian culture to "two literatures," his idea of Berlin embodying a "juncture" (styk) of various cultural trajectories rings true. The present book focuses on this very juncture, exploring the ways in which Russian writers, artists, and intellectuals living in Weimar-era Berlin negotiated their own spaces, roles, and understandings of themselves as being "apart together" during this German city's tumultuous and culturally complex period. As a "stepmother of all Russian cities," Charlottengrad was less a nurturer or incubator than a symbol of displacement—a substitute for a native city, a resented haven. Its Russian stepchildren, among them Boris Pasternak, Marina Tsvetaeva, Viktor Shklovsky, Marc Chagall, and Vladimir Nabokov, also described Berlin in memorable ways—as a transfer train station, a garrison barrack, a zoo, a caravanserai, a department store, and a living hell.[17]

These metaphors evoke the image of Weimar Berlin as the depraved and deprived metropolis the German Expressionists recorded, because that same Berlin contained Russian Berlin. Whereas alienation from one's immediate environment functioned as a marker of modern cosmopolitan belonging for the German modernists and many others, it was largely a byproduct of life in a foreign city for Russian Berliners. Unlike, say, American writers of the Lost Generation in Paris, who valorized (self-)exile for its artistic potential, their Russian contemporaries were in a much more precarious position. Among them were émigrés who left Russia deliberately, political exiles whom the Bolsheviks banished, and refugees driven from their homeland by the ongoing armed conflict. Restricted in their ability to travel, they experienced firsthand such stereotypical traits of modernism as "unsettlement, homelessness, solitude and impoverished independence."[18]

Drawing on archival research in Germany, Russia, and the United States, *Charlottengrad* elucidates the crucial period during which Russian cultural dynamics abroad were most dynamic—when individuals changed their minds about staying abroad or returning to Russia and formed identities capacious enough to be artistically generative without hard and fast political labels, at least for some time.

Exiles, Émigrés, Squatters

Viktor Shklovsky, after a little over a year in Berlin, alluded to the inadequacy of the terms "emigration," "émigré," and "exile" to characterize the community of displaced Russians. In his novel *Zoo, or Letters Not about Love* (1923), Shklovsky wrote, "We are refugees. No, not refugees, but fugitives and now squatters."[19] The abbreviated syntax of this sentence and the use of "squatters" (sidel'tsy) to describe Russians in Berlin captures their uncertain position in the space between emigration, which denotes departure (usually for good) from the home country, and immigration, which means entrance into a new state. The word "exile" (izgnanie) brims with pathos in Russian—as does "scattering" (rasseianie)—and these terms gain prominence a little later, mostly among conservative émigrés.[20] Before 1917, being an "émigré" was associated with seeking political refuge abroad for plotting to undermine and overthrow the tsarist autocracy; let us recall that Bolshevism was born in emigration.[21] After the triumph of those revolutionary emigres in 1917, the terms "emigrant" and "emigration" began to denote individuals who were living abroad because they were unable or unwilling to stay in Soviet Russia.[22] Shklovsky's metaphoric description of his compatriots as squatters in Berlin alludes to their cultural (and legal) difference and suggests that their experience of modernity, registered in art and literature, was also different from that of their German contemporaries.

Most Russian subjects who found themselves abroad had to leave the former Russian Empire under conditions of coercion—political, financial, or psychological. Therefore, I use the terms "exiles" and "émigrés" interchangeably, even though, technically speaking, the term "exile" implies forced and politically motivated migration, and the term "émigré" emphasizes agency in one's decision to move abroad.[23] Perhaps because coercion is implicitly understood in both, the terms "exile" and "émigré" are traditionally used interchangeably in Anglophone scholarship as well. In Russian, the preferred term is "émigrés," or "emigranty." But as will be apparent in chapter 2, not everyone wanted to adopt the term "émigré" for self-appellation.

Externally, Russian refugees presented an unprecedented diasporic formation that posed the modern problem of statelessness. The League of Nations responded by instituting in 1922 the "Nansen Passport," which enabled stateless individuals to cross borders and protected them from deportation, but without granting them citizenship. In view of their qualifying for this relative privilege, Hannah Arendt later referred to the Russian émigrés as the "aristocracy" of all European stateless persons during the interwar period.[24]

By the time High Commissioner for Refugees Fridtjof Nansen undertook to solve the European refugee crisis, Russians had already dispersed all over the world. Berlin was one among many cities that harbored displaced Russians in the aftermath of the 1917 events. Major émigré clusters sprang up in Belgrade, Sofia, Istanbul, San Francisco, London, Cairo, Prague, Harbin, and Paris. Each city acquired a specific diasporic flair.[25] Belgrade, Sofia, and Cairo became the strongholds of the "White" army veterans defeated by the "Reds" during the Russian civil war. Istanbul constituted a large hub for all those escaping the civil war via Crimea and the Black Sea. San Francisco offered a destination for the refugees fleeing Russia through the Far East. London and Copenhagen sheltered surviving Russian royals. Prague formed the nucleus of Russian academic life in exile, taking on the character of a university town. Harbin had become a Russian outpost in northeastern China long before the Revolution—after which it grew in size and influence. Paris, a perennial magnet for artists and writers, in the 1920s also offered numerous employment opportunities to unskilled immigrant laborers.

In 1921–24, Berlin became a crossroads in a way that the other cities did not and a meeting place for the civil war's losers and winners alike—a transitional place where political views could be renegotiated and artistic practices tested. Crucially, the Berlin experience shows that Russian culture outside Russia developed not linearly but as a series of encounters that seem extraordinary from today's vantage point. While the literary critic Yuly Aikhenvald was lecturing at Berlin's Russian Scientific Institute, funded by the YMCA, his son, the leading Marxist economist Alexander Aikhenvald, was attempting to persuade him to return to Moscow, in vain. In Berlin, Boris Pasternak published the second edition of his major poetry collection, *My Sister—Life* (*Sestra moia—zhizn'*), which propelled him to fame while he was trying to decide whether to stay abroad as his parents and sisters had or to return. For a few years, Berlin functioned as a giant publishing house that supplied both the diasporic and Soviet markets.[26] The printing infrastructure made possible a proliferation of journals and magazines, the most daring of which was the trilingual *Veshch'/Gegenstand/Objet*, edited by the writer Ilya Ehrenburg and the artist El Lissitzky. Perhaps the most promising project was *Colloquy* (*Beseda*), conceived by none other than Maxim Gorky, eventually canonized as the founding father of Soviet literature but living in exile near Berlin in 1921–24. His journal—aimed at informing readers in Russia about literary, philosophical, and technological developments elsewhere in the world—failed spectacularly: despite encouraging abundant print runs, Soviet officials never allowed it to be imported and thereby bankrupted the publisher. Another important Berlin journal of the early 1920s, *The Russian Book* (*Russkaia kniga*), and its successor *The New Russian Book* (*Novaia russkaia kniga*), edited by the Moscow lawyer Alexander Yashchenko, served as a public bulletin board where one could find information about contemporary writers and about books published in Berlin and in Russia, in addition to literary essays and summaries of newspapers from both sides of the border.

Social life was just as colorful. Picture the Soviet celebrity poet Sergey Esenin and his wife, the American dancer Isadora Duncan, bar-hopping with the budding composer Nicolas Nabokov, whose family had lost most of its vast fortune after the Revolution.[27] Or consider the photograph of a "Russian Artists' Ball" with Ehrenburg in the lower right corner and the poet Vera Lourié sitting on Lissitzky's lap. Later in life, Lourié would say that during this time Ehrenburg was a "Soviet Russian" and had nothing to do with the émigrés.[28] In the center of this festive gathering we see the Berlin publisher Abram Vishniak, who was about to be immortalized in Marina Tsvetaeva's poetry after their tumultuous love affair in Berlin (fig. 1).[29] What may not be visible in this snapshot is the queer life of Russian Berliners. Indeed, Charlottengrad brought together many queer cultural producers. Their strategies of self-representation, previously unknown or simply

Figure 1. Russian Artists' Ball in Berlin, ca. 1924. Berlinische Galerie—Museum of Modern Art, Photography and Architecture; Artists' Archives; BG-Ar 22/91,2.

ignored, can tell us much about belonging in exile, as will be discussed in chapters 3 and 5.

Poets of all sorts gathered in the city's cafés, such as the Prager Diele on the Prager Platz and Café Landgraf in Kurfürstenstraße 75.[30] Café Leon on the Nollendorfplatz hosted the House of the Arts, a club modeled on Dom Iskusstv or DISK in Petrograd. Berlin's House of the Arts, where Vladimir Mayakovsky, Andrei Bely, and Vladislav Khodasevich read their poetry, declared itself above political differences. Remembering this social milieu later, Chagall said that in 1922 Berlin was a place where aristocrats, miracle-working rabbis, and Constructivist artists crossed paths.[31] Comparing Berlin to Paris of the 1930s and New York of the 1940s, Chagall added, "at times it seemed that we lived in a dream and at others, in a nightmare."[32] From Dovid Bergelson's Yiddish prose we learn that in a Berlin boarding house the victim and the perpetrator of a pogrom might occupy rooms across the hall from each other.[33] The White Guard general Alexey von Lampe paints a less horrifying but equally surreal picture of Berlin's communal living in his memoirs: "Here there was a former director of a ship's chandlers, with his family, a sportsman, a landowner, a property owner from Ekaterinburg, the owner of the house where the family of the tsar was lodged and murdered, a forceful police captain from the imperial Duma, belonging to the Guards regiment, with his estranged wife, a ballerina who now worked in a second-hand bookshop. There was a lady singer from the St. Petersburg music theatre, a film commission agent who showed the young ladies how to dance the foxtrot. Anyone and everyone was here. It's impossible to enumerate them all."[34]

This unlikely cultural ecosystem was made possible by a diplomatic rapprochement between the Weimar Republic and Soviet Russia. The Treaty of Rapallo, signed on Easter Sunday, 1922, freed both republics from all territorial and financial claims against each other that had been pending since the Treaty of Brest-Litovsk, which had ended Russia's participation in World War I. The 1922 treaty gave Russian subjects a legal route from Russia to other European countries through Germany—a significant benefit for ordinary citizens. (Travelers could reach Berlin by water via Szczecin, by rail via Riga, and by air via Königsberg with DeRuLuft, a German-Russian airline that operated from 1922 to 1937.) Russia had been ostracized after the Bolshevik takeover and diplomatically cut off from the rest of the world. Germany was likewise a pariah up to this point, stung and shamed as the perpetrator of World War I by the Treaty of Versailles. The new alliance improved Russia's international standing, much to the chagrin of the Entente Powers, and turned Berlin into a major travel and trade hub between Russia and the West.

Financial circumstances also played a key role in drawing Russians to Berlin. In postwar Germany's ravaged economy, travelers with foreign currency or valuable possessions they could trade or sell found Berlin exceedingly affordable. During the infamous hyperinflation of the early 1920s, money was not worth the paper it was printed on, unless it was a dollar, which was worth millions of marks. In September 1922, the artist Pavel Tchelitchew wrote to his sister, "Everything in Berlin is getting very expensive. I just don't understand it, the German mark seems to be getting stronger, but the prices of goods are growing unimaginably high . . . in August a pair of shoes cost 1,500, but the same pair of shoes now costs 8–10,000—it looks as though everything will have unreal prices soon."[35] Diamonds, pearls, furs, rugs, rare postage stamps, gold cigarette cases, precious decorative trifles, and other easily transportable luxury items fueled Charlottengrad's economy, as the advertisement supplements of Berlin's Russian-language dailies make clear. The diplomatic and financial infrastructure rendered Berlin a predetermined destination, in most cases chosen out of necessity, not desire.

Why Berlin?

Paris has been the focal point of much of the scholarship on modernist culture in general and on Russian émigré culture in particular.[36] After World War I, major European cities provided vibrant, complex, and cosmopolitan spaces for conversations and collaborations that were unavailable elsewhere. As Raymond Williams suggests, the city allowed "a sophistication of social relations, supplemented in the most important cases—Paris, above all—by exceptional liberties of expression.... Within the new kind of open, complex and mobile society, small groups in any form of divergence or dissent could find some kind of foothold."[37] Before Paris evolved into the capital of Russia Abroad around 1925, Berlin was the most important center of Russian culture outside Russia that offered opportunities for a wide range of dissenting groups to flourish.

It is perhaps ironic that Berlin gained such prominence in the artistic imagination of its Russian residents in the early twentieth century. After all, the city had no notable medieval or early modern past and gained stature chiefly as the capital of a recently unified Germany and a site of accelerated industrial modernization. While the Weimar Republic is unimaginable without Berlin, it was chartered, symbolically and deliberately, in Weimar, famed for Goethe and Schiller's friendship and collaboration, which produced German Classicism.[38] As the Russian Berliner Roman Gul wrote in 1927, Berlin was truly famous for "the Ufa movie theaters with the magnificent 'Ufa-Palast am Zoo'; radio towers; natural gas storage tanks; the Junkers, Siemens, and Schwarzkopf factories; electric trains; underground trains; bars; and dance halls."[39] What it lacked in the elegance and beauty of Paris, Vienna, or London and in the political vanguardism of Petersburg or Moscow, Berlin compensated for with its urgent modernity—as a frontier of the industrial revolution, of social democracy, and of large-scale migration from the crumbling Russian Empire.

While there were already thousands of Russians in Berlin before the Treaty of Rapallo, mainly monarchists and other anti-Bolshevik émigrés, the improvement in German-Soviet relations and the attendant fresh influx of Russians made Berlin's Russian contingent much more diverse politically and culturally. Some came to Berlin voluntarily for official and private reasons, on the one hand. Khodasevich, for example, came as a representative of the Soviet Ministry of Education (Narkompros). Chagall secured an exit permit through his Narkompros connections. On the other hand, Soviet authorities exiled in fall 1922 scores of intellectuals the government deemed untrustworthy and potentially counterrevolutionary. Because many of these intellectuals were philosophers or philosophically minded thinkers, such as Nikolay Berdyaev, Nikolay Lossky, Ivan Ilyin, Pitirim Sorokin, and Fyodor Stepun, the ship that carried them to Germany became known as the Philosophy Steamer.[40] Despite being exiled, many of these influential thinkers remained committed to the ideal of Russia's revolutionary transformation. Without subscribing to the communist worldview, they were critical of the anti-Bolshevik Whites and pushed back against other émigrés' depictions of total devastation in Russia. Pavel Miliukov, the leader of the Constitutional Democrats and a prominent émigré, called the passengers of the Berlin-bound Philosophy Steamer "Russia No. 2½," meaning that their views landed them somewhere beyond both Russia No. 1 (Bolshevik Russia) and Russia No. 2 (Russia Abroad), where they constituted half of a third alternative.[41]

The Change of Landmarks (Smena vekh) movement, established in 1921, made Russian Berlin even more heterogeneous. The movement's title refers to a provocative 1909 collection of articles, *Landmarks* (*Vekhi*), which reappraised the role of Russia's intelligentsia in the revolutionary movement following the failure of the 1905 Revolution. The adherents of the Change of Landmarks, who were especially active in Berlin, urged the émigrés to reconcile with the Bolsheviks, return to Russia, and join in the effort to make utopia a reality.[42] The Soviet government welcomed this initiative, as the country needed skilled professionals to advance the New Economic Policy that had replaced war communism.[43] While moderately successful in meeting this goal, the Change of Landmarks fractured further an already divided Russian Berlin. The émigré writer of aristocratic background Alexey N. Tolstoy, the future triple recipient of the Stalin Prize, publicly and shockingly announced his support of the Bolsheviks by publishing in the movement's newspaper, *On the Eve* (*Nakanune*). Tolstoy's high-profile conversion earned him the nickname of the "Red Count" and made it exceedingly difficult for everyone else to maintain any semblance of political neutrality.[44] The movement's activity was met with hostility by radical monarchists and liberal émigrés alike. Maxim Gorky dismissed the proponents of the Change of Landmarks as "'bourgeois' writers who knew nothing of realities inside Soviet Russia."[45] As a result, though, among the centers of Russia Abroad, Berlin embodied a unique site of encounter for itinerants of all stripes. Nowhere else were the divergent understandings of Russia, its past, present, and future, argued as vehemently and changed as dramatically as in Berlin of the early 1920s.⁴⁶

Charlottengrad—the Capital of Russia No. 2½

This book focuses on Berlin as the capital of this Russia No. 2½—as a space of multiple cultural and political possibilities that bridges the rigid opposites of Soviet Russia and Russia Abroad. In telling the story of Charlottengrad, I trace the variety of ways literature and art sustained connections to Russia, real and imagined. One of the great challenges of this task involves the continuous transformation of Russian culture abroad: the evolution of viewpoints and of the semantic charge of the terms "émigré," "Soviet," and "Russian" as descriptors of individuals and works of art. To grasp these nuances, my book explores not only the aesthetic premises but also the cultural networks that underlay much of the cultural activity of this time.

The First Exhibition of Russian Art, which took place in Berlin's Van Diemen Gallery in fall 1922, was pivotal. The show brought together an astonishing one thousand items, including nineteenth-century realist paintings and the latest avant-garde abstract compositions. Organized to raise money for famine relief in Russia's Volga region, the exhibition was a highly successful collaborative venture between Narkompros and the German Foreign Office.⁴⁷ The emphasis on "first" and "Russian" (rather than "Soviet") in the exhibition's title suggests an argument in itself: there can be only one true Russian art—now, by default, Soviet. Anatoly Lunacharsky, the head of Narkompros and the exhibition's driving force, shaped the narrative of the show's success as a triumph of Soviet art. In the Soviet daily *Izvestiia*, he wrote, "it can be said that the average German viewer rejoiced at finally seeing a little slice of life in Soviet Russia. Apparently the German viewer has grown so tired of the White Guard's version of 'Russia No. 2,' and is sufficiently conscious that this is not the real Russia, that he hurried to see the confirmation of his suppositions at our exhibition."⁴⁸

Yet the show included a number of artists who had left Soviet Russia without plans to return—Chagall, David Burliuk, Ksenia Boguslavskaia, Ivan Puni, Vasily Kandinsky, and several others. That expatriate artists were conscripted into a cultural diplomacy event of the highest caliber points to the dexterity of the organizers. Importantly for this study, their participation not only highlights that the Soviets exploited the émigrés to advance their own propaganda; it also underscores the elasticity of Russian culture caught between Russias No. 1 and No. 2. Scores of artists and writers lived permanently in Berlin who are today conventionally labeled émigrés, but more often than not they were sympathetic to the cause of revolutionary renewal and felt little nostalgia for imperial Russia.

Roman Gul, a White Guard officer who became a maker of émigré cultural politics after World War II, was one such writer who maintained close ties with key Soviet writers—Konstantin Fedin, Boris Pilniak, Alexey N. Tolstoy—and took advantage of publishing opportunities in Moscow but never moved back. As late as 1927 Gul doubted the viability of émigré culture. He ended his reminiscences of Berlin life published that year in Moscow with a chapter about an imitation Russian village, Alexandrovka—Gul calls it the "Alexanderdorf Colony"—which was established in the 1820s in Berlin's aristocratic suburb of Potsdam. An open-air museum with Russian-style izbas, an Orthodox church, and German-speaking "Herr Gavriloff, Herr Makaroff, and Herr Kramarenkoff," Alexandrovka was as Russian as Gul was German—not at all. Gul was convinced that Charlottengrad would become another Alexandrovka—a performative stylization of ethnicity devoid of substance—and that being an émigré was a culturally doomed existence.

"How long can a person be an emigrant?" Gul asked. In 1927 his own answer was "Not long. The person either dies or becomes a German, Frenchman, Italian, or an Arab. And this happens much faster than the person thinks."[49] Fifty years later, however, when writing his three-volume memoirs (significantly titled *I Carried Russia Away*), Gul changed his outlook completely. He now maintained that being an émigré was the only culturally appropriate and even ethical stance.[50] He was able to do so not least because by the 1970s Russia Abroad had been joined by two additional waves of emigration out of the USSR: one right after the war and the other during the 1970s.[51] But in the late 1920s, lacking the benefit of hindsight, Gul produced prose that was more ambivalent and therefore more revealing of the cultural complexities of Russian culture in its postrevolutionary transition. Recovering a contemporary perspective such as Gul's in 1927 offers invaluable insights for understanding the historical trajectories of Russians in Berlin.

Although Gul wrote about Alexandrovka to make a rhetorical point, he may have been inspired, or perhaps frustrated, by the (short-lived) German fascination with everything *à la russe*. Much as Lunacharsky exaggerated the weariness with Russia No. 2 among the Germans in his review of the First Exhibition of Russian Art, his statement was accurate in that Charlottengrad quickly became an exoticized stereotype. In May 1923, the German satirical magazine *Ulk* featured a caricature called "Russian Berlin" (fig. 2).

Figure 2. "Russian Berlin." Published in *Ulk: Wochenschrift des Berliner Tageblatts*, May 4, 1923.

Spanning two pages, the drawing depicts a busy intersection in Berlin's western part. Two street signs suggest the location of the neighborhood: one refers to Tauentzienstrasse, the other to the Kurfürstendamm. The street name endings and spellings are Russianized and read "[Ulitsa] Tauentzienskaja" and "Kurfürstendamski Prospekt," reinforcing the impression that this part of Berlin was overrun by Russians: we see cartoonish troikas speeding through the street carrying cartoonish Cossacks; a disheveled peasant selling "Caviar for the People"; a woman dressed in national costume walking a polar bear on a leash; and a horse-drawn wagon carrying crates of "wodka." The composition is crowded by the massive gingerbread house of an Orthodox cathedral, toward which a bearded priest leads a procession. Save for the restaurant called Red Sarafan on the left and a Russian bathhouse on the right, every building in the background houses a cabaret—the Russian Cabaret, the Red Bird, the Green Bird, and the Big Bird. In fact, Berlin had three major Russian cabarets in Berlin, but only one of them was avian-themed, the Blue Bird.[52]

A significant element of the picture is the newsstand located to the left of center. A sign in German, "German Spoken Here," seems to beckon to a Berliner lost in this thoroughly Russified part of the city. As remarkable as this linguistic detail is, it is the selection of newspapers for sale that deserves special attention. Although the newspaper titles are misspelled in Cyrillic, the titles themselves offer a glimpse of Charlottengrad as the politically diverse locus of a global Russia Abroad: *The Sun* (*Solntse*) was published in Shanghai, while *Comrade* (*Tovarishch*) hailed from newly independent Lithuania. *The*

Voice of Russia (*Golos Rossii*), *On the Eve*, and *Time* (*Vremia*) were based in Berlin and aligned with the Socialist Revolutionaries, the Change of Landmarks, and liberal democrats, respectively. Perhaps the cartoonist had simply copied the newspaper titles sold at Russian newsstands without intending to show how omnivorous Russian Berlin's reading public was. Be that as it may, the image shows that, despite their sartorial similarity, these émigré Russians were not as cohesive a group as they might appear to outside observers.

The image also poses a question that preoccupied Gul and other Russian Berliners: can a geographically displaced community be culturally productive, or is diasporic culture always derivative, endlessly reproducing the original left at home? Charlottengrad's complexity notwithstanding, it remained mostly a novelty for the Germans, and Russian Berliners were aware of this fact even while many of them capitalized on Slavic exoticism at restaurants, cabarets, and fashion ateliers that they established.[53] Russian-German transactions with Berlin's landladies, bankers, and police officers occurred on a daily basis, but artistic interactions remained limited.

German intellectuals found the developments in the Soviet Union far more stimulating than the work of the Russians living among them, to which they paid less and less attention.[54] In 1922 Thomas Mann made an appearance at Charlottengrad's House of the Arts and read his short story "Das Eisenbahnunglück," as well as an excerpt from his essay "Goethe and Tolstoy." His precocious son Klaus frequented émigré salons. In a letter of November 9, 1924, the Socialist Revolutionary activist and journalist Vladimir Zenzinov wrote to his friend Amalia Fondaminskaia that he had attended a Russian charity event where "Thomas Mann's seventeen-year-old son read his rather naïve short story."[55] In contrast, the most intensive, and visible, intercultural exchange happened along the Communist International (Comintern) channels, continuing well into the 1930s.[56]

This ideological divide becomes apparent in Russian Berlin's historiography, too. We find little overlap between the studies of cultural figures who criticized the Soviet project and studies of those who embraced it, even though a great deal of ambivalence existed on both sides. The literature gives us the Berlin of Nabokov, Tsvetaeva, and Bely or the Berlin of the filmmaker Sergey Eisenstein, the artist El Lissitzky, the poet Vladimir Mayakovsky, and the writer Larisa Reisner. While these individuals existed in separate social circles, they shared a city, however briefly. Berlin's Russian bookstores carried titles from the Soviet Union, and German movie theaters screened Soviet films, many of them produced by a Moscow company headquartered in Berlin, Mezhrabpom-Rus. But the implications of this cultural coexistence rarely play a role in the debates on the diasporic and national accounts of Russian culture.[57]

Scholarship on Russian Berlin reflects the realities of the Cold War. Needless to say, the official study of émigrés was impossible in the USSR until Perestroika. Soviet historians framed Russian connections in Berlin as part of a Soviet–East German cultural dialogue.[58] In Anglo-American academic circles, an interest in émigré culture developed only gradually—a 1973 special issue of *TriQuarterly*, for example, opened with a foreword titled "Who Are the Émigré Writers?"[59] The 1983 appearance of a remarkable volume of letters called *Russian Berlin, 1921–1923* offered a treasure trove of documents for assessing the significance of Berlin for Russian literature in the 1920s, but it did not lead to a revision of either émigré or Soviet literatures. Published in the Literary Heritage of the Russian Emigration series with YMCA-Press in Paris, the volume was inaccessible to readers in the Soviet Union and was not taken up by Western Russianists at the time.[60]

Meanwhile, both East and West German scholars underscored Berlin's role as an international leftist circuit.[61] West German publications on the topic focused on documenting avant-garde art, which was being rediscovered as part of the leftist turn in Western European intellectual life that fueled the student protests in 1968.[62] Ten years after German unification, the historian Karl Schlögel brought together Berlin's various Russian groupings in his impressive *Berlin, Europe's Eastern Station*.[63] In this work, Schlögel offers an encyclopedic account of Berlin's Russian life, replete with case studies of émigré taxi drivers as urban sociologists, Comintern agents and undercover political operatives, and Grand Duchess Anastasia pretenders. It is one of the most valuable books for understanding Russian and Soviet activity in the sociopolitical landscape of interwar Germany.

Charlottengrad complicates and enriches previous cultural historiography in two important ways. First, it explores the wide range of political and personal positions that émigré authors adopted relative to the Soviet project, from enthusiastic loyalty to questioning ambivalence to pessimistic alienation. Second, it highlights the ways in which Russian authors abroad sought to engage with Weimar-era cultural energies while sustaining a distinctly Russian perspective on modernist expression. Especially notable within these analytical frameworks is the community of queer Russian and German modernist artists in Weimar Berlin, who engaged in rich intercultural interactions and charted a continuous evolution in political and cultural attitudes toward both the Weimar and Soviet states. The legend of Weimar Berlin rests in no small part on its reputation as a sexually uninhibited city; a consideration of "queer exile" reveals how the lives and experiences of marginalized figures change familiar stories and bring the past much closer to the present.

Mapping the Unloved Metropolis

Russian Berliners, even those who chose to stay permanently, seldom expressed any fondness for Germans or Berlin. During his eight-month stay in 1922–23, Boris Pasternak observed that disparaging Berlin had become the "most hackneyed habit" in Russian circles, and his fellow sojourner Ilya Ehrenburg reported that complaining about the city was considered "good form" among Russians.[64] Andrei Bely called Berlin a "bourgeois Sodom."[65] Nina Berberova wrote about "sickly Germany, sickly money, the sickly trees of Tiergarten."[66] Vladimir Nabokov, who spent fifteen years in Berlin, likened Russians in the city to film extras—unnoticeable, superfluous, and marginal—and later in life declared there was "no real communication, of the rich human sort," between his émigré compatriots and the "perfectly unimportant strangers, spectral Germans and Frenchmen."[67]

This insistence on isolation, so prominent in exile narratives from Berlin, functioned as both a coping mechanism and an artistic device. New work on Nabokov, for example, reveals that he was very aware of contemporary developments in Germany but chose to cultivate an image as a blissfully ignorant émigré who spoke almost no German.[68] The idea of cultural isolation operated as a bulwark against assimilation, but it also suggests a particular mode of engagement with the city—a deliberate and steadying maintenance of a sense of disruption, which (paradoxically) promotes the negotiation of a desired cultural identity. As *Charlottengrad* demonstrates, disruption in identity is a function of a particular physical location: as a large city, Berlin fostered the "radical coexistence," to use Raymond Williams's phrase, of diverse groups.[69] Berlin provoked, offended, disrupted, and stimulated. For some Russians, the sense of disruption translated into a permanently peripheral existence and the preservation of conservative cultural values. For others, disruption also meant a reevaluation of old values that led to an exploration of new themes, perspectives, and manners of representation.

The central aim of this book is to tell the story of the dispersal of Russian cultural activity beyond Russia proper, as it was counterbalanced by the centripetal pull of interwar Berlin, exploring the meanings of disruption. Without minimizing the alienation, displacement, and statelessness that characterize exile, I develop a case-study-based approach that uncovers the generative aspects of community, artistic networks, and creative cross-pollination. While my archive stems chronologically from modernism and technically from diaspora, I rely on both terms as keywords. I use modernism to denote the time of the early twentieth century and innovative aesthetic principles shared by various groups, and I use diaspora to encompass a community held together by language and cultural background in a foreign nation. Following recent scholarship in diaspora studies, I proceed with an understanding that diasporas are far from static or uniform entities.[70] As Brent Edwards has argued, emphasizing a diasporic genealogy—a shared geographic descent—assumes an internal coherence that is rarely there. The utility of the term diaspora, he maintains, is "not in that it offers the comfort of abstraction, an easy recourse to origins, but that it forces us to consider the discourses of cultural and political linkage only through and across difference."[71] In Charlottengrad, the encounters and clashes of the Russian Empire's former subjects worked as such linkages through and across difference.

Accordingly, I privilege primary texts from and about Berlin and, in the first two chapters, frame them with contemporaneous critical essays by Russian formalists striving to conceptualize Russian culture's postrevolutionary transition. When turning to subjects who made their careers entirely abroad, I use insights gleaned from queer studies to make visible the intersections of politics and gender overlooked in previous studies guided by a well-worn belief in the linguistic-cultural insularity of Russian émigré culture between the wars.

Charlottengrad consists of an introduction, five chapters, a conclusion, and an appendix. In the chapters I analyze poetry, fiction, journalism, set design, photography, and private correspondence produced in and about Berlin. Russian Berliners' ideas about the changing world order found clearest expression in their representations of Berlin. This made the city a singular site of knowledge about Russian national identity and cultural sensibility—which were in a state of transition.

As a transit zone between East and West, Berlin in the 1920s became a place of what I call "trial emigration": a political and cultural environment that enabled deliberations about whether to emigrate permanently or to return to Soviet Russia. The first chapter outlines three typologies of trial emigration by bringing together three poets who spent a considerable amount of time in Berlin: Pasternak, Mayakovsky, and Khodasevich. Each has acquired a strong posthumous mythology: Pasternak is known as the dissident poet, whereas Mayakovsky and Khodasevich have come to epitomize the Soviet and the émigré poet, respectively. Yet their poetic careers were significantly affected by the experience of trial emigration in Berlin. This chapter's analyses highlight the interplay of Soviet and nascent émigré cultural sensibilities in Berlin and offer a record of aesthetic and ideological positions that show the inadequacy of the Soviet/émigré binary.

The second chapter turns to narrative prose to examine aesthetic differences between exilic and non-exilic perspectives in representing the space and time of the city. Although some Russian Berliners, such as Ehrenburg, hail Berlin as "the most contemporary city in Europe," most dislike the city, regardless of their ideological agendas. In his Berlin novel *Zoo*, Shklovsky likens the city to a menagerie. Bely calls it a "kingdom of shades" in his whimsically macabre Berlin travelogue. In his classic short story "A Guide to Berlin," Nabokov paints Berlin as the modern version of Dante's hell. Larisa Reisner provides an emphatically partisan account of Berlin as a site of a failed communist revolution. I analyze these authors' texts as literary maps—not only of Berlin but of their own aesthetic conceptions of form, time, and language.

The third chapter considers the use of the Russian classical literary past in debates about the present and future of Russia abroad. It undertakes an archival reconstruction and analysis of Pavel Tchelitchew's 1923 staging of Rimsky-Korsakov's opera *The Golden Cockerel*, based on Pushkin's fairy tale, at the Berlin Opera. I read Tchelitchew's visual world by contextualizing the iconography of the surviving scenic and costume designs, applying cultural-historical analysis. This examination of the interrelation of the literary and visual arts reveals how the exiled Russians attempted to sway Germans' fascination with the Soviet Union. In tracing the rise of an exilic sensibility, I show how Tchelitchew's staging links art and ideology in a discourse that transcends the stage and expresses political and social anxieties about the interconnection of power and gender.

The fourth chapter draws further connections between Russian Berlin's émigré and non-émigré authors, focusing on the people and places of Vladimir Nabokov's actual and fictional German milieu. Nabokov is arguably the most successful Russian émigré author and one who always identified as an exile. Yet he took his exilic position to an extreme, maintaining an autobiographical narrative of total cultural isolation in Berlin, where he lived from 1922 until 1937. However, the intertwining of tradition and modernity that can be discerned in the structure of Nabokov's Berlin novels, especially

The Gift, conveys a deliberately hybrid conception of temporality and the space of the city, as well as indebtedness to his German and Soviet contemporaries. Focusing mainly on *The Gift*, I consider how Nabokov's perception of language and time in Berlin shaped his ideas about exilic authorship. Whereas *The Gift* is the most studied of Nabokov's Russian novels, previous scholarship has yet to account for the novel's dependence on Berlin's urban space and its cultural environment. To understand Berlin's role in *The Gift* is to appreciate the extent to which Nabokov used exile in Berlin for imagining a Russian literary renewal.

After World War I, Berlin evolved into the center of European queer life, the site of a "masquerade of perversions," as Christopher Isherwood put it. At the forefront of the modern gay rights movement, gay Berliners exemplified international modernity. The fifth chapter situates émigré culture within the city's international queer community by focusing on the figures of the queer and the exile. Notable Russian visitors such as Sergey Eisenstein and Sergey Esenin were known to have visited Berlin's famed gay bars and cabarets. But our knowledge of Russian responses to contemporary German discourses of sexuality is limited to the pervasive homophobic currents in Nabokov's Berlin oeuvre, from the clichéd gay couple in *Mary* to the tragic ménage-à-trois in *The Gift*. Supported by archival research, I turn to Nabokov's brother Sergey Nabokov to uncover how queer Russian artists and intellectuals challenged established conventions of representation while negotiating relations with the diasporic and host communities in interwar Berlin. I also discuss the life and oeuvre of Vera Lourié, Nikolay Gumilev's pupil in St. Petersburg, who lived in Berlin from 1921 until her death in 1998. In 1985–86 she wrote *Letters to You*, a collection of autobiographical epistolary prose addressed to her visiting medical nurse and modeled on Shklovsky's *Zoo, or Letters Not about Love*. Having survived twentieth-century Berlin, Lourié deliberately engages with Shklovsky but writes *about* love— in German, queerly, and without nostalgic sentimentality. I synthesize the concepts of queerness, modernism, and diaspora to develop an approach to analyzing émigré culture that helps illuminate the Berlin Russophone community's role in shaping modern queer culture but also grapple with its Russianness. This final chapter establishes the ways in which the discourse on sexuality connects Russian authors across borders.

The appendix contains a transcription and translation of handwritten meeting minutes of Berlin's Russian Poets Club from 1928 that offers an unmediated glimpse into Charlottengrad.

1

Unsentimental Journeys

Berlin as Trial Emigration

"The blockade of Russia is ending," the writer Ilya Ehrenburg and the artist El Lissitzky proclaimed in a 1922 editorial in the inaugural issue of *Veshch'/ Gegenstand/Objet*, a Berlin-based cultural journal aiming to bridge the divide between artists and writers in Soviet Russia and the West.[1] The "blockade," the nearly five years of global isolation that Russia faced following the 1917 Bolshevik Revolution, was being symbolically lifted in Berlin after Soviet Russia established diplomatic relations with the Weimar Republic. This new Russian-German alliance made Berlin Russia's modern "window onto Europe."[2] In Berlin more than anywhere else, the line separating émigrés from non-émigrés shifted over time.[3] As a European capital open to all travelers from Russia, regardless of political belief and artistic practices, Berlin enabled the overlap of pro-Soviet revolutionary avant-gardism, traditionalist Russian culture, and everything in between.

    A journal like *Veshch'* is emblematic of that diversity. While *Veshch'* is considered an artifact of the Soviet avant-garde, its ideological attachments were less stable than they seem. The journal was conceived as an explicitly international project to publicize emergent Soviet culture abroad. Even though *Veshch'* appeared in Russian, German, and French, the bulk of its text was in Russian, and it was published by an émigré press.[4] The publisher eventually distanced itself from the journal because it mocked anti-Soviet Russian exiles, but some of its authors, including the critic Viktor Shklovsky and the poet Alexander Kusikov, soon also found themselves in exile. Ehrenburg and Lissitzky effectively lived abroad, and their collaborators the poets Vladimir Mayakovsky and Boris Pasternak spent prolonged periods of time in the city.[5] As a journal with conflicting loyalties, *Veshch'* was hardly unique. There was

Figure 3. Cover of *Veshch'/Gegenstand/Objet*, no. 1–2 (1922). Amherst Center for Russian Culture.

Figure 4. Cover of *Zhar-Ptitsa*, no. 7 (1922). Beinecke Rare Book and Manuscript Library.

also the World-of-Art-inspired *Firebird*, a lavishly illustrated multi-lingual review of Russian literature, art, and theater. In contrast to the saturated red cover of *Veshch'*, with its abstract geometric forms, *Firebird*'s ornately styled front page epitomized conservative Russian émigré chic (figs. 3 and 4). Yet both were financed by the Bolshevik government.[6]

The coexistence of these diverse artistic networks in Berlin highlights the fluidity of Soviet identity abroad in the years immediately following the 1917 Revolution; it also points to the instability of what it means to be an émigré. Not every émigré bemoaned the loss of Russia, not every Russian living abroad considered him or herself an émigré, and not every author living abroad and supporting the Soviet cause agreed with the Bolshevik policies. The sharp distinction between Russian culture in Russia and Russian culture abroad did not yet exist in the way we understand it today.

Existing scholarship tends to document the role of Russian Berlin as the place where the conflicting possibilities of art and life after the Revolution meet.[7] A great many cultural producers visited the city. Some returned to Soviet Russia; others chose to remain abroad. Berlin's sociocultural context clearly influenced Russian literary dynamics before the firm separation of émigré aesthetic principles from the non-émigré cultural modality. But the implications of that impact remain neglected.

This chapter argues that Berlin afforded a particular way of living and writing abroad that can be called a trial emigration: a political and cultural environment that enabled deliberations about whether or not to return to Russia. Berlin was positioned as a transitional space—a buffer zone between East and West, a city both imperial and democratic, both conservative and progressive, where it was possible to understand what a life in emigration might entail.[8] The very notion of permanent emigration consisted less in a hard, either-or choice than in the articulation of this binary distinction over the course of the interwar years. That is, the category of "emigration" was itself on trial. Accordingly, I view trial emigration in Berlin as a sort of historical intermission, an interlude directly tied to the contemporaneous experience in Russia. I aim to show that the ideas of a number of authors, whose approach to writing evolved during their sojourns in Berlin, affected the postrevolutionary cultural order.

Trial emigration is possible in an environment where multiple allegiances, viewpoints, and identities coexist, rooted in the contradictions between the promise of the Revolution and the realities of life in and outside Russia. Fyodor Ivanov, a Berlin-based critic reviewing contemporary Russian literature in 1922, approached poetry and prose written in Soviet Russia in a remarkably balanced manner, while writing that "the process of fermentation in the emigration is at its peak, and who knows in what new forms it will flow."[9] This unbiased and welcoming anticipation of new developments in literature written across borders points to the artifice of the Soviet/émigré divide. What matters at this time is the new and unprecedented literature itself.

This chapter outlines three typologies of trial emigration associated with three poets of the same generation—Boris Pasternak (1890–1960), Vladimir Mayakovsky (1893–1930), and Vladislav Khodasevich (1886–1939)—extremely distinctive poets whose oeuvres conditioned further literary developments in the Soviet Union and what would come to be known as Russia Abroad. Each poet belongs to the canon of twentieth-century literature for different reasons. A discussion of Soviet cultural history would be incomplete without including the work and legacy of Mayakovsky. Khodasevich is indispensable for understanding émigré literature. Pasternak stands as a canonical author and a Soviet-era poet who later became an important figure for anti-Soviet intellectuals. All three spent extended periods of time in Berlin at pivotal moments in their careers. Exploring trial emigration through the lenses of their Berlin poetry shows the enmeshment of the Soviet and nascent émigré cultural sensibilities. Reading their poems in the context of trial emigration reveals their own conflicted aesthetic and ideological positions in the early 1920s. Their Berlin texts comprise a salient archive of period and space that highlights the interlude when émigré and non-émigré poetics take shape.

POETICS AND POLITICS OF THE INTERLUDE

The competing visions for Russian culture during this moment of transition are especially discernable in poetry. Poetry is a privileged genre in Russia, and poets enjoy special prominence among Russian authors. Their texts and personal mythologies animate narratives not only of literature but of history. Despite the achievements of great Russian novelists, it is notable that the "Silver Age" of Russian culture at the turn of the twentieth century is named similarly to the poetry-dominated Golden Age of the early nineteenth century. In a 1924 essay, the literary critic and writer Yuri Tynianov, taking stock of the first peaceful years following the civil war, turned to contemporary poetry and introduced the term "interlude" (or "interval," *promezhutok*) to understand the significance of aesthetic styles and their historical interpretation. Tynianov argued that during moments of historical transition, poetry is capable of capturing the world as it is. He likened the emergence of new poetic forms to the development of a "new vision" stemming from a new language: "Poetry is speech transformed; it is human speech that has outgrown itself. Language in poetry has thousands of unexpected shades of meaning; poetry gives language a new dimension. New poetry is new vision. And the growth of these new phenomena happens only in the interludes when inertia loses its grip. The action of inertia is, essentially, all we know—in skewed historical perspective, an interlude without inertia seems like a dead-end. (Every innovator is ultimately working for inertia; every revolution is produced for the canon.) But there are no dead-ends in history. There are only interludes."[10]

Tynianov's argument concerns historical narratives as much as it does poetics. Interludes punctuate periods of cultural and historical change, but the "skewed historical perspective"—what translates literally as the "optical laws of history"—prevents us from seeing those periods for what they are because we rely on retrospectively observed historical phenomena shaped into convenient narratives. By these "optical laws of history," the first wave of Russian emigration is implicitly seen in cultural historiography as a spectacular (if inevitable) "dead end." As the losers of the civil war, émigrés move to the margins of history where, deprived of a wide readership, they dwell in nostalgic conservatism until dying, switching from Russian to another European language and assimilating into their host societies. Such a characterization, although exaggerated, sums up the prevalent assumptions about émigré culture.[11]

But these assumptions crumble if we consider Berlin in all its remarkable diversity as a spatialized iteration of Tynianov's interlude—a crossroads where everything is in flux and new traditions are being invented before inertia can again take shape. Tynianov further explains this through his theory of the interlude: "During an interlude, 'successes' or 'ready-made objects' are the last things we need. We don't know what to do with good poems, just as children don't know what to do with toys that are too fancy. What we need is a way out. Poems can be 'unsuccessful'—what matters is that the failures bring closer the possibility of successes."[12]

Following Tynianov's argumentation, linguistic and thematic shifts in poetry are signs of cardinal change in Russian literature across borders, indicating the failures and successes of poems as they come into existence. He discusses formal aspects of poetry, but at the same time he draws our attention to temporality. As Yaroslava Ananko points out in her analysis of Tynianov's concept, the interlude at once describes and announces a new phenomenon, thereby bringing new literary reality into existence.[13] Tynianov's goal is therefore two-pronged, combining affective and practical needs: to sense the moment of revolutionary openness in aesthetic innovation and to devise a nomenclature of this moment. Tynianov examines poetics and temporality to make sense of the postrevolutionary, post-civil-war, liminal mid-1920s in Soviet Russia. By considering Berlin through the prism of the interlude, by merging locality and temporality, I aim to elucidate how a paradoxical impulse to maintain the openness of the postrevolutionary present in the face of more pragmatic needs structured the meanings of emigration in Berlin.

The poets discussed here existed in an environment where the political and cultural definitions of emigration evolved against the background of the Bolsheviks' consolidation of power in the Soviet Union, a process that gradually but inevitably required clear political commitments and rejected hermeneutic complexity in art.[14] In Berlin, Pasternak, Mayakovsky, and Khodasevich were suspended between the cultural hegemony of traditionalist exiles and the cultural hegemony of the Soviets. But Berlin was also a place where the avant-garde conception of art (and revolution) was still alive and vibrant. In three distinct ways, and with different outcomes, these poets navigated the city in search of "a way out." I begin with Pasternak, whom Tynianov singled out as the most promising voice of new Russian poetry by dedicating "Interlude" to him.

Berlin Juncture—Pasternak

Pasternak's seven-month sojourn in Berlin offers a conspicuous example of ambivalence toward both emigration and Soviet Russia. Pasternak traveled to Berlin in August 1922 to visit his parents, who had emigrated a year earlier; he returned to Moscow in March 1923.[15] While in Germany, he wrote ten poems, and although he did not consider them a thematically unified cycle, taken together they reflect the development of Pasternak's "new vision," to use Tynianov's expression.[16] The poetry he wrote before 1923 cannot be easily placed on the political spectrum. But his Berlin writings reveal subtle but decisive shifts indicative of the emerging émigré and non-émigré aesthetic dynamics. Moreover, Pasternak's Berlin poems help refine our perceptions of chronology, temporality, and causality in both émigré and Soviet literature and show how deeply interconnected they are.

Pasternak arrived in Berlin at a pivotal moment in his career. His formal affiliation with futurism had hurt his reputation at home and abroad: there was a growing campaign against futurism in Soviet Russia, while among the more conservative émigré critics all avant-garde experimentation was dismissed as propaganda.[17] In Berlin he was marked as a "red" poet for publishing his poems in leftist venues, and in Moscow he faced escalating criticism from the Bolshevik establishment for avoiding the themes of the proletariat, the Revolution, and social renewal in his writings.[18] Arriving in Berlin under pressure to demonstrate his ideological commitments, Pasternak enters a personal and historical interval that informs what can be called a pivotal aesthetics of his Berlin poems: he repeatedly turned to Berlin's urban space as the site of his ambitions and anxieties in an attempt to reconcile the highly subjective lyrical pitch of his poetry with political commitments.

Commenting on the mounting pressure on Pasternak in Russia in the early 1920s, Lazar Fleishman has suggested that the poet traveled abroad to reassess his career from the geographical distance Berlin afforded. Fleishman has examined the poet's previously unknown correspondence to explain the major change that occurs in Pasternak's poetics on his return to Moscow: after Berlin, he is no longer a seemingly detached lyric poet, but one who engages with the topic of the Revolution directly, as if conforming to the establishment's expectations of a Soviet poet.[19] As a result, Fleishman explains the outcome of Pasternak's Berlin sojourn as the poet's "refusal to emigrate" (otkaz ot emigratsii).[20] Fleishman emphasizes that this refusal grows out of Pasternak's doubts about the viability of culture in exile and his initial belief in the historical potential of the USSR, the first socialist state in the modern world. Pasternak's troubled relations with the Soviet authorities would worsen later in his life, however, and Fleishman's framing of Pasternak's return as a refusal to emigrate serves a deeper purpose, demonstrating Pasternak's significance as a Russian poet. Fleishman underscores that in Berlin Pasternak came to a "clear understanding of the connection between the historic choice and the fate of the poet" and chose to be in Russia despite the difficulties of living and writing there.[21] But Pasternak's Berlin poetry, which Fleishman does not discuss, suggests instead an overwhelming sense of ambivalence and uncertainty.

The memoir of Pasternak's sister Josephine Pasternak, who lived in Berlin in the 1920s, confirms that Pasternak did indeed consider emigrating. To his brother Alexander, Pasternak wrote about the high quality of life in Berlin, something that "even the liveliest imaginations cannot fathom" in Russia, where basic conveniences have fallen by the wayside during War Communism.[22] In Josephine's account, however, the appeal of being in Berlin diminished the longer he lived in a crowded boardinghouse shared with parents, siblings, and an inquisitive German landlady. The situation was complicated by his wife's pregnancy, the news of which apparently distressed Pasternak.[23] The growing family began to reconsider their plans of a life abroad, and Josephine remembered that "the main theme" of the couple's altercations was their inability to "make up their minds as to whether and when to return to Moscow."[24] To make matters worse, the critical reviews of his poetry were mixed at best. Whereas Ehrenburg opined in *Veshch'* that Pasternak's "magic is in his syntax," such influential poets and critics as Andrei Bely and Khodasevich failed to be enchanted and branded his writing incomprehensible.[25] Pasternak felt undermined, moreover, by the editorial politics of expatriate publishers.[26] German publishers seemed uninterested. This may be unsurprising because in Berlin Pasternak limited his public appearances and publications as much as he could. He did not publish his texts in either the anti-Soviet press or the infamous newspaper *Nakanune*, whose mission was to encourage Russians abroad to come to terms with the Bolshevik victory and return to Russia.[27] Pasternak's attitude toward Berlin was also ambiguous: at times he criticized the city as an "impersonal Babylon" while at others he found its social fabric and technological advances immensely inspiring.[28]

By taking these biographical insights into account but focusing on poetry, I approach Pasternak's trip as a trial emigration. His Berlin poems from this period build on his earlier poetry and offer a view of the poet searching for the right method to order his overwhelming surroundings. Pasternak's main interests in Berlin comprise representation of urban space versus untamed nature, poetry as memory, and historical present and timeless past. Rather than condemn life abroad as futile or eulogize the Soviet project, Pasternak experimented by composing poetry that thematically and formally expressed an anticipation of change. While his poems register the looming transformation—be it the change of seasons ("Arrival of Winter" and "Autumn"), transition from night to dawn ("Roosters"), travel ("Sailing Away" and "The Calm Sea"), construction ("The Butterfly-Tempest"), or the workings of poetry ("Vigor" and "Flight")—his lyric subjects invariably occupy the center of semantic shifts and are on the verge of transition. Although this sense of transformation is critical to Pasternak's poetics in general, I trace this common feature through three of his Berlin poems by situating them in the city to show that the idea of transformation undergirds his pivotal poetics abroad. One of these poems, "Gleisdreieck," he wrote as a memento in a private album of his Berlin acquaintance Nadezhda Zalshupina, and it first appeared in Russia only in a posthumous collection of his poems. It is among the most remarkable city poems he ever wrote. Two other poems, "The Butterfly-Tempest" and "Sailing Away," Pasternak deemed worthy of publication soon after returning to Moscow; the fact that he continued revising them throughout the decade suggests their importance.[29]

Viacheslav V. Ivanov has identified "The Butterfly-Tempest" as a poem that holds the answers to Pasternak's lyrical oeuvre.[30] The poem also effectively captures Pasternak's aesthetic of this period. As Ivanov has observed, despite seeming "dark and intelligible" at first sight, the poem is extraordinarily rich:

Бывалый гул былой Мясницкой
Вращаться стал в моём кругу,
И, как вы на него ни цыцкай,
Он пальцем вам—и ни гугу.

Он снится мне за массой действий,
В рядах до крыш горящих сумм,
Он сыплет лестницы, как в детстве,
И подымает страшный шум.

Напрасно в сковороды били
И огорчалась кочерга.
Питается пальбой и пылью
Окуклившийся ураган.

Как призрак порчи и починки,
Объевший веточки мечтам,
Асфальта алчного личинкой
Смолу котлами пьёт почтамт.

Но за разгромом и ремонтом,
К испугу сомкнутых окон,

Червяк спокойно и дремотно
По закоулкам ткет кокон.

Тогда-то сбившись с перспективы,
Мрачатся улиц выхода,
И бритве ветра тучи гриву
Подбрасывает духота.

Сейчас ты выпорхнешь, инфанта,
И, сев на телеграфный столб,
Расправишь водяные банты
Над топотом промокших толп.

The old-time buzz of the old Miasnitskaia Street
began to whirl around me,
and it doesn't matter how you shush it
it'll wag its finger at you—and that's that.

I dream of it behind the massive movements,
I see it in the rows of numbers burning up to the roofs,
it pours the ladders like in childhood
and makes terrible noise.

In vain they banged in frying pans
and the stove poker saddened.
The pupated storm
feeds on gun shots and dust.

Like a specter of damage and restoration
that ate through the sprigs of dreams,
like asphalt's avaricious caterpillar
the post office drinks tar by the cauldron.

But behind the rubble and repair
to the fright of shut windows
the worm weaves the cocoon
in nooks calmly and drowsily.

And then having stumbled out of perspective,
the exits of the streets grow gloomy,
and mugginess tosses up
the cloud's mane to the wind's blade.

Now you will fly out, Infanta,
and, having landed on a telegraph pole,
will straighten your watery bows
above the tramping of soaked masses.

In Pasternak's signature bewildering syntax, which Tynianov affectionately called "monstrous," the poem captures a complex image of a Moscow neighborhood under construction, the heat of the febrile day about to be relieved by an invigorating thunderstorm. The action of the gathering storm parallels the poet's search for the appropriate means of expression for his powerful vision. High and low diction collide like the frying pan with the saddened stove poker; rhymes combine such incongruous images as dreams and the post office (mechtam / pochtamt); and the mischievous "old-time noise" becomes animated and blurs the difference between the subject and object of representation. It is typical of modernist texts to self-reflect on their own status as artworks, and at this time Pasternak writes many poems about poetry and the process of creation.[31] In the urban sensorium of "The Butterfly-Tempest," he writes about the birth of a poem to capture the image of two temporalities merging: the Moscow past and the Berlin present. Rather than simply privileging Moscow or disparaging Berlin, Pasternak renders the general European historical moment.

In his extensive analysis of the poem, Ivanov mentions Berlin and its precarious temporality only in passing.[32] Yet, Pasternak's text suggests a link between private memory and public history as captured in urban spaces. The spatiotemporal location of the metamorphosis addressed in the first two stanzas is of particular importance. One of Moscow's central avenues, aristocratic Miasnitskaia, home to the Pasternak family for many years, was renamed The First of May Street (Pervomaiskaia) in 1918 to honor International Workers' Day and formally register the historical change in the new Russian government's value system.[33] And it is Miasnitskaia, not Pervomaiskaia, that the poet sees and hears. He recognizes the street in the throes of construction through the oneiric gaps in Berlin's cityscape ("I dream of it behind the massive movements, / I see it in the rows of numbers burning up to the roofs"). The burning numbers suggest overlapping images of NEP-era Moscow with the illuminated signs of the German mark's swelling exchange rate during the infamous hyperinflation of the early 1920s.[34] The poet is aware of these immediate concerns, but he ignores them in favor of his imagination. He does not mourn the lost world of imperial Russia as a reactionary exile would, nor does he use this as an occasion to reflect on the significance of the Revolution. Instead, he conveys the sense of the nearly palpable physical movement of ongoing transformation, but without clarifying what is changing.

As the poem progresses, it reveals the environment from an almost Cubist perspective. The suspension of linear perspective is announced in the line "And then, having stumbled out of perspective" to reinforce the overall confusion of linguistic multiplicity. Then, the poet transcends the disorienting bustle by elevating his gaze above the city, finding a stable point of view from a telegraph pole. But even as he attempts to carve out an independent position, he remains part of the poem's linguistic environment, embodied in the image of the "pupated storm" (okuklivshiisia uragan). The irregular rhythm of "pupated storm," caused by the missing stress in two of the four iambic feet, renders this already arresting image even more striking. The storm-in-the-making absorbs all sensory impressions so that they can be transformed into an edifying verbal shower. The poet signals that the storm is coming but stops short of delivering the downpour itself. While the final image of the Infanta-like butterfly bursting free from its cocoon promises heavy rain, that rain occurs outside the poem. The interior of the poem is a dynamic screen, "the mass of movements," which reflects several simultaneously unfolding metamorphoses: those of the butterfly, the weather, the city, and human perception. But the ultimate stage of these metamorphoses is not represented, and the text's buzzing confusion does not become ringing clarity. We are left with a delicate record of salient ambiguity—this poem—in which Pasternak hesitates to cross the boundary separating before and after.

Pasternak's meditation on the boundary dividing past and future continues in another poem from Berlin, "Sailing Away." Here he also describes a pivotal moment before a big change using some of the same tropes, relying particularly on water imagery. As the title suggests, "Sailing Away" anticipates a sea adventure:

Слышен лепет соли каплющей.
Гул колес едва показан.
Тихо взявши гавань зá плечи,
Мы отходим за пакгаузы.³⁵

The lisp of dripping salt is heard.
The noise of paddle wheels is barely shown.
Taking the harbor by its shoulders gently,
We leave behind the warehouses.

The topoi of the road, new beginnings, and origins are prevalent in Pasternak's poetics. His classic book of poetry *My Sister—Life*, for example, is organized as a journey through Russia during which his surroundings, experiences, and observations merge and reveal a dynamic vision of the world.³⁶ In "Sailing Away," the journey corresponds to an artistic journey through traditions of Russian writing. From the beginning, the poem betrays a recognizable precursor: as Evgeny and Elena Pasternak have observed, the metrical pattern and the imagery of "Sailing Away" are modeled on Nikolay Gumilev's poem "By the Shore" from the cycle *The Return of Odysseus* (1909).³⁷ Whereas Gumilev depicts a return home, Pasternak describes a departure. But in the poem, it is unclear where the speaking "we" are headed, except into an increasingly stormy open sea. This description evokes the imagery of a Romantic poet confronting untamed nature, such as in Pushkin's "To the Sea" (1824) and Lermontov's "The Sail" (1832). However, "Sailing Away" fashions itself as a post-Symbolist modernist poem that simultaneously emphasizes and revokes the aesthetic experience of the restless poet. There are no wrenching negotiations between the poet and the sea: his voice, embodied in the collective pronoun "we," gradually dissolves into a third-person speaker as he relinquishes himself to the forces of nature.

Pasternak is known for suggesting awareness of various preceding artistic traditions, mostly from the Russian and Western European canons, and subverting them in his own poems.³⁸ In "Sailing Away" he goes further by turning the physical surroundings upside down and flipping the sea and the sky, as in the lines "the sea, darkly idling, / looks from up above at the travelers" (море, сумрачно бездельничая, / смотрит сверху на идущих).³⁹ This flipping of the elements conveys an image of the poet looking at his own reflection in the water, whereas the water "looks from up above." Caught between reflections and in a liquid continuum, the poet chooses to submit to the elements, not rebel, fight, or escape. The ending of the poem welcomes the seafarers to a terrifying expanse of the unpredictable sea:

Страшным полуоборотом,
Сразу меняясь во взоре,
Мачты въезжают в ворота
Настежь открытого моря.

Вот оно! И в предвкушеньи,
Сладко бушующих новшеств,
Камнем в пучину крушений
Падает чайка, как ковшик.[40]

With a frightening half-turn,
suddenly changing their gaze,
the masts ride into the gates
of the wide-open sea.

This is it! And in expectation
of sweetly raging novelties,
like a stone into the abyss of shipwrecks,
drops the seagull like a little scoop.

Following the "frightening half-turn" of the ship and the changing gaze, "sweetly raging novelties" appear on the horizon. Unlike in "The Butterfly-Tempest," the picture here is clear, but the syntax precludes identifying a single point of view. Who is overjoyed to enter the open sea: the seafarers, the ship masts, or the seagull? This confusion adds to the emotional charge of the text, which syntactically, phonetically, and lexically depicts change, fragmentation, and uncertainty.

This sort of sea imagery, often of biblical proportions, is characteristic of writing about the revolutionary change during this period. Authors in exile, many of whom left Russia by sea, compare the vanished Russian Empire to Atlantis.[41] Those who are sympathetic to the Soviet Union compare the Revolution to the biblical story of the Great Flood and Noah's Ark, underscoring the apocalyptic cleansing of the past.[42] Pasternak's contemporaries in Berlin, Shklovsky, Ehrenburg, and Mayakovsky, each compared the Russian revolutionary period to the Great Flood. Ehrenburg wrote that Berlin resembled a Noah's Ark whose passengers, divided by the Revolution into the "pure" and "impure," met peacefully in the city's cafés.⁴³ Mayakovsky wrote about a flood obliterating Berlin from the face of the earth in his play *Mystery-Bouffe*. Shklovsky, before finding himself in Berlin, attempted to convince Roman Jakobson to return to Russia by writing, "the flood is nearing its end. The animals are leaving their arks."⁴⁴ But Pasternak does not partake in this metaphorical flow of ideas.⁴⁵ The high tension of the stormy seascape in "Sailing Away" ends suddenly with an image of a seagull plunging into the water like a little dipper (kovshik). The dipper is a metaphor for a vessel, not unlike a personal ark, which here stands for both an actual boat and a container of private memories.⁴⁶ Although it is unclear who the poem's subject is, the subject remains inside the vessel, as if in a hermit ship traversing the seas on his own.

This emphasis on eroding independence and artistic ambivalence reaches its apogee in "Gleisdreieck"—the only poem in which Pasternak does not merely allude to Berlin but engages the city directly. Gleisdreieck is a Berlin transit station whose name indicates a triangle where three different railroad tracks converged, all significantly elevated aboveground (fig. 5). The station itself was suspended in the middle of the industrial triangle. In the early 1920s it was one of Berlin's technological wonders and fascinated Pasternak and other modernists immensely.⁴⁷ In the poem, Pasternak taps into the powerful topoi of the city and the railroad. Important as they are individually, once combined, the urban railroad represents a crucial intersection of private life and modernity at large. And so, in "Gleisdreieck" a busy train station bursts into the intimate domestic quarters:

Чем в жизни пробавляется чудак,
Что каждый день зá небольшую плату
Сдает над ревом пропасти чердак
Из Потсдама спешащему закату?

Он выставляет розу с резедой
В клубящуюся на версты корзину,
Где семафоры спорят с красотой
Со снежной далью, пахнущей бензином.

В руках у крыш, у труб, у недотрог
Не сумерки, — карандаши для грима.

Туда из мрака вырвавшись, метро
Комком гримас летит на крыльях дыма.
        30 января 1923
        Берлин

How does an odd fellow get by in this life,
who every day for modest pay
rents an attic above the roaring abyss
to the sunset rushing from Potsdam?

He puts out roses and mignonettes
into a basket that steams for miles,
where the semaphores vie in beauty
with the snowy vista reeking of gasoline.

In the hands of roofs, of chimneys, and of impatiens
is not twilight—makeup pencils.
There as a lump of grimaces flies the subway,
free from the darkness, on the wings of smoke.
        January 30, 1923
        Berlin

Whenever Pasternak writes about trains, train stations, and railroads, from his early poems to *Doctor Zhivago*, he signals profound change. But whereas the train trope typically entails a journey, the station in "Gleisdreieck" is merely a transitional zone, suspended in the air above the city. The poem comprises a series of such unexpected discrepancies, beginning with form: "Gleisdreieck" is written in a traditional iambic pentameter with a basic a/b/a/b rhyme pattern, but the complexity and succession of the imagery approaches cinematic montage.[48] The rhythm and sound resemble the tempo of a moving train as the sunset rushes from the aristocratic countryside of Potsdam into the thicket of metropolitan Berlin. The country/city opposition then parallels the quarrel between the worlds of industrial technology and nature that vie for dominance, each offering its own version of beauty. Furthermore, the vastness of a "roaring abyss" confronts the enclosed space of the attic, and the dynamism of the surrounding environment expends itself in the static idling of the impoverished "odd fellow" (chudak; an eccentric, strange man). These clashing metaphors culminate in the final image of the elevated train that moves so fast it appears to fly, but it is unclear where it is headed. Pasternak's Gleisdreieck typifies Berlin's elaborate transportation infrastructure and symbolizes movement without direction. His contemporaries recall that he dubbed the Gleisdreieck station a "subway to nowhere."[49] Although the Gleisdreieck station was a major transfer hub with many alternative routes to choose from, very few trips originated here.

Within the poem's conflicting imagery, Alexander Dolinin has identified the leitmotif of the demise of Western civilization. He sees the poem as a depiction of a feverish sunset above the "demonic megalopolis" and writes, "though Pasternak never brings the theme of doom into the open, the imagery of the poem and the sound structure of its last stanza . . . indicate that he read the city in eschatological terms close to those of Oswald Spengler's famous *Decline of the West*."[50] Matthias Freise and Britta Korkowsky have

Figure 5. A view of the Gleisdreieck station in 1902. Landesarchiv Berlin, F Rep. 290 (02) Nr. II3294. Photo by Waldemar Titzenthaler. The station was rebuilt in 1912 and would have looked somewhat differently with an added two-level terminal when Pasternak wrote about it. But the station's signature curved railways still formed a triangle in 1923.

expanded Dolinin's analysis, anchoring their reading of the poem in the idea that Pasternak was responding to the irrevocable transformation of Europe.[51] They have found that the image of the "odd fellow" is borrowed from the German Romantic vocabulary and that Pasternak inscribed him and his bourgeois habits of putting red and yellow flowers on the windowsill into the context of rapidly industrializing modernity.[52] Freise and Korkowsky suggest that the image of the odd fellow in the iron grip of the crisscrossing railroads stands for the loss of the Biedermeier-like idyll and, simultaneously, for uncertainty about the future.[53]

As tempting as it might be to see the poem as Pasternak's indictment of Berlin as a demonic metropolis, a subtler message can be found in his interrogation of the role of the human in the machine age through the figure of the odd fellow. The future remains mysterious in "Gleisdreieck," as in "The Butterfly-Storm" and "Sailing Away," but the odd fellow is anyone but an indifferent observer—he is a poet. The liminal space of the attic, which the odd fellow inhabits, and the window, which displays the unrelenting force of industrial progress, are privileged spaces in Pasternak's poetics.[54] For example, in his poem "About These Verses," the lyric subject also lives in an attic and is seemingly disinterested in the external world in the fateful year 1917, preferring to spend his time reading Romantic poets. When he leans out the window, he asks, "What millennium is it / out there, my dears?" (Какое, милые, у нас / тысячелетье на дворе?). For generations, critics used these lines as proof of Pasternak's political aloofness. At a certain point this phrase even became an idiom meaning inappropriate behavior in a given historical context.[55] However, as Timothy Sergay has argued, Pasternak borrowed these lines from Dickens's short story "A Christmas Carol," and, according to Sergay, the seemingly ahistorical poem in fact depicts Russian revolutionary change fashioned after the spiritual rebirth of Ebenezer Scrooge.[56]

Pasternak's use of similar imagery of an absent-minded poet observing a city from the attic in "Gleisdreieck" invites sociohistorical interpretation of the Russian cultural situation in Berlin. The poem offers a view of the city that telescopes out from the attic and the station: the odd fellow's apartment opens onto the railroad, which expands into an urban panorama at sunset, which in turn stands for the entirety of Berlin, a transitional city grounded in the present. The odd fellow is thus in the middle of an existential crossroads signified by the triangular shape of the train station. The idea of an intersection is further implied by the allusion to four cardinal directions because the image of the sunset rushing from Potsdam suggests the East-West axis.

The importance of the odd fellow's predicament is further underscored in the last stanza, where he stands apart from the mob of commuters collectively depicted as a "lump of grimaces," faces seen in the window of the rushing subway car. On the whole, we see that the odd fellow is positioned in the complex network of relations, is aware of them, and is uninterested in fitting in.

As is the case with Pasternak's other Berlin poems, and indeed most of his early poems, "Gleisdreieck" resists unequivocal interpretations. Within the context of Berlin, this aspect of his poetry acquires special significance that anticipates a looming shift: the reader recognizes certain images, words, and sounds as multivalent and comprehends the need to choose one interpretation among the available options. But commitment to a single reading cancels out other interpretative paths. The resulting hesitation only strengthens the impression of the text's importance. All three poems discussed here show the extent to which the poet can be imbricated in his medium. In all three, Pasternak is committed to a highly personalized and ambiguous poetic mode. We do not know what the odd fellow of "Gleisdreieck" is going to do, where the seafarers of "Sailing Away" will arrive, and how the world will change once the rainstorm begins in "The Butterfly-Tempest." But this uncertainty is the most important, authentic, and aesthetically valuable thing.

Soon after leaving Berlin, Pasternak wrote "The First of May," a poem that was promptly published in *LEF*, the journal of the Soviet organization the Left Front of the Arts. As it opens, the poem presents a modern city as a force of nature and an arena of historical transformation that is imperceptible to the untrained eye:

О город! О сборник задач без ответов,
О ширь без решенья и шифр без ключа![57]

O city! You are a set of problems without answers,
a vastness without solution, and a cipher without a key.

These enigmatic lines challenge the reader to decipher the city at the same time that they proclaim the task impossible: there are no definitive answers, solutions, or keys to the cityscape. Reading Pasternak's Berlin poetry cannot provide conclusive evidence about why he chose to leave Germany. However, rereading his poetry in historical context does provide an illuminating case study in exploring Berlin as a site of Russian writing in transition, after the Revolution but before the sharp opposition developed between Russian literature in Russia and Russian émigré literature. For Pasternak, that transition begins as early as the second stanza of "The First of May," when the ambiguous lyrical rumination characteristic of his Berlin poems, which are in tune with his early poetry, turns into heavy-handed proletarian messaging borrowed from "The Internationale," which is characteristic of his particular take on historical poetics. This sharp rhetorical turn would not last very long, but in 1923 it signaled the end of his trial emigration.

Red Berlin—Mayakovsky

Pasternak was not unique in traveling to Berlin and (re)evaluating abroad his career and standing as a poet in Soviet Russia. The turn against futurism in the country had consequences for Pasternak's friend (and rival) Mayakovsky, too. Whereas Pasternak's poetry was criticized for its lack of political awareness, Mayakovsky's ideologically overzealous work could not be faulted as politically aloof. However, Lenin himself deemed Mayakovsky's writings a reflection of his "hooligan communism."[58] If Pasternak was too lyrical and not revolutionary enough, Mayakovsky was too revolutionary. As Bengt Jangfeldt suggests, Mayakovsky traveled abroad seeking new publishing opportunities and exposure after suffering a public scolding in the newspaper *Pravda* for alleged excessive avant-gardism.[59] Considering that Mayakovsky was nevertheless committed to the revolutionary, transformative potential of art, a look at his accounts of Berlin in juxtaposition to Pasternak's can reveal illustrative instances of urban poetry from a profoundly non-émigré perspective. Mayakovsky's Berlin is rarely included in discussions of Russian culture in Berlin, even though his writing is centrally important for understanding the émigré and non-émigré positions in the early 1920s. Reading Mayakovsky's Berlin texts alongside Pasternak's ambivalent Berlin poems yields surprising evidence of Mayakovsky's own ambivalence about his participation in the strictly regulated Bolshevik cultural initiatives.

In *Veshch'*, Mayakovsky and Pasternak were singled out as the most original voices of contemporary Russian letters.[60] Mayakovsky's poem "This Is to You" opened the journal's poetry section.[61] The pathos of this poem, which declared an urgent need for new forms for proletarian art, underscores the drastic difference between the two poets. Unlike Pasternak's highly subjective diction, Mayakovsky's style is declarative and totalizing:

Товарищи,
дайте новое искусство:
такое чтоб выволочь Республику из
　　　　　грязи.

Comrades,
give us new art:
such art that can drag the Republic out of the
　　　　　dirt.[62]

The "dirt" the country needs to expunge can be understood literally and metaphorically. The Soviet Republic was ravaged economically after the Great War, the Russian civil war, and the years of international blockade. Many individuals, including Pasternak and Mayakovsky, headed to Berlin in part to improve their impoverished material condition. But metaphorically, dirt can also refer to the many efforts to undermine the Soviet project abroad.[63] Soviet Russia was a pariah state for much of the 1920s; Germany, another pariah nation, was virtually alone in establishing diplomatic relations with Russia in 1922. Mayakovsky saw his mission as not only to create and demand new forms of art, but also to defend the Revolution.[64]

Before ever visiting Germany and before the two countries became strategic partners, Mayakovsky turned to Berlin as an instructive example of a compromised revolution. Due to the failure of the 1918 November Revolution, Weimar Berlin was home to a sharply divided German Left. The city demonstrated what Petersburg could have become had the Provisional Government not been ousted by the Bolsheviks. This fact made Berlin an easy target of Mayakovsky's biting political satire in his 1921 verse play *Mystery-Bouffe: A Heroic, Epic, and Satiric Representation of Our Time*. An outlandishly utopian text originally written in 1918, the play was part of Mayakovsky's attempt to reinvent Russian futurism and produce new art for a new world.[65] However, there was no place for Weimar Berlin in Mayakovsky's conception of the future. In the 1921 version of the play, Berlin, "an uneasy sea of delirium," was to be annihilated by a revolutionary force, represented allegorically as the Great Flood.[66] According to the logic of the play's biblical imagery, Berlin's sin was the betrayal of the true Revolution.[67] Appropriately, a politically dubious German bourgeois paints this portrait of the city on the eve of its destruction:

Так вот—сижу я это у себя в ресторане
на Фридрихштрассе.
В окно солнце так и манит.
День,
как буржуй до революции, ясен.
Публика сидит и тихо шейдеманит.
Суп съев,
смотрю я на бутылочные эйфели.
Думаю:
за какой мне приняться беф?
Да и приняться мне за беф ли?
Смотрю—
И в горле застрял обед:
Что-то неладное с Аллей Побед.
Каменные Гогенцоллерны,
стоявшие меж ромашками,
вдруг полетели вверх тормашками.[68]

So yes—There I was today sitting in a restaurant
On Friedrichstraße.
The sun through the window was so enticing.
The day was as bright as a bourgeois before the Revolution.
The public was sitting there and quietly Scheidemannizing.
Having finished my soup,
I looked at the bottles, those Eiffel towers,
and pondered
what *boeuf* I should try.
And should I even try *boeuf* today?
I looked again,
and my supper got stuck in my throat:
Something's wrong with Victory Avenue.
The stony Hohenzollerns,
which had been standing among the daisies,
suddenly flew up, head over heels.

The familiar modernist urban imagery of the Eiffel Tower is presented here in a remarkably negative key. The satiated German burgher sees multiplied Eiffel

Towers in the presumably empty wine bottles. The iconic tower captured the imagination of many avant-garde artists, but in *Mystery-Bouffe* Mayakovsky considers the tower part and parcel of Western bourgeois culture. Another modernist landmark, the impressive, elevated train station on Friedrichstraße, is simply ignored. Instead, Mayakovsky mocks the fashionable promenade, a staple of nineteenth- and early twentieth-century European bourgeois modernity, as a stand-in for the shallow capitalist lifestyle and meaningless discussions of politics in cafés, or "Scheidemannizing." This satiric neologism derives from the name of Philip Scheidemann, a Social Democrat and the first Chancellor of the Weimar Republic—hence the Communists' ideological enemy. In this depiction of Berlin, Mayakovsky is charting a new political history by means of a favorite futurist device: the obliteration of the old.[69]

The 1921 edition of *Mystery-Bouffe* reached a wide international audience. This "first Soviet play," as it was advertised, was translated into German and performed for the delegates of the Third Congress of the Comintern in Moscow. Vsevolod Meyerhold directed this remarkable avant-gardist production, with sets and costumes by Kazimir Malevich.[70] The play received a sympathetic review in the German press.[71] However, the Soviet authorities disliked Mayakovsky's attempt to reconcile futurism with a pragmatic ideological agenda. The performance was too avant-garde for proletarian tastes and its message too heavy-handed for the intelligentsia. Mayakovsky was denied his royalties and subsequently sued Gosizdat (the State Publishing House). In part to escape this scandal, he headed abroad. Although Party officials did not approve of Mayakovsky as an ambassador of Bolshevik culture, he was perceived and acted as one during his extensive travels throughout the 1920s.[72] He spoke no foreign languages, but as his German publisher Wieland Herzfelde remembered, his charisma and power of expression in Russian were such that after meeting him one immediately understood that he was "a revolutionary artist and the artist of the Revolution in one person."[73]

Far from being an émigré, Mayakovsky nevertheless showcased his commitment to the revolutionary cause in a way that highlights his attempts to find new audiences outside Russia. His first trip to Berlin, in 1922, coincided with the opening of the First Exhibition of Russian Art at the Gallery van Diemen, which featured his window posters made for ROSTA, the state news agency. (The exhibit was an official affair, jointly organized by Narkompros and the German Foreign Office to raise funds for famine relief in Russia.) During this trip Mayakovsky also signed a contract with the leftist publishing house Malik Verlag and met the leading German avant-gardists, including Otto Dix, Ernst Toller, John Heartfield, and George Grosz.[74] Most importantly, after this trip Mayakovsky's attitude toward Berlin changed drastically. During the visit he wrote a poem called "Germany," conceived as his personal gift to the country, a text free from the obfuscations of bureaucratic rhetoric:[75]

> Германия—
> это тебе!
> Это не от Рапалло.
> Не наркомвнешторжьим я расчетам внял.
> Никогда,
> кикогда язык мой не трепала
> комплиментщины официальной болтовня.[76]

> Germany!—
> This is for you.
> This is not from Rapallo.
> I did not account for the interests of the Ministry of Foreign Trade.
> Never,
> Never were my lips at the service of
> The protocol compliments of officialdom's babbling.

The poem consists of two parts, an extended Dedication and "The Workers' Song." From the start, the author aligns himself with the German working class and startlingly dismisses the official Soviet institutions of trade and diplomacy as meaningless, though their official titles offer sonic material for cacophony. Though full of hyperbole, as is typical of Mayakovsky, the poem has no clichés about Germany or the Germans of the kind that are otherwise ubiquitous in contemporaneous Russian texts on the topic (Germany as a nation of soldiers and callous burghers).[77] The poem makes a genuine gesture to reach ordinary Germans and empathize with the suffering proletariat. Strikingly, the expression of solidarity with the Germans turns into an attack on the French and the British, presumably a comment on the Treaty of Versailles, infamous for humiliating the Germans.[78] Mayakovsky achieves solidarity with Berlin by identifying Germany as a fellow victim in the aftermath of the Great War. He also makes sure to attack Alexander Kerensky, the exiled leader of Russia's Provisional Government, thus implicitly criticizing political exiles as well. But he does so from a cosmopolitan position, writing "I have long ago / discarded / the ragged clothes of nationalities" (Я давно / с себя / лохмотья наций скинул). Furthermore—and rather shockingly—Mayakovsky, who wrote *Mystery-Bouffe* a year earlier, not only declares his love of Germany, but even depicts himself as a German, "Germany's own son" in composing the poem.[79] Considering the overwhelming Germanophobic sentiment in Russian society during and after the Great War, these proclamations are unexpected. (Only a few years earlier Mayakovsky engaged in making anti-German wartime propaganda posters ridiculing Berlin and the German military.)[80] Yet here Mayakovsky consciously draws a parallel between Russia and Germany as kindred nations united by victimhood. If we take at face value Mayakovsky's intention in "Germany" to make an honest statement free of diplomatic motives, then his insistence on universalizing the challenges of the Revolution in Russia and Germany appears to be a move toward securing for himself the role of the poet of the international Left.[81]

As if trying to realize his own earlier appeal for "new art," Mayakovsky composes the second part of the poem as "The Workers' Song" and sets it in Berlin, which is presented as the dormant center of a future revolution. "The Workers' Song" is the main part of Mayakovsky's gift to Germany: the text is positioned explicitly on the border between music and verse and can be read as a chant, a utilitarian medium intended to inspire and organize the proletarian masses awaiting the "Red Revenge" in the face of stalled historical progress:

Мы пройдем из Норденов
Сквозь Вильгельмов пролет Бранденбургских ворот.
У них доллáры.
    Победа дала.
Из унтерденлиндских отелей
ползут,
вгрызают в горло доллáр,
пируют на нашем теле.
Терпите, товарищи, расплаты во имя . . .[82]

We will come from the Nordends,
and walk through the Kaiser-Wilhelm passageway of the Brandenburg Gate.
They have dollars.
    The victory gave it to them.

They crawl
from hotels on Unter den Linden,
they chew the dollar's neck,
and feast on our body.
Endure, comrades, in the name of payback . . .

The phonetic inventiveness here is staggering: pronouncing "walk through Kaiser's passageway of the Brandenburg Gate" in Russian is a challenge that pays off—the explosive combination of the consonants "v," "b," "r," and "t" is militantly thunderous, turning German toponyms into Russianized literary weapons. In addition, "The Workers' Song" is as rhythmically captivating as some of Mayakovsky's comparable earlier texts, such as the "Left March" (1918). But unlike the universalizing "Left March," "The Workers' Song" is topographically very specific and underscores Mayakovsky's familiarity with Berlin, especially with the impoverished blue-collar districts in Berlin-Nordend.[83] Surprisingly, however, Mayakovsky does not so much offer a vision for a new proletarian Berlin as reclaim the city's landmarks, including the Brandenburg Gate and the luxury hotels on Unter den Linden, for the working class.[84] This iteration of Berlin is certainly more imaginative than the one in *Mystery-Bouffe* where the city was simply annihilated, yet since Mayakovsky's inspired incantation of the "Red Revenge" does not presuppose a new form of the city, his "Germany" sounds like wishful thinking. Nevertheless, the poem remains a singular example of Mayakovsky's self-proclaimed internationalism as he branches out to Berlin to overcome a political and creative impasse at home.

During his subsequent journey to Berlin in 1924, however, Mayakovsky will articulate an innovative project for communist Berlin. His "Two Berlins" anticipates the birth of a "Red Berlin," or a "Third Berlin" that will emerge as a Hegelian synthesis after the clash of bourgeois and proletarian versions of the city embodied, respectively, by Kurfürstendamm and Nordend. The poet's confidence in the inevitable rise of Red Berlin was supported by contemporary events. In the May 1924 federal election, the Communist Party of Germany received historically strong support.[85] Blending current politics and verse, the final lines of "Two Berlins" are the confidently stressed "The first news: / there are / three million votes / for the Communists."[86] The idea of the Third Berlin is arguably borrowed by Mayakovsky from home. Moscow was long regarded in Russia as the Third Rome, and the 1917 Revolution renewed the capital city's image as the alternative center of the world.[87] Berlin is by no means a substitute for Moscow here, but the overlapping urban images offer yet another glimpse into Mayakovsky's attempts to claim the urban space of Berlin for the international Left.

What appears to be truly original in "Two Berlins" is Mayakovsky's invention of a poetic subject as a politically engaged flâneur: unlike the Baudelairean flâneur as detached observer, Mayakovsky's poetic subject walks the streets as a political agitator, helping to realize the coveted goal of a communist future.[88] In "Two Berlins" Mayakovsky records his Berlin impressions from the street level. The opposition between the two Berlins is based on differences in the modes of movement in the city. At first the poem's subject is not walking but driving around Berlin's wealthy neighborhoods.[89] But once the poet reaches the working districts of Nordend, it is stressed that he is walking ("I'm idly walking / and bustling / in the workers' Nordend").[90] In fact, walking makes his observations all the more powerful as he witnesses the egregious poverty and overhears the news of one family's collective suicide. Whereas Pasternak's lyric subject strove to distance himself from the city and observed the sprawling and impersonal metropolis from the height of his attic, Mayakovsky engages with Berlin on the ground level, and the act of walking translates into cognition and communication.[91] Walking spatializes the poet's affective state and, overwhelmed by the movement in the deprived Nordend, the subject of "Two Berlins" cries out that anyone who has walked here even a mile will understand—

> что должен
>   отсюда
>   родиться третий—
> третий родиться—
>   Красный Берлин.[92]

> that a third—
>   a third city
>   must be born
> from here—
>   a Red Berlin.

Mayakovsky's Berlin flâneur is not a solitary figure alienated in the crowd, but a partisan visionary of an organized collectivity. He reassures the reader that nothing will stop Red Berlin from coming to life. The imagined city is presented as a force that will break through all obstacles, be it a bayonet or imprisonment. Importantly, however, this proletarian force transforms Berlin not through violence but through democratic elections, and the poem ends with the proclamation of an impressive three million votes for the Communists. Life, politics, and art merge in the polarized world of "Two Berlins" as Mayakovsky dissolves the borders separating them in order to reach the ideal of Red Berlin.

Always at the vanguard, Mayakovsky looked to Weimar Berlin as a new frontier for the affirmation of his ideas about international left art. A prodigious futurist in imperial Russia, he found it exceedingly difficult to fit into the postrevolutionary Soviet Russian cultural scene. As debates about the relevance of the avant-garde were becoming more hostile in proletarian Moscow, Berlin offered Mayakovsky an opportunity to export and test his brand of artistic expression, often applied to the cityscape.[93] His depictions of Berlin evolved from the center of the failed revolution in *Mystery-Bouffe* to the site of a brooding revolt in "Germany," and to a hopeful rebirth of the city in "Two Berlins." However, in his popular reports on contemporary Europe for Soviet audiences, he downplayed his international forays. For example, his article "Berlin Today" (1923), published in several newspapers across the Soviet Union, compared Berlin to a cemetery and a slowly decaying organism and implied that the Germans were losing their national identity as their famed punctuality disappeared in the overgrown railroad tracks.[94]

The title of Mayakovsky's 1924 lecture on his international travels, "On *LEF*, White Paris, Gray Berlin, and Red Moscow," suggested furthermore that there was only one true Red capital in Europe: Moscow.[95] In this talk, Paris was assigned the "white" label for being the citadel of the anti-Soviet monarchist emigration, while Berlin's "gray" was a comment on both the city's divisive politics and the heterogeneity of its Russian émigré community. Mayakovsky was actually instrumental in making Berlin "gray." He appeared several times at Russian expatriate literary gatherings, never failing to amplify the differences among émigrés undecided about returning to Russia. At a meeting with Berlin's Union of Russian Students in Germany, he defined his position unequivocally: "One can only be a Russian poet and writer if one lives with Russia, in Russia. Let those authors who have settled abroad not think that they will enter Moscow riding on a white horse of their multivolume works."[96] In a feat of aggressively patriotic rhetoric, Mayakovsky simultaneously encouraged Russian authors abroad to return to the motherland and informed them that they were inferior to those working in the Soviet Union.

Mayakovsky had a difficult time defending his vision of Russian postrevolutionary literature as the Bolshevik leaders grew intolerant of the avant-garde, and he was concerned that the returning émigré intellectuals would bring their conservative tastes with them.[97] Mayakovsky's gray Berlin was in many respects the site of his own trial emigration, understood not as the kind of ambivalent contemplation of life abroad discernible in Pasternak's highly subjective pivotal aesthetic, but as an opportunity for Mayakovsky to exercise the avant-garde internationally and demonstrate its potential for fomenting revolution on the street. As such, Mayakovsky's gray Berlin was also a battlefield for Red Moscow. But there were still writers in Berlin who were neither red nor white, such as Khodasevich, who wanted a Russian literature free of ideological intrusion and would not, metaphorically speaking, accept a return to Russia on Mayakovsky's terms.

Berlin as the Stepmother of Russian Cities—Khodasevich

Vladislav Khodasevich is celebrated as one of the most influential Russian émigré poets. Although he wrote relatively little poetry after leaving Russia, focusing on literary criticism instead, the poetry he did write is so bleak that it easily supports the idea that émigré literature embodies the despair, alienation, and resentment of life in exile.[98] Khodasevich's Berlin poems are among his cruelest and most hopeless, and they appear in his last collection of verse with the suggestive title *European Night*.[99] The dark and cynical mood of these poems colors Khodasevich as a tragic version of the poet in exile.[100] He also authored Russian Berlin's famous epithet, "the stepmother of Russian cities"—a twist on the medieval description of Kyiv as the "mother of Russian cities."[101] As "the stepmother," Berlin becomes a substitute for a native city and the center of orphaned Russia Abroad.

Khodasevich did not, however, embrace émigré values overnight. In a way, emigration chose him. As David Bethea underscores, "Khodasevich's status as émigré writer was never something he bore lightly, and by the 1920s he realized that he was living in a world of rapidly vanishing options. At first he would not, and later he could not, return to the Soviet Union."[102] Khodasevich's cryptic diary, known as the *Kammerfurier's Journal*, which he kept from the time he arrived in Berlin in 1922 until his death in Paris in

1939, shows that he avoided socializing with anti-Soviet intellectuals until the mid-1920s.[103] Gradually, his attitude toward emigration changed, and eventually it became apparent that the Soviet government would have exiled him regardless.[104] Yet he left Moscow as that government's official delegate, collaborated in Berlin with Gorky, and had nothing but contempt for the tsarist-sympathizing exiles.[105] Khodasevich was not fond of new experimental poetry, and he certainly loathed Mayakovsky and came to dislike Pasternak. But like them, he supported the overthrow of the tsar in 1917 and worked at developing his own understanding of postrevolutionary art. And it was in Berlin that he could reflect on and propagate his artistic position within the conflicting movements in contemporary literature and culture. Shortly after his arrival in Berlin in June 1922, Khodasevich wrote to a friend in Russia: "Literature here is but a province. I'll have to turn everything upside down and induce the revaluation of values. I'm preoccupied with real routine troubles so far; not writing poetry and not glimpsing into 'other worlds': *nicht hinauslehnen!* [do not lean out]. It's written inside all streetcars to bring the likes of us to our senses."[106]

Russian literature produced in Berlin was what Khodasevich found hopelessly provincial. The writers he admired and respected remained in Petersburg.[107] He cited Nietzsche's "the transvaluation of values" slogan, meaning a thorough revision of fundamental beliefs, to stress his contempt for anti-Soviet intellectuals living in Berlin. Very soon Khodasevich would begin a revaluation of his own values and never again return to Russia, which in 1922 seemed to him "grueling, murderous, repulsive, but wonderful nonetheless, as always."[108] Berlin was a crucial space where Khodasevich began his transformation from a patronizing fellow traveler to a bitter stateless refugee.

What is even more fascinating in Khodasevich's letter is that it is peppered with various formulaic phrases from German public spaces—*Rauchen verboten!* [smoking prohibited], *Bitte Deckel schliessen!* [please put the toilet lid down]—which he weaves into his narrative. Berlin's urban space permeates the spatial, linguistic, and temporal dimensions of his being. He paradoxically resists the foreign space—*nicht hinauslehnen!*—by deliberately following the militaristic proscriptions governing everyday life in the city. He is drawn to Berlin but can only access its surfaces in the form of signs regulating all manner of bodily activities.

In keeping with this play on surfaces and in-betweenness, Khodasevich's trial emigration in Berlin yields an aesthetic that can be conceptualized as "extraterritorial." A term of legal coinage, extraterritoriality implies exemption from the laws of a country in which an international subject is physically present.[109] The concept of extraterritoriality has also been productively used in cultural studies for exploring configurations of space and time unbound by political borders and nationalist attachments.[110] Extraterritoriality is nevertheless far from being a post-national utopia of free migration. In fact, in literary criticism the extraterritorial condition is associated with the paradox of simultaneous inclusion and exclusion that characterizes exile: inhabiting a foreign place and becoming a foreign local.[111]

For example, Khodasevich's poem "Sorrento Photographs" gives shape to this phenomenon through the image of a double-exposed snapshot. This accidental photograph contains the shots of two distinct worlds at once, pre-revolutionary Russian and contemporary European—one overlaid onto the other in an extraterritorial formation. Both images are interdependent and exist in a spatiotemporal limbo of inclusive exclusion. Greta Slobin has observed that this sort of double exposure is a hallmark of Russian émigré literature, which is steeped in a nostalgia for the vanished Russian world.[112] I argue that it is more productive to approach this sort of double exposure as a sign of an extraterritorial aesthetic, which illuminates not only the distress of displacement but the fissures in the very idea of home. Khodasevich's Berlin poems, in particular, grapple with the universal alienation that accompanies life in any big city. He arrived at his extraterritorial aesthetic as he was exploring the contradictions of belonging in exile.

Khodasevich scholars acknowledge the poet's uneasy stance toward emigration during the first few years of life abroad and his uncertainty about going back or staying, yet until recently his Berlin poems tended to be analyzed primarily in the exilic register with emphasis on the poet's anguish and disillusionment. This tendency can be traced to Khodasevich's partner Nina Berberova. In her influential memoir *The Italics Are Mine* (1969), she reproduced his existential outcry, "*Here* I cannot, cannot, I cannot live and write, *there* I cannot, cannot live and write."[113] But Khodasevich was unusually prolific in Berlin, writing some of his finest poems there, though developing mostly the same themes of spiritual alienation of his earlier poetry. Nevertheless, his commitment to the classical literary heritage earned him the reputation of a "traditionalist, if not an outright reactionary," as Michael Wachtel has put it.[114] His contemporary Soviet critics faulted his poetry for sounding ahistorical. In "Interlude," Tynianov all but dismissed Khodasevich as a nineteenth-century epigone, and Nikolay Aseev characterized his poetry as "ominous, exhausted to the state of thorough impotence, refusing any movement."[115] Recent studies of the poet's oeuvre suggest that he was highly aware of such criticism and responded to it in his Berlin poems.[116] Berlin's cultural milieu as the space of trial emigration is just as important to repositioning Khodasevich as an author attempting to withstand the ideological polarization of Russian literature.

In Berlin, Khodasevich developed a renewed sense of kinship, tradition, and modernity. Consider for example his poem "All is Stony. Into a Stony Passage," which often serves as shorthand for discussions about the plight of Russian exiles in Europe:

> Всё каменное. В каменный пролет
> Уходит ночь. В подъездах, у ворот—
>
> Как изваянья—слипшиеся пары.
> И тяжкий вздох. И тяжкий дух сигары.
>
> Бренчит о камень ключ, гремит засов.
> Ходи по камню до пяти часов,
>
> Жди: резкий ветер дунет в окарино
> По скважинам громоздкого Берлина—
>
> И грубый день взойдет из-за домов
> Над мачехой российских городов.
>
> <div align="right"><i>23 сентября 1923
Берлин</i>[117]</div>

> All is stony. Into a stony passage
> the night departs. In entryways, by gates—
>
> stand like statues—couples stuck together.
> And heavy breath. And heavy cigar smell.
>
> The key clinks against the stone; the door bolt rumbles.
> You must walk upon the stone till five o'clock, and

wait: the brisk wind will blow into an ocarina,
pass through the keyholes of cumbersome Berlin—

and a coarse day will rise from behind the houses
above the stepmother of Russian cities.

September 23, 1923
Berlin

The persistence of stone imagery renders the city a cold and alienating space. It is a realm of shadows locked out of the building, perhaps by a strict German landlady. The poem has been the subject of several analyses, and they focus on Berlin's stony environment as a marker of stillness, harshness, and infertility.[118] It is hard to ignore this stony imagery since the poem opens with the unsettling hypermetrical stress in the first line's first word "vse," underscoring that indeed everything is stone. The highly original rhyme "okarino/Berlina," however, links the city with a musical instrument. Ocarina is a type of flute. There are not that many names of musical instruments that would rhyme with the word "Berlin." The use of "ocarina" is striking both because it is rare and because it is a wind musical instrument that, despite a limited sound range, can produce moving lyrical melodies. In the poem, then, the wind blowing into the "keyholes of cumbersome Berlin" turns the foreign city into a musical instrument. The resulting music accompanies the dawn of a new, "coarse" day. As gloomy as this scene may seem, the rising sun in the poem's last stanza also suggests the forthcoming renewal and continuity Khodasevich so cherished. Furthermore, while it is true that dawn exposes Berlin as the "stepmother," familial bonds are nonetheless implied.

The notion of surrogate motherhood is in fact an important motif in Khodasevich's poetics. Though half-Polish and half-Jewish, he identified as Russian and underscored his connection to Russia in a 1922 poem, writing "Not by my mother, but by a peasant woman from Tula / Elena Kuzina was I nursed."[119] As the émigré critic Vladimir Weidle has noted, although the image of the peasant woman is effective, the language of Khodasevich's poetry originates not in Elena Kuzina's but Pushkin's innovative Russian.[120] Meanwhile, Pushkin is not only *the* Russian poet, but a poet who also was highly aware of his African ancestry. In other words, literary language is the vital thread that connects Khodasevich to Russia, irrespective of geography.[121]

Khodasevich's vision of the language of poetry as a mediator even in the face of Berlin's stoniness is in stark contrast to the ambivalence about the present in Pasternak's poems from Berlin, expressed in the images of the brewing storm, the hermit ship, and the attic, which the poet is reluctant to leave. It also contrasts with Mayakovsky's visceral experience of walking in the city, translated into versified avant-garde agitation. Whereas both Pasternak and Mayakovsky experiment with incorporating Germanic words associated with industrialization and urban modernity ("pakgauzy," "unterdenlindskie oteli," etc.) into their Berlin poems, Khodasevich depicts the city through the sound of a musical instrument that cannot be tied to one specific location. The urban space of Berlin forms and informs Khodasevich's poetic sensibility as extraterritorial.

Arguably more than any other Russian poet who matured after the Revolution, Khodasevich insisted on the primacy of language—not territory—in a national tradition. In a 1933 essay, "Literature in Exile," he passionately argued against the growing consensus about the extinction of Russian literature in exile, claiming that "a literature's national character is created by its language and spirit, not by the territory where the literature's life unfolds and not by the *byt* reflected in it."[122] He then cataloged major exiled authors who wrote in Italian, French, Polish, Hebrew, and Yiddish and eventually shaped respective literary traditions. In private correspondence, he shared doubts about the validity of his own claims, but in his public work, he strove to envision an unbroken tradition persevering in and through language. A decade earlier, in 1924, while still uncertain about repatriating or emigrating, Khodasevich wrote to Viacheslav Ivanov: "I am equally depressed by what goes on in Russia and by what I've had ample opportunity to witness here, in emigration. There—deliberate and systematic destruction of culture, here—complete idiocy.... Russia is split in two, and both halves are rotting; each in its own way. It is tormenting that no *words* will help here: a 'historical process' is taking place. And such a process is like bad weather—one can only wait till it's over, sit it out. But will we sit it out?"[123] Khodasevich sent this letter after leaving Berlin, but the notion of "waiting out" (peresizhivat') historical calamities is akin to trial emigration, and the trial period was coming to an end. Still, despite his declared linguistic helplessness in the face of a "historical process," the poems he wrote in Berlin offer more than a surrender to the rot of history.

The rotting metaphor Khodasevich uses in his letter to Ivanov, and which permeates his Berlin texts, can be linked to his major 1917 poem "Grain's

Way," which encapsulates his idea that culture depends upon meaningful engagement with preceding traditions and is sustained by cultivation.[124] Continuing Pushkin's classical notion of the poet as prophet, Khodasevich imagines the poet as the prophetic wise sower who ensures that the grain's way leads to a better time and place. The poem's final lines are haunting yet hopeful: "And you, my country, and you, her people, / will die and will come alive, having gone through this year" (И ты, моя страна, и ты, ее народ, / Умрешь и оживешь, пройдя сквозь этот год). The biblical connotation of the seed that dies to bear more fruit (John 12:24) reinforces the message that suffering can bring strength and regeneration.

The process of disintegration is unavoidable for this agricultural metaphor to work, and so is fertile soil. Yet as Bethea and others underscore, Khodasevich's Berlin consists of impenetrable stony surfaces.[125] In the central Berlin poem "Underground," for example, Khodasevich employs the imagery of masturbation to emphasize the futility of writing in exile. The poem ends with the striking image of an old man, ousted from an underground toilet for indecency, ascending the stairs like "Hades's shadow" into the "brilliant delirium" of the Berlin day:

А солнце ясно, небо сине.
А сверху синяя пустыня . . .
И злость, и скорбь моя кипит,
И трость моя в чужой гранит
Неумолкаемо стучит.

And the sun is bright, the sky is blue.
and up above is a blue desert . . .
And my rage and my grief seethe,
and my walking stick on the alien granite
Incessantly taps.

Bethea argues that "Underground" is an extensive inversion of the core principles of "Grain's Way" and calls the poem Khodasevich's "most terrifying and powerful expression of the condition of exile."[126] He posits that instead of the wise sower, we encounter a version of the biblical Onan spilling his "seed" on the ground, the "alien granite" upon which the poem's subject taps his walking stick.[127] While Bethea's interpretation is compelling, to read this poem so pessimistically is to miss the extraterritorial complexity of Khodasevich's aesthetic. Let us recall that in 1923 Khodasevich does not yet consider himself an émigré and continues to entertain the possibility of returning to Russia. In Berlin he also works on the second edition of his book of poems *The Heavy Lyre*. The title evokes the image of a weary Orpheus. Considering that in "Underground" there is a direct reference to Hades, the poem can be understood in terms of the mythological story of Orpheus and Eurydice. Khodasevich replaces the tragic ancient Greek lovers in the underworld with a depraved old man in an underground toilet and an old woman who chases him away from it. Even so, as a disgraced Orpheus returns to the world, the tapping of his walking stick is modified with the adverb "neumolkaemo"—which can be translated as "incessantly," while also meaning "without ceasing to speak." The poem's subject might be unable to penetrate the foreign soil, but he retains his voice and searches for alternative means of expression.

In Germany it became clear to Khodasevich that the old models of representation had exhausted themselves. However, presenting "Underground" as a thorough revaluation of the core principles expressed in "Grain's Way" is somewhat shortsighted. As Sarah Bishop has argued, "Grain's Way" was not originally written as a programmatic poem, but it became one in emigration. In her analysis of the book of poems as a genre, Bishop finds that "Grain's Way" had a decidedly different tonality in its earlier editions. The poem was placed toward the end of the original book of poems, such that a reading of the entire volume before arriving at "Grain's Way" showed the poet's "path from despair and doubt to a shaky, tentative hope."[128] But in the final 1927 edition, the poem opens the book. Instead of delaying the reveal of the pattern of cyclical rebirth, this placement points to an outcome that is never in doubt. Bishop concludes that the "result is a more epic view of the poet in general."[129] If "Grain's Way" only gained strength after Khodasevich left Russia, his Berlin poems are likewise indicative of the broader shifts in his aesthetics.

Duality is at the heart of Khodasevich's poetry, and as Robert Hughes observes, the theme of "the discrepancy between appearance and reality, the imprisonment of his soul in a despised environment" is present even in his earliest texts.[130] In his later European poetry this duality is no longer a lyrically subjective internal conflict but a symptom of extraterritoriality as part of the modern human condition. These poems are set in the present, but the sense of time is distorted, unable to communicate the past and much less the future. Extraterritorial displacement is especially evident in the settings of Khodasevich's Berlin poems: the poetic subject can be found in the transitory public spaces of the street, café, bar, and the underground, but never in a home.

These ambiguous environs also affect the physical wholeness of his characters. His Berlin is grotesque, populated with "little freaks, huge freaks, and regular freaks," including Cain with skin disease, night strollers with dogs' heads, a young barmaid raped and murdered in the woods, and a decapitated poet.[131] And yet in his seemingly dreary Berlin tableaux Khodasevich does not so much emphasize a crisis of poetry as articulate an alternative futurity for literature outside Russia. He turns to scandalous and unpoetic imagery, experiments with classical rhyme and meter, and mixes contemporary parlance with archaic vocabulary. In doing so, he joins the cohort of other European modernists.

Khodasevich's overwhelming fascination with Berlin's gritty side is in keeping with Weimar Berlin's zeitgeist. John Malmstad has observed that Khodasevich's Berlin is so terrifying it reminds one of George Grosz's Berlin.[132] One could easily include the Berlin of Otto Dix, Max Beckmann, Ludwig Meidner, and other German expressionist artists and poets. Khodasevich's representation of Berlin shares much with the established expressionist practice of depicting city life, and it is also inflected with the aesthetics of Russian fin-de-siècle.[133] In "A Berlin Poem," a sick poet finds himself in a smoke-filled café and stares out the window until he recognizes in the windows of a passing streetcar the reflection of his own severed head. In "An Mariechen," the poet directs his gaze at another person. He is so repulsed by the thought of Mariechen, the young barmaid, ending up in a bourgeois marriage with an "honest man" that he wishes her to be attacked at night and to experience shame and death at once. He then imagines her corpse in a birch forest with a knife stuck under her virgin breast. In describing his disturbing vision, Khodasevich uses the most endearing vocabulary and soothing rhythm. This depiction of female sexual mutilation draws on Alexander Blok's poetry and echoes narratives of sexual murder (*Lustmord*) in Weimar-era expressionist art and literature.[134] Like his German counterparts, Khodasevich mined the depths of human depravity as an artistic strategy for channeling the vulnerability of modern city life. His use of macabre imagery, coupled with classic Russian iambs and trochees, morphed into texts brimming with anxiety and irony as he realized the universality of postwar political instability. The title of his final collection of poems, *European Night*, thus covers the entire continent to emphasize the geographical breadth of what he perceived as a universal spiritual condition, which extends beyond the expatriate Russian milieu.

But the uncertainty of belonging in a rapidly changing world can be overcome through writing. This message is strongly suggested in "All is Stony. Into a Stony Passage," analyzed earlier. The poem's restless subject cannot return to his boardinghouse until early morning; he does not fit in among the "couples stuck together," but he witnesses a dawn. As "cumbersome Berlin" emerges from the darkness, the city, with its many gutters and keyholes, is likened to a flute (ocarina) played at night. The anti-lyrical scene of the coarse day rising above the "stepmother of Russian cities" may seem to vocalize the blues of exile. But this urban musical reference evokes another poem with strikingly comparable imagery: Mayakovsky's "And Could You?" Mayakovsky wrote this poem in 1913 and included it in his avant-garde book *For the Voice*, designed by Lissitzky and published in Berlin in spring 1923 (fig. 6).[135] The poem ends with a provocative question: "And you, / could you / perform a nocturne / on the drainpipe flute?" (А вы / ноктюрн сыграть / могли бы / на флейте водосточных труб?). Lissitzky's typographic treatment of Mayakovsky's text, including the grid of question marks and the interdependent positioning of the pronoun "vy" and particle "by," establishes the subjunctive

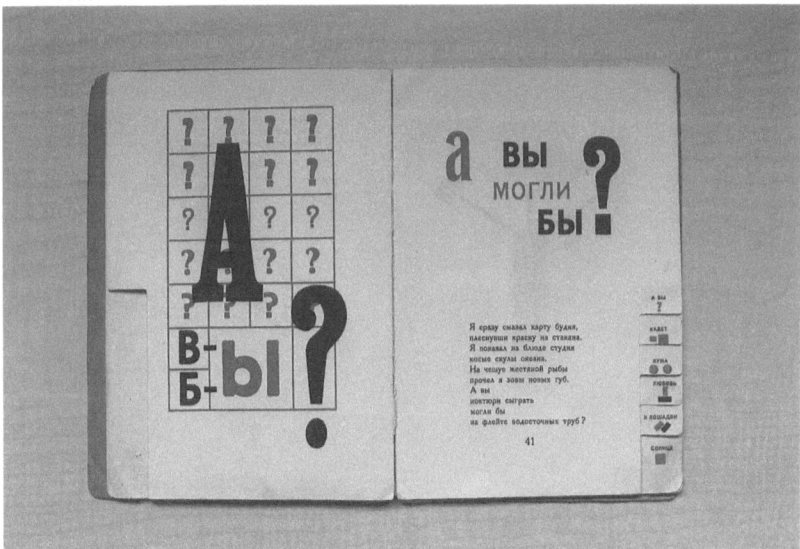

Figure 6. Mayakovsky's poem "And Could You?" with Lissitzky's typographical design in *For the Voice* (1923). Amherst Center for Russian Culture.

mood and intensifies the poem's interrogative message. Whether intentionally or not, in "All is Stony. Into a Stony Passage" Khodasevich delivers a resounding "yes" to the question posed by his avant-gardist rivals: he can indeed perform a "nocturne on the drainpipe flute," even in foreign, cumbersome Berlin. He fashions Berlin's drainpipes into ocarinas and uses them as instruments in his improvised poetic orchestra, even if they play in a mostly minor key.

For Khodasevich, as for Pasternak and Mayakovsky, Berlin became a referent in defining aesthetic and ideological positions after the Revolution. But those positions were not always fixed. Berlin's multidimensional artistic networks suggest the fluidity of the émigré/non-émigré identities, which oscillate between sameness and difference. Russian Berlin's transitional nature in the years 1921–23 facilitated trial emigration, creating a singular moment in the development of Russian modernist poetry. This moment is characterized by spatial indeterminacy and, when examined closely, it disrupts the Soviet/émigré binary as we know it. This moment also exposes how these poets' active engagement with Berlin's topography distinctly marks their artistic practices—Pasternak's pivotal ambiguity, Mayakovsky's internationalist avant-gardism, and Khodasevich's extraterritorial aesthetic. Their Berlin texts contribute to the urban mosaic of interwar Berlin and simultaneously highlight the growing fissures in the fabric of Russian postrevolutionary literature.

2

Guides to Berlin

Exiles, Émigrés, and the Left

On March 28, 1922, Vladimir D. Nabokov, a prominent Russian statesman, was shot and killed during a public émigré event at Berlin's Philharmonic Hall. The violent attack echoed terrorist tactics used by many Russian revolutionaries in their struggle against the tsarist autocracy since the nineteenth century. In Berlin, the tables had turned: the perpetrators were the monarchists and their victim was a key member of the Constitutional Democrats (Kadets).[1] Nabokov's assassination was a tragic reminder that while the Bolsheviks had ultimately seized power in October 1917, they were but one group within the multifaceted Russian revolutionary movement. The Kadets belonged to the most conservative of progressive parties. For the monarchists, though, they were as bad as any Bolshevik for supporting the 1905 Revolution and welcoming the abdication of the tsar in 1917.

As the civil war drew to a close in 1921, all non-Bolshevik political parties were increasingly unwelcome in Soviet Russia. Berlin sheltered the losers of the Revolution, including the monarchists and liberals as well as the Mensheviks and Socialist Revolutionaries. Among the centers of the Russian postrevolutionary emigration, Berlin of the early 1920s was the most heterogeneous. Scholars typically acknowledge Russian Berlin's cultural and political diversity, but many of its residents' leftist commitments remain insufficiently explored. The existing accounts of Russian émigré culture privilege its anti-Bolshevik ethos, the sense of uprootedness, and cultural conservatism.[2] Yet, the exiled liberal intelligentsia and non-communist leftists were engaged in permanent soul-searching as Russia was being reimagined without them and on terms that were not theirs. Once the goal of the Revolution was no longer propelling leftist ideas and aesthetics, what sort of diasporic identities and sensibilities did they shape?

Interwar Berlin is especially important for answering this question in its role as "Europe's Eastern train station," as Karl Schlögel has put it. Although Berlin was a hub for exiles, the city also maintained consistent Soviet ties thanks to its geographical proximity to Russia, railroad infrastructure, and diplomatic agreements. Following the Treaty of Rapallo in 1922, Berlin grew more diverse, flooded with a new wave of Russian visitors and émigrés whose support or condemnation of the Soviet project was tentative.[3] The majority of Russian Berliners arguably favored the Revolution as a necessary step in establishing a democratically governed Russia, but they continually differed over the acceptability of Bolshevik policies and methods. Yesterday's political exiles from the Soviet Union were today's enthusiastic supporters of the Bolshevik state and vice versa.[4] These conditions shaped a diasporic community that shared not only the experience of displacement but also the exposure to multiple ideologically irreconcilable political organizations, as well as the ability to cross borders. Far from being an insular and apolitical émigré enclave, Russian Berlin was a site of transnational encounters that prompted cultural producers to interrogate their positions as well as the purpose of their art in the wake of the Bolshevik takeover in Russia. In the previous chapter, the case studies of Pasternak, Mayakovsky, and Khodasevich demonstrated that during this interlude period in Berlin, ideological positions were not static but continued to evolve. In this chapter, I turn to narrative prose produced in Berlin to examine the ways politically progressive, non-Bolshevik Russian writers in Berlin negotiated their stance vis-à-vis Soviet Russia and emigration by writing about Berlin.

Guides to Berlin: Migration and Travel Writing

A particularly salient archive of the geohistorical contradictions of this time and place can be found in literary representations of the city. Writing about Berlin, usually in autobiographically inflected genres, became an outlet for ordering the inherently disorienting experience of life abroad. That some émigrés could return to Russia—that the permanence of their exile was not definitive—meant that city writing also functioned as a rhetorical staging ground for conceptualizing this historical moment, finding new means of artistic expression, and exercising political agency despite being in exile.[5]

Consider Viktor Shklovsky's epistolary novel *Zoo, or Letters Not about Love* (1923), which catalogs the romantically rejected narrator's disappointments with diasporic politics in Berlin and ends with an "official" application requesting permission to return to Russia.[6] Andrei Bely's pamphlet travelogue

One of the Mansions of the Kingdom of Shades (1924) chronicles the author's decision to leave Germany and return to Russia as he feverishly dances through Berlin's cafés and cabarets.[7] Ilya Ehrenburg's travel sketches gathered under the title "Letters from Cafés: Germany in 1922" (1923) conjure up a methodical description of Berlin's inferiority by an author unwilling to relocate to Moscow.[8] These authors belonged to differing political and aesthetic camps, but their narratives about Berlin and its Russian contingent reflect a universal sense of conflicted indeterminacy about the future.

Admittedly, some avowedly anti-Bolshevik writers also turned to Berlin for similar purposes. In 1925, Vladimir Nabokov, whose father was assassinated three years earlier, published his seemingly austere short story "A Guide to Berlin," an exile's tour of a foreign city interspersed with shrewd observations on the nature of art, history, and memory.[9] Although Nabokov's text precludes a leftist reading—the narrator has nothing but contempt for communism—the story offers an original approach to structuring a day in the life of an émigré as a city guide. Utilitarian at its core, the city guide genre is a form of tourist propaganda that promises to unlock foreign spaces and that models ways of discovering culturally significant sites ranging from museums to restaurants. Nabokov inverts city guide logic by focusing on the mundane aspects of city living: navigating streets under construction, riding on public transit, visiting a zoo, and getting a drink at an unremarkable pub. Nabokov's protagonist cannot overcome the foreignness of the city in which he lives as a permanent stranger. Unfamiliarity with foreign surroundings, the same feeling that might excite a tourist, only reaffirms the exile's alienation. That alienation is nevertheless valuable as a bulwark against assimilation. Therefore, the frame of a city guide stabilizes the uncertainty of exile while offering an outlet for maintaining difference.

On the opposite end of the ideological spectrum are discursive guides to Berlin written by Soviet visitors. For example, Larisa Reisner's essays from Berlin published under the title "Berlin in October of 1923" have an emphatically communist tone.[10] In Berlin as a special correspondent for the Soviet newspapers *Izvestiia* and *Krasnaia zvezda*, Reisner dispenses sharp critique of German socialists and provides heartbreaking descriptions of the urban poor. Whereas in his "A Guide to Berlin" Nabokov deliberately avoids any sort of social commentary, Reisner visits the Reichstag and Berlin's working-class neighborhoods to describe the politicians' cowardice and the workers' poverty. She compares the Reichstag to a zoo, a casino, and a museum—anything but a functional legislative body. Her style is agitational, sharp, and accusatory. In her eyes, in Berlin "Everyone is ready to do anything to avoid a social revolution" (79). This statement concerns both the deputies from the Social Democratic Party of Germany, who are consumed with "sausage, coffee, and anxiety" in the Reichstag's cafeteria, and the petty bourgeois, who dream of margarine at night. She sees no possibility for a revolution in Berlin, a city that in her view represents a failed promise. At the same time, she draws attention to the plight of women, many of whom were pregnant, malnourished, or socially trapped: "Very often the man does not withstand the famished devastation—the crying of the unfed children, of hunger, and of dirt. Thousands of women workers are abandoned by their husbands and lovers after a few months of unemployment" (82). Although her impressions of Berlin are thoroughly pessimistic, Reisner retains some hope for a better future by implying that it can be achieved through gender equality. She imagines strong future women, mothers struggling against "hunger and degeneration" with "all the strength of youth and love, all the stamina and culture of the world's singular working class," unencumbered by "not only unenlightened men but also . . . unenlightened women" (83).

Given how partisan Reisner's Berlin writing is, her text, while thematically fascinating, leaves little room for interpreting the possibilities of émigré identities. Unsurprisingly, her brief description of "Russian émigrés" is condescending, albeit playfully so. She describes seeing some Russian émigrés at the zoo giving a baboon "empty match boxes, pieces of old paper, and cigarette butts." The "old and smart" baboon quickly loses interest and signals his disdain by turning his "crimson-blue" behind to them (84). In Reisner's account, the émigrés are no more worthy of attention than the discarded items they offer the baboon. In contrast to Reisner, Ehrenburg, Shklovsky, and Bely consider the identities of Russians abroad a subject worth exploring. Like Reisner (and Nabokov), they elaborate their difference abroad by writing about the city. But compared to politically uncompromising Reisner and Nabokov, Ehrenburg, Shklovsky, and Bely represent Berlin as a zone of negotiation of Russianness in the postrevolutionary moment.

When read as city guides, Ehrenburg's, Shklovsky's, and Bely's Berlin texts lend themselves to tracking the shifts in aesthetics and politics at a moment of extraordinary geopolitical flux. The three authors position themselves as neither nostalgic exiles nor agents of newly defunct empires.[11] In a world where newly redrawn national borders trigger transnational mobility and sharpen national identities, these writers describe the foreign city to map the development of their understanding of what it means to be a Russian writer abroad. Indeed, reading these texts as guides opens a fresh critical perspective on the time when Russian literature was splintering into divergent Soviet and émigré modalities. As a result, these texts function as guides *out* of Berlin as much as guides *to* Berlin.

Shklovsky, Bely, and Ehrenburg arrived in Berlin in the early 1920s out of necessity. The literary critic Shklovsky fled Bolshevik persecution as a Socialist Revolutionary in 1922. Bely, the renowned Symbolist poet and anthroposophist, was allowed to leave Russia in 1921 to improve his health and settle marital affairs with his estranged wife. Ehrenburg, a former Bolshevik but a committed socialist, settled in Berlin after being expelled from Paris in 1921. Unlike Nabokov and those who spent the rest of their life in exile, Shklovsky, Bely, and Ehrenburg returned to Moscow in 1923, though Ehrenburg went back to Western Europe almost immediately and continued to live and work there as a foreign correspondent for the Soviet press until 1940. Shklovsky was to become an inimitably controversial Soviet author, while Bely died in 1934 after a series of failed attempts at ideological conformism.

Shklovsky's *Zoo*, Ehrenburg's "Letters from Cafés," and Bely's *Kingdom of Shades* are not labeled as guides to (Russian) Berlin and are not meant to provide practical advice to tourists. Instead, by mixing literary and nonliterary prose—as well as overtly ideological statements with intimately personal ruminations—Shklovsky, Ehrenburg, and Bely use city writing as an occasion to reflect on their own presence in Berlin at a pivotal historical point. Approaching these texts as city guides allows us a look into what the Formalist critic Boris Eikhenbaum called "the literary everyday" (literaturnyi byt), understood as the dialectics of an author's embeddedness in the literary marketplace.[12] Consequently, the spatial perception registered in Shklovsky's, Ehrenburg's, and Bely's texts and these texts' publication histories reflect the development of the concepts of "Soviet" and "émigré" authorship in relation to Berlin's cityscape.

The Literary Everyday: In Search of a Genre

Russian prose genres experienced a revival in the early 1920s. The literary historian D. S. Mirsky observed in 1925, while still in emigration himself, that the "most important event in Russian literary life of the last three years is the decline of poetry and the rise of prose," which followed "the bookless years of the civil war."[13] In Russia proper, however, Boris Eikhenbaum was far less optimistic in his assessment of contemporary prose. In his programmatic essay "The Literary Everyday" (1927), Eikhenbaum argues that in a society reshaped by the Revolution, the question of "how to write" had been superseded, "or at least complicated," by the problem of "how to be a writer."[14] As Serguei Oushakine has pointed out, Eikhenbaum's argument was less about extra-literary materialist concerns, such as the importance of information on book contracts and the makeup of the reading public, and more about "directing the readers' attention to the forms of authorial self-reflection regarding the writer's positionality within the system of literary production."[15] Inspired by the rapid expansion of the periodical press in the Soviet Union, Eikhenbaum puts this theory into practice in his 1929 hybrid text *My Periodical*. In her analysis of *My Periodical*, Alyson Tapp has observed that Eikhenbaum's approach to writing "dissolves the boundaries between scholarship, autobiography and literary prose ... allowing critic, author and perhaps even literary character to mingle and move between these three modes of writing."[16] Oushakine interprets Eikhenbaum's disregard for strict genre boundaries as an advantage afforded by publishing in periodicals, whether newspapers or journals, which allowed authors to connect the disparate elements of their biographies and writerly activity.[17] This experimentation with genres and media, conceptualized as the theory of the literary everyday, was meant to underscore the unprecedented historical and social environment that required new forms of representation.[18]

Although Eikhenbaum's critical concept of the literary everyday is rooted in Soviet realities, extending his theory to Russian Berlin helps us recognize how writers who lived outside Russia searched for representational forms adequate for the times. The problem of authorial agency, "how to be a writer," only sharpened in a context of diasporic displacement, especially because the likely duration of that displacement was unclear in the early 1920s. Whereas writers in Berlin opted for city writing as a way of cultural mapping, in his *My Periodical*, Eikhenbaum chose the format of an idiosyncratic periodical publication for ordering heterogeneous literary material, wandering across various modes of writing within the same text to anchor the authorial experience of a rapidly changing Russia. In Berlin, the motif of wandering extends beyond metaphor and into daily practice. The texts about Berlin thus reflect the literary everyday of migrant writers.

The Migrant Literary Everyday of Russian Berlin

When D. S. Mirsky wrote about the revival of Russian prose after the civil war, his knowledge of contemporary Russian literature—the writing of Evgeny Zamiatin, Mikhail Zoshchenko, Vsevolod Ivanov, Lev Lunts, Boris Pilniak, and Lydia Seifullina—came almost exclusively from books published in Berlin.[19] The Russian publishing business flourished in Berlin from 1920 until 1924, as the city's presses supplied books to the global diaspora and, for a brief period of time, the Soviet market. The Kadet community leader and publisher Iosif Gessen states in his memoir that in 1921 there were as many as seventy-two Russian publishing houses in the German capital, a city of four million.[20]

The major publishers had a variety of distinct profiles and rosters of authors. For example, Ivan Ladyzhnikov Press was nominally Marxist. Zinovy Grzhebin Press, Gelikon, Petropolis, Epokha, and Otto Kirchner & Co. were established in Russia and permanently moved their operations to Berlin, where they served diasporic markets while hoping to distribute their books in the Soviet Union. In fact, most of Grzhebin's books bore a "Berlin-Petersburg-Moscow" imprint. Slovo was established by the Kadets and partially owned by the German Ullstein Verlag; it published nineteenth-century classics, early Nabokov, and the monumental *Archive of the Russian Revolution* series. Obelisk specialized in Russian religious philosophy. Mednyi Vsadnik was a monarchist press. Olga D'iakova & Co., a rare example of a publishing house run by a woman, supplied the diaspora with house manuals, family calendars, and reprints of middlebrow bestsellers.[21]

This robust publishing environment reflects the complexity of Berlin's postrevolutionary Russian community. The abundance of publishing venues also suggests that authors had a choice in aligning themselves with particular presses serving specific segments of the reading public. This meant that authors had a general sense of their audience, and presses, without pigeonholing their authors, offered an affiliation that gave some indication of mutual political dispositions. Someone like the anti-Bolshevik Nabokov, for example, never published with pro-Soviet publishing houses such as Grzhebin or Gelikon. And Shklovsky and Ehrenburg never published with Slovo, but both Nabokov and Ehrenburg published with Petropolis.[22] Eikhenbaum might have called this publishing reality "literature's social mode of being," and to grasp its dynamics, it is imperative to consider how the authors conceived of their roles as writers in the polarizing Russian-language community.

Ehrenburg, Shklovsky, and Bely were remarkably prolific in Berlin. From 1921 to 1923, Ehrenburg wrote and edited nearly twenty books; Shklovsky published a volume of memoirs, a novel, and a collection of essays; and Bely published sixteen books.[23] The city's thriving publishing market facilitated much of this activity, especially considering that most of what these authors published then was written earlier, as was the case with Ehrenburg's *The Extraordinary Adventures of Julio Jurenito* (Gelikon, 1922), the revised edition of Bely's *Petersburg* (Epokha, 1922), and Shklovsky's *A Sentimental Journey* (Gelikon, 1923).[24] The time these writers spent in Berlin, however, yielded a number of texts about Berlin itself. In his Author's Preface to *Zoo, or Letters Not about Love*, Shklovsky wrote that his novel originated as "a series of essays on Russian Berlin" but evolved into a "book on a dispute between people of two cultures" (3–4; 267). Similarly, Bely and Ehrenburg focused on migrant encounters in Berlin in their respective narratives. And much as Shklovsky's *Zoo* turned out to be a book about more than Russian émigré life, Bely's *Kingdom of Shades* and Ehrenburg's "Letters from Cafés" employed the theme of exile in Berlin as a motivation to express broader concerns about postwar, postrevolutionary European modernity.

Ehrenburg and the End of "Spatial Patriotism"

The interconnection of the political and the poetical undergirds all three of these Berlin texts. This entanglement is especially evident in the work of Ehrenburg. For most of his life, Ehrenburg acted as a bridge between the Soviet Union and the West.[25] Even before becoming an indispensable figure of Soviet cultural diplomacy under Stalin, Ehrenburg tirelessly promoted abroad the literature, art, architecture, and theater produced in Soviet Russia. He was very active when he lived in Berlin in 1921–23. In addition to publishing his own poetry and fiction, editing with El Lissitzky the international journal *Veshch'/Gegenstand/Objet*, and writing countless book reviews, Ehrenburg secured Russian publishers in Berlin for the poetry of Boris Pasternak, Marina Tsvetaeva, and Sergey Esenin. Though Ehrenburg took advantage of the opportunities to publish in Germany, he publicly declared that "Russian culture is being created there, in Russia, and not outside it."[26]

Ehrenburg's own national status as a writer in Berlin was somewhat ambiguous. As a reviewer for *Izvestiia* put it, "the Whites consider Ehrenburg to be Red, and the Reds think he is White."[27] Ehrenburg broke with the Bolsheviks long before the Revolution, in 1909, and was not enthusiastic about the October 1917 coup. After a brush with the secret police, he left Russia in 1921 but never self-identified as an émigré and maintained his Soviet citizenship. In Soviet Russia of the 1920s, however, he was considered a friendly but deeply mistaken fellow traveler.[28] Some of these contradictions are captured indirectly on the cover of Ehrenburg's collection *Six Stories* about *Easy Endings*, published in Berlin in 1922: illustrated by Lissitzky, the text is typeset in the prerevolutionary orthography, bringing together the avant-garde abstraction linked with revolutionary change and archaic letters (such as *yat*) associated with the imperial past. Many émigré writers, including Nabokov, signaled their commitment to prerevolutionary Russia by never accepting the new orthography.

Ehrenburg was consistently critical of conservative émigrés. But he also shared a certain sensibility with them. As Ehrenburg's biographer Joshua Rubenstein has observed, "underlying his work for most of the 1920s is a brooding sadness over the fate of his country."[29] However, Ehrenburg's pessimism was of a different sort than that of the exiles bemoaning the loss of old Russia. He was attached to the idea of pan-European unity and was concerned about Soviet Russia's isolation from the wider world. He later commented on this period by writing that "spatial (prostranstvennyi) patriotism" died in the trenches of the Great War: "the notion of 'motherland' (rodina) was swiftly replaced with 'modernity' (sovremennost')."[30] For Ehrenburg, Russia's isolation meant temporal incongruity with the rest of Europe.

Strikingly, in "Letters from Cafés" Ehrenburg placed the center of modernity in Berlin, not in Moscow. He wrote that "there is only one contemporary city in Europe—Berlin" (123).[31] With backhanded praise, he called Berlin "the only imaginable capital of Europe. Among other big cities, it is Karl Schmidt, Paul Durand, Ivan Ivanovich Ivanov" (123) or, one might add, "John Smith." Finding Berlin remarkably average, Ehrenburg saw the city as an "enormous nodal train station" at the intersection of nationalism and internationalism, socialism and capitalism, republicanism and monarchy. In the space of rival political systems, Ehrenburg's sympathies lay with the working-class districts of eastern and northern Berlin, with the singers of "The Internationale." His speculation that perhaps the people who "fiercely reject the notion of motherland are the genuine patriots" exposed his own beliefs: he lived abroad to advance the cause of a class struggle unbound by national borders.[32]

In the impoverished Berlin of 1922, he saw a city on the brink of an all-out class conflict. Berlin appeared to him as a "messenger (gonets) into the most delightful uncertainty" (133). The uncertainty of the future eventually proved to be far from delightful, but the messenger metaphor was fortuitous. Ehrenburg's idealism would be tempered with time—and he would leave Germany once France issued him a visa—but in post–Great War Berlin, he came to realize his own role as a messenger from and for Moscow.

Shklovsky and Diasporic Celebrity

Shklovsky was also a leftist but not a Bolshevik. He actively participated in the Revolution and the civil war on behalf of the Socialist Revolutionaries.[33] His support of the Provisional Government and opposition to the Bolsheviks eventually forced him into exile in Berlin, where he, nevertheless, kept his distance from the anti-Soviet émigrés. Shklovsky socialized instead with Maxim Gorky, himself an exile of sorts, and published primarily with the Soviet-friendly Berlin press Gelikon. Despite Shklovsky's ambivalence about the Soviet government—his wife was arrested and refused a permit to leave Russia, and his brother was repeatedly arrested on political grounds—he chose to return. He lived in Berlin from March 1922 until September 1923. His celebrated novel *Zoo*, published by Gelikon, secured his return to Moscow as its last chapter was stylized as an official application to be allowed to repatriate.[34] On the eve of his departure to Moscow, Shklovsky wrote to Gorky, "I am leaving. It will be necessary to lie (pridetsia lgat'), Alexei Maximovich. I know, it will be necessary to lie. I don't expect good things."[35]

Once back in Russia, Shklovsky was eager to point out the deficiency of émigré life and the foreignness of Germany. While the original 1923 edition of *Zoo* defies easy categorization as a piece of either émigré or Soviet literature, the subsequent editions of the novel in 1924, 1929, and 1964 were made distinctly Soviet with numerous additions and strategic cuts.[36] In 1924, moreover, Shklovsky added to his Berlin corpus such lines as "We [the émigrés] were plucked from Russia like a sieve from the water. Dark and incomprehensible is the smoke of northern, working-class Berlin."[37] Working-class northern Berlin arguably remained incomprehensible to Shklovsky even after his exile because he never showed genuine interest in German proletarian culture. But when he lived in Berlin's wealthy and heavily Russian western part, he was fully aware of the diasporic dynamics and pursued publishing opportunities that promised to reach a wide readership.

Several chapters from *Zoo* first appeared in the journal *Beseda*, an uncensored international journal aimed at informing readers in Russia of the latest developments in the arts and sciences abroad. *Beseda* was a phenomenon typical of Russian Berlin in that it brought together as editors such seemingly ideologically incompatible writers as Gorky, Khodasevich, and Bely.[38] In 1923 they all had enough in common to work together on a journal intended for distribution in Soviet Russia. (Notably, the journal's working title had been *Putnik*, or "the wayfarer," suggesting the editors' consideration of a travel guide as metaphor.)³⁹ To secure access to Moscow and to attract émigré contributors and readers, it was very important to the editors that *Beseda* maintain political neutrality. Initially, Shklovsky was on the editorial board as well, but his colleagues excluded him after he jeopardized the journal's apolitical stance by causing a scandal during a public lecture on Russian futurism.⁴⁰ Following this incident, Shklovsky wrote to Gorky to apologize and added, "I think that this whole affair won't compromise the journal, more so because on the Berlin market I am a relatively insignificant and easily erasable entity."⁴¹ Shklovsky's behavior did not, in fact, affect the journal, and his marketplace value only increased after the publication of *Zoo*. But since *Zoo* ended with the author's declaration "it is not right that I should be living in Berlin," he effectively erased himself from the city and the émigré community.

BELY AND THE LIMITS OF IDEOLOGICAL ECUMENICALISM

The Soviet authorities delayed allowing—and ultimately never allowed—*Beseda* to be imported into the USSR. The newly instituted censorship directorate Glavlit suspected the journal of carrying out subversive anticommunist propaganda. Among its many concerns, Glavlit took note of Andrei Bely's consistent defense of anthroposophy on the pages of the journal. Formally, Bely was a supporter of the Soviet project, living in Berlin as a Soviet citizen. He was one of the few authors with reputations firmly established before 1917 who accepted the October Revolution. Yet, as an ardent adept of anthroposophy, Bely saw revolutionary change in Russia as spiritual rejuvenation. The Marxist understanding of reality in terms of competing economic forces was alien to him.⁴² Although he had little in common with the Bolsheviks ideologically, he nevertheless welcomed the transformation of Russia and went abroad to improve his health, not necessarily to emigrate.⁴³

Arriving in Berlin in November 1921, Bely discovered in the city a "swarm of Russians—a chaos."⁴⁴ Despite the chaos of social divisions, it appears from Bely's Berlin diary that he knew well the distinctions among the anti-Soviet émigrés and Soviet-sympathetic intelligentsia.⁴⁵ While he stayed away from the monarchists, he had numerous contacts with liberals and non-Bolshevik leftists. Bely's literary everyday in Berlin reveals a writer positioning himself above political differences on the left, if not disregarding those differences as insignificant details. As soon as he arrived in Berlin, he accepted the invitation of the Kadet Gessen to deliver two public lectures, one on Alexander Blok and the other on the "contemporary crisis," in support of

Russian student associations abroad.[46] He was a board member of the short-lived House of the Arts, billed as an apolitical organization that functioned as an informal trade union of Russian writers, artists, musicians, and actors outside Russia.[47] In addition to serving as an editor of the politically neutral *Beseda*, he had his own monthly literary journal, *Epopeia*. He also contributed book reviews to the Socialist Revolutionary daily *Dni*. His publishers during the Berlin years 1921–23 included the Kadet press Slovo, the Menshevik Epokha, Soviet-friendly Grzhebin Press and Gelikon, and the Soviet Gosizdat. Despite not having much sympathy for either the Soviets or émigrés, Bely worked with both.[48]

Bely's ideological ecumenicalism ended abruptly with his decision to return to Moscow in October 1923. As many of his contemporaries noted, Bely was emotionally unstable in Berlin, and his sudden departure from Germany has occasioned various speculative explanations.[49] Be that as it may, in 1922 he believed that the possibility of going back to Russia was forever foreclosed for him, but a year later he was in Moscow, praising the spectacular achievements of the Soviet state.[50] His impressions of life in Berlin were gathered into an eccentric pamphlet, *One of the Mansions of the Kingdom of Shades*, published by Gosizdat in 1924. In this book, Bely depicts Berlin as the heart of the émigré community embedded within the "kingdom of shades." The narrator located this community's topographical center at the spire of Berlin's Gedächtniskirche: "The spire of the remarkable church is a crossing of times and spaces: the antediluvian past is crossed here with the approaching future.... The spire of that church is a point from which run (razbegaiutsia) the radii of Russian resettlements in Berlin within the circumference of the Charlottenburg reality. One radius is Kurfürstendamm. Another radius is Tauentzienstraße. The third radius is Kantstraße. The fourth radius—and so forth" (31).

Bely envisioned Berlin in transnational terms as a mythopoetic space of intercultural encounter embodied in geometric shapes, similar to the way he described Petersburg in his eponymous novel. He saw Berlin of 1923 in the agony of cultural exhaustion, the same way he saw Petersburg of 1905. The pessimism and hopelessness that imbued Bely's Petersburg—the city unable to contain the forces of entropy—came to haunt him in Berlin. Both cities are inhabited by shades (teni), but in Berlin the accent is on the degenerate copies of real humans losing themselves in the "rhythms of foxtrot" and cocaine (60). Echoing the pessimism of *Petersburg*, Bely's narrator found Berlin, and the European civilization for which it stood, to be but a thin veneer over the "savage chaos of real decay and death" (69).

In a marked difference from *Petersburg*, however, *Kingdom of Shades* ends on an improbably cheerful note. The narrator moves back to Moscow, which he describes as "the source of life" and "a creative laboratory of future, perhaps never-before-seen, forms" (69; 73). The book's cover cartoonishly emphasized the difference between black Berlin (bourgeois men and a lady in fancy hats promenading in front of a "Berliner Kafe") and red Moscow (gender-ambiguous workers in front of a massive construction site) (fig. 7).[51] The pro-Soviet bias of Bely's narrative, finished in Moscow and published in Leningrad, is so hyperbolic that one Bely scholar, Monika Spivak, has even characterized it as a "servile Soviet collection of essays."[52] Having made the choice to return, Bely was diligently performing the role of a class-conscious writer in contrast to his ideologically flexible stance in Berlin.

Paradoxically, Bely, who was much more ambivalent about politics than Shklovsky and Ehrenburg, wrote the most explicitly propagandistic text against Russians in Berlin. Yet Bely's text, narrated by "Someone," is so maniacally agitational and so structurally peculiar in its condemnation of Berlin as a "bourgeois Sodom" that it borders on parody. It is likewise difficult to take at face value Ehrenburg's "Letters from Cafés" and Shklovsky's *Zoo* because these texts struggle to maintain the separation of the fictional and documentary narrative elements. In various proportions, all three texts contain a blend of autobiographical observations, historical commentary, and political insight. They are produced by authors navigating a precarious political landscape: unwilling to become émigrés, they are reluctant to embrace the Bolsheviks as all the while Russian culture is becoming increasingly divided.[53] Although these authors ultimately sided with the Soviets, the record of their publishing and public activity in Berlin shows how circuitous their paths to Moscow were. Their texts' generic inconsistency, moreover, reflects the search for representational means of synthesizing the period's contradictory cultural dynamics. To guide the reader through (Russian) Berlin in a reassuring way, Ehrenburg, Shklovsky, and Bely chart the city's topography and inscribe themselves into it. Importantly, as Shklovsky's "letters not about love" and Ehrenburg's "letters from cafés" indicate, the figure of the personal letter plays a major role in navigating the cityscape. Therefore, before turning to these writers' spatial conceptions of Berlin, I explore the epistolary strategy of plotting the urban narrative.

Figure 7. Cover of Andrei Bely's *One of the Mansions of the Kingdom of Shades* (1924).

A Guide to the City: The Letter

In Russian Berlin, autobiographically inspired novels and memoirs fueled the publishing industry's continuous stream of books about the origins and indignities of the Great War, the Revolution, and the civil war. Shklovsky's *A Sentimental Journey*, for example, was one such autobiographical book published in Berlin that covered the eventful years 1917–22. In the novel that followed, *Zoo, or Letters Not about Love*, Shklovsky switched from describing the recent past to narrating the present and, as the critic Yan Levchenko has put it, "the adventurous mode changed to the psychological mode."[54] The confessional quality of *Zoo* was intensified by the novel's epistolary form, which allowed Shklovsky to experiment with various modes of writing within the same text. In one of the first reviews of *Zoo*, Yuri Tynianov underscored the fundamental ambiguity between the personal tone and public exposure present in Shklovsky's letters, writing that they "do not actually make the impression of *private* letters." He then praised Shklovsky for producing a narrative that was simultaneously "a novel, a feuilleton, and a piece of scholarship."[55] With similar results, Ehrenburg also chose to arrange his narrative about contemporary Germany, "Letters from Cafés," as a series of letters. And although Bely's *Kingdom of Shades* is not an epistolary narrative, it did originate as a public lecture about Bely's time in Berlin.[56] That these texts are shaped as variations on types of address suggests a desire to establish channels of communication and convey privileged information about Berlin—to guide the reader through the city.

The literary form of travel impressions presented as letters had been in existence long before these Russian writers found themselves in Berlin.[57] But in its modernist take, the epistolary genre facilitated open experimentation with writing conventions to mediate the disorienting reality of a foreign environment. In her analysis of epistolary modes in twentieth-century fiction, Linda Kauffman has argued that letters enabled writers to "self-consciously dramatiz[e] the processes of textual production and reception to undermine the tenets of representation."[58] Shklovsky's admission in *Zoo* that "it's impossible to write a book in the old way" (23) illustrates Kauffman's point but also highlights the transnationalism of his new approach. Even before writing *Zoo*, Shklovsky tapped the narrative possibilities of private correspondence by publishing a personal letter to his fellow theorist Roman Jakobson in three different journals based in Prague, Odesa, and Berlin.[59] As the literary scholar Asiya Bulatova has shown, Shklovsky used the open letter to create a discourse that united quotidian speech, criticism, and fiction; moreover, by publishing the letter in multiple venues simultaneously, he bypassed conventional mechanisms of publication and dissemination.[60] A similar dynamic is at play when it comes to narrating the experience of displacement in Berlin.

Letters Not about Love and a Russian Public Sphere Across Borders

Zoo is written to a woman named Alya, the fictional embodiment of the writer Elsa Triolet, who forbids Shklovsky to write to her about love. Struggling to contain his romantic feelings for her, the narrator writes instead about the city around him. Shklovsky is impossibly self-ironic throughout the novel, but his obsessive letter writing in and about Berlin is indicative of an earnest attempt to outline a Russian public sphere across borders. That is, as Shklovsky cycles through a diverse range of topics in his letters, the letters themselves formally act as rhetorical bridges connecting people and ideas across space and time. This public sphere is conjured by letter writing in linguistic and cultural terms, not in a geographical space. Indeed, there is little of Berlin in the novel. Shklovsky mentions Berlin's boroughs, landmarks, and streets, but it is otherwise a Russian city with Russian inhabitants. (Both Ehrenburg and Bely, as well as Pasternak, appear on the pages of *Zoo*, along with many other Russian writers and artists who were in Berlin at the time.) Some scholars have taken the novel's central metaphor of a zoo to mean that the novel represents "an allegory of exile" and "a model émigré narrative."[61] Nevertheless, it is important to remember that *Zoo* is not only an account of the Russian neighborhood surrounding the Berlin Zoo, but also an homage to the futurist poet Velimir Khlebnikov and his poem "Menagerie" (1909). The long poem depicts a transhistorical world in which past, present, and future converge in a panoramic vision of human and animal cohabitation. The civilizational reach of Khlebnikov's "Menagerie" is important to Shklovsky, and he cites the poem in full in the novel's epigraph.[62] Likewise, Alya's letters from Tahiti underscore the primacy of linguistic connection over geographic distance.

The tragedy of *Zoo* lies in the consistent failure of the narrator's letters to spark meaningful connections. Shklovsky includes the actual letters Elsa Triolet wrote him as rare responses from Alya. Her honest indifference to him, expressed in the same breath as her boredom with the things around her, is as funny as it is devastating: "The pile of books which I can read and don't read, the telephone into which I can speak and don't speak, the piano on which I can play and don't play, the people whom I can see and don't see and you, whom I should love and don't love" (59). The numerous cultural figures about whom Shklovsky writes in *Zoo* are likewise preoccupied with their own lives and art projects and have little interest in anything else. Despite being an epistolary novel and formally facilitating a dialogic exchange, *Zoo* constantly enacts a short-circuiting of dialogue. The only actual dialogue to be found in the novel occurs in Letter Ten between Alya's slippers and water during a flood in Berlin.

By the middle of *Zoo*, Letter Seventeen of Twenty-Nine, the narrator declares that he feels stuck in Berlin and downgrades Russian Berliners to the status of squatters (sidel'tsy): "We are refugees. No, not refugees but fugitives—and now squatters" (63). Presumably, genuine refugees, exiles, and émigrés would have been galvanized by a common sense of righteous indignation and a resolve to fight for shared ideals.[63] But in Shklovsky's estimation, "Russian Berlin is going nowhere. It has no destiny. No propulsion" (63). This lack of propulsion stalls all mobility.[64] Toward the end of the novel, Shklovsky supplements the propulsion metaphor with that of a dying battery: "Our batteries were charged in Russia; here we keep going around in circles and soon we will grind to a halt" (95). The futility of "going around in circles" coupled with the lack of propulsion means that Shklovsky's letters cannot circulate properly, rendering him powerless and isolated. As Alya writes in her last letter to him, "A lot of letters have accumulated. I have filled the drawer of my writing desk; my pockets and my purse are overflowing" (101).

Only the novel's last letter, Shklovsky's "Declaration to the All-Russian Central Executive Committee" that he cannot live in Berlin and wants to go back to Russia, achieves the intended result: the author is allowed to repatriate. In switching his addressee from the person to the state, Shklovsky styles his last letter as a declaration of defeat: "I raise my arm and surrender" (104). His surrender to the authorities reflects a deep crisis. While he experiences Russian Berlin in such a way as to conclude that "poor Russian emigration" "has no heartbeat" (95), he also concedes that "the revolution has lost its propulsion," too (63). This admission of the Revolution's exhaustion, which was cut from all subsequent Soviet editions of *Zoo*, betrays Shklovsky's recognition that the utopian aspirations of the Revolution are over, together with his illusions about the possibility of life abroad.[65] Thus, the planetary scale of Khlebnikov's "Menagerie," as well as an attempt at starting a transnational Russian public sphere, crashes against the fragmentation and inertia of Russian Berlin and the Realpolitik of Soviet Russia. *Zoo* remains to show how Shklovsky exploited the malleability of the personal letter to rehearse arguments about history, politics, literature, film, and art and to record his intellectual itinerary out of Berlin.

Letters from Cafés and a Commonly Shared Modernity

The generic capacity of the letter to incorporate conflicting modes of writing while allowing the author to articulate private concerns publicly was taken up by Ehrenburg as well. Whereas Shklovsky failed to see much past Russian Berlin, Ehrenburg focuses on Germany and Germans. Addressed to an imaginary "dear friend," his postcard-like "Letters from Cafés" combine journalistic reportage, personal ruminations, and art criticism. They describe Berlin, the mountain of Brocken, the cities of Hildesheim and Magdeburg, and Weimar. The seriality of Ehrenburg's letters sustains the narrator's investigation of several recurring themes: the unfolding of history in cities, the role of art in society, and the place of Russians in postwar Europe. Ehrenburg writes from the perspective of a cosmopolitan Russian traveler whose presence in Germany remains unexplained. He is neither a regular tourist nor an émigré, and his letters are written in a spontaneous and informal style. Moreover, he manages to create a sense of immediacy and interconnectedness by assuming that his unnamed interlocutor—any reader of his text—agrees with him.

Unlike Shklovsky, who privileged the linguistic community across borders, Ehrenburg dutifully describes geographical differences. He denigrates most Russians abroad with equal fervor by pointing out the cynicism of those patriots who extol either the virtues of Orthodoxy or the achievements of the Revolution but prefer to live in Baden-Baden. Ehrenburg himself experiences Germany from the position of an outsider: he eavesdrops on debates about "Europe's destiny" in Berlin's cheap cafés, follows organized excursions into the mountains, and observes guided tours for schoolchildren in provincial towns. He references tourist information from the Baedeker travel guide but instantly dismisses it. By underscoring his position as an outside observer, Ehrenburg implies that his letters provide an authentic and unmediated view of Berlin and other German cities.

Taken together, Ehrenburg's letters resemble a portrait of postwar Germany in transition.[66] The picturesque medieval towns are miniature representations of the uncertainty Ehrenburg observes in the industrially advanced but ideologically conflicted Berlin. Magdeburg is in the throes of what Ehrenburg terms "expressionist" urban redevelopment headed by the modernist architect Bruno Taut. Weimar is divided between "respectable burghers" and "blockheads" studying at the Bauhaus, the progressive art school headquartered in Weimar from 1919 until 1925. Although Ehrenburg qualifies Bauhaus as Germany's "sole live art school," he compares it unfavorably to its Moscow counterpart Vkhutemas.[67] That is not to say that Ehrenburg necessarily finds Soviet art superior. As he visits Berlin's famed modern art gallery Der Sturm and witnesses the life of art in the provinces, his letters reflect a growing disappointment with the general popularity of leftist art. He mocks the avant-garde's resolute utilitarianism by claiming that "not a single constructivist would agree to sit on a 'constructivist' chair for more than five minutes" and goes so far as to suggest that geometric abstraction can be violent: "the leftists have beaten feeling (izdubasili chuvstvo) with a ruler" (148). It is striking that Ehrenburg, who championed contemporary European art in 1922 in a book of essays, *And Yet It Spins*, and his own journal *Veshch'/Gegenstand/Objet*, disparages the avant-garde once he sees it against the background of the pastoral German countryside in 1923.[68]

Ehrenburg is quick to reassure the reader of his letters that he did not switch his loyalties to the political right, but he insists on criticizing the left. Traveling through politically torn Germany makes him realize that the commitment of leftist art to "produc[ing] manifestos, excommunicat[ing] the heretics, and cover[ing] walls and hearts with diagrams, equations, and charts" leads to nothing more than unusable "pseudo-constructivist" furniture (148–49). In criticizing the superficiality of such artistic practice, Ehrenburg implies that bad art translates into bad politics. And even though he is ostensibly writing about Germany, there is nothing that stops the reader from extending Ehrenburg's analysis to Russia, especially considering the international ethos of leftist art. These letters might have been written in German cafés, but they concern a commonly shared modernity.

Reports of a Refugee from the Realm of the Undead

In contrast, Bely's *Kingdom of Shades* is a damning report on Berlin that positions Soviet Russia outside the bounds of a supposedly declining Western Europe. After describing Berlin's stagnation and depravity in three compact chapters, the narrator delights in Moscow's bustling activity, which generates "stability and the presence of firm soil" (71). Bely opens the book with "A Few Explanatory Words" for readers in Russia: "I will attempt to conduct in front of you my 'myth' or *skaz* about Berlin" (10). The hesitation about designating his narrative as either a myth or *skaz*, an improvisational oral discourse, points to the centrality of direct communication in Bely's text and grounds it in a particular kind of performance. As noted earlier, *Kingdom of Shades* originated as a public lecture in Moscow. Bely's narrative might not be technically epistolary, but the author frames it as a sequence of informal and at times disturbingly personal messages about a foreign city and its large Russian diaspora. As such, the text strives to affirm Soviet state building at the expense of denigrating Berlin while mapping Bely's journey from Moscow to Berlin and then back to Moscow. In doing so, Bely presents himself not only as a returnee but as a refugee from the soon-to-collapse West.

From the book's first paragraph, Bely announces Berlin's decisive impact on him: "It's very difficult for me to share my impressions of being in Germany," he states, because his entire life he considered himself a Westernizer and repeatedly wrote about the intellectual "poverty of Slavophilism" (5). Postwar Berlin, "this little slice of Europe," convinces Bely of the inaccuracy of his previously held beliefs. It comes as some surprise that Bely announces the challenge of narrating his life abroad by referencing the central sociophilosophical debate of the nineteenth century between the proponents of the Western model of development (Westernizers) and the adherents of the idea of Russia's exceptionalism (Slavophiles). Not only is the relevance of this debate questionable in 1924, invoking it to announce the primacy of the nationalist Slavophiles contradicts the Soviet ambition of a global revolution and therefore undermines Bely's own aim of aligning himself with the Soviet authorities.[69] This rhetorical incongruity arguably points to the naïve superficiality of Bely's political awareness. But Bely needs the binary of Russia versus The West to justify his return from Berlin and to stage his ideological transformation.

As Alexander Dolinin has observed, the theme of Europe's demise is an important presence in Bely's oeuvre from the early 1900s onward.[70] David Bethea has analyzed the apocalyptic tendencies of Bely's fiction, particularly in *Petersburg*, and underscored that "his view of history as spiraling toward an end" can be detected in the structure and the language of his prose.[71] But prior to moving to Berlin in 1921, Bely lamented the prospect of a European apocalypse as a tragic, if inevitable, event. It is in Berlin that Bely adopts the idea that Europe is in irredeemable decline. Monika Spivak attributes Bely's sudden Europhobia to a string of personal misfortunes, primarily the breakup with his wife, Asya Turgeneva, and with his mentor, the founder of anthroposophy, Rudolf Steiner.[72] Yet, for all its flaws, *Kingdom of*

Shades avoids the topic of personal troubles and reflects instead Bely's thorough familiarity with contemporary German art and culture. In fact, Bely's narrative is squarely within the gloomy millennial expectation of Oswald Spengler's widely popular treatise *The Decline of the West* (1918; 1922). Bely writes pages dismissing German philosophers, poets, musicians, politicians, and artists as derivative, concluding, "and then one begins to understand the core mood of such books as Spengler's *Decline of the West*" (43).[73] This is not to say that Bely accepts Spengler's ideas wholesale. In an essay, "The Elements of My Worldview," written in 1922 but never published in his lifetime, Bely outlined the main lines of his disagreement with Spengler.[74] However, in *Kingdom of Shades*, Bely follows Spengler's model of cyclical historical evolution and identifies Berlin as the locus of Western civilizational decay. For example, Bely claims that the popularity of such past civilizations as Egypt, India, and China among German Dadaists and expressionists is a telltale sign of a dying society (44). According to this logic, Russian Berlin becomes an illustration of multicultural contamination and Western degeneration (26–38).

Bely's support of Spengler in *Kingdom of Shades* stands out among contemporary Russian responses to *The Decline of the West*. Ahead of the appearance of its Russian translation in 1923, the intellectuals Nikolay Berdyaev, Fyodor Stepun, Semyon Frank, and Yakov Bukshpan published in 1922 a volume of essays recognizing the importance of Spengler's achievement but largely disagreeing with his prophecies.[75] The reviews in the leading Soviet literary journal *Red Virgin Soil* were mixed, though in a 1923 essay titled "Today's Berlin," S. Chlenov lauded Spengler's analysis as brilliant urban history.[76] The extent of Bely's knowledge of the Spengler debates in Russia while he lived abroad is unclear. Nevertheless, read in the context of Spengler's reception in Russia, Bely's description of Berlin in terms of darkness, shadows, and decline, in comparison to the brightness and ascent of Moscow, appears to be part of a systematic effort to confirm Spengler's theory on the ground. Unaware that the Soviets would ultimately ban *The Decline of the West*, Bely renounces his past attachment to Europe by way of concurring with Spengler and discursively enacting his escape from Berlin.

In his "Letters from Cafés," Ehrenburg also invokes Spengler and associates his name with the theme of travel: "Spengler wrote his book right here, nearby, at the train station bar" (132). For Ehrenburg, however, Spengler is just one writer among many others trying to make sense of the postwar, postrevolutionary present in Berlin, the city resembling a big train station where disgruntled travelers await future, better destinations. Accordingly, the narrative space of Berlin is marked by impermanence and mobility. Indeed, physical movement through Berlin underpins the texts by Ehrenburg, Bely, and Shklovsky regardless of the authors' degree of familiarity with the city. The state of permanent wandering that envelops these texts is reinforced in their organization as letters, understood as publicly addressed private messages, in search of their readers. It is worth recalling that Nabokov's "Guide to Berlin," which is likewise kept together by the narrator's movement through the streets of Berlin, also anticipates readers—indeed, Nabokov's narrator has an actual, if bored, listener. But Nabokov positions himself as someone whose creations can be read both at the time of writing and "in the twenties of the twenty-first century," like the works of the great masters of the past (93). Meanwhile, Shklovsky, Ehrenburg, and Bely are preoccupied with declaratively contemporary matters. Their experiments with city writing tend to follow the same pattern: their aesthetic and spatial considerations of Berlin map ways out of it.

A Guide to the City: The Map

Ever since the advance of industrialization and urban growth, cities have served as the main locus for writing about the present.[77] In the Russian literary tradition, Petersburg exerted an outsized influence on paradigms of city writing. Bely certainly turned to some of the same tropes he used in his novel *Petersburg* when writing about Berlin in *Kingdom of Shades* and even deliberately confused the two cityscapes: "there the street extends to the spire of the Admiralty—no, pardon me, to the spire of Gedächtniskirche" (30). Admittedly, St. Petersburg of the nineteenth-century classics was represented uniformly as an un-Russian and unreal place, but it was also a crucial site of personal crisis rooted in religious ethics of rebirth.[78] Berlin, a major diasporic center, was a genuinely foreign city where existential crises were of a more immediate nature.[79] Russians flocked to Berlin not out of admiration for Prussian urban planning and lifestyle, but because the city was affordable and accessible, and because it allowed for the possibility of returning to Russia. Many Russian Berliners faced a choice between living outside Russia indefinitely or surrendering to the Bolshevik state. As we have seen, Ehrenburg repeatedly wrote about Berlin as a buzzing train station, and Bely commented on its confusing mix of multiple temporalities. Shklovsky memorably compared Berlin's residential architecture to a heap of luggage: "The houses are as alike as suitcases" (304; 66). Such literary mappings of

Berlin were dependent on topographical mapping, and the combination of the two was perhaps the most universally employed and productive way of narrating the circumstances surrounding the pivotal moments of the writers' lives abroad.

The historian Karl Schlögel has observed that Russian writers in Berlin generally turned to some of the same landmarks and phenomena of the "urban interior" as they navigated the city.[80] To be sure, the Berlin Zoo, the Gedächtniskirche, streetcars and underground trains, as well as pubs and cafés appear frequently across various texts. What distinguishes the spatial experience of those Russian Berliners who eventually left for Moscow, however, is that they were highly aware of the social discrepancies of the areas within which specific landmarks are located. Most immediately, the Berlin Zoo and the Russian enclave adjacent to it happened to be located in Berlin's wealthy western district, primarily in the borough of Charlottenburg. Whereas in his "Guide to Berlin" Nabokov ignores the socioeconomic aspect of his exiled narrator's milieu, Ehrenburg, Shklovsky, and Bely emphasize the fact that Berlin is divided into the working-class north and bourgeois west, and that the majority of Russians live in the west. In Bely's description of his arrival in Berlin, he wrote that from the train station he reached "that part of Berlin that the Russians call 'Petersburg' while the Germans call it 'Charlottengrad'" (26). He later added, "for several months I lived in the most bourgeois quarter of Berlin" (63). Shklovsky reported laconically, "In Berlin, as everyone knows, the Russians live around the zoo. The notoriety of this fact is no cause for joy" (66; 303). Ehrenburg alluded to staying in the city's western part by sharing that he lived on the Kaiserallee, near Hohenzollernplatz (127). This topographic connection between Berlin's upscale neighborhood and its Russian pocket established a deliberate metonymical relation between the German bourgeoisie and the Russian expatriate community.

All three writers pushed their class-informed observations further as they constructed their narratives over Berlin's existing social hierarchies embodied in urban space. As Ehrenburg wryly put it, "as in any other city, in Berlin there are 'nationalists' and 'internationalists.' They live in different parts of the city." He explained that the "nationalists," otherwise known as "respectable people," live in the west. The "internationalists" are factory workers living on the city's northern and eastern outskirts (126–27). This fraught geography provided a paradoxically stabilizing coordinate system in a city where everything else seemed to be in flux. In mapping the movement of their narrators within this space, Ehrenburg, Shklovsky, and Bely outlined how their respective aesthetic, social, and political considerations were simultaneously shaped by and reflected in Berlin's urban environment.[81]

For example, Ehrenburg was aware of the irony of living on the street honoring the kaiser, but he pointed out that the symbolism of the toponyms in the postwar city was being renegotiated: "At one point the leftists proposed renaming questionably named streets. The rightists declined the proposal by citing the greatness of history and the interests of cabbies" (125). Ehrenburg's observation suggests that the insufficiency of history's greatness to justify the street's royal name—indeed, the need to pair the kaiser and the cab driver—indicates the disintegration of the link between the signifier and signified, street name and kaiser. As he witnessed, the very idea of German patriotism, "which was previously so solid it was used as granite for the monuments to Bismarck," was undergoing a fundamental transformation, "becoming an unclear, changing form," in the wake of the Great War (127–28).

Furthermore, Ehrenburg questioned the validity of any rigid political platform. He ridiculed the disintegrating monarchy and called the forces of fascism and communism competing for dominance in Berlin's streets the "redeeming agendas" (spasitel'nye raspisaniia) heralded by the swastika and the red star. Despite sympathizing with the workers' movement, he warned that "all those who declare their calculations and dreams to be genuine itineraries (raspisaniia) lie—some lie sincerely, others not" (132). Recognizing a universal desire for change on the left and on the right, Ehrenburg presents Berlin as a city where all meaning is contingent, where "everything is ersatz," a substitute for something else: the street names invoke nonexistent royalty, tobacco is made of cabbage, the political parties are interchangeable, coffee is brewed from kidney beans, churches function as commercial concert venues, and pastries taste of potatoes (130–31). This contingency thrilled Ehrenburg because it mediated the uncertainty of the historical moment—and rendered the present negotiable.

Bely was far less charitable in his view of Berlin's intersecting spatial and social planes. In his eyes, the Wittenbergplatz in the city's western part was dominated by black marketeers and rich foreigners. A rare communist demonstration disrupting the feast of consumerism appears to Bely as a mirage: "Red flags get raised and flow into the open abyss of neighborhoods" (29). He exacerbates this hallucinatory gaze by writing in a macaronic language peppered with German toponyms and idioms both in German and transliterated Russian. Easily distracted from his thoughts on class struggle by "the rhythms of foxtrot," Bely takes the reader on a tour of various "Diele" (cafés) and "Nachtlokals" (night clubs) where "Annuschkas" and "Nataschas" sing songs about "Wolga" and visitors enjoy "Kuljebjakas" (26–29). This lifestyle is summarized in the couplet, "Nacht! Tauenzien! Kokain! / Das ist Berlin!" (29) and reinforced in the oft-repeated slogan "Bum-Bum," the soundtrack to the imploding city.[82]

The grotesque imagery of Berlin is counterbalanced by Bely's portrayal of a sober countryside. In a passage that reads like a proletarian pastoral, Bely finds reprieve in the suburban town of Zossen. There he discovers working-class Germany full of contempt for the bourgeois capital. Living alongside German workers, Bely reports learning from his hosts about economic ties that bind together all capitalists—what he calls "the black international of Europe" (63).[83] He is told that regardless of their nationality, bankers and factory owners have more in common with each other than with the proletariat. By traveling outside Berlin, Bely encounters two different ways that postwar Germany is coping with the burden of reparations imposed by the Treaty of Versailles: while Berlin is losing itself in dancing and drinking, Zossen undergoes political education. Hence, despite finding in Berlin a "voluptuous anticipation of a revanche, which makes one pay hopeful attention to *Sowjetrussland*" (60), Bely declares that the city is capable only of a "masquerade under the revolutionary banner" (42). However, the memoirs of Bely's contemporaries reveal that he despised Zossen.[84] In his own diaries he called the town "a village of undertakers" and lived there for only two months.[85] It is clear that Bely's favorable comparison of Zossen to Berlin, as well as his presentation of the city as a den of sensual excess, was a strategic move necessary to create a structural pattern showing Berlin's spatial inferiority and suggesting that it is incapable of fostering meaningful social life.

The principle of inscribing social relations into urban topography, which marks Ehrenburg's and Bely's texts, dominates Shklovsky's narrative as well. It is noteworthy that these writers envision themselves as outsiders without identifying a clear center of the city, its locus of power. Instead, they conceptualize their marginality by describing their difference in the middle of a foreign space. As Shklovsky writes, "we huddle among the Germans like a lake between its shores" (67; 303). Searching for an anchoring center throughout *Zoo*, Shklovsky's narrator travels restlessly across Berlin's western neighborhoods from Wittenbergplatz to Nollendorfplatz to arrive at Gleisdreieck, the engineering marvel of a train station and the novel's lyrical crescendo:

> All around, along the roofs of the long yellow buildings, run tracks; tracks run along the ground and along high iron platforms, where they intersect other iron platforms as they rise to platforms still higher.
>
> Thousands of fires, lanterns, spires, iron balls on three legs and semaphores—semaphores everywhere.
>
> Despair, émigré love and streetcar no. 164 have brought me here; I have walked a long time on the bridges over the tracks that intersect here, just as the threads of a shawl drawn through a ring intersect. That ring is Berlin. (68; 305)

The crisscrossing bridges and train tracks represent the space of a personal and historical crossroads where the narrator finds himself. Rather than provide a shrewd analysis of the historical situation, he is deeply conflicted about love and politics. And Berlin, conceived of as a ring through which biographical threads intersect, sharpens the sense of indeterminacy about national belonging. There is also a notable similarity between Shklovsky's and Pasternak's renditions of Gleisdreieck. Both authors turn to this industrial landmark to express the tension between one's private, inner world and the outward, modern world at large. This Berlin location becomes the center of geographies, temporalities, and identities as they converge here and open new paths forward. In Shklovsky's case, describing Berlin as a ring and tracing the narrator's circular trajectory within it allow him to break through that circle.

As Gary Saul Morson has suggested, *Zoo* exemplifies Shklovsky's theory of literature and constitutes a "menagerie of literary species."[86] Throughout the novel, the narrator inserts vignettes of literary analysis in unexpected contexts. In one of the chapters following the Gleisdreieck passage, there is a discussion of Voltaire's *Candide*. Shklovsky writes that the novel "has a nice circular plot (kol'tsevoi siuzhet): while people look for Cunégonde, she is sleeping with everybody and aging. The hero winds up with an old woman, who reminisces about the tender skin of her Bulgarian captain" (92; 319). Given that the premise of *Zoo* is the narrator's own futile quest for the affection of Alya, his indifferent love interest, the reference to Cunégonde implies that Alya is similarly preoccupied with other men. Furthermore, this literary example extends to geography: while Shklovsky struggles to find a place for himself in hollow Russian Berlin, life in Russia goes on. The pattern of his walks around Berlin suggests that *Zoo*, the novel he is writing, is in danger of having a circular plot, too.[87]

However, as the novel's author and protagonist, he guides the reader to recognize the narrative's underlying structure and also shows that he is in a position to manipulate it. The critical reference to *Candide* occurs in the same chapter as Shklovsky's discovery of proletarian Berlin: "It's nice to follow the canals to the workers' districts. . . . There, at the Hallesches Tor, out beyond the place where you live, stands the round tower of the gasworks, just like those at home on the Obvodny Canal. When I was eighteen, I used to walk my beloved to those towers every day" (90; 318). The adjective "obvodnyi" (which denotes the quality of bypassing something) reiterates the notion of circularity but also introduces the idea of circumvention. More importantly, this passage provides a space to insert a message of solidarity with the German workers and to remind the narrator of his youthful romantic exploits in Petersburg. The invocation of workers reads almost like an afterthought here, but it is consistent with Shklovsky's sustained effort to weave together the personal and political to find a way out of the exilic impasse. The emphasized affinity with the workers, even if strained, conjures up memories of personal fulfillment. By linking industrial labor and the labor of love, Shklovsky reshapes the circularity of the plot into a linear progression toward his decision to leave Germany.

The invocation of class-based solidarities in *Zoo*, "Letters from Cafés," and *Kingdom of Shades* does not mean that Shklovsky, Ehrenburg, and Bely were Marxist thinkers. Rather, their "migrant literary everyday" reflects a performance of class-consciousness. Nevertheless, in *Literature and Revolution*, Trotsky dismissed Bely as a representative of prerevolutionary bourgeois culture, calling him "a corpse [who] will not be resurrected in any spirit."[88] As a formalist, Shklovsky was hostile to Marxism until he had little choice but to adopt it in the late 1920s.[89] Even Ehrenburg, who had credentials as a revolutionary exile before 1917, was criticized by his communist peers for paying insufficient attention to the "economic conditions determining the morals, customs, political system, philosophy, and culture" of the European countries he visited.[90] It is reasonable to assume that by the time the Soviet Union was established in 1922, indicating some awareness of class-based solidarity was necessary for authors living abroad wishing to receive Soviet book contracts or to repatriate. The fact that each one of the three authors acknowledged in their Berlin texts local forms of class conflict indicates that they foresaw readers interested in labor issues and strained to accommodate that interest. Although this pseudo-Marxist impulse complicates the exilic aspects of these texts, it does not negate them. For instance, the uniform focus on urban exteriors and the lack of domestic interior spaces showcases the authors' outsideness. And while Ehrenburg, Bely, and Shklovsky reach the same conclusion that they must leave Berlin, their individual approaches to mapping the city produce three distinct conceptions of social agency that Berlin conditions. Ehrenburg finds that the present is negotiable as he hops from one café to another. For Bely, Berlin is a city best not visited because it is the realm of the undead. And romantically rejected Shklovsky shows how reading the city opens up ways of navigating it.

Exploring Ehrenburg's, Shklovsky's, and Bely's writerly activity in Berlin has demonstrated that city writing offered them versatile plotting strategies for capturing the complexity of the social worlds they inhabited. I approached their texts through the figures of the letter and the map, both of which are subsumed into the broader structure of a city guide. Like Nabokov's "A Guide to Berlin," the narratives of Ehrenburg, Shklovsky, and Bely are not meant to entice visitors or facilitate seamless experiences of consumerism. Instead, the internal logic of the guide provides a way of organizing the literary everyday in exile and, to an extent, exposing the precarious infrastructure of modern life. Berlin's landmarks, streets, and neighborhoods turn into discursive tools used to produce an urban space that allows for assembling disjointed urban impressions into a coherent whole. For Ehrenburg, Shklovsky, and Bely, Berlin becomes an embodiment of their dashed hopes, broken hearts, and other misfortunes—a negative city and a place "not about love." To use another of Shklovsky's locutions, they find that in Berlin "'we' is a funny word. . . . 'We' is I and somebody else. In Russia, 'we' is stronger" (54; 296). United by a desire for collectivity, these authors imagine it differently: as an international collectivity in "Letters from Cafés," a union with the beloved in *Zoo*, and a rapturous arrival home in *Kingdom of Shades*. As such, these texts also evade an easy classification into Soviet and émigré modalities. They show instead how intertwined those modalities were in the early 1920s.

3

Performing Exile

The Golden Cockerel *at the Berlin State Opera*

Berlin's community of opera connoisseurs was scandalized in 1923 when the city's premier musical venue, the Berlin State Opera, presented its audience with an ambitious production of Nikolay Rimsky-Korsakov's last opera, *The Golden Cockerel* (1907). Iosif Gessen writes in his memoirs that at that time "the Germans strenuously cultivated Russian music: Tchaikovsky, Rimsky-Korsakov, Mussorgsky, Stravinsky, and Prokofiev were ubiquitous on various opera stages and in concert halls."[1] In Gessen's opinion, the German approach to staging Russian operas was hopelessly clichéd in its mobilization of "improbable stereotypes" (razvesistaia kliukva). When it came to *The Golden Cockerel*, it was the German public who was disturbed. Gessen recounts his wealthy German companion's confused outrage during an intermission: "I adore Rimsky-Korsakov, but this is a real farce!"[2] The reviews of this classic fairy tale about the foolish Tsar Dodon, the conniving Tsarina of Shemakha, the enigmatic Astrologer, and a magical bird were mostly harsh.[3] And the production, the most expensive to date in the company's history, was pulled after only seven performances over the course of two consecutive seasons.[4] For his own part, Gessen disliked the production, calling it "a coarse tomfoolerish grotesque."[5] This notion of the grotesque, however, was central to the creative vision of the person hired to design the sets and costumes for the opera, the Russian artist Pavel Tchelitchew.

The previous two chapters explored primarily the Berlin oeuvres of Russian authors who grappled with possible exile but eventually chose to return to Moscow. Here I analyze the same pivotal moment in the development of Russian culture's exilic ethos in Berlin using Tchelitchew's *The Golden Cockerel* as a rich case study. I also take my analysis from the streets of Berlin to the interior of a cultural institution that enabled remarkable cultural collaborations. It is unknown exactly how Tchelitchew gained access to the city's most prestigious performance space. Once he did, he experimented with artistic forms in pursuit of political aims and weaponized the staging to undermine the newly established Soviet Union. Tchelitchew used the opera as a vehicle for criticizing the growing acceptance of the Bolshevik government and for reminding everyone of recent historical events in Russia, such as the Revolution and the civil war, that had created the vast expatriate community in Berlin in the first place. Moreover, contrary to the prevalent assumption that émigrés were isolated from the local communities, the Berlin Opera's production of *The Golden Cockerel* underscores the extent to which Russian culture outside Russia developed in a cross-cultural milieu.

Images lose less in translation than words, and as a painter, Tchelitchew was at an advantage when compared with his fellow exiled countrymen who were writers. Yet, as an émigré without an established reputation, Tchelitchew had to make his visual ideas unexpected and outstanding. He bridged the fin-de-siècle aesthetics with a more radical contemporary avant-garde idiom while tapping into the opera's capacious interpretative possibilities. Drawing on Bakhtin's theory of the carnivalesque, queer studies, and theories of camp, I will describe Tchelitchew's approach to *The Golden Cockerel* as "fabulous dissent" to account for his production's sartorial extravagance, political antagonism, and subversive imagery—what some contemporaries summed up as "grotesque."

Certain challenges arise when it comes to analyzing this particular production. The ephemeral nature of any time-limited performance, especially before recording technology could fully capture choreography, acting, and sound, complicates the task of accurate historical examination. To complicate matters further, very little physical material from this opera survives because the Berlin Opera House and its archives sustained irreparable damage during World War II. In my analysis of Tchelitchew's *The Golden Cockerel*, I rely primarily on the visual record—sketches and photographs—as well as memoirs, critical reviews, and other archival materials.[6] This chapter is concerned with the interrelation of the literary and visual arts, and my methodology is rooted in close readings of the libretto and formal visual analyses of Tchelitchew's surviving drawings of sets and costumes.[7] Before discussing the production itself and contextualizing Tchelitchew's career in Berlin, I will provide a brief overview of the opera's genesis and explain this chapter's theoretical premise.

Cultural Migrations of *The Golden Cockerel*

Rimsky-Korsakov's opera has been called many things since its opening night in 1909 at the Zimin Opera Theater in Moscow. Critics and scholars have referred to the opera as a "magical mirror," a "very modern fairy tale," a "tragic fairy tale," a "trifling parody," and a "political opera."[8] These contradictory responses to the seemingly lighthearted fairy tale—"a tall tale personified" (nebylitsa v litsakh), as the author of the libretto, Vladimir Belsky, subtitled it—reveal the opera's rich subversive potential.

Beginning with the libretto's source text, Pushkin's *The Fairy Tale of the Golden Cockerel* (1834), this story has been a mysterious text inviting interpretation, as demonstrated by its famous lines "Although this fairy tale is a lie / It contains a hint and a lesson for virtuous young men" (Сказка ложь, да в ней намёк / Добрым молодцам урок).[9] Yet, it is unclear what the lesson is and who it is for. There are no outright positive characters in this fairy tale, which is named after a magical bird that secures the aging Tsar's military power. The Astrologer gives the Cockerel to the Tsar in exchange for the Tsar's promise to grant his every wish. The Astrologer ultimately claims the foreign Tsarina as a reward, but the Tsar refuses this, wanting to marry the Tsarina himself, even though his sons have killed each other for her. There is no "happily ever after": the story ends with the Tsar murdering the Astrologer, the Cockerel pecking the Tsar to death, and the Tsarina simply disappearing.

From the rich body of scholarship on Pushkin we know that the fairy tale presents itself as a simple native Russian folktale while drawing on foreign literary models, mainly Washington Irving's "The Legend of the Arabian Astrologer" (1832), and packing a symbolic punch against Nicholas I and his court.[10] Rimsky-Korsakov's opera with Belsky's libretto expanded the coded political expression inherent in Pushkin's fairy tale. Rimsky-Korsakov used Pushkin's and other Russian fairy tales for his operas before working on *The Golden Cockerel*: examples include *The Tale of Tsar Saltan* (1900) and *Kashchei the Deathless* (1902). With *The Golden Cockerel*, the composer was more interested in contemporary satire and a new urban folklore than in magical tales. Rimsky-Korsakov was fired from the St. Petersburg Conservatory for defending students involved in the political demonstrations of 1905. Moreover, Russia's defeat in the Russo-Japanese War coupled with the empire's loss of access to the Suez Canal impacted Rimsky-Korsakov, a navy man, to such an extent that the staunchly conservative professor for most of his life turned into an oppositional figure.[11]

The opera comprises scenes that exaggerate inept and corrupt governing, senseless wars, and libidinal tension. Tsar Dodon makes a pact with the Astrologer because he has aged, can no longer satisfy his desires, and does not wish to relinquish his power. The refusal to accept change causes Dodon's ultimate demise. As Simon Morrison and others have pointed out, Dodon's portrayal embodied much that was wrong with the rule of Nicholas I's great-grandson Nicholas II, from Russia's humiliating defeat in the Russo-Japanese war of 1904–5 to the outsized influence of the self-proclaimed holy healer Grigory Rasputin on the royal family.[12]

In contrast to stubborn Tsar Dodon, the character of the Tsarina of Shemakha represents flexibility and new ideas. She seeks change. Her stated mission is to conquer Dodon's realm, but because she disappears after achieving her ostensible goal, her plotline is open-ended and offers possibilities for various interpretations. Depending on one's point of view, she can be a villain or a heroine.[13] The figure of the Astrologer is even more bewildering because he exists both in and outside of the performance: his appearances in the prologue and epilogue—before the curtain goes up and after it goes down—frame the spectacle. The Astrologer seems omnipotent in Act One but is struck dead in Act Three. More than any other character, he encourages the audience to find the hint and lesson of the performance, but he offers no direct guidance. The general meaning of the opera is malleable because the final act ends with the chorus wailing, "What will a new dawn bring? / How will we live without a tsar?" (Что даст новая заря? / Как же будем без царя?).[14] This looming sense of change in the finale can be suspended in uncertainty, staged as an unfortunate end of an era, or shown as the beginning of a bright future. In any event, the ending makes it clear that change is inevitable.

Justin Weir has observed that on the level of form, too, *The Golden Cockerel* embodies change. Weir argues that the opera "thematizes an aesthetic in transition" from realism to modernism, and this transitional quality enables a range of conflicting interpretations.[15] From the modernist perspective, the fantastic tale is hermetically self-sufficient. The realist approach, on the other hand, considers its fantastic elements as means of political commentary. To reconcile those contradictory aspects, Weir applies Gary Saul Morson's notion of "threshold art" to *The Golden Cockerel*. Works that belong to this hybrid generic category lend themselves to mutually exclusive readings, much like homonyms but on the scale of a text. According to Morson, a threshold text is to be understood not by choosing one interpretation of it over another, but via the dialectic between the two.[16] Performance inherently activates this kind of dialectic between contradictory readings while emphasizing the elements of the story chosen as important for a given production. For instance, for the opera's premiere in 1909 at the Zimin Opera, the libretto was severely censored after being rejected from the imperial theaters for the provocative portrayal of royalty, and the staging was executed as a lush magical tale, removing the production's narrative from the contemporary moment. Nevertheless, the fraught romantic relationship between the elusive Tsarina, the Astrologer, and the Tsar was, below the surface, as much a biting commentary on contemporary events as it was a magical fairy tale, especially considering the striking parallel between the Astrologer and Rasputin.[17]

Fabulous Dissent

In remaking Pushkin's fairy tale into an opera, Rimsky-Korsakov and Belsky added to the opera's title a seemingly innocuous subtitle: "nebylitsa v litsakh," or a "tall tale personified." It is difficult to capture the subtitle's linguistic play in translation fully, not least because the meaning of the phrase is tantalizingly unclear in the original. The alliterative effect, akin to "nonsensical sense," intensifies the paradox that this "tall tale" (nebylitsa) is nevertheless based on realistic—and publicly performed—representation (v litsakh: literally, "in faces"). Therefore, from the tongue-in-cheek subtitle and onward, the opera disrupts expectations and challenges the audience to take itself seriously while not committing to any degree of credibility. The very image of the Golden Cockerel is entertaining as a fairy-tale character while being provocative as a sexual symbol. This self-aware game of recognition with elements of parody resembles an aesthetic similar to what we might now identify as camp.

Camp historically has the capacity to empower and render visible those who are marginalized and invisible. Following Susan Sontag's classic "Notes on Camp," it is through the mixture of the exaggerated, the fantastic, the passionate, and the naïve that camp, which is always open to double interpretation, both entertains and serves to make a point.[18] To explain the effect of camp, Fabio Cleto has turned to formalist narrative theory, writing that if there is a distinction between the chronological order of events in a story (fabula) and the narrative arrangement of the story's events (plot), then "the fabula of camp may well turn out to be utterly misaligned and topsy-turvy. Or maybe just *fabulous*? For the history of camp is indeed a gesture of fabulation: the story of fabled stages, of marvelous imaginary performances, and of extraordinary identities."[19]

By engaging with the campy ambiguity of *The Golden Cockerel*, Tchelitchew could exploit it to his advantage as an impoverished exiled aristocrat and an unapologetically gay artist. His staging is associated with a particular form of stylized critique, which I call *fabulous dissent*. I use *fabulous* to invoke both spectacular appearance and fabulation, understood as fictionalized, speculative rearrangement of a world as it is—of a world that excludes those who deviate from the accepted norm (of race, gender, sexuality, class, ability, and so on).[20] Given the opera's sexually subversive themes centered on the image of the golden cockerel—these themes are obvious, yet the logic of public propriety circumvents their discussion—it would be productive to interpret Tchelitchew's approach with the help of queer theory. As a school of thought concerned with recovering marginalized voices and disrupting traditional belief systems, queer theory offers useful tools for recognizing signs and patterns of dissent, often hidden in plain sight.

In *Fabulous: The Rise of a Beautiful Eccentric*, Madison Moore defines "fabulousness" as a queer aesthetic that "allows marginalized people and social outcasts to regain their humanity and creativity."[21] Being fabulous has to do with an intentionally different appearance, flamboyant style, and the use of art for making ideologically motivated statements. As Moore explains, fabulousness has many commonalities with camp; however, "fabulousness is never there just for the sake of being fabulous. It is never just art for art's sake, nor is it style over content. . . . Fabulousness is art created in states of duress, and this is its political edge."[22] Even though Moore writes about "beautiful eccentrics" today, Tchelitchew in Weimar-era Berlin meets these criteria, too, as a destitute gay Russian exile eager for professional recognition. In 1923 Tchelitchew's spelling of his surname in German, as "von Tschelitscheff," is but one example of the aspiring artist's attempt at fabulous visibility. Regardless of the historical period, to be fabulous is to claim agency by pushing the limits of conventions. In Tchelitchew's case, these conventions concern both socially conservative anti-Bolshevik exiles and non-Bolshevik leftists ousted from Russia. Tchelitchew interacted with Russian Berlin's various constituencies, reluctant to join any one faction.

Being fabulous is also about creating fables and crafting fantastic stories. Developed by feminist and Black queer studies scholars, the concept of fabulation allows for constructing stories unburdened by the constraint of verity as a way of producing narrative strategies for survival.[23] Broadly understood, fabulation might address dissatisfaction with a political regime or with social scripts of normative behaviors, such as gender role expectations. In the absence of political agency, fabulous dissent is a mode of artistic expression that subverts existing signifying practices to restructure established meanings and thus register disagreement. My use of the term *dissent* implies an unwillingness to accept social, cultural, and political realities as they manifest themselves in power relations.[24] However, it does not entail an adherence to a consistent ideological worldview, as Tchelitchew's work will demonstrate. This kind of dissent is not an organized movement aimed at undermining the state, but an artistic practice of embedding hints and cues to provide social insight and tap into art's potential to empower.[25] It is a search for ways of exercising agency.

Fabulous dissent operates in the realm of the aesthetic and flourishes in the conspicuous excess of theatricality. In its playfulness and liberating spirit, fabulous dissent resembles the carnivalesque as described by Mikhail Bakhtin. The carnivalesque applies to the literary representation that Bakhtin traced to the tradition of the medieval European carnival, the all-encompassing street performance festival wherein power structures are reversed or destabilized by being mocked.[26] While the Bakhtinian carnivalesque relies on performing transgressive social behavior to temporarily suspend the dominant authority, fabulous dissent aims for a more lasting effect. In the case of *The Golden Cockerel*, fabulous dissent draws on the fairy tale as a genre because fairy tales perform several functions simultaneously: they entertain, educate, strengthen social bonds, and communicate messages packaged as moral lessons. Moreover, fairy tales are addressed to two groups at once: children and adults.[27] Audience members who recognize these messages coalesce into a public, a group of strangers linked by a shared set of values.[28] Fabulous dissent likewise shapes a discourse. And with his elaborate and outrageous set and costume designs, Tchelitchew staged *The Golden Cockerel* as a cultural gesture toward such a discourse seeking its public. He mobilized stereotypes about Russia to direct his fabulous dissent against the political status quo of the day and molded the sexual undertones of the story into an instrument of attack.

Performance/Transposition

Scholars of performance have considered how the true, allegorical nature of a work of art emerges during its transfer from the page to the stage. Caryl Emerson has defined a retelling of a story in a different genre or medium as "transposition," a process akin to translation during which the "meaning of events and personalities within [the story] is transformed."[29] A transposition of a story is historically conditioned and inevitably reflects the concerns of the time when the transposition occurs. She writes, "different elements emerge and expand at different times to carry the weight of the story."[30] Shifts in thematic accents generate new meanings of the original text. Emerson underscores that it is the changes in the spatiotemporal organization of the text—what Bakhtin has called the chronotope—that lead to significant changes in the meaning of a narrative.[31] It should be added, however, that when the libretto is performed on the stage, the textual chronotope is realized within the space and time of the stage. Therefore, the staging and performance of the same opera in different historical periods will necessitate substantial changes in the ways the characters are conceived and perceived.

In Berlin, the theater critics were aware of Rimsky-Korsakov's troubles with censorship but thought the parody of the royal court was simply spicing up the performance. One critic wrote in a preview of the opera's premiere that "today it seems to us that the satire, even if one were to attempt to direct it at particular countries and individuals, is spicy seasoning [pikante Würze]; but in its burlesque unintentionality this satire is so removed from any point in time that we can heartily laugh at it without any concerns."[32] Emphasizing the entertainment value of the opera, the critic continued, "the German audience should also accept the opera as a cheerful spectacle. Then, without much pondering, the audience will discover many a 'wise lesson' under the cover of facetious humor and, in particular, effortlessly enjoy musical pieces of rare appeal."[33] Musical appeal was undoubtedly the deciding factor in the Berlin Opera's decision to produce *The Golden Cockerel*. The Opera's management needed a reputable contemporary piece to complement the classical repertoire of German and Italian operas.[34] They also needed to fill the void left after French composers had been purged from the German stage at the height of the postwar, post-Versailles Francophobia. Favorable comparisons of Rimsky-Korsakov to Wagner likely made him stand out among contemporary Russian composers.[35]

The Germans were also determined to claim the staging of *The Golden Cockerel* in Berlin as the opera's first international performance. Berlin critics knew that Sergey Diaghilev's *Ballets Russes* had presented *The Golden Cockerel* as *Coq d'Or* in Paris and London in 1914. But they maintained that Diaghilev had grievously misinterpreted Rimsky-Korsakov's masterpiece by turning it into a ballet with singers relegated to either side of the stage: "an opera that is celebrated as a dance pantomime without vocal performance is, in essence, not an opera."[36] As a result, no expense was spared in producing *Der goldene Hahn*, as *The Golden Cockerel* was billed in German.[37] Indeed, Tchelitchew greatly exceeded the allocated production budget and mounted a production that eclipsed the Berlin Opera's existing shows with its originality, complexity, and ambition. Even so, the much-anticipated premiere was a flop.

Finding the performance dazzling but thoroughly perplexing, Berlin theater critics who had eagerly anticipated opening night panned the show the following day for lacking a coherent narrative thread. Reviewing the opera for *Deutsche Allgemeine Zeitung*, Walter Schrenk wrote that "it is always dangerous for the success of a stage performance not to know what is actually going on."[38] Edmund Kühn complained in *Germania: Zeitung für das deutsche Volk* that despite reminders about the fairy-tale-opera's "hint and lesson," "absolutely no deep meaning could be deciphered [herausrätseln]."[39] The costly production had a very short lifespan, leaving the repertoire permanently after 1925. This disappointing outcome was partly due to the German critics' inability to understand Tchelitchew's conception of the piece.

Nevertheless, some Russian critics in Berlin also emphasized the sense of confusion and disappointment: "The opera's audience was international, with Germans and Russians prevailing. The performance was met with restraint. The Germans did not know how to perceive the staging that contradicted everything else they have seen at the State Opera. The Russians, meanwhile, did not recognize their 'Cockerel.'"[40] Writing in *Dni*, R. Engel was positively dismayed by the production's playful inventiveness: he objected to the costumes, to the prosthetic noses that the actors wore, and to the pink horses made of cardboard. He recognized that the staging was trying to be "fantastic" but found it to be "exaggerated, caricature-like, and in bad taste."[41] He declared that such a frivolous approach to the work of a "great Russian composer" was most incongruous with the "traditions of the State Opera."

Yuri Ofrosimov's review in *Rul'* was much gentler, though short of actual praise. Rather than decry the staging's stylized primitivism, as Engel did, he saw in it the spirit of the Russian lubok, a popular print, taken up by "someone with modern taste and, even, through the eyes of an ironic European."[42] Tchelitchew's bright colors and puppet-like costumes delighted Ofrosimov. He also hinted that Tchelitchew might be after some deeper meanings in his staging, which was imbued with theatrical contradictions and paradoxes. He summed up his review by saying that Tchelitchew's work on the opera was "in any case significant and interesting—both for us and for the artist himself."

While the confusion of the German critics may be understandable in that they were ill-equipped to follow the important Russian opera from the outset, the contradictory responses of the Russian critics reflect the fraught complexity of Berlin's expatriate community. It is particularly striking that a negative review, written in a reactionary tone, was published in the Socialist Revolutionary *Dni*, while the more conservative *Rul'* published the positive review, commending the liberties the artist took in his staging. These ostensibly misaligned Russian responses highlight Russian Berlin's complexity, in which such terms as "progressive" and "reactionary" are shaken loose from historical meta-narratives. The political ambiguity and inconsistency of Tchelitchew's *The Golden Cockerel* illustrates this complexity well. He was addressing multiple publics at once. To untangle the meanings of Tchelitchew's staging, it may help to consider the beginning of his artistic trajectory in exile.

(Russian) Berlin and Its Many Publics

Der goldene Hahn spread its wings at a time when Berlin served as a major railroad nodal point connecting Russia and the West. In the words of the composer Nicolas Nabokov, in Berlin the umbilical cord between the Soviet Union and the émigré community was not yet fully severed.[43] Conversely, prolific artistic exchanges among leftist cultural producers in both countries contributed to the Germans' increased interest in Russian culture.[44] The same year *The Golden Cockerel* premiered at the Berlin Opera, the competing opera companies in the city produced Tchaikovsky's *Eugene Onegin* (Deutsches Opernhaus) as well as Rimsky-Korsakov's *The Tsar's Bride* and *The Snow Maiden* (both at the Grosse Volksoper).[45] The Berlin Opera's decision to produce *The Golden Cockerel*, rife with its Russian exoticism, is but one indication of this heightened curiosity about Russia, which had expounded a radically new conception of state- and nationhood in the wake of the October Revolution of 1917.

Tchelitchew settled in Berlin in fall 1921 at age twenty-three after four years of roaming—from his ancestral estate in Dubrovka near Kaluga, to a Kyiv torn by the civil war, to Constantinople on the eve of Atatürk's Reforms, and to monarchic Sofia.[46] Many of his compatriots arrived in Berlin after similarly circuitous routes. Others came directly from Moscow as emissaries of the nascent Soviet Union. This convergence of imperial and postrevolutionary Russias in Berlin led to competing visions of Russianness, where tradition and modernity collided. Although Soviet intellectuals strove toward internationalism, Europeans still considered their work Russian. The more conservative émigré Russians, on the other hand, were invested in preserving their classical imperial heritage, as Mark Raeff has argued, and tended to exploit "Old Russian" folk motifs.⁴⁷ Laurence Senelick has called this use of inherited images a "Slavic Disneyland."⁴⁸ A kaleidoscope of garish colors and hyperbolized traditional dresses and settings in the spirit of Nikita Balieff's touring revue *La Chauve-Souris* was evident in the offerings of Berlin's Russian cabarets *Van'ka-Vstan'ka*, *The Blue Bird*, and the Russian Romantic Theater. Tchelitchew was steeped in this hybrid environment of radical avant-gardism and commercialized figurative representation as he developed his painterly technique.

His politics was similarly hybrid. One the one hand, he came from an old aristocratic family that the Bolsheviks persecuted as an enemy class (the Soviets exiled the Tchelitchews from their estate and forbade them to settle anywhere near it). He also served in the White Army as a cartographer at the insistence of his father. On the other hand, he maintained friendship with various European leftists, as well as the non-Bolshevik Russian-speaking leftists whom he met during the year he spent in Kyiv, before the Bolshevik takeover of independent Ukraine. Once in Constantinople, witnessing the harrowing penury of the refugees, he wrote to a friend: "But I—we—can't return [to Russia], can we? I think about the hundreds, maybe even thousands of my poor compatriots, including women, who don't have any money, any hope, and, possibly, any friends. Everyone is in the same boat, practically starving."⁴⁹ These biographical details reveal a young man grappling with displacement and exile, but they do not paint a portrait of a stereotypical "White émigré." They do help, however, to contextualize his artistic output during this time.

Before his breakthrough onto the contemporary European art scene at the 1925 Salon d'Automne in Paris, Tchelitchew worked primarily as a set designer at Russian cabarets in Berlin. Given the allure of the archaic Slavic aesthetic at such establishments, Tchelitchew's early oeuvre demonstrates his propensity for vibrant color and presents an array of onion-dome cupolas, ornate headscarves, and merry peasants. But if his émigré cabaret designs are thematically somewhat predictable, their formal execution deserves attention. Most of his designs from the early 1920s share a striking feature: the fusion of traditional subject matter with modernist form, which positions him within both the Russian and the broader European avant-garde.[50] His work on a dance piece called *The Boyar's Wedding Feast* at the Russian Romantic Theater (1922) is especially notable. It featured barefoot female dancers in angular *sarafan*s (sleeveless dresses) and *kokoshnik*s (traditional head-dresses) on the background of Muscovy-inspired interiors plastered with contemporary newspapers. In addition to the entertainment value of the set, the incorporation of newspapers suggests a desire to preserve and document Russian heritage that is under threat. Visible in Tchelitchew's design is a collage of folk and avant-garde aesthetics, modernist flatness and reverse iconographic perspective, and premodern and modern historical contexts (fig. 9). In its use of line and color, this production reveals the distinct influence of Fernand Léger as well as Alexandra Exter, who tutored Tchelitchew in Kyiv.[51] Yet despite these common influences, *The Boyar's Wedding Feast*, with its bright whites, scarlets, and blues and the detailed ornamentation of Old Russian architectural elements, represented Russian exotica and was therefore easily put into a niche for Russian and Russia-curious audiences.

In some of his other projects, Tchelitchew had the opportunity to connect to the common European heritage of his Berlin audiences. For example, he designed the set and costumes for Pyotr Suvchinsky's stage adaptation of Arthur de Gobineau's *Savonarola* (1877) at the Theater on Königgrätzer Straße (1923). The German public warmly received Tchelitchew's iteration of *Savonarola*, a play based on the life of Girolamo Savonarola, a Dominican friar and a forerunner of the Reformation. Although the play's subject matter had to do with the Renaissance, Tchelitchew's costume designs, with their voluminous geometric shapes and deep blues and browns, as well as the arrangement of the actors on multiple stage levels, strongly echoed the constructivist theater designs of Exter. In his modernist rendition of the Italian Renaissance, Tchelitchew was certainly drawing on the sharp lines and signature surfaces of Exter's stage organization, aligning himself in form, in this instance, with the Russian non-émigré avant-garde (fig. 8).

While unrelated, *The Boyar's Wedding Feast* and *Savonarola* demonstrate the thematic versatility and formal consistency of Tchelitchew's approach to set design. Overall, his cabaret and chamber theater work can be interpreted as an effort to reconcile nationalism and modernism, the roots of which might be found in the artist's exposure to primitivism and his brief affiliation

Figure 8. A fragment of a page from *Berliner Illustrirte Zeitung*, January 7, 1923, 7, picturing Tchelitchew's costume design for *Savonarola*. Staatsbibliothek zu Berlin.

Figure 9. Pavel Tchelitchew, set design for *The Boyar's Wedding Feast*, Berlin, 1922. Gouache and newspaper collage on cardboard; 28.5 × 45.5 cm. Alexander Kuznetsov and Pavel Melyakov Collection.

with the Eurasianist movement.[52] Tchelitchew was friends with Suvchinsky, one of the main Eurasianist thinkers, and designed the cover for the first programmatic publication of the Eurasianists, *Exodus to the East*, in 1921. As it was initially articulated in exile in the 1920s, Eurasianism, part philosophy and part ideology, rejected Bolshevism and sought to provide an illiberal alternative to communism and capitalism. Eurasianism was hardly a homogeneous movement, but at its core was the premise that Russia is neither European nor Asian but a civilization of its own.[53] On the cultural front, Eurasianism was anticipated by turn-of-the-century literary and artistic developments in search of a genuinely Russian style. Much of Russian modernism is informed by and mediated through a move against the imaginary West and toward an equally imagined East.[54] In other words, there was little ethnographic accuracy in the modernist attempts to channel ideology into aesthetics by artists and intellectuals educated primarily in the European tradition. Yet, the desire to transcend Russia's ambiguous position between Europe and Asia drove art and politics alike.

As a firsthand witness to the commercialization of Russian Orientalized exotica in exile, Tchelitchew eventually abandoned national themes after he moved from Berlin to Paris, but only after his work on *The Golden Cockerel*. In a way, his work on the opera became a turning point in his career that allowed him to overcome his exploitation of folk themes for the sake of commercial success. This turnaround coincided with his growing resentment against Soviet Russia, deepened by his involvement with Eurasianism. Rimsky-Korsakov's opera was already a product of the proto-Eurasianist cultural moment shaped by the Revolution of 1905 and the Russo-Japanese War.[55] In 1923, when the opera made it into the Berlin Opera's repertoire, *The Golden Cockerel* offered convenient material for a Eurasianist allegory: the performance is set in a timeless and boundless Russian kingdom threatened by a mysterious foreign queen (the Tsarina of Shemakha). In order to survive, the Tsar has to recognize this threat and embrace the uniqueness of his realm without help from the outside (neither from the Astrologer, nor the Golden Cockerel). However, *The Golden Cockerel* also exposed a paradox inherent in Eurasianist thought: for all the fetishization of the East, the East is seen as inferior and therefore underestimated. As a result, the Tsar cannot survive direct contact with the region personified by the queen. Tchelitchew affirmed this paradox on the Berlin Opera's stage. He drew on a subversive tradition—of disguising *The Golden Cockerel* as a colorful fairy tale while trying to convey a timely political critique—to warn his audiences of the dangers posed by the Bolsheviks. In crafting his message, Tchelitchew turned to Russia's cultural heritage—Pushkin's fairy tale, folkloric forms and tropes, and symbolic use of color—as an heir reaching out toward a shared cultural past for the purposes of the present. Beneath the layers of deliberately excessive Eurasian imagery, one finds in Tchelitchew's staging an attempt to reclaim agency as a Russian artist in a city that was opening up to the Soviets.

THE GOLDEN COCKEREL IN BERLIN

Earning a commission from one of Germany's most prestigious opera houses provided Tchelitchew with an opportunity to address Weimar Berlin's many publics, from German intellectuals and Soviet sympathizers to staunch Russian monarchists and those who were still unsure whether to stay in emigration or return to now-Soviet Russia. The opera was to be sung in German, but the visual language brought together multiple national traditions. Both the Weimar Republic and Soviet Russia were fresh examples of nations reconstructed in the aftermath of failed monarchies; and Pushkin's story of the whimsical and inept Tsar Dodon was remarkably adaptable to contemporary events. *The Golden Cockerel* is in many ways a masquerade of skillfully constructed identities. Tchelitchew, caught between a desire to be universally recognized and his status as an exile, might have seen this commission as an opportunity to bridge the old and new Russias with Germany, a space where the work could also hold universal meaning.

The opera premiered on June 17, 1923, with an illustrious international cast: Zinaida Jurjewskaja as the Tsarina of Shemakha, Albert Fischer as Tsar Dodon, Leonardo Aramesco as the Astrologer, and Ethel Hansa as the Golden Cockerel. The supporting roles of the Tsar's sons Gvidon and Afron, the housekeeper Amelfa, and General Polkan were sung by Hans Batteux, Herbert Stock, Ljuba Senderowna, and Herbert Janssen, respectively. Leo Blech conducted, and Ludwig Hörth directed the performance. Ekaterina (Catherine) Devillier devised choreography. Tchelitchew, who designed sets and costumes, envisioned the piece as puppet theater, perhaps in an homage to Stravinsky's *Petrushka*, staged by the *Ballets Russes* (1911). But unlike the elegantly nimble dancers of Diaghilev's troupe, the Berlin Opera singers were dressed in thickly padded voluminous costumes.[56]

For his production of *The Golden Cockerel* in 1923, Tchelitchew engaged with existing designs for this opera by three prominent Russian artists: Ivan Bilibin, Konstantin Korovin, and Natalia Goncharova. Bilibin designed his exuberant sets for the opera's world premiere in Moscow at the Zimin Opera in 1909; Korovin presented his grand vision of Slavic tsardom at the Bolshoy Theater a month later in 1909; and Goncharova reimagined Korovin's and Bilibin's stagings for the *Ballets Russes* in 1914. Bilibin was praised as the finest specialist of his time in the imagery of Old Rus. Korovin was a recognized master of interpreting Russian folk themes in the impressionist style for the imperial theaters. Goncharova played with and exaggerated expectations of Russian folk imagery. Tchelitchew's vision for *The Golden Cockerel* emerged in contrast to Korovin's and Bilibin's opulent, ornamental costumes and sets, and was more aesthetically aligned with the ethos of the World of Art and Goncharova's highly detailed and densely populated primitivist designs. To emulate the success of these predecessors, Tchelitchew also reinvigorated Russian folk clichés with a modernist vocabulary (fig. 10).

Tchelitchew distinguished his design from the preceding designs with intentionally angular shapes and the near-absence of any symmetrical or parallel lines. This sort of frustrated precision and the lack of an easily identifiable center in the swaying perspective affirm the sense of instability and

Figure 10. Pavel Tchelitchew, set design for *The Golden Cockerel*, Act Three, 1923. Gouache and gold-colored speckles on paper; 36.8 × 58.4. Alexander Kuznetsov and Pavel Melyakov Collection.

ominous suspense that defined Tchelitchew's interpretation of the opera. The entire space seems decentered from its anchoring axis. Rather than a theatrical "cube," we have something much closer to cubofuturist disorientation: at once flat and three-dimensional, closed off and open, stable and dynamic. In comparing Tchelitchew's sketches with those of Korovin, Bilibin, and Goncharova, one can see the extent to which an individual's staging approach can intervene in the understanding of the source text—and the rich ways performance can inform artistic transposition.

Tchelitchew's primitivist styling of the fairy-tale setting draws on recognizable images of Russia's archaic past to underscore contemporary concerns. For instance, in contrast to the conventional depiction of the Golden Cockerel as a delicate bird (the part is sung by a soprano), Tchelitchew's Golden Cockerel is distinguished by its impressive physical build and its traditional bast shoes, *lapti*. This ethnographic detail suggests the artist's engagement with the primitivist aesthetics he shared with Goncharova, who frequently used *lapti* in her designs.[57] Tchelitchew, however, embraced the archaic imagery in a peculiar way: acutely aware of both the Soviet and exilic perspectives in Berlin, his use of archaic visual vocabulary suggests a sociopolitical critique of the present. His Tsar Dodon, for example, appears as if copied from the caricatures of Russian monarchs and aristocrats that proliferated when early Soviet propaganda was widespread.[58] The implied peasant origins of the *lapti*-wearing cockerel also anticipate the murder of Dodon by the common people later in the performance. In this vein, the bespectacled Astrologer can be seen as a representative of the progressive intelligentsia, someone who advocated for the common people (the narod) and was active in the revolutionary movement until the Bolsheviks came to power and forced intellectuals like him into exile. To audience members familiar with these images, these particular representations of Pushkin's Tsar Dodon, the Golden Cockerel, and the Astrologer might have appeared as direct references to the aftermath of the October Revolution, thus setting the tone for the entire performance.

Some of the references to Russia's recent past were so heavy-handed that at the time of the opera's Berlin premiere it was rumored that the entire show was a political skit.[59] No wonder some of the German critics were confused and irritated by the seemingly inappropriate mixing of tragedy and comedy in the performance.[60] This sort of mismatch of high and low stylistic registers was especially evident in Act Two, when Dodon first discovers his dead sons on a pitch-black stage, only to be distracted by the singing Tsarina of Shemakha. In the sketch representing the ominous scene of fallen soldiers, we see the figures of two brothers who have murdered each other (fig. 11). In 1923, the representation of fraternal conflict recalls the Russian civil war (1917–22), when familial bonds were often broken and siblings found themselves fighting against one another. The positioning of the bodies is reminiscent of Bilibin's illustration of Pushkin's fairy tale, with two young men interpenetrating each other with their swords. In Tchelitchew's representation of the brothers and fallen soldiers, we observe arrows placed in a way that suggests arousal caused by the presence of the Tsarina, visually identifying sexual frustration as the source of the deadly conflict. As a result, the scene looks both tragic and comical.

The comedic effect, the ambiguous ambiance, and the skewed perspective of Tchelitchew's image is reinforced by a recognizable visual source from the Western canon, Pieter Bruegel's *The Land of Cockaigne* (1567). Many of the images Tchelitchew includes in his set design have multiple points of reference that demonstrate his awareness of the Western canonical and avant-garde pictorial models. These images also bring together Eastern cultural touchstones with contemporary geopolitical developments. In this connection, the opera's subversive potential hinges on its representation of

Figure 11. Pavel Tchelitchew, set design for *The Golden Cockerel*, Act One, 1923. Gouache and silver-colored speckles on paper; 40 × 59.2 cm. Alexander Kuznetsov and Pavel Melyakov Collection.

the Tsarina of Shemakha. The scene of Tsar Dodon discovering his dead sons at the beginning of Act Two is followed by a scene in which the Tsarina enters the stage (fig. 12).

When she appears, the somber battlefield becomes a cheerful Orientalized setting. Numerous crescents adorn the Tsarina's tent and a maroon rug by its entrance features stylized Arabic writing. Yet, what looks like Arabic script can also be read in Cyrillic as the Tsarina's initials, ШЦ (Шемаханская царица). The big sun in gold-speckled paint rising behind the Tsarina's tent correlates with the image of the Golden Cockerel itself—the cockerel is traditionally the harbinger of the sun. Considering the resemblance of Tchelitchew's Golden Cockerel to a hardy peasant (a muzhik), the looming victory of the Tsarina foreshadows the victory of the common people. Metaphorically, Tchelitchew is capturing the victory of the sun; yet, his is not the genuine sun, but rather something like the mechanistic sun from Mikhail Matiushin and Alexey Kruchenykh's "first futurist opera," *Victory over the Sun* (1913).[61] That avant-garde opera rejected all tradition, including "the sun of Russian literature" (Pushkin), and welcomed a wholly new world order. In Tchelitchew's design, the false sun is returning to haunt the present as an embodied force: a gaudy, seductive, and dangerous idea from the East.[62]

Figure 12. Pavel Tchelitchew, set design for *The Golden Cockerel*, Act Two, 1923. Gouache, gold and silver-colored speckles on paper; 38 × 59.2 cm. Alexander Kuznetsov and Pavel Melyakov Collection.

When the Tsarina reveals herself, it becomes clear she is meant to be taken as a composite parody of Soviet symbols (fig. 13). Red and gold predominate in the surviving sketch of her costume. Although the colors of her turban, the lining of her cape, and her pants are vermilion, her belt, her shoes, and the ribbons on her arms and turban are a strikingly different shade of red, closer to the saturated maroon of the initialed rug. These maroon ribbons, belt, and shoes are stylized to resemble the fabric the Soviets would have used for banners and decorating newly occupied towns. Soviet forces were also, of course, dubbed the Reds during the civil war, in contrast to the anti-Bolshevik Whites. The golden wheat spikes adorning the Tsarina's head and waist, and her golden sickle-shaped nails (not present in the image, but described in the reviews) make her costume appear as if derived from the state emblem of the Russian Socialist Federative Soviet Republic, adopted in 1922, with its distinctive red colors and golden hammer and sickle.[63] Because it is evident from the plot that Dodon's sons have killed each other fighting for the Tsarina, the civil war clues become all the more substantial and poignant, forming an overarching political allegory for Tchelitchew's transposition of Rimsky-Korsakov's opera in exile.

Figure 13. Pavel Tchelitchew, costume design for the Tsarina of Shemakha, 1923. Gouache and golden speckles on paper; 50.1 × 32.3 cm. Alexander Kuznetsov and Pavel Melyakov Collection.

The Golden Cockerel offered plenty of the exotic for audiences interested in an unusual opera. Tchelitchew's Tsarina was a nesting doll of exotic images, well suited for Berlin's many publics: she stood for the Russian imperial Orient; she was an Amazon warrior queen; and in color scheme and adornment she symbolized the young Soviet Russia. At the opera's end, the chorus sings in anxious anticipation of a new dawn "without a tsar." In Tchelitchew's transposition, it is the Tsarina who comes to embody that new, red dawn. But to trust the light of the Tsarina's dawn also means death. Tchelitchew's interpretation of *The Golden Cockerel* can thus be read as a warning from the stage of the Berlin Opera to audiences intrigued by the Bolsheviks' ideas. It is in this warning that much of the artist's critique, his fabulous dissent, lies. Tchelitchew addressed his message to those Russians who were considering a return to the Soviet Union. Those who had intended to see a lighthearted depiction of popular Russian exotica encountered veiled historical commentary on recent political events. Tchelitchew reanimated the deep critical intent of Pushkin's fairy tale and Rimsky-Korsakov's opera and used the staging of *The Golden Cockerel* as an opportunity to undermine the reconciliatory rhetoric of accepting Soviet Russia and returning there after the Whites effectively lost the civil war.

In the context of bourgeois Weimar Berlin, such an interpretation of the opera seems experimental in form but conservative in content. This discrepancy, however, is part and parcel of Russian Berlin's sociopolitically heterogenous environment. While not a monarchist, Tchelitchew articulates his critique against Soviet Russia by means of monarchic tropes. Moreover, his conception of the Tsarina of Shemakha has decidedly misogynist undertones. But if looked at closely, the Tsarina of Shemakha's role in Tchelitchew's production has yet another, deeper aspect that further reinforces his fabulous experiment.

In Pushkin's fairy tale, the Tsarina is a consequential but minor character, and this is in stark contrast to her role in the opera. However, both Pushkin and the librettist Belsky underscore the Tsarina's beauty, sensuality, and otherness. Tchelitchew stayed close to her image as suggested by Pushkin and elaborated by Belsky but vastly expanded the Tsarina's agency by centering the Berlin performance on her. In her stunning aria in Act Two when she first appears, the Tsarina begins her song by asking the sun whether the natural beauty of her native realm is as marvelous as she remembers it; soon she asks whether the women in her realm still enjoy the dreams of "forbidden love" (любви запретной страстный сон) and rush to see their lovers at night "with sweet confession on their lips" (с признаньем сладостным в устах).⁶⁴ The libretto, coupled with Rimsky-Korsakov's Orientalist clarinet roulades, contributes to the image of the Tsarina as an odalisque. At the same time, she introduces herself to Dodon as an independent woman aiming to conquer his tsardom: "I am my own maiden / the Tsarina of Shemakha / I am moving like a thief / To conquer your city" (В своей воле я девица / Шемаханская царица / Пробираюсь же, как тать, / Город твой завоевать).⁶⁵ Despite her stated independence, she is overtly sexualized and yearns for a strong man "Where could I find someone who would be able / To contradict me in everything" (Где сыщу, кто б мог перечить / Мне во всем противоречить).⁶⁶ Her image is situated textually within the patriarchal framework: her existence depends on male characters and their approving attention.

In Tchelitchew's staging, the Tsarina of Shemakha is anything but the submissive and pleasing female archetype. She is much more than the mere subject of the male gaze, the symbolic ideal: she is a woman warrior and a ruler in her own right.⁶⁷ Her sensuality is only pretense. Tchelitchew's notion of the Tsarina as an emancipated woman is particularly clear in comparison with depictions of her by his contemporaries. The artist Wasyl Masjutyn (Vasily Masiutin) represented the Tsarina as a sensual Orientalist female figure in his woodcut illustrations for a lavish edition of Pushkin's *The Golden Cockerel* published in Berlin in 1923. The two images are very similar in their use of imagined Orientalia, but in Tchelitchew's version, the Tsarina is threatening because she is such an independent woman. She embodies danger: for Tchelitchew in Berlin, she is the new, fearsome Soviet Russia.

This sort of representation of the Tsarina of Shemakha is remarkably similar to another female icon of modernity—Salomé. From Oscar Wilde's play (1891) to Richard Strauss's opera (1905) to Alla Nazimova's Hollywood film of the same name (1922), the spectacular reemergence of Salomé in the modernist period has been interpreted as an indication of the "crisis of human agency and freedom in a radically changed, secular, modern world."⁶⁸ (Incidentally, the Moscow Chamber Theater toured Berlin with its production of *Salomé* in 1923.) Lawrence Kramer has argued that the abundance of Salomé adaptations and interpretations at the turn of the century made her into a "monstrous sexual icon" who reflected a "bundle of instabilities produced by the fin-de-siècle gender system."⁶⁹ The modernist obsessions with sexuality, gender fluidity, women's emancipation, murder, and Orientalism were channeled through the image of Salomé. Rachel Morley has suggested that "the Salomé craze enabled early twentieth-century women to dramatize for themselves, and for their audiences, their desire for various kinds of emancipation."[70]

If we consider the Tsarina of Shemakha alongside the equally transgressive Salomé, we will see that *The Golden Cockerel* is preoccupied not only with death and desire but also with the representation of power and, by extension, the gender dynamics that undergird the maintenance of that power. Yet, there is a sizable difference: Salomé is brutally murdered after manipulating men to achieve her goals, whereas the Tsarina of Shemakha makes it to the end of the performance alive and victorious—indeed, she is the only character to do so. As the early twentieth-century music critic Igor Glebov wrote, in an attempt to rationalize the Tsarina's unruly figure, "with the expressive music characterizing the Tsarina of Shemakha, [Rimsky-Korsakov], having dismissed all hypocrisy, laid bare the covers of the female soul and asserted . . . that in a woman's vital juices there are seeds capable of leading both to heaven and to hell."[71] In Tchelitchew's transposition, the Tsarina of Shemakha brings about the implosion of the patriarchal order. Her disappearance at the opera's end suggests that she is uninterested in the newly acquired tsardom—she uses war and destruction only to underscore the flaws of male dominance. She manages to do so by forging an alliance with the Golden Cockerel, an instrument and symbol of the patriarchy.

Figure 14. Ivan Bilibin, "Sic transit . . . ," published in *Zhupel*, no. 2 (1905). Beinecke Rare Book and Manuscript Library.

The overarching hint and lesson of *The Golden Cockerel*, then, might be directly connected to the use and misuse of phallic power. As Sona Hoisington has observed, Pushkin was also fully aware of his Golden Cockerel's phallic connotations: he sketched phallic images on the title page of the fairy tale's fair copy.[72] For the opera's libretto, Rimsky-Korsakov and Belsky emphasized the crisis of masculinity implicit in Pushkin in a satirical vein by significantly expanding the role of the Tsarina of Shemakha. Bilibin, who experimented with depicting Dodon in fin-de-siècle satirical journals before working on the opera, underscored the need to curb cocky political ambition by drawing caricatures depicting a regal cockerel's transformation into cooked chicken (fig. 14). Applying the framework of fabulous dissent enables us to see these and similar "hints and lessons" when *The Golden Cockerel* undergoes transposition and is performed onstage. In Weimar Berlin, *The Golden Cockerel* became a repository of this shared cultural heritage that helped uncover political and social anxieties concerning the interconnection of power and gender and opened up spaces of protest, spaces of fabulous dissent, from the margins.

4

Nabokov, Berlin, and the Future of Russian Literature

> Almost everything I can say about the Berlin period of my life (1922–37) I exhausted in the novels and short stories I wrote during that time.
>
> —VLADIMIR NABOKOV, *Drugie berega*

The question of Russian literature's viability outside of Russia has always troubled Russian writers in exile. As discussed in chapters 1 and 2, Pasternak, Bely, Shklovsky, and others who left Berlin for Moscow justified their departure by stressing the inadequacy of culture in exile. By the mid-1920s, the hope for an imminent Soviet collapse that had initially energized the diaspora was dimming among émigrés. With the approach of the October Revolution's tenth anniversary, the debate about the future of Russian literature outside Russia intensified. Whereas the older, well-established, and more influential émigrés favored isolationism from contemporary European life for the sake of preserving Russian cultural values, the younger writers tended to reject a nostalgic mode of writing about the Russia they had lost.[1]

In one fiery speech in 1926, Nina Berberova reminded her fellow writers in exile that the younger generation of Russian authors could not write about the old Russia because her generation—born at the turn of the century—simply lacked many memories of it.[2] She called on émigré writers to take advantage of the "fullest freedom of speech," which they enjoyed outside Russia, unlike young Soviet writers bound by the state's "special command."[3] A year later, Vladimir Nabokov echoed Berberova's sentiment in his essay on the tenth anniversary of Soviet rule. He wrote, "we are celebrating ten years of freedom. Such freedom as we know perhaps no other nation has known. . . . Our scattered nation, our nomadic state, is fortified by this freedom."[4]

At the same time, Nabokov treaded carefully when it came to engaging with his immediate environment. In 1934, he went so far as to call Berlin's émigré cultural scene an "almost idyllic backwoods" in a letter to Vladislav Khodasevich, who then lived in Paris.[5] The intensity of Russian literary life in Berlin paled in comparison with that of Paris, but there was no shortage of aspiring young poets in either city. Two literary groups that gathered in Berlin in the late 1920s and early 1930s, the Russian Poets Club and the Aikhenvald-Tatarinov Circle, attest that a considerable number of intellectuals who came of age in exile continued to write in Russian and did so deliberately.[6]

One view of the literary situation that captures the attitudes of younger émigrés in Berlin can be found in a playful poem written on a scrap of paper and taped into the journal of the Russian Poets Club, which documents its meeting minutes. The first stanza reads, "in emigration / we live in prostration / all the world's nations / are foreign to us" (мы в эмиграции / живем в простраций / не знаем нации / мы никакой).[7] This unsigned poem was likely meant as a joke and not intended for publication. But its clichéd observations about the emotional and economic hardships of living and writing in exile expose a stark reality: younger Russian authors faced greater difficulty in getting their work published and reviewed, and hence in becoming professional writers. Having left Russia in early adulthood, they found themselves seen as not German (or French, or British, etc.) and, often, not Russian enough.[8] Nabokov, his Russian oeuvre, and the critical responses to it exemplify many of the contradictions and paradoxes of interwar émigré literature. He was by far the most successful of the émigrés who began publishing in exile, paving the way for other young writers to be taken seriously by their elders.[9] Nonetheless, his prose was routinely criticized as "un-Russian," even though he was one of the fiercest defenders of the Russian classical literary legacy.[10] Nabokov's contemporaries detected in his novels the influences of modern European writers, including Proust, Kafka, and Stefan Zweig.[11] And although Nabokov admitted to having an interest in Proust, he insisted that he never read German books and that he barely spoke any German.[12] While he was well versed in contemporary European and Soviet literatures, he systematically cultivated a public image as an aloof writer.[13] His position in this broader context suggests an understanding of self and culture in exile as performative and unfixed: as both isolated and integrated; as Russian and cosmopolitan; and as outside nation and tradition, yet planted within classical Russian literature.

Nabokov elaborates his views on exilic aesthetics most fully in his novel *The Gift* (*Dar*, 1937; 1952), which is generally considered one of his finest achievements.[14] At its core, this novel is the story of a young Russian émigré writer in Berlin caught at the nexus of alienation, nostalgia, and literary ambition. Nabokov wrote *The Gift* between 1933 and 1937, but the narrative itself covers the years 1926–29.[15] From its first chapter, it chronicles the processes of creating and disseminating literature. The narrative builds as the protagonist, Fyodor Godunov-Cherdyntsev, reads, writes, and analyzes poetry—and, importantly, as he anticipates reviews of his books, attends literary salons, and engages in sophisticated discussions with literary critics. As Alexander Dolinin has put it, *The Gift* is "a Magna Carta of an exiled writer's artistic freedom."[16] In it, Nabokov presents exile as an aesthetic problem and provides strategies for solving it.

It is often overlooked that *The Gift* is a Berlin novel and that this location is not accidental. Perhaps more than any other Nabokov novel, *The Gift* shows just how alienating an unloved foreign culture can be and how that very alienation spurs breathtaking creativity. Berlin in *The Gift* leads Nabokov's hero—and us—to recognize the gifts of exile. In this sense, *The Gift* is centrally important for understanding Russian Berlin's pull on the poetic imagination of émigrés beyond its heyday of the early 1920s. Through meandering across Berlin, mocking Berliners, and lodging in typical Berlin apartments, Nabokov finds the space to position himself as an heir to the Russian literary tradition.

Although it was not meant to be Nabokov's last finished novel in Russian, *The Gift* also concludes the writer's Russian period. In biographer Brian Boyd's words, *The Gift* is "a tender love story, a portrait of an artist as a young man, a meticulous inventory of a social milieu, a vivid travel fantasy, an exploration of fate, a passionate tribute to a whole literary heritage, an original investigation of the relation between art and life, half a shelfful of biographies, nostalgic, panegyric, tragic, and polemical."[17] Two conflicting tendencies animate *The Gift*'s multilayered narrative. On one hand, the novel depicts the life and work of a young poet, a dreamer living in complete isolation from the surrounding world. On the other, it is highly aware of that world and is steeped in debates ranging from contemporary émigré issues to philosophical approaches to time.[18] The literary scholar Simon Karlinsky tried to reconcile these tensions in 1963, in what is the pioneering scholarly treatment of the novel in any language. Karlinsky outlined the complex structure of the novel's main themes and underscored that, on the whole, *The Gift* should generally be understood as a sui generis work of literary criticism.[19]

For the purposes of this chapter, I am especially interested in Karlinsky's comments on the role of Berlin in *The Gift*, shown "in a number of imaginative, personalized cityscapes," and on the problem of "the possibility and validity of an émigré literature."[20] Archival research reveals that Nabokov liked Karlinsky's interpretation. In a letter to Karlinsky, Nabokov's wife and devoted assistant, Véra Nabokov, writes: "My husband asks me to thank you for your great kindness in sending him your article on DAR. He wants me to say that he found it very interesting and extremely well written; and also that it was a great pleasure for him to find that his book has been read by you (and written about) with such admirable care, insight, and attention to the details which are dear to their creator."[21] There are admittedly passages in Karlinsky's article that would be difficult for any Russian writer to dislike. The article's concluding statement, for example, reads, "this study cannot convey the unique value of [*The Gift*], its very special humor or the great elegance of its prose writing, which is in the Pushkin-Tolstoy tradition of terseness and precision."[22] But Karlinsky makes other observations as well, and Nabokov, known for his strong opinions, uncharacteristically objects to none of them. In this chapter, by focusing mainly on *The Gift*, I will consider how Nabokov's perception of language and time in Berlin shaped his ideas about exilic authorship. Whereas *The Gift* is the most studied of Nabokov's Russian novels, the existing scholarship has yet to account for the novel's dependence on Berlin's urban space and its cultural environment.[23] To understand Berlin's role in *The Gift* is to appreciate the extent to which Nabokov used exile for imagining a Russian literary renewal.

NABOKOV'S *FAUST*: THE ÉMIGRÉ TEMPORALITY

Interwar Berlin harbored Nabokov during his formative years as a writer. As Stanislav Shvabrin points out, "what is customarily referred to as Nabokov's 'Russian years' . . . might just as well be called the 'German' chapter of his biography."[24] Nabokov moved to Berlin following his graduation from Cambridge in 1922 and remained there until the Nazi threat left no other choice but to leave, which he and his family did in 1937.[25] But many aspiring Russian authors left Berlin either for Moscow or Paris much earlier, in the mid-1920s. The historians Catherine Andreyev and Ivan Savicky have explained Russian Berlin's decline by pointing out that "the political position of Germany was too weak, its ties with the Soviet Union were too strong, and its economic situation offered little chance of good employment [to stateless refugees]."[26] Returning to Soviet Russia was never an option for

Nabokov, but he chose to stay in Germany. He explained that his initial reason for staying in Berlin and not relocating to Paris in the 1920s was to use his German-speaking surroundings as a bulwark against assimilation: he did not know much German and therefore his Russian remained untarnished in Berlin.[27] He would later write about this period: "Upon moving to Berlin I was beset by a panicky fear of somehow flawing my precious layer of Russian by learning to speak German fluently. The task of linguistic occlusion was made easier by the fact that I lived in a closed émigré circle of Russian friends and read exclusively Russian newspapers, magazines, and books. My only forays into the local language were the civilities exchanged with my successive landlords and landladies and the routine necessities of shopping: *Ich möchte etwas Schinken* [I would like some ham]. I now regret that I did so poorly; I regret it from a cultural point of view."[28]

According to this well-worn narrative, the "task of linguistic occlusion" would not have been possible in Paris because Nabokov was fluent in French. Paraphrasing Nabokov's words, his cousin the composer Nicolas Nabokov wrote in his memoir, "in Germany [Nabokov-Sirin] could remain a mum observer, and, as it turned out, he was a brilliant one."[29] Even though Nabokov minimizes Berlin's influence on his art by stressing the city's strictly utilitarian function in his life, Berlin's landladies, shopping venues, and trams nourished Nabokov's modernist vision of the author as exilic outsider who transcends the present. Berlin appeared as an urban Wunderkammer in "A Guide to Berlin" (1925); a metaphoric boarding house in *Mary* (1926); a soulless department store in *King, Queen, Knave* (1928); a site of memory in *Glory* (1930–32); a destructive metropolis in *Laughter in the Dark* (1932); and a delirious city of Doppelgänger in *Despair* (1934).[30] Long after World War II and in the wake of Nabokov's worldwide fame, the Weimar sensibility of some of his Berlin novels was rediscovered by arthouse film directors, who adapted *King, Queen, Knave* and *Despair* for the screen.[31]

Notably, Nabokov cultivated the image of an enigmatic author detached not only from Berlin and the broader European context, but also from his émigré milieu. The journal of the Russian Poets Club contains a manuscript of a poem by Evgenia Zalkind describing the atmosphere of the club's meetings and providing satirical characterizations of its members. In the stanza devoted to Nabokov, Zalkind emphasizes the aura of mystery surrounding his guarded demeanor: "Only Sirin very meekly / very politely kept silent / and for no one raised / a steel grille from his face" (Только Сирин очень кротко, / Очень вежливо молчал—/ И с лица стальной решетки / Ни пред кем не подымал).³² This quatrain is accompanied by a drawing of a young man smoking a pipe and wearing a steel grille on his face—a perceptive visual emblem of Nabokov's presumed aloofness (fig. 15).³³

The pseudonym Nabokov adopted in Europe, Sirin, a mythological creature that was half maiden and half bird, underscored his self-fashioned exoticism in ostensibly culturally superfluous Berlin.³⁴ But much as he tried to distance himself from Berlin, his contemporaries saw him as a Berliner. Consider this portrait of Sirin offered by the Parisian journalist Andrey Sedykh to introduce the writer to the readers of the newspaper *Segodnia*: "A thirty-three-year-old athletic youth, very agile, nervous, and impulsive [poryvistyi]. His polite manners and refined, slightly French-sounding style of speech (grassiruiushchaia rech') remained from his Petersburg upbringing; his athleticism came from his time at Cambridge; and from Berlin came his manner of dress: there was a sturdiness and certain bagginess to his suit. Rarely in Paris would someone wear such a mackintosh with a detachable lining."³⁵

While Nabokov's clothes betray his Berlin residence, his translation work suggests a thorough familiarity with German. A number of scholars emphasize that Nabokov, who spent fifteen years in Germany in addition to childhood trips, understated his exposure to German literature and culture as well as his knowledge of German.³⁶ He clearly felt comfortable correcting the English translation of Kafka's "The Metamorphosis" while teaching at Cornell.³⁷ Earlier in his career, in Berlin, one of Nabokov's first translations was a Russian rendition of Goethe's "Dedication" to *Faust*.³⁸ Considering his stance on being a lonely genius, it is not surprising that Nabokov turned to Faust: the classical German hero's nonconformism, self-awareness, and marginality corresponded to his own aesthetic values. Coincidentally, this

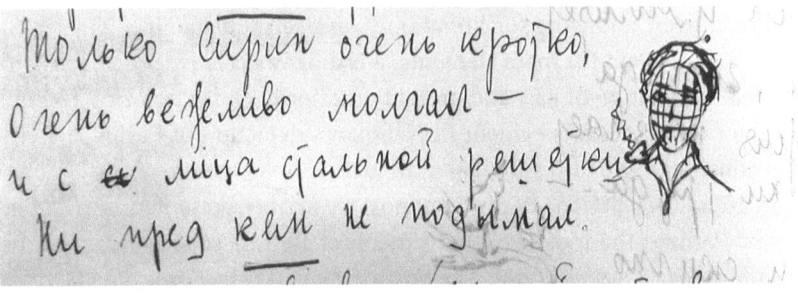

Figure 15. A fragment of a manuscript showing Evgenia Zalkind's poem "My zateiali pirushku" from May 15, 1928, with a caricature of Sirin (Nabokov). Beinecke Rare Book and Manuscript Library.

undertaking inscribed Nabokov into the distinguished line of Russian translators of Goethe from Vasily Zhukovsky and Alexander Pushkin to Afanasy Fet and Valery Briusov. It also afforded him the opportunity to articulate his thoughts and feelings about exile.

Robert Louis Jackson has noted that in translating the "Dedication" to *Faust*, "Nabokov translated himself into the poem: his exile, the loss of his native cultural milieu, the scattering and death of friends and family."[39] Indeed, Nabokov historicizes Goethe's poetry to suit his own exilic condition, so that in spite of his great losses Sirin-the-bard can continue singing away from home. Emphasizing the foreignness of his environment, Nabokov renders Goethe's line "Mein Lied ertönt der unbekannten Menge" (My song sounds to an unknown crowd) as "Для чужих, / неведомых, звучит мой стих печальный" (For the alien, and the unknown, my sorrowful verse resounds). He changes the brightly nostalgic tone of the original to the deeply melancholic sound in his translation. And though he envisions the bard's audience as not only "unknown," as in Goethe, but also "foreign," he nevertheless acknowledges that that audience exists.

Nabokov translates the final lines of the "Dedication," "Was ich besitze, seh' ich wie im Weiten, / Und was verschwand, wird mir zu Wirklichkeiten" (What I possess, I see as if in the distance, and what has disappeared becomes realities to me), as "Все настоящее вдали пропало, / а прошлое действительностью стало" (All that is real vanished in the distance, and the past became the reality). The poignancy of the juxtaposition of "nastoiashchee" (the real, the present) and "proshloe" (the past) is intensified by the implication that the past has replaced the present. In this moment of poetic engagement with Goethe's *Faust*, Nabokov charts his own temporal dimension, in which time is relativized to convey the trauma of dislocation and to convert a longing for home into a universal belonging. The translation also displays the main elements of Nabokov's creative process as continuous negotiation of past and present, interiority and exteriority. The full scope of this process is evident in Nabokov's depiction of Berlin as a city that constrains, but also stimulates, his artistic imagination.

In Nabokov's fiction, Berlin is almost invariably presented in negative terms. Perhaps the most extreme version of Berlin's superficiality can be found in *King, Queen, Knave*. The novel's Russian title, *Korol', dama, valet*, abbreviates to KDV, which stands for Berlin's luxury department store Kaufhaus des Westens, or KaDeWe. Here Nabokov's disdain for the German bourgeoisie and dislike of its urban domain converge. However, as Luke

Parker has shown in his study of the novel, only an insider, someone well informed about Berlin's opportunities for consumerist escapades, could have written about the city and its media environment with such insight.[40] Parker argues that in *King, Queen, Knave*, Nabokov mines the commonplaces of Weimar commercial urban culture such that the novel functions as a discursive "shop window, as both reflective surface and frame for the phantasmagoria staged within."[41] The tendency to deprecate Berlin's cityscape while taking inspiration from it runs through most of Nabokov's texts featuring the city. This tendency is already evident in his programmatic short story "A Guide to Berlin," as discussed in chapter 2.

A remarkable example of Nabokov's openness to Berlin can be found in his poem "Berlin Spring," written and published in May 1925.[42] Similar to "A Guide to Berlin," which appeared later that year, the poem is a manifesto-like proclamation of a writer in exile:

Нищетою необычной
На чужбине дорожу.
Утром в ратуше кирпичной
За конторкой не сижу.

Где я только не шатаюсь
В пустоте весенних дней!
И к подруге возвращаюсь
Все позднее и позней.

I value an unusual poverty
in a foreign land.
In the morning I don't sit
at a desk in the brick city hall.

There are few places where I don't wander
in the emptiness of spring days!
And I return to my girlfriend
later and later each time.

In these first two stanzas, the poet announces his pride in not working a mundane bureaucratic job at the city hall. The phrase "brick city hall" ("ratusha," or "Rathaus") refers to Berlin's Red City Hall, known for its distinctive red brick facade. Another Germanic word, "kontorka" (work desk, derived from "das Kontor," an office), further specifies the German setting. Against this setting, the poet cherishes his "unusual poverty" and lack of conventional employment, which enable him to explore the city. The poem ends with the poet's recapitulation of his main point, "that to everything I will prefer / my wild path / my golden poverty" (что всему я предпочту / дикую мою дорогу, / золотую нищету). In his order of priorities, absolute freedom is far greater in value than material wealth. The effect of the paradoxical epithet "golden poverty" is strengthened by the very word "nishcheta," which is not just poverty, but extreme poverty.[43] Despite this cavalier revaluation of values, there is a hint of the poet's precarious position in "Berlin Spring" as well. For example, it is uncertain that a foreigner would have qualified for a job at the city hall. Moreover, the words used to describe the poet's roaming around the city convey a sense of ambivalence: the verb "shatat'sia" denotes aimless wandering and implies instability, while the "pustota" (emptiness) of spring days in Berlin evokes total solitude. He is a flâneur of a new type: unlike the financially independent city strollers of the nineteenth century, Nabokov's poet has nothing left to lose.[44] The poet's penury is compensated, however, by his unmediated access to the city.

In "Berlin Spring" Nabokov also shows that his "golden poverty" enables him to create an alternative temporality that helps transform the foreign city into his own space. The poet might not have any money, but his literary heritage is more precious than gold. The poem alludes to the Romantic poet Fyodor Tiutchev's "By the winter's magic" ("Charodeikoiu zimoiu," 1852). Nabokov's metrical pattern of trochaic tetrameter and the unusual phrasing of the opening line in the instrumental case leave no doubt about that. One of Nabokov's favorite poets, Tiutchev was rediscovered at the turn of the century by the Symbolists, who were astounded by his poetry's metaphysical depth.[45] "By the winter's magic" depicts a snowed-in forest as if enchanted by winter. With effortless simplicity, the poet unveils nature's beautiful complexity and vitality below the seemingly lifeless frozen surface. Nabokov transposes Tiutchev's winter landscape onto his own Berlin's springtime cityscape to show that his poetic imagination is likewise capable of discerning life's gifts hidden in plain view. For instance, when in "Berlin Spring" the poet's neighbor airs a red feather bed through the window, the poet sees the mattress as a raspberry-colored tongue—and in so doing he endows the unremarkable urban scene with speech (tongue, language). The only way to persevere in exile, Nabokov tells us, is by realizing that cultural wealth is superior to material riches. He will extensively elaborate this outlook on exile in *The Gift*, on the first page of which the protagonist signals his values: "in *my* suitcase there are more manuscripts than shirts" (3).

INTO THE CROSSWORD PUZZLE: NABOKOV'S BERLIN IN *THE GIFT*

The Gift opens with a scene of a couple moving into a new apartment in "Number Seven Tannenberg Street, in the west part of Berlin" (3). The novel's protagonist Fyodor has moved into the same building earlier that day, but the particulars of his move are omitted. Nabokov introduces Fyodor "in the still unaccustomed state of a local resident" (4). For Fyodor, however, his new street had begun "to settle down as an extension of his new domicile," following a period of "revolv[ing] and glid[ing] this way and that, without any connection with him" (4). The scene is complete with the image of a moving van; and even the moving company's name painted on the van's side suggests a move: the letters spelling the company's name are "shaded laterally with black paint," creating the illusion of being three-dimensional and exposing, in Fyodor's eyes, a "dishonest attempt to climb into the next dimension" (3). The narrator hints at an example of an "honest" attempt a few lines earlier: "a foreign critic once remarked that while many novels, most German ones for example, begin with a date, it is only Russian authors who, in keeping with the honesty peculiar to our literature, omit the final digit." Although Fyodor's new address is shared in the opening sentence in detail, including not only the house number but the specific neighborhood, such an address never existed in Berlin.[46] Given that *The Gift* begins on "April the first 192–" but Berlin's Tannenberg Street is fictional, our narrator's honesty is compromised. The contrast of the German and Russian novelistic traditions loses its sharpness, too, and reminds us that our narrator is writing in Russian in Berlin. The theme of relocation is thus firmly established from the beginning, but on Nabokov's terms: his Berlin is an imaginatively multidimensional textual domain.[47]

Among the many metaphoric descriptions of Berlin in *The Gift*, one is particularly revealing. In the third chapter of five, the narrator finds himself in a neighborhood "in the vicinity of Grunewald," also in Berlin's western part, and compares "the massifs of the houses" to "dark crossword puzzles, in which not everything was yet filled in by the yellow light" (176). Nabokov was an avid composer of crossword puzzles, for which he coined the Russian neologism "krestoslovitsy." Many of Nabokov's puzzles appeared in Berlin's

Russian daily *Rul'*.⁴⁸ In *The Gift*, the likening of a multi-story tenement building to a crossword puzzle is a witty description of the building's street-facing wall with many windows, some lit and others dark, which create the image of a checkered puzzle. But there is an additional interpretative possibility here as well. Architecturally, Berlin's tenement buildings, called the *Mietskaserne*, are organized as labyrinthine clusters with interconnected courtyards.⁴⁹ If seen from above, as on an aerial photograph or on an entrance plaque showing the arrangement of the inner courtyards for visitors, these "massifs of the houses" would also resemble one big crossword puzzle (fig. 16, 17, and 18). That is to say, Nabokov's crossword puzzle metaphor extends to the

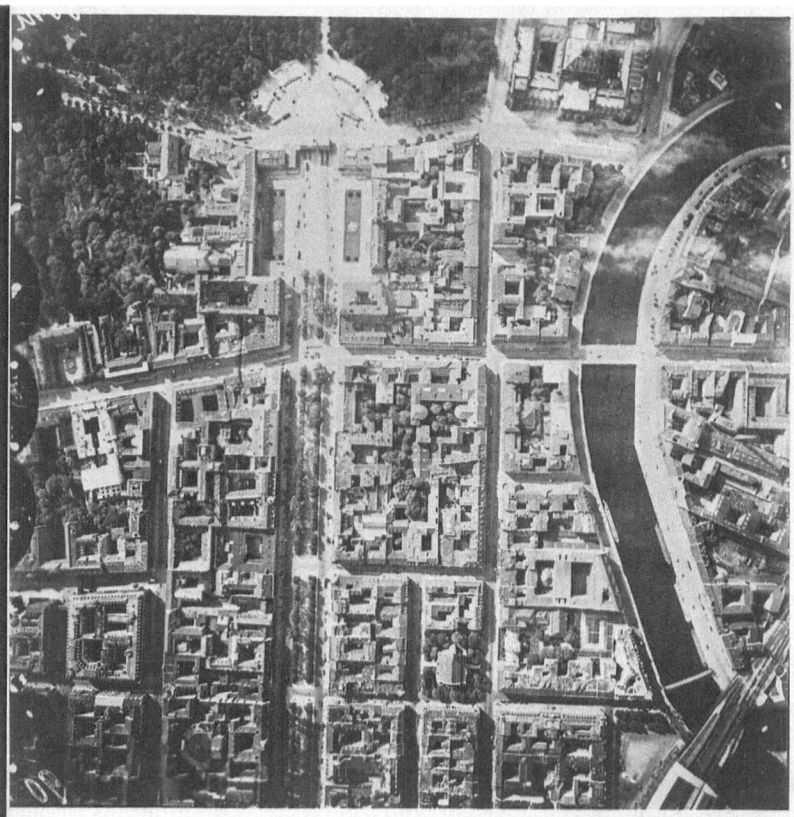

Figure. 16 Aerial view of Berlin from around 1928 showing parts of the Tiergarten, the Reichstag building, the Brandenburg Gate, Pariser Platz, Unter den Linden, and the Spree. Landesarchiv Berlin, F Rep. 290 (02) Nr. II1463. Photo by Horst Siegmann.

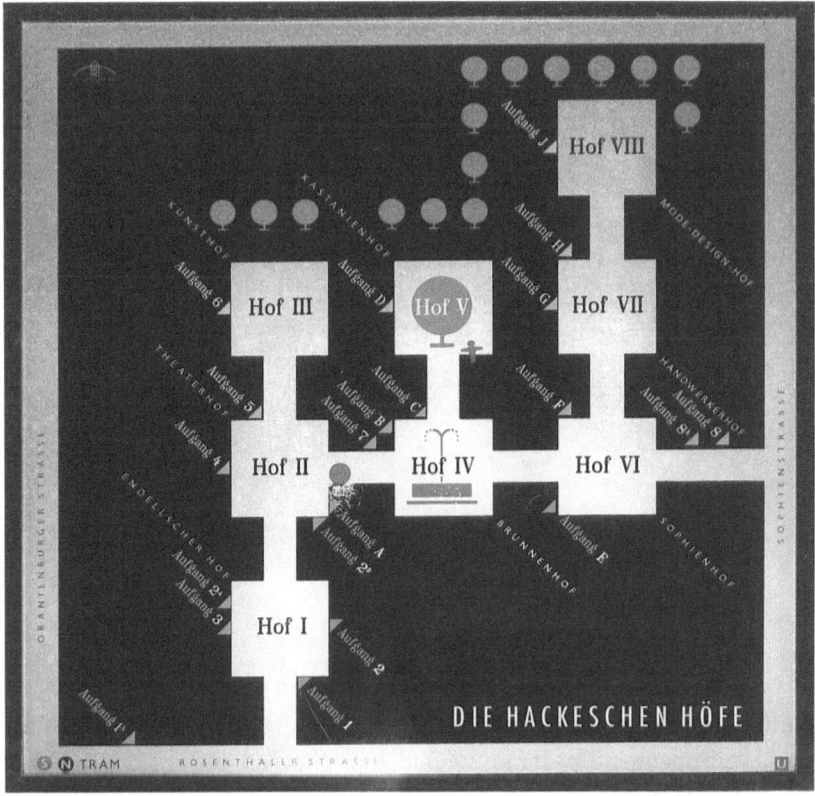

Figure 17. A courtyard map of the Hakesche Höfe residential buildings in Berlin Mitte. Wikimedia Commons.

formal composition of *The Gift*, which famously consists of several interconnected texts, including poems, a short story, and two biographies.[50]

This comparison of apartment buildings to crossword puzzles indicates Nabokov's conception of Berlin's urban space as a text that is ciphered and divided into discrete units. Although these units remain for the most part isolated, there are always points of intersection that yield new knowledge. As in a crossword puzzle, such individual units appear to be self-enclosed, but are in fact fragments of a larger textual whole. The image of the crossword-puzzle-like tenements suggests, moreover, Fyodor's orientation within the city as both horizontal (seeing from within) and vertical (seeing from above), enabling him to move between urban exterior and personal interior. In keeping with his self-fashioning as an aloof writer, Nabokov's representation of

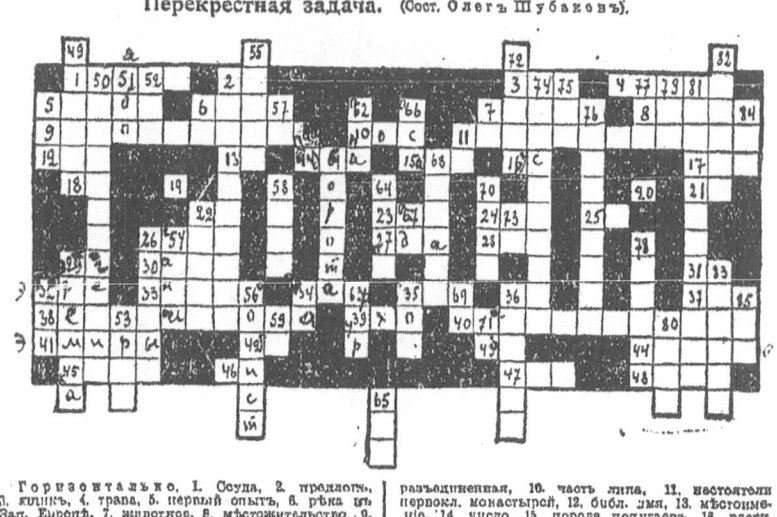

Figure 18. A crossword puzzle published in *Rul'* on May 10, 1925. Staatsbibliothek zu Berlin.

Berlin (and everything German) is largely negative. Only three pages after the novel's opening, Fyodor says, "God, how I hate all this" (5). Various versions of this statement are repeated throughout the novel. Yet, while at first glance Nabokov rejects a correlation between his Berlin surroundings and his narrative imagination, upon a closer look that correlation becomes apparent.[51] As I will show, the artistic vision of Nabokov's hero is dialectically dependent on his urban environment, which he conceives in literary terms. Such an urban conceptualization suggests that spatiality, textuality, and identity are interlinked in *The Gift*. This conceptualization offers a concise demonstration of how Berlin exerts influence on Russian émigré culture despite being portrayed as a profoundly foreign place.

At the novel's beginning, as Fyodor continues to familiarize himself with his new neighborhood, it is said that his new street begins with a post office and ends with a church, and the narrator likens such an urban layout to an epistolary novel (4). This literary observation underscores that Fyodor, himself a writer, will be residing within a novelistic space. As Fyodor's panoramic vision expands, he famously contemplates the compositional sequence of stores on the block and ponders whether "such a sequence followed its own law of composition" and whether it would be possible to "deduce the average cycle for the streets of a given city" (the "average rhythm," in the Russian original—5; 193). He further observes that the "rhythmic swarming" (roenie ritma) of Tannenberg Street has not yet established itself, but he foresees that with time, the tobacco shop, pharmacy, and greengrocery will rearrange themselves, "forming a typical line":

> The greengrocery, with a glance over its shoulder, would cross the street, so as to be at first seven and then three doors away from the pharmacy—somewhat the same way as the jumbled letters find their places in a film commercial; and at the end there is always one that does a kind of flip, and then hastily assumes its position . . . and thus they will wait until an adjacent place becomes vacant, whereupon they will both wink across at the tobacco shop, as if to say: "Quick, over here"; and before you know it they are all in a row, forming a typical line. (5; 193)

This description of the street wherein the shops occupy specific numbered positions is analogous with poetry: the rhythm in poetry is achieved by stressing particular syllables in a given line. The arrangement of vacant buildings on Tannenberg Street ("at first seven and then three doors away") is comparable to how syllables might be accented in a line of verse.[52] When Fyodor is introduced in the novel, the reader learns that he is an amateur Russian poet in exile whose first book of poems has recently been published. Fyodor's understanding of the surrounding world in poetic terms supports his development as a poet. As the novel unfolds, Fyodor's versification grows ever more sophisticated. Ultimately, *The Gift* ends with an Onegin stanza typeset as prose—an homage to Pushkin, considered to be one of the most gifted of all Russian poets, in whose footsteps Fyodor, as well as Nabokov, follows.[53]

It is also significant that in the novel's introductory scene Fyodor writes about the future "rhythmic swarming" of Tannenberg Street by coupling a poetic term (rhythm) with an entomological one (swarming, as in bees founding a new colony).[54] Such a pairing conveys the twin image of a new poem and a new home coming into being.[55] Furthermore, the playful shops that move around Tannenberg Street enliven it and suggest that Berlin is more than a conventional narrative setting. The city is an animated presence similar to a character in its own right.[56] In this connection, it is not incidental that throughout *The Gift* Nabokov evokes Andrei Bely's *Petersburg*, a contemporary Russian novel in which the city becomes a meta-protagonist.[57] Like the city in *Petersburg*—a revised edition of which Bely published in Berlin in 1922—Nabokov's Berlin is charged with prosody and becomes a significant player in the novel. Berlin in *The Gift* is admittedly less sentient than Bely's Petersburg. Nabokov's Berlin is nevertheless both textual material and the text itself.

The passage describing Tannenberg Street also illustrates the impact of Berlin's media environment on Fyodor's imagination, particularly when the tobacco shop, pharmacy, and greengrocery are compared to "jumbled letters [that] find their places in a film commercial." That is, much as Fyodor is steeped in Russian literary history, he is also aware of contemporary German advertisement practices.[58] The reference to a "film commercial" (reklamnaia fil'ma) serves a larger purpose, too. From the novel's beginning, the narrator signals that he will be organizing the city's "jumbled letters" into a coherent text. By chapter 5 of the novel, Fyodor even tries his hand at putting jumbled letters into spectacularly long words, following the example of German compound words: "The illuminated sign of a music hall ran up the steps of vertically placed letters, they went out all together, and the light again scrambled up: what Babylonian word would reach up to the sky? . . . a compound name for a trillion tints: diamondimlunalilithlilasafieryviolent-violet [brilliantovolunnolilitovosizolazorevogroznosapfiristosinelilovo] and so on—and how many more!" (325; 500).[59]

The appearance of this astonishingly multisyllabic word is possible thanks to the blueprint of German grammar and Berlin's dramatic illuminated advertising. This compound principle is already evident in Nabokov's 1935 short story "Recruiting" ("Nabor"), which can be considered a study for *The Gift*. In it, he practiced writing about Berlin by stringing together seemingly disconnected images. The short story's Russian title "Nabor" connotes both "recruiting" of images and "typesetting" of various jumbled letters.[60] Accordingly, the short story's narrator describes the process of scanning his Berlin surroundings for noteworthy phenomena and incorporating them into his writing. *The Gift*'s narrative develops very similarly, emphasizing Berlin's role as a warehouse of urban impressions.

In the recruiting and typesetting mode, Fyodor continuously negotiates the meaning of Berlin's verbal textures and pictorial surfaces. For instance, he twice draws the reader's attention to signs over various shops. At the beginning of chapter 2, commercial signage underscores Berlin's foreignness as Fyodor, suddenly paying attention to what he sees from a tram window, cannot read the German shop signs and "only one [sign] could still appear to be written in Russian: Kakao" (80). Since the word "cocoa" is written identically in German and Russian, this easily legible advertisement deepens the sense that all other signs require more effort to be read. On another occasion, in chapter 3, Fyodor notices a "live blackbird" sitting on one of the "vertical yellow letters" spelling the name of a car maker above a gas station (174). Dolinin has identified the car firm as Daimler-Benz AG.[61] Fyodor wishes that the bird were sitting on the letter "B" instead of the "E" because that way the image of a blackbird sitting on the "B" "would have made an alphabetic vignette." This imaginary urban alphabet reinforces Berlin's textuality and Fyodor's ability to put foreign letters into legible words. Naturally, the focus on the letters "B" and "E" also produces the verb "be," as if encouraging Fyodor.[62] In the Russian original, the letters are "D" and "A," resulting in an approving "da" (yes). If these German letters are read in Russian, moreover, they spell the novel's working title *Da* and hint at the word *Dar* (the gift)—the novel's final title and the affirmative gift of creative imagination that endows Fyodor's life with meaning.[63]

Nabokov tests Fyodor's ability to read his surroundings in one memorable episode when Fyodor rides in a crowded tram. Late for an appointment, a disgruntled Fyodor contemplates Berlin's giftlessness (bezdarnost'): the tram is the "least gifted of all methods of transport"; the streets he sees in the window are "hopelessly familiar" and "hopelessly ugly"; and the passengers are but "the feet, sides and necks of the native passengers" (80).[64] Huddled together in the "cattle-like crowding," the passengers and their "cold, slippery eyes" make Fyodor feel threatened (81). For a moment, Fyodor reasons with himself: "The Russian conviction that the German is in small numbers vulgar and in large numbers—unbearably vulgar was, he knew, a conviction unworthy of an artist." Nonetheless, once a newly boarded passenger accidentally bumps him with his knee and "with the corner of a fat briefcase with a leather handle," Fyodor's irritation turns into "pure fury." The physical touch of another person prompts Fyodor to stare at him, "reading his features." As he does so, he spews a long list of graphic anti-German stereotypes, his "sinful hatred (for this poor, pitiful, expiring nation)." Fyodor's screed is interrupted when the clumsy passenger takes a Russian émigré newspaper out of his pocket and coughs "unconcernedly with a Russian intonation" (82). Fyodor is delighted with this transformation, since he had assumed that the passenger was German. He marvels at life's graceful slyness and swiftly recognizes in the passenger's features "compatriotic softness"—"it became at once both funny and incomprehensible how anyone could have been deceived." But Fyodor was deceived, and his failure to distinguish between form and content, German and Russian, indicates that in Berlin, stereotypes are as treacherous as ever and the metropolis, an urban jungle, can be deceptive.

Indeed, much later in the novel, Fyodor will mistake a German for a Russian (343). Although the Germans among whom Fyodor lives are physically repulsive and morally suspect—they long for physical work (189); have "excellent sanitary conditions" (326) but awful hygiene (189; 362); they have disfigured bodies (336); and are prone to torturing animals (80; 350)—the Germans of Fyodor's childhood are almost idyllic people: "what has happened to those originals who used to teach natural history to Russian children—green net, tin box on a sling, hat stuck with pinned butterflies, long, learned nose, candid eyes behind spectacles—where are they all, where are their frail skeletons—or was this a special breed of Germans, for export to Russia, or am I not looking properly?" (102). Fyodor's admission that he may not be looking properly is confirmed when he mistakes Russians for Germans and Germans for Russians. As a result, his many xenophobic proclamations about Berlin and Germans are thrown into question. When Fyodor is riding on the tram, moreover, the public spheres that he inhabits are refracted through the image of the newspaper, which serves as an iconographic symbol rather than a text. The tram episode thus serves to educate Fyodor about the city's multimedia complexity and reveals the limitations of his abilities. In particular, his self-fashioning as a completely independent émigré artist is compromised as he is shown to be at once an outsider and an insider.

Fyodor's exilic identity can be illuminated by Mikhail Bakhtin's discussion of otherness and outsidedness, especially as outlined in his essay "Author and Hero in Aesthetic Activity."[65] Bakhtin argues that all experience is mediated by the intertwined relationship between self and other. The position of outsidedness and the experience of alterity are innate to the human's perception of the self and the surrounding environment. In fiction, the self's relation to the other and the self's outsidedness are modified by what Bakhtin calls "aesthetic empathizing (*Einfühlung*)" (esteticheskoe vzhivanie).[66] This aesthetic activity consists of "seeing from within," assuming the interiority of the other and achieving a moment of simultaneous being with the other; in turn, this process allows for a properly aesthetic experience. So, if we look at Nabokov's hero in this episode through the optics of aesthetic empathy, we can see that Fyodor manipulates the process of aesthetic empathizing. When Fyodor sees the "native passengers" as a disintegrated, Cubist-like mass of "feet, sides, and necks," he denies them their wholeness as humans and deliberately positions himself as a disinterested outsider, until he notices that one of the passengers he thought was German is reading a Russian-language newspaper. The symbolic recognition of the newspaper leads Fyodor to identify the other as a fellow man, at which point the outsidedness of Nabokov's hero is rapidly transformed into a creative force. The verticality of the self intersects with the horizontality of the other, and as a result of this fusion, from onlooker Fyodor turns into insider. This process additionally demonstrates that Fyodor's disinterested contempt for Berlin and Berliners, "a conviction unworthy of an artist," impedes his creative vision.

This recognition passage takes place in a tram, a signature urban space in the modernist imagination. Enclosed, but also open and dynamic, the tram is a location that embodies the liminality between exterior and interior. Immediately preceding this passage, Fyodor is daydreaming about his parents at their country estate in Russia. With cinematic effect, the narrator depicts Fyodor's awakening when, through the falling snow, he sees "a dim yellow blotch approaching, which suddenly came into focus, shuddered, thickened and turned into a tramcar" (80). And a few sentences later, Fyodor reemerges from his memories to board the tram: "straight from the hothouse paradise of the past, he stepped onto a Berlin tramcar." On the surface level, the comparison between the hothouse paradise of the past and the Berlin tramcar is not in favor of the Berlin present. The warm botanical paradise of the past is further contrasted with the cold "Berliner animal luxury" of the present (83). But the bygone paradise is contained within a hothouse (called "oranzhereia," an orangery, in the original), which is an artificial and largely decorative space. It requires meticulous care, the labor of memory, to maintain its beauty.[67] And as the encounter on the tram demonstrates, Fyodor learns that the present can be delightful in its deception only if he pays attention to it and reads it with care.

The same logic applies to Fyodor's notorious obliviousness to the signs that would have led him to meet his lover, Zina Mertz, much earlier than he did (363–64). Indeed, the connection between Zina and Berlin is implied in one of Fyodor's poems. As is often the case in *The Gift*, the poem is formally unmarked but embedded in the narrative's prose. Fyodor composes it in a state of euphoria once he learns that Zina is one of the few people who had bought his first chapbook. Ostensibly addressed to Zina, the poem's first line is "Love only what is fanciful and rare"; by the lines "Beyond that gate lies Baghdad's crooked shade, and yon star sheds on Pulkovo its beam. Oh, swear to me . . ." the poem is disrupted by a telephone call only to continue after this break with the lines, "What shall I call you? Half-Mnemo*syne*? There's a half-shim*mer* in your surname too. In dark Berlin, it is so strange to me to roam, oh, my half-fantasy with you" (156–57). Nabokov italicizes the syllables "syne" and "mer" to emphasize the anagrammatic reference to "Zina Mertz."[68] But there is also a crucial rhyme in these lines, evident especially in the Russian: "polu-Mnemozina / Berlina" (Half-Mnemosyne, Berlin). This rhyme establishes a connection between Zina and Berlin, as well as between Berlin and Mnemosyne, the mother of nine muses and the goddess who embodies memory in Greek mythology. Berlin thus emerges as a space that facilitates Fyodor's cosmopolitan imagination ("Baghdad's crooked shade") and stimulates his memory (Pulkovo was a village outside Nabokov's native St. Petersburg and the site of a major observatory since 1839).[69]

The rest of this poem reappears some twenty pages later and is again occasioned by Fyodor's thinking about Zina and his observations about Berlin: "Waiting for her arrival. She was always late—and always came by another road than he. Thus it transpired that even Berlin could be mysterious" (176). In this backhanded compliment there is a recognition of Berlin's complexity that continues to surprise Fyodor. By the novel's end Fyodor will tacitly acknowledge his inability to grasp Berlin fully as his "restless wanderings [with Zina] carried them in ever widening circles into distant and ever new corners of the city" (327). Furthermore, Fyodor's multiple encounters with Berlin's urban space give way to moments of creativity, and the city's felt reality coalesces into poetry.

An earlier example of this poetic process can be found in chapter 1, when Fyodor forgets the keys to his room in a boarding house and, due to the late hour, is forced to wait for an unlikely opportunity to get inside. As he paces the street at night, he is overcome with poetic inspiration and begins composing his strange lyric poem with civic undertones, beginning with the line "Thank you my land; for your remotest / Most cruel mist my thanks are due" (54–56). The imagery of this scene—the stony pavement, forgotten keys, wind that plays the street like a musical instrument, and forced nocturnal flânerie—is reminiscent of Khodasevich's poem "All is made of stone. Into the stony street" (1923). The poem refers to Berlin as "the stepmother of all Russian cities," and Nabokov may be consciously evoking Khodasevich's metaphor as Fyodor is thanking his cruel fatherland (otchizna) and sharpening his poetic skill with the help of his stepmother-city. Overall, the prosody of *The Gift*'s poetic segments functions as a mnemonic device that both constitutes the poetic rhythm and accentuates the verbal nature of Nabokov's Berlin: "Our poor nocturnal property—that wet asphaltic gloss, that fence and that street light—upon the ace of fancy let us set to win a world of beauty from the night" (157).

These affinities notwithstanding, for Fyodor Berlin always remains a city of exile, and he rarely fails to underscore its foreignness. Berlin appears to be more undesirable when compared to Paris, the major center of the Russian diaspora: "When, three years ago, still during his existence here as a student, his mother had moved to Paris ... she had written that she just could not get used to being liberated from the perpetual fetters that chain a Berliner to the door lock" (29).[70] This somewhat enigmatic image is eventually explained when Fyodor realizes that he is locked out of his apartment building late at night: "In those days Berlin janitors (shveitsary) were for the most part opulent bullies who had corpulent wives and belonged, out of petty bourgeois considerations, to the Communist Party" (54). Unable to count on the presumably friendlier Parisian concierges, Fyodor is locked out of his apartment twice, in the novel's beginning and end.[71] All this imagery of forgotten keys and locked doors would seem to underscore Fyodor's marginality in the city, and yet Berlin almost literally chains itself to Russian Berliners and eventually becomes an inseparable part of Fyodor's life: "He was walking along streets that had already long since insinuated themselves into his acquaintance—and as if that were not enough, they expected affection (raschityvali na liubov'); they had even purchased in advance, in his future memories, space next to St. Petersburg, an adjacent grave" (53). Unconcerned with Fyodor's consent, Berlin's streets are animated in their expectation of affection from the novel's narrator and protagonist—and, arguably, from the author. Regardless of what Fyodor (or Nabokov) might have wished, Berlin will occupy a space next to St. Petersburg in his memory.

This equivalence between Berlin and St. Petersburg is evoked again when Fyodor visits a bookshop near Wittenberg Square, a "region ... rich in encounters, so that it seemed as if on this German street there had encroached the vagabond phantom of a Russian boulevard." But before any conclusions can be made about émigrés as sad apparitions, the narrator adds, "or as if on the contrary a street in Russia, with several natives taking the air, swarmed with the pale ghosts of innumerable foreigners flickering among those natives like a familiar and barely noticeable hallucination" (166).

By implying that the two streets, one in Germany and one in Russia, could be interchangeable, Fyodor allows for a possibility of making Berlin his own. Nabokov describes the area by Wittenberg Square featured in many Russian narratives about Berlin, from Bely's pamphlet/travelogue *One of the Mansions of the Kingdom of Shades* to R. G. Batalin's crime novel *Petersburg on Wittenberg Square* (1931).[72] In a departure from his predecessors, Nabokov rejects the pervasive narrative of cultural decline in exile and instead enlists Berlin to showcase the liberating complexity of his exilic imaginary. But like many of his contemporaries in Russian Berlin, his representation of the city configures it as an in-between location in space and time.

As the preceding examples show and as I have been suggesting, the specificity of references to Berlin and their function in *The Gift* extend beyond that of a conventional narrative backdrop. In a sense, Nabokov shows that Berlin embodies exile—in the novel, the city is filled with boundaries, borders, and partitions of various kinds. Such spatiotemporal organization reminds its (Russian) inhabitants of their difference physically and discursively.[73] And Nabokov's aesthetic conception of exilic writing rests on simultaneous elaboration and violation of the borders of exile. For example, early in the novel, when Fyodor speculates about a future return to Russia "on foreign-made soles," he states that "there is one thing I shall definitely not find there awaiting me—the thing which, indeed, made the whole business of exile worth cultivating: my childhood and the fruits of my childhood" (25; 212). These fruits are Fyodor's juvenilia, his amateur poetry, which he shares so liberally in the first chapter. It would appear that cultivating exile enabled Fyodor to preserve his precious childhood memories in his Berlin poems. However, the Russian original of this sentence reveals a double entendre: the phrase "the business of exile was worth cultivating" is "stoilo gorodit' ogorod izgnaniia," which translates as "it was worth putting up a fence of exile" and contains the Russian proverb "gorodit' ogorod" (literally, "putting up a fence around a vegetable garden"). Colloquially, this proverb means that the activity at hand is senseless and doomed to fail.[74] In the novel, the senseless activity is the business of cultivating exile. Furthermore, the word "gorod" (city) is repeated twice in the phrase "*gorod*it' o*gorod*." Since *The Gift* is set in Berlin, such reiteration reinforces the interrelation between the city and exile. It conveys Fyodor's equal awareness of the creative potential of exile and the futility of achieving isolation in the city. That this linguistic play is lost in translation indicates how important it is that *The Gift* is written in Russian in Berlin, because the punning awkwardness of the novel's Russian is inevitably smoothed out in the English translation.

Nabokov brings the problem of cultural translation to the forefront also by means of references to borderlines and partitions. In chapter 3 Fyodor spots a peculiar fence while waiting for Zina, and the lengthy description of that fence presents a deft elaboration of Nabokov's vision of self and art in exile:

> A remarkable fence made out of another one which had been dismantled somewhere else (perhaps in another town) and which had previously surrounded the camp of a wandering circus, but the boards had now been placed in senseless order, as if nailed together by a blind man, so that the circus beasts once painted on them, and reshuffled during transit, had disintegrated into their component parts—here there was the leg of a zebra, there a tiger's back, and some animal's haunch appeared next to another creature's paw: life's promise of a life to come had been kept with respect to the fence, but the rupture of the earthly images on it destroyed the earthly value of immortality. (176)

The randomly reassembled mural of exotic animals once painted on that fence is a salient allegory of expatriate Russians in Berlin.[75] Although isolation, alienation, captivity, and deterritorialization are implied in the image of the chimeric creature with the leg of a zebra and a tiger's back, this fence description goes beyond a lyrical rumination on the condition of exile. This fence presents a crude mixing of visual aesthetic models and therefore can be viewed as a statement about modernist fragmentation and collage, similar to the earlier description of tram passengers as a mass of "feet, sides, and necks." That is not to say that Nabokov is advocating for the primacy of mimetic representation, especially considering that he is writing *The Gift* during the violent valorization of realism in the Third Reich and the Soviet Union.[76] Instead, by alluding to the tension between the abstract and figurative aesthetic practices, Nabokov reminds the reader of Fyodor's earlier shortsightedness on the tram and hints at the crucial importance of seeing the seemingly familiar in an unfamiliar light.[77] As Fyodor puts it while continuing the description of the fence, "at night, however, little could be made out of it [the fence], while the exaggerated shadows of the leaves (nearby there was a streetlight) lay on the boards quite logically, in perfect order—this served as a kind of compensation, the more so since it was impossible to transfer them to another place, with the boards, having broken up and mixed the pattern: they could only be transferred *in toto*, together with the night" (176).

Fyodor's vision of wholeness is predicated on the power of the imaginary and the ability to see the entire picture. Although this multi-layered and multiply exposed image is ephemeral and "impossible to transfer," Fyodor captures it verbally such that its delicate texture is safeguarded from being disrupted again. On the metaliterary level, this episode displays the reparative potential of exilic writing—its compensatory value. The reference to the "exaggerated shadows" lying logically on the illogically reassembled fence elaborates Fyodor's conception of artistic practice: the totality of this image represents the tension between form and content, genre and medium, and tradition and the individual talent, to use T. S. Eliot's famous formulation. Fyodor gestures toward these tensions without resolving them because resolving them would break up and mix the pattern, while engaging with them advances artistic innovation.

The image of the fence provides a commentary on the afterlife of the Russian literary tradition in exile, too. After all, Sirin, Nabokov's alter ego in Berlin, was also a chimeric creature—half maiden and half bird—who came of age in exile, a stateless Russian poet in Germany. And Fyodor is haunted by the "everlasting, chilly thought: there he is, a special, rare and as yet undescribed and unnamed variant of man" who is forced to waste his talents on mediocre tutoring (163). Perhaps to soften the pathos of the self-observation that he belongs to a new human species, Fyodor adds, "I am a simply poor young Russian selling the surplus from a gentleman's upbringing (*izlishek barskogo vospitaniia*), while scribbling verses in my spare time, that's the total of my little immortality" (164). He will make the point about his immortality again almost at the end of the novel, quoting himself in a letter to his mother in Paris: "'I lust for immortality—even for its earthly shadow!'" (350-51). Fyodor frames this point about immortality and its earthly shadow as a "historical hope, a literary-historical one"—because just as the imperfect fence with the perfect shadows upon it survives in the reader's memory, Fyodor's, and by extension Nabokov's, writing will survive in the form of books "or at least in some researcher's footnote" (350).

In the task of achieving immortality by means of creative writing, Fyodor turns to Berlin both to emphasize the difficulty of living in "this country, oppressive as a headache" (350) and to showcase how he recruits Berlin's topography, landmarks, and residents to structure the entirety of *The Gift*:

at the end, it is apparent that Fyodor is writing the novel we are reading.[78] The variety of Berlin realia listed in the novel explicitly and implicitly is impressive, and I have discussed only those directly related to Berlin's textuality. Fyodor additionally presents a number of striking cityscapes, scatters references to contemporary literature and cinema, exhibits his nude body in the Grunewald forest while referencing the German body culture (Freikörperkultur), and shares his thoughts on political activism ("exhibition of civic excitement").[79] Fyodor's final topographic trajectory in Berlin is also significant.[80] After he discovers that he is, once again, locked out of the apartment, he goes to meet Zina at the train station, which is unnamed but likely the Stettiner Bahnhof.[81] His route takes him from Tauentzien Street in the western part of town to Unter den Linden in the east via the Potsdamer Square and then back through the "*defile* (tesnina) of the Brandenburg Gate" (361).[82] This is the farthest point east to which Fyodor ventures in *The Gift*, albeit only for a brief moment and, notably, without going to the train platform itself, as if to avoid the temptation of leaving the city.

He returns to Berlin's western part with Zina. Neither of them knows that they both have no house keys. While Fyodor and Zina are locked out of the apartment, they are locked in the city, for the novel ends with a circular reference to its beginning. This tricky ending includes an obvious reference to Pushkin's *Eugene Onegin*: the final paragraph is composed as an Onegin stanza and includes the lines alluding to the ending of Pushkin's novel-in-verse: "Onegin from his knees will rise—but his creator strolls away" (366). At the end of Pushkin's novel, significantly, Eugene and his beloved Tatyana never consummate their love. Fyodor and Zina, deprived as they are of their apartment keys, are prevented from consummating their relationship as well, even though Fyodor eagerly anticipates it throughout chapter 5.[83] This purposefully sex-less ending hints at Nabokov's vision of creative evolution and the fact that texts (re)produce by literary, not biological, means.[84] Indeed, the description of the sun licking Fyodor's nude body in the Grunewald, as eroticized as it is, can be read as a version of Pushkin's programmatic poem "Prophet" (1826), as Priscilla Meyer has noted. Nabokov exploits the erotic to describe "the poet's access to the sublime through nature, framed by artistic vision which is itself a prelude and means to a writer's future spiritual insight to be understood through his art."[85]

Just as *Eugene Onegin*, with its unhappy ending, nonetheless stands at the beginning of the modern Russian novelistic tradition, so does *The Gift* not only continue that tradition but also attempt to engender a new way of writing outside Russia proper, in Berlin exile. *The Gift*'s ending therefore opens up a question about the future of Russian literature. Or rather, it leaves that question open, since the reader is encouraged to reread the novel *ad infinitum*, "and no obstruction for the sage exists where I have put The End: the shadows of my world extend beyond the skyline of the page, blue as tomorrow's morning haze—nor does this terminate the phrase. The End" (366). Reading retrospectively, beyond "The End," the reader is soon reminded that Fyodor, for all his forgetfulness, did take away the keys to Russia itself (350). In the next and concluding section, I will explore some implications for *The Gift*'s futurity and its importance for Russian Berlin by situating the novel in its broader cultural context.

WHAT IS TO BE DONE? *THE GIFT* AND THE FUTURE OF RUSSIAN LITERATURE

As noted earlier, Simon Karlinsky has observed that one of the overarching themes Nabokov presents in *The Gift* is "the possibility and validity of an émigré literature."[86] I have aimed to show that Nabokov's Berlin writing demonstrates a search for a new urban idiom in Russian literature, now in exile. *The Gift*'s overt preoccupation with its own status as a novel is a signature modernist feature, but unlike most major modernist city novels, Nabokov's is the product of genuine exile. While Nabokov minimized the role of Weimar-era Berlin in *The Gift*, he captured the entire universe of Russian Berlin and Russia Abroad in writing it. When read with the knowledge of émigré cultural politics, *The Gift* presents a marketplace of ideas whose only legitimate currency is Russian literary fame. Although Fyodor avoids acknowledging it directly, he stakes his future on the record of his urban experience in Berlin.

Nabokov implies his awareness of literary futurity in the Foreword to *The Gift*'s English translation in writing that the novel's "heroine is not Zina, but Russian Literature" (ii). As important a character as Zina is, however, she can hardly be considered a proper heroine given her decidedly secondary role and limited appearance on the book's pages.[87] By instructing the reader not to see Zina as the heroine, Nabokov only draws attention to the fact that the novel's hero is Fyodor, and that all of Russian Literature is channeled through him.[88] Fyodor's recurrent wish is to return to Russia: "Some day, interrupting my writing, I will look through the window and see a Russian autumn" (175); "and when will we return to Russia? . . . I shall live there in my books" (350).[89] Zina articulates his innermost literary desire:

"I think you'll be such a writer as has never been before and Russia will simply pine for you—when she comes to her senses too late" (364). This emphasis on the future reveals the magnitude of Fyodor's ambition: he imagines himself as the future of Russian literature. Fyodor estimates that his motherland will come to her senses "in a hundred, two hundred years" (350), but in the meantime he outlines his aesthetic ideology by means of reevaluating modern Russian literature.[90]

Fyodor's archnemesis in Russian literature is Nikolay Chernyshevsky, whose literary biography constitutes chapter 4 of *The Gift*. A progressive Russian intellectual of the 1860s, Chernyshevsky wrote *What Is to Be Done?* (1863)—"the novel that has had the greatest impact on human lives in the history of Russian literature," as Irina Paperno has put it.[91] "It was read the way liturgical books are read—not a single work by Turgenev or Tolstoy produced such a mighty impression," writes Fyodor in the "Life of Chernyshevsky" (277). After being first published in 1863, the novel was banned in Russia until 1905. For his political activity, Chernyshevsky was mock-executed and exiled to Siberia for over twenty years. These revolutionary credentials play against Chernyshevsky in *The Gift*. Through Fyodor, who explains writing about Chernyshevsky as "firing practice" (196), Nabokov traces the causes of the Russian Revolution and the postrevolutionary emigration to Chernyshevsky and his novel: "Why had everything in Russia become so shoddy, so crabbed and gray, how could she have been so befooled and befuddled? Or had the old urge 'toward the light' concealed a fatal flaw, which in the course of progress toward the objective had grown more and more evident, until it was revealed that this 'light' was burning in the window of a prison overseer, and that was all? When had this strange dependence sprung up between the sharpening of thirst and the muddying of the source? In the forties? In the sixties? and 'what to do' now?" (175).

"What to do?" is an alternative translation of "what is to be done?" In the world of *The Gift*, Chernyshevsky's "muddying of the source" is directly responsible for the emergence of the Soviet Union. Therefore the novel dramatizes the paradox of so many Russian émigré liberals who revered Chernyshevsky without holding him accountable for their exile. The character of Alexander Chernyshevsky, Fyodor's well-meaning but misguided friend, is meant to be a living embodiment of this paradox (197). The poet Koncheyev, with whom Fyodor identifies, ventriloquizes the author's position in his review of the "Life of Chernyshevsky," and Fyodor's inclusion of Koncheyev's name in square brackets only betrays Fyodor's own presence in the cited review: "He began by drawing a picture of flight during an invasion or an earthquake, when the escapers carry away with them everything they can lay hands on, someone sure to burden himself with a large, framed portrait of some long-forgotten relative. 'Just such a portrait [wrote Koncheyev] is for the Russian intelligentsia the image of Chernyshevski, which was spontaneously but accidentally carried away abroad by the émigrés, together with other, more useful things,' and this is how Koncheyev explained the stupefaction occasioned by the appearance of Fyodor Konstantinovich's book: 'Someone suddenly confiscated the portrait'" (308).

In this respect, *The Gift* reflected the situation in real life, too. As Dana Dragonoiu has observed in her study of Nabokov's engagement with the tradition of liberalism, "By having Fyodor launch his career with a biography of Chernyshevsky, Nabokov targets . . . the radical intelligentsia whose all-encompassing positivism and utilitarianism came to be regarded by many as having laid the groundwork for the Soviet tyranny."[92] Fyodor's difficulty in finding a publisher for his "Life of Chernyshevsky" in the novel was prophetic, as Nabokov faced nonnegotiable censorship at the Parisian émigré journal *Sovremennye zapiski*, where *The Gift* was being printed serially in 1937–38. The editors were so outraged by Nabokov's irreverence toward the progressive icon that they suppressed the entire fourth chapter.[93] Nabokov later recounted this episode as "a pretty example of life finding itself obliged to imitate the very art it condemns" (i). In Nabokov's view, Chernyshevsky's main transgression is his belief in the inferiority of art to life, his utilitarian aesthetic. That is why in *The Gift* Nabokov stages Fyodor's artistic trajectory against that of the historical Nikolay Chernyshevsky and fictional Yasha Chernyshevsky, the tragically mediocre gay poet who shoots himself in the Grunewald—an example of the ruinous effects of the utilitarian conviction that art is bound by life.[94] The guiding principle of Fyodor's aesthetic education in the novel is that genuine art is free from pragmatic demands.[95]

For all his methodical insistence on artistic autonomy, however, Fyodor is writing *The Gift* both as an answer and a rival to *What Is to Be Done?*—"this dead little book," as he calls it (282). After finishing his Chernyshevsky biography, Fyodor is wondering what he should write next. In Brian Boyd's succinct words, "in the last chapter of the novel, where he thinks up the idea for *The Gift* itself, he muses for a moment that he should write 'a practical handbook: *How to Be Happy*' [328]. In a sense *The Gift* is that book."[96] Nabokov scholars often cite Fyodor's musings about the literary recipe for happiness as the essence of the novel, and rightfully so, though Boyd neglects to reproduce Fyodor's question mark following *How to Be Happy*?⁹⁷ To be fair, the question mark is placed at the end of an interrogative sentence—"Use them immediately for a practical handbook: *How to Be Happy*?" (328)—and it is not entirely clear whether that question mark belongs to the title of the prospective book or whether it simply indicates the end of that sentence. It must also be added that Nabokov's "how" is in response to Chernyshevsky's "what," as Fyodor himself writes in chapter 4: "What to do? Live, read, think. What to do? Work at one's own development in order to achieve the aim of life, which is happiness. What to do? (But Chernyshevsky's own fate changed the businesslike question to an ironic exclamation)" (282). That Fyodor prefaces his own potentially interrogative title of *How to Be Happy*? as a "practical handbook," subjecting literature to utilitarian means, makes one think that he uses the question mark ironically.

The resulting ambiguity may be the point, since Fyodor explains to Zina that he would like to write Chernyshevsky's biography while keeping "everything as it were on the very brink of parody.... And there must be on the other hand an abyss of seriousness, and I must make my way along this narrow ridge between my own truth and a caricature of it" (200). Let us recall that *What Is to Be Done*? opens with a prefatory chapter called "The Fool" (Durak), in which the narrator describes the apparent suicide of a young man, whose body cannot be found, and how "One couldn't make any sense whatever of this whole affair; he was both a fool *and* very clever" (i durak, i umno).⁹⁸ While Fyodor's balancing between his "own truth and a caricature of it" is a very sophisticated act, it is formally reminiscent of the simultaneously foolish and clever ways of Chernyshevsky's character Dmitry Lopukhov, who, by the way, escapes to Berlin after staging his suicide.⁹⁹ That is to say, the correspondences between the two novels, of which there are many, make it clear that Fyodor takes Chernyshevsky's novel seriously, and not only as the material for parody.¹⁰⁰ Marina Kostalevsky has underscored that "since the literary-critical component of *The Gift* is directly related to the problematics posed in 'The Life of Chernyshevsky' [the novel] becomes, to a certain extent, a commentary on it."¹⁰¹ One can go a step further and say that Fyodor rewrites *What Is to Be Done*? to show *how it must be done*. After all, Fyodor identifies himself as a new "variant of man," undescribed and unnamed, and Chernyshevsky is describing and naming "the new people" of nineteenth-century Russian society. (The full title of Chernyshevsky's novel is *What Is to Be Done? From the Stories about the New People*.)¹⁰² Fyodor perfects the structure of *What Is to Be Done*? too—instead of Vera

Pavlovna's clumsy dream sequences containing details necessary for advancing the plot, as well as discursive writings on a socialist utopia, in *The Gift* there are dream-like encounters between Fyodor and the poet Koncheyev that serve to present Fyodor's aesthetic program.[103] Furthermore, *The Gift*'s circular narrative, which guides the reader to continue rereading Fyodor's creation, is arguably an elaboration of Chernyshevsky's narrative conceit in which the reader must return to the novel's detective fiction-like beginning to understand the plot's peripeties.[104]

The traces of Chernyshevsky's novel in *The Gift* point toward Nabokov's literary ambition to change the rules of Russian literature. In the passage in which Fyodor quips about writing a practical handbook titled *How to Be Happy?*, he immediately contemplates another writing project: "Or getting deeper, to the bottom of things: understand what is concealed behind all this, behind the play, the sparkle, the thick, green grease-paint of the foliage? For there really is something, there is something!" (328). Boris Maslov has analyzed this episode as an integral part of Nabokov's aim to rehabilitate "literary dilettantism," the practice of writing fiction and poetry free from utilitarian, moral, and economic demands. Such an approach to literary practice, encapsulated in the slogan "art for art's sake," was traditionally exercised by financially independent aristocrats who ignored the demands of the literary marketplace.[105] As Maslov argues, Nabokov was not interested in valorizing aristocracy; rather, he attempted to rid the notion of aesthetic autonomy, the key tenet of "literary dilettantism," of the advantages afforded by an author's socioeconomic privilege. Therefore, the nobleman Fyodor defends Chernyshevsky, the son of a priest, from the class-biased criticism of the landowning Turgenev, Grigorovich, and Tolstoy, but faults him for being "a complete bourgeois in his artistic and scientific tastes" (240).[106] Nabokov uses the term "bourgeois" free from "any politico-economic Marxist connotation," to mean "people preoccupied with the material side of life and believing only in conventional values"—regardless of their class background.[107] This rhetorical maneuver allows Fyodor to bypass the class-based aristocratic critique of Chernyshevsky, Maslov maintains, and thus uphold the autonomy of art and the writer's independence from history.[108]

As insightful as Maslov's reading of *The Gift* is, it misses a foundational contradiction in Fyodor's attack on Chernyshevsky and on the utilitarian approach to art. The representation of Berlin complicates Nabokov's anti-utilitarian animus because he clearly instrumentalizes the city to advance his practical goals, which coincide with his aesthetic aims. Like Nabokov,

Fyodor is an exile—and not in Siberia but in Berlin. Put crudely, Fyodor can mount his defense of literary dilettantism and artistic autonomy precisely because he is an impoverished Russian exile.[109] His novel emerges as the result of his fraught relationship with Berlin. If we return to the episode where Fyodor thinks about writing *How to Be Happy?*, we will see that it is a stunning cityscape that moves him to write:

> The sun played on various objects along the right side of the street, like a magpie picking out the tiny things that glittered; and at the end of it, where it was crossed by the wide ravine of a railroad, a cloud of locomotive steam suddenly appeared from the right of the bridge, disintegrated against its iron ribs, then immediately loomed white again on the other side and wavily streamed away through the gaps in the trees. Crossing the bridge after this, Fyodor, as usual, was gladdened by the wonderful poetry of railroad banks, by their free and diversified nature: a growth of locusts and sallows, wild grass, bees, butterflies—all this lived in isolation and unconcern in the harsh vicinity of coal dust glistening below between the five streams of rails, and in blissful estrangement from the city coulisses above, from the peeled walls of old houses toasting their tattooed backs in the morning sunshine. (328)

This urban pastoral also includes three elderly postal workers who enjoy the outdoors before work. The narrator then exclaims, "Where shall I put all these gifts with which the summer morning rewards me—and only me?" Nabokov decouples people and objects from their utilitarian functions; the natural and the mechanistic join in a "poetry of railroad banks" removed from the theatricality of the city-stage. Crucially, Fyodor is capable of making these observations because he rejects steady jobs and is free to spend his days daydreaming while sunbathing in the Grunewald.[110] (Arguably, his most stereotypically anti-German act is his refusal to work.) To emphasize his aesthetic independence, Fyodor showcases his ways of nonutilitarian appropriation of the surrounding world. But he insists on his singularity so forcefully that he inevitably undermines his coveted goal of freedom from his times.

Furthermore, the Chernyshevsky biography and the range of critical reviews of it presented in chapter 5 serve a concrete function: a multipronged polemic with contemporary émigré critics and Soviet writers.[111] As Justin Weir has observed, the "Life of Chernyshevsky" traps Fyodor's opponents because "it reveals the ideological baggage one carries into the reading of it."¹¹² It is also worth recalling that when Zina first learns of Fyodor's intention to write *The Gift*, she warns him that "that will result in an autobiography with mass execution of good acquaintances" (364). Nabokov's lampooning of easily recognizable historical and contemporary figures never reaches the level of "mass execution," but the novel contains a plethora of more and less harmful jabs at specific critics, writers, filmmakers, political movements, and cultural phenomena, plentifully cataloged in Dolinin's book-length commentary to *The Gift*. In return, Nabokov offers dazzlingly innovative prose. Fyodor fulfills his reassuring promise to Zina to "so shuffle, twist, mix, rechew and rebelch everything, add such spices of my own and impregnate things so much with myself that nothing remains of the autobiography but dust—the kind of dust, of course, which makes the most orange of skies" (364). As if returning to an earlier juxtaposition between the "orangery" (hothouse) of the past and the Berlin tram (80), Fyodor colors the entirety of Berlin in his personal palette.

The author's presence indeed saturates the novel. As is visible in the episode surrounding the *How to Be Happy*(?) project quoted above, the novel's narrative perspective fluctuates. Fyodor's first-person narration is frequently displaced via deliberately unmarked transitions to the third-person perspective. Stephen Blackwell has proposed that Nabokov created a "multistable narrator," "an 'inner author' figure who merges with and diverges from the narrator and the main protagonist."¹¹³ Such an approach eludes definitive interpretation and ultimately teaches the reader to "discover that there is 'no boundary' at the novel's end and [to] proceed into the unknown and open future." As Blackwell shows, moreover, Nabokov's modernist innovation in prose owes much to another nineteenth-century giant whom Nabokov notoriously despised: Fyodor Dostoevsky. This pattern of engaging with literary predecessors—Fyodor's "rebelching" of historical material, so to speak—follows the logic of literary evolution put forth by the Russian Formalists, as Irina Paperno has demonstrated.¹¹⁴ Unlike the Formalists, though, who believed in making apparent the ways literary texts are made, Nabokov invested in skillful patterning, camouflage, and misleading clues. The delight and torment of reading *The Gift* is that it is seemingly inexhaustible: the novel's multistable narrator encourages the reader to participate in a never-ending game of hide-and-seek. The unknown and open future that follows the novel's formal end reinforces Nabokov's aesthetic ideal of ahistorical timelessness.¹¹⁵ It also exposes the precarity of existence in a world that is infinitely more complex than people are able to perceive. In stripping the literary tradition of the comfort of the Chernyshevskian positivist causality, Nabokov nevertheless aims to safeguard the future of Russian literature by building a verbal infrastructure of cultural renewal. What weakens his position, however, is his reluctance to admit that he instrumentalizes the condition of exile to break the molds of established ways of seeing and storytelling.

Far from celebrating exile and Berlin, Nabokov presents Fyodor as a lone genius waiting to be discovered by future readers. As if being embedded in the broader cultural context would diminish the value of *The Gift*, Nabokov warns in the novel's Foreword that his "young man [Fyodor] is moreover influenced by the rise of a nauseous dictatorship belonging to the period when the novel was written [1933–1937] and not the one it patchily reflects [1926–1929]" (ii). Nabokov appears to prevent any attempt to read *The Gift* as unduly influenced by the modernist 1920s. If anything, however, Nabokov's firsthand experience of involuntary exile gives his fiction a unique and valuable perspective on some of the same artistic problems being faced by his Soviet and German contemporaries who were not in exile.[116] When Nabokov leaves Europe in 1940 for the United States, though, he attempts to shed the label of an author in exile altogether, writing, "The term 'émigré writer' has an air of tautology about it. Any true author emigrates into his art and exists within it."[117] He further asserts that "the love of a Russian writer for his homeland had always been nostalgic, even if he never left it. Not only Kishinev or the Caucasus, but even Nevsky Prospekt have seemed like far-flung exile."[118] Nabokov boldly draws a parallel here between himself and Pushkin, Russia's national poet who wrote some of his best poetry and prose during his many domestic exiles. In fact, all Russian writers from Nabokov's personal canon flourished and rose to prominence during and after their years of internal exile (Pushkin), prolonged life abroad (Gogol), or self-imposed isolation (Tolstoy). Nabokov was very much aware of the creative potential of exile, and that writing from the margins often secures a place in the center. Seeing continuity in originality, Nabokov put Berlin on the map of Russian literature. By doing so, he also inscribed himself, and Russian Berlin, into Weimar modernity.

5

Queering the Russian Diaspora

In late summer 1921, a young Russian émigré, Pyotr Yuritsyn, summed up his thoughts on living in exile in a letter to a friend. He wrote: "It's so boring here, such melancholia [toska], that even cocaine stopped helping. Pavlik, why did we end up in this idiotic country?"[1] The country in question is Bulgaria, and Pavlik is Pavel Tchelitchew. Their sojourn in Bulgaria was typical of this time: Yuritsyn and Tchelitchew were among the hundreds of thousands of Russian émigrés who fled Russia after the Bolshevik Revolution, traveling via the Black Sea to the Balkans and beyond. However, in addition to the precariousness of being stateless émigrés, Yuritsyn and Tchelitchew happened to be gay. Eventually, they became lovers, and their brief romance alleviated Yuritsyn's substance abuse problem until Tchelitchew left for Berlin later that fall. Yuritsyn stayed behind in Bulgaria, unable to secure funds to move to Berlin himself. Their correspondence dwindled as Tchelitchew remained indifferent to Yuritsyn's queries, such as this one: "Do you remember our last kiss by the door when we walked to the landlady's room? Remember?" He followed up with a litany of self-deprecating speculations: "You are in Berlin now. You see many handsome men and you probably forgot me, my boring and ugly, crooked-nosed and thick-lipped self," adding, "You know, I'm almost certain you're no longer mine. You get interested in others so easily. For example, in Belgrade you immediately got interested in some Englishman. And in Berlin there are so many handsome men [muzhschin] (I do not know how to spell this word) . . ." By drawing attention to his insecurity about spelling "this word," Yuritsyn emphasizes his struggle to find appropriate vocabulary to express the confusing and all-consuming desire for men that also feeds his image of Berlin as a gay haven.

The intimate drama that plays out in this correspondence is at once mundane and extraordinary. Presumably, heartbreak is a universal human experience, regardless of one's sexuality. One would be hard-pressed to find, however, readily available, nonjudgmental Russian narratives of queer relationships in the 1920s and 1930s, especially in spaces of emigration.[2] To be sure, this is not a uniquely Russian phenomenon. Although Weimar-era Berlin is now celebrated as the birthplace of the modern LGBTQ+ emancipation movement, the city was perceived as "Sodom and Gomorrah in a Prussian tempo," to quote Thomas Mann's son Klaus Mann.[3] As the drama scholar Mel Gordon has put it, "Moralists across the widest spectrum of political and spiritual beliefs have condemned by rote this chimerical metropolis [Berlin] as a strange city, built on strange soil."[4] The historian George Mosse has explained that in the postwar period, Berlin undermined the national and moral revival sought by the German right:

> Through [Weimar Berlin's] night life, for example, homosexuality and lesbianism were highly visible. Homosexual bars increased from some forty in 1914 to about eighty in 1929. At the same time, those who wanted to pry into the recesses of a hidden female sexuality had the choice of about a dozen lesbian bars and Cook's Tours of Berlin included visits to some of these establishments.... It was the visibility rather than the mere existence of a homosexual or lesbian subculture that was important, for London and Paris also contained such a culture, but in Berlin it was more readily inspected, photographed, and written about.[5]

In this final chapter, I bring together Queer Berlin and Russian Berlin during the Weimar era to take a step toward recovering a history of Russian queer subjectivity—however preliminary such a history may be—as it was shaped by and in German exile. One of my aims is to document the very existence of Russian queer exiles and their standing within Charlottengrad and the broader European community. In doing so, I wish to reclaim their right to "historical citizenship." The historian Anna Hájková has proposed the concept of historical citizenship to make visible the stories of people whose lives are often deemed unworthy of being part of history.[6] Hájková focuses on writing a queer history of the Holocaust. However, her methodological approach to existing historical narratives and deliberate omissions from those narratives helps to recast Russian Berlin, and indeed Russia Abroad, as the complex, diverse, and nonnormative cultural space that it was. Reinscribing

Russian queer émigrés into the narratives of Russian diasporic culture sheds brighter light on the in-between position in time and space of interwar Berlin and its Russian-speaking residents.

The existing Russian accounts of Berlin from this period make no secret of the city's openness to and relative tolerance of sexual experimentation. But they do so in terms of failure, perversion, and deviance—terms that perpetuate homophobia. Even ostensibly socially progressive Russian writers chose to comment disapprovingly on Berlin's "most perverse abominations," to use Andrei Bely's phrase. In *Kingdom of Shades*, Bely branded Berlin a "bourgeois Sodom" where "hundreds of homosexual and lesbian cafés operate openly."[7] Ilya Ehrenburg observed that in Berlin a regular prostitute "begins to look like a model of virtue" because "in the cafés where women love women and men love men, she is simply the most ordinary and traditional prostitute." Ehrenburg noted additionally that in Berlin one could buy "an academic journal, *Freundschaft*, devoted to homosexualism"—but one had to do so "without blushing."[8] Viktor Shklovsky hinted at the utility of writing about homosexuality in Berlin in the postscript to his novel *Zoo, or Letters Not about Love*: "In the dark public toilets of Berlin, men indulge in mutual onanism. They are suffering from a devalued currency and hunger; their country is perishing."[9] The homophobic aspects of Shklovsky's, Ehrenburg's, and Bely's texts serve to underscore the supposed depravity of Europe since all three writers chose to return to Soviet Russia.

Meanwhile, the Yuritsyn-Tchelitchew correspondence offers a rare glimpse of same-sex desire between two Russian men in exile. Most importantly, Yuritsyn's letters to Tchelitchew—in their content and materiality—bring together ideas about geography, sexuality, and history in cities, provincial (Sofia) and cosmopolitan (Berlin) alike. They suggest not only the existence of queer émigrés, but also their negotiation of their own spaces and selves in ways that raise questions about the more traditional accounts of émigré culture: Is it possible to understand exile without an understanding of what it is like to be an exile within exile? How did the queer émigrés navigate normative expectations of sexuality and negotiate belonging in big cosmopolitan cities with large Russian-speaking émigré populations, such as Berlin and Paris? What sorts of configurations of family and community did they imagine and participate in?

In answering these questions, I aim to identify how Russian queer artists and intellectuals in exile envisioned and practiced alternative lives and to show how they challenge standard assumptions about communal affiliation in the diaspora, and by extension, in the homeland. This sort of imagined community has been called the Homintern, or the "international presence of lesbians and gay men in modern life."[10] Although the analogy to the Communist International, or Comintern, is largely tongue-in-cheek, it is fitting in Berlin, which was, along with Moscow, one of the major centers of the global leftist circuit where the communist agenda sometimes overlapped with queer activities. For instance, the filmmaker Sergey Eisenstein met with the German sexologist Magnus Hirschfeld at his Institute for Sexual Science, while the poet Sergey Esenin is said to have explored Berlin's gay bars with his wife, the American dancer Isadora Duncan.[11] Eisenstein repeatedly returned to images of Berlin's gay bars and the gender bending he witnessed there in his graphic work later in life (fig. 19). But our knowledge of Russian émigré responses to contemporary German discourses of sexuality is severely limited.[12]

The search for documentary evidence to tell the stories of queer exiles is impeded by the twin problems of invisibility and erasure: frank depictions of nonnormative acts, desires, and expressions, already rare, have often been suppressed. I recover them by retracing the routes of their marginalization in the historical record. That is, my work is informed by archival research that is attuned to absences, omissions, and gaps as much as to the presence of evidence. As Daniel Marshall, Kevin Murphy, and Zeb Tortorici put it in their editors' introduction to a special issue of *Radical History Review* on queering archives, "Fragments of information float unfixed—historically unraveled—and we form archives when we pull the fragments into the orbit of efforts to know."[13] For instance, while Yuritsyn's letters offer a rich insight into queer exile, there is no reliable information about his own biography. Tchelitchew became a prominent painter, leaving Sofia for Berlin before moving to Paris and then to New York, as discussed in chapter 3. There is no indication that the two of them ever met again. However, Tchelitchew valued the several handwritten pages from his one-time lover enough that he saved them in his personal archive through his many peregrinations around the world. Preserved as if in anticipation of queer historicism, these letters contest the perceived heteronormativity of Russian émigré culture and announce the need to reframe the approaches to its study.

Recalcitrance

As discussed in the opening chapter of this book, the semantic distinction between "exile" and "émigré" is an important one. For Russians forced to live

Figure 19 (*above and right*). Sergey Eisenstein, "Cosy Corner Berlin," ca. 1930. The Russian State Archive of Literature and Art, Moscow.

abroad following the 1917 Revolution, self-identifying as émigré (as opposed to "living in exile") implied a certain ideology and commitment to "preserve the values and traditions of Russian culture and to continue in creative efforts for the benefit and ongoing spiritual progress of the homeland."[14] Gradually, the term émigré came to mean any Russian living abroad by choice, but the politically conservative connotations of the term never fully dissolved. However, any notion of Russia Abroad as a benevolent Orthodox Slavic patriarchy is contradicted by the cosmopolitan and ethnically diverse reality of émigré life.

While mainstream Russian émigré culture preserved the imperial heritage, it also advanced Russian art and literature unburdened by Soviet censorship and became embedded within European and Anglo-American contexts. Russia Abroad boasts such influential cultural figures as the composer Igor Stravinsky, the painter Marc Chagall, the writer Vladimir Nabokov, and the choreographer George Balanchine. No less illustrious are the queer members of the émigré intelligentsia, such as the founder of the Ballets Russes, Sergey Diaghilev; the dancers Ida Rubinstein, Vaclav Nijinsky, and Serge Lifar; the actress Alla Nazimova; the painters Konstantin Somov and Pavel Tchelitchew; and the poet Marina Tsvetaeva, among many others.[15] Ironically, however, singling out the stories of individual success obscures the larger implications of queer collectivity in exile, and queerness itself becomes merely a biographical detail, if it is mentioned at all. The standard narrative thus remains heteronormative, even as recent scholarship has expanded to consider émigré culture's transnationally networked nature.[16]

There are challenges to researching queer dimensions of émigré culture in the interwar period because of the relative scarcity and, in some cases, inaccessibility of archival sources. But sometimes even the known artifacts can surprise one with laconic suggestions of queer potential. Consider the photograph taken in the 1920s in Berlin by Roman Vishniac (fig. 20). Captioned "Recalcitrance," the snapshot presents a quotidian scene in the city. Passersby are busily walking in every direction conjuring up a sense of the everyday. The dog refusing to comply with its leash anchors the composition. Standing stubbornly in the middle of the sidewalk, the recalcitrant dog disrupts mindless movement and animates the image's perspective. The image is shot from the liminal space of a threshold with the camera cautiously yet curiously peeking into the street. On the left, the building partially blocks the view of a sign that reads "inden Bad," directly above the

Figure 20. Roman Vishniac, *Recalcitrance*, ca. 1929. Gelatin silver print. Gift of Mara Vishniac Kohn © The Magnes Collection of Jewish Art and Life, University of California, Berkeley.

stubborn dog. The cut-off sign intensifies the effect of spontaneity but also draws attention to itself and its message, which advertises "Linden Bad," a Russian bathhouse. The positioning of the sign across from the entrance to the building from which the street is observed suggests that the camera, and the viewer along with it, are on the doorsteps to that bathhouse. And while the bathhouse is a communal space unlike any other in Russian culture, it can also be an elusive and illicit queer space.[17] Berlin's Russian bathhouses served as cruising sites for men long before the émigrés moved to the city en masse.[18] That is not to say that Vishniac's photograph necessarily documents a cruising spot. Rather, his image of the bathhouse hidden in plain view and the stubborn dog conveys the tension between historical (and archival) presence and absence, suggesting that the conflict we see is only part of the story, full of unruly subjects hiding in the margins.

As necessary as finding the instances of queer presence is, my study goes beyond simply cataloguing the appearances of gay and lesbian characters in fictional and documentary texts produced in exile. What is far more important than "homo-spotting" is understanding the logics of location and identification that diverge from (or unexpectedly align with) the scripts of normative behavior and aesthetic practices. What, then, makes a queer diasporic subject? Gayatri Gopinath has argued that the work of diasporic queers is marked by "their inhabiting of multiple times and places, and the double vision it affords."[19] In the context of Russian emigration, however, the framework of doubled temporality can be and has been applied to all cultural producers who saw themselves as out of sync with history, rendered irrelevant by the uncertainty of their legal status as exiles.[20] As Leonid Livak has observed, "Russian exiles obtained de jure what European modernists cultivated artificially, namely, the notions of crossed borders, of breaking with the past, of cultural uprootedness, solitude, and crisis."[21] Consequently, the alienating experience of exile often entailed adherence to an imaginary set of ideals of wholesome Russianness exacerbated by the condition of displacement. Perhaps one of the most famous articulations of a fantasy of national coherence in exile can be found in Vladimir Nabokov's autobiography *Speak, Memory*: "As I look back at those years of exile, I see myself, and thousands of other Russians, leading an odd but by no means unpleasant existence, in material indigence and intellectual luxury, among perfectly unimportant strangers, spectral Germans and Frenchmen in whose more or less illusory cities we, émigrés, happened to dwell."[22]

Although exaggerated, Nabokov's position regarding the "perfectly unimportant strangers" is symptomatic of constructing a normative exilic identity in opposition to the local and the cosmopolitan. Even in carving out a parallel temporality for himself and "thousands of other Russians," Nabokov envisions the nation in exile within the traditional bonds of relationality based on language and genealogy: despite being immersed in the foreign environment, he claims detachment from the "illusory cities" by rejecting difference and privileging sameness.

Queer exiles, on the other hand, already always excluded from the rituals of reproductive life cycle, practice alliances and sustain solidarities across the demarcation lines of nation, class, gender, sexuality, and language as a means of survival. That is, being an exile within exile presupposes existing within multiple worlds and temporalities as a way of continuously forging hospitable forms of affiliation and collectivity. Given their participation in various, often overlapping, international networks, it is tempting to see queers in exile as "mediating figures between the nation and diaspora, home and the state, the local and the global," as Arnaldo Cruz-Malavé and Martin Manalansan have proposed.[23] At the same time, making any claims about queer exile that assume universality of diasporic experiences and practices, queer or otherwise, would be shortsighted. Meg Wesling has cautioned against conflating the categories of queerness and diaspora since doing so prevents a context- and site-specific understanding of sexual difference.[24] For example, Russian émigrés, who lacked the option of returning to Russia, experienced different conditions of possibility for sexuality than did expatriate Americans in Paris (e.g., the salon of Gertrude Stein and Alice B. Toklas and that of Natalie Clifford Barney) or Britons living in Berlin (e.g., Christopher Isherwood, W. H. Auden, and Stephen Spender). When their paths intersected—as they did, for instance, when Gertrude Stein and Pavel Tchelitchew entered into a tumultuous friendship in 1925—they shared ideas about belonging and kinship, but they hardly constituted a diaspora. Natalie Clifford Barney's cool reception of Tsvetaeva in her Parisian salon in the 1930s is likewise indicative of the limits of queer diasporic solidarity. Moreover, Barney's indifference to Tsvetaeva's remarkably (anti)queer essay *Letter to the Amazon*, which Tsvetaeva addressed to her, highlights the differences between (wealthy) expatriates and (impoverished) émigrés.[25] Yet, as Brent Edwards has demonstrated in the context of black transnational culture of the 1920s and 1930s, the term diaspora can be used in a way that avoids "the comfort of abstraction, an easy recourse to origins" and does not promise "foolproof anti-essentialism."[26] Following Edwards, I use the term "diaspora" in a historically acute way, emphasizing cultural connections across differences, not cultural coherence rooted in the shared idea of a homeland.

The term queer is, of course, itself the queerest of them all, and my use of it in this context is necessarily ahistorical.[27] However, I use this term for the purposes of legibility while being mindful that its analytical capacity in application to the early twentieth-century material is limited, especially when that material is primarily about white cisgender homosexual men. The word gay is similarly problematic, but Russian terminology that circulated at the turn-of-the-century is tied to legal, medical, and theological vocabularies that were not used for self-identification. These terms included such words as Urning, sodomite (sodomit and muzhelozhets), pederast, the third sex (tretii pol), Sapphist, and the moonlight people (liudi lunnogo sveta).[28] The issue of language of self-presentation becomes even more slippery on the cross-cultural terrain of exile but, to quote Heike Bauer, "I deploy *queer* to denote something of the sharedness of experience—however historically, socioculturally, and somatically contingent and emotionally inflected—that comes with living lives that are figured as being against accepted norms."[29]

When it comes to the representation of the lives that unsettle accepted norms in exile, the most visible record of queerness produced in emigration is to be found in the oeuvre of Vladimir Nabokov. For someone who professed aversion to the "sorrows of homosexuals," Nabokov could not stay away from the topic.[30] Gay characters are present in his entire body of work, invariably pathetic, laughable, inept, or evil—from the gay ballet dancers in his first Russian novel (*Mary*), the quirky English Russophile Archibald Moon in *Glory*, the despicable gay imposter in *Laughter in the Dark*, and the tragic young student Yasha Chernyshevsky in his last completed Russian novel *The Gift* to the ruthless dictator in *Bend Sinister*, the inverted double of Humbert Humbert in *Lolita* (Gaston Godin), the sad art teacher Lake in *Pnin*, and the deranged poet Charles Kinbote in *Pale Fire*.[31] Outside of his fiction, Nabokov had a number of gay relatives—his uncles Ruka (Vasily Rukavishnikov) and Konstantin Nabokov, as well as his brother Sergey—about all of whom he writes with varying degrees of acerbic charm in *Speak, Memory*.

Furthermore, Nabokov's father, the prominent jurist Vladimir Dmitrievich Nabokov, was among the unlikely pioneers of gay liberation in late-imperial Russia: although he maintained that homosexuality was socially undesirable, unnatural, and unhealthy, he nevertheless argued that that was insufficient reason to punish it by law.[32] He pointed out that if gay men—women were never subject to this law—were to be persecuted on moral grounds to prevent damage to the institution of marriage and procreative family, then bachelorhood should be outlawed as well.[33] The elder Nabokov was committed to the cause of decriminalization of homosexuality to such a degree that he translated his article on the topic into German and published it in the 1903 volume of the *Yearbook of Intermediate Sexual Types* (*Jahrbuch für sexuelle Zwischenstufen*).[34] This unique annual journal was Hirschfeld's project, initiated in 1899, before the Institute for Sexual Science was established in 1919. In supporting Hirschfeld's efforts from Russia, Vladimir D. Nabokov indirectly contributed to making Berlin into interwar Europe's queerest city.[35] It is in this city that the Nabokov family settled once in exile. Arguably, the urban environment of Berlin shaped much of Nabokov's fiction and especially his conception of gay characters. But his openly gay younger brother Sergey, who moved from Berlin to Paris as soon as he could, helps us conceptualize queer exile unmediated by Nabokov's fiction. The relationship between the two Nabokov brothers—one based in Berlin and the other in Paris—is paradigmatic for our understanding of exile and being queer in exile.

A Tale of Two Brothers

Russian émigré culture is unfathomable without Vladimir Nabokov. His brother Sergey, nine months his junior, is a ghost-like shadow of Vladimir. Both of them were brought up in the world of aristocratic privilege of pre-revolutionary St. Petersburg. They both spent their adult lives in exile. Before moving to Berlin, each completed his undergraduate education at Cambridge (though Sergey started at Oxford, transferring to Christ's College during his first year). After university, their paths diverge: under the penname Sirin, Vladimir quickly established himself as one of the most promising writers of the Russian emigration. In contrast, Sergey never wrote or published anything of note, although he reportedly was a prolific translator of Russian into English, German, and French. If any of his translations were published, they are yet to be found. While Vladimir plays a main role in Russian émigré cultural history, Sergey is merely a footnote to that history: a famous writer's gay brother.[36]

Their unequal relationship stretches back to their childhood. In *Speak, Memory*, Vladimir wrote, "For various reasons, I find it inordinately hard to speak about my other brother.... He is a mere shadow in the background of my richest and most detailed recollections. I was the coddled one; he, the witness of coddling."[37] In the same passage, Vladimir also wrote surprisingly honestly about "certain oddities of behavior" on Sergey's part, about him outing Sergey "in stupid wonder" after reading Sergey's diary, and about his mixed feelings about it all.[38] In his own diary, recording the minute details of the day their father was assassinated in Berlin on March 28, 1922, Vladimir recalls that one of the last conversations he ever had with him was about Sergey: "We chatted through the open door, talked of Sergey, of his strange, abnormal inclinations."[39] Strikingly, immediately after the comment about Sergey, Vladimir writes, "Then Father helped me put my trousers under the press, and drew them out, turning the screws, and said, laughing: 'That must hurt them.'"[40] The juxtaposition of the image of the device that straightens pants and the mention of his brother's "abnormal inclinations" comes across as almost cruel, especially considering the joke that the forced straightening must hurt the pants—this juxtaposition makes one wonder about Sergey's feelings about existing in a society that operates not unlike such a straightening press. Vladimir never fully accepted Sergey's sexuality and, if anything, was profoundly conflicted and anxious about same-sex desire. While he famously mythologized his childhood, the specter of his queer brother was always an uneasy presence.

Vladimir's struggle to write about Sergey with any degree of familial affection and affirmation manifests itself in a variety of ways, at times in forms other than narrative. Consider, for example, the caption to the family photograph of the Nabokov siblings reproduced in *Speak, Memory*: in it, Nabokov identified all his siblings, and in describing Sergey, he added that Sergey is "unfortunately disfigured by flaws in the picture" (fig. 21).[41] The earlier drafts of the manuscript show that before settling on this phrasing, he tried "She [Elena] and Sergey are disfigured by flaws in the picture" and then "Flaws in the picture disfigure Sergey," choosing to focus only on Sergey in accounting for slight paper discoloration and the photographer's botched retouching of the printed image.[42] Yet the semantic impact of the word "disfigure," coupled with his choice of the grammatical passive voice in the caption, mark Sergey's image as an aberration of the norm. Moreover, this disfigurement is at once an intrinsic quality of the photograph and the evidence of tampering with the original. Vladimir's acknowledgment that the damage is unfortunate nevertheless suggests that Sergey's flawed image compromises the integrity of the whole. As a result, Sergey's incompleteness haunts the entire picture.[43] In turn, this haunting makes Sergey a muted social figure

The author aged nineteen, with his brothers and sisters, in Yalta, November 1918. Kirill is seven; Sergey (unfortunately disfigured by flaws in the picture), wearing a rimless pince-nez and the uniform of the Yalta Gymnasium, is eighteen; Olga is fifteen; Elena (firmly clasping Box II) is twelve.

Figure 21. Photograph of Vladimir and Sergey Nabokov with their siblings in 1918. Reproduced from *Speak, Memory: An Autobiography Revisited* by Vladimir Nabokov (G. P. Putnam's Sons, 1966).

that is not allowed to speak for itself, but is inevitably spoken through, about, and for. Such a denial of agency and marginalization tells us more about Vladimir than Sergey, of course. Nevertheless, untangling the ways in which the record of Sergey's queer life was managed helps uncover the complexity of power relations that characterize the processes of remembering and forgetting in exile. Sergey may not have left a literary legacy himself, but the ephemeral archive of his life can tell us much about émigré culture, as well as about the forms of kinship forged in exile.

Whatever shame and contempt Vladimir might have felt about Sergey, they were never estranged and saw each other regularly until the outbreak of World War II. Vladimir left Europe with his wife and son via Paris in 1940 without being able to say goodbye to his brother in person: "It so happened that he [Sergey] learned of our departure only after we had left. My bleakest recollections are associated with Paris, and the relief of leaving it was overwhelming, but I am sorry he had to stutter his astonishment to an indifferent concierge."[44] As fate would have it, Sergey would never again stutter anything to Vladimir. Three facts of Sergey's biography are remembered and usually invoked whenever his name is mentioned: he was gay, he had a bad stammer, and he died in 1945 in a Nazi concentration camp. Vladimir would find out about Sergey's gruesome end only after the war. In a letter to the American critic and writer Edmund Wilson, he wrote: "[My brother] was placed by the Germans in one of the worst concentration camps (near Hamburg) and perished there. This news gave me a horrible shock because Sergey was the last person I could imagine being arrested: he was a harmless, indolent, pathetic person who spent his life vaguely shuttling between the Quartier Latin and a castle in Austria he shared with a friend."[45]

The friend was Sergey's longtime partner, Hermann Thieme, whom Vladimir variously refers to as Sergey's friend, boyfriend, and husband in his letters to his wife Véra Nabokov. In one of them he provides some additional details: "I had lunch today near the Luxembourg garden with Sergey and his husband. The husband, I must admit, is very pleasant, quiet, absolutely not the pederast type, with an attractive face and manner. But I felt somewhat awkward, especially when one of their acquaintances, a red-lipped and curly-headed man, approached us for a minute."[46] Note that Vladimir feels fine so long as his masculinity is not threatened by the presence of a fabulous queer, even for a minute.

There are other direct references to Sergey's sexuality in Vladimir's private correspondence. After visiting his mother and youngest brother Kirill in Prague, Vladimir reported to Véra that "Kirill is strikingly handsome and refined, reads a lot, is relatively well educated and very high-spirited. He tells me that my brother Sergey (who arrived stout, with a fat neck, looking like Shalyapin) asked where there was a café where men met and strongly advised him to sniff cocaine. Fortunately, Kirill is absolutely normal."[47] Sergey is clearly not normal in Vladimir's eyes on many counts. He is oddly shaped, he has a drug problem, he stutters, and, above all, he is interested in men (and knows that any big city has a café where men meet). But what about Sergey's perspective?

Recovering Sergey's voice is a challenging task because almost none of his own writings survive. Most of what is known about him comes from

Vladimir's *Speak, Memory*, his letters, and a few other memoirs.[48] Vladimir and Sergey's cousin, the composer Nicolas Nabokov, provided the following description of the two brothers in his *Bagázh: Memoirs of a Russian Cosmopolitan*:

> Of my two elder cousins, Vladimir and Sergey, in those Berlin years I was closer to Sergey. Sergey loved music and Vladimir did not. Rarely have I seen two brothers as different as Volodya and Seryozha [nicknames for Vladimir and Sergey]. The older one, the writer and poet, was lean, dark, handsome, with a face resembling his mother's. Seryozha, although as lean in his angular way, and handsome, looked more like Babushka. He was not a sportsman. White-blond with a reddish tint to his face, he had an incurable stutter. But he was gay, a bit highly sensitive (and therefore an easy butt for teasing sports).... Sergey also knew a great deal about literature and history, and conversations with him were always interesting and profitable to me.[49]

Nicholas's son, Ivan Nabokov, recently shared that his mother always claimed that Sergey was "the nicest of all the Nabokovs, a sweet, funny man, much nicer, much more dependable and funnier that all the rest of them."[50] In his detailed biographical reconstruction of Sergey's life, Dieter Zimmer has found another portrait of Sergey and Vladimir provided by one of their émigré friends, the fashion critic Lucie Leon Noel, who moved to Paris from Moscow in the early 1920s:

> No brothers could have been less alike than Volodya and Serge. At that time (Cambridge-Oxford), however, they went around together. Volodya was the young *homme du monde*—handsome, romantic in looks, something of a snob and a gay charmer—Serge was the dandy, an aesthete and balletomane. Volodya's conversation was gay and amusing and even when he was serious, there was a kind of lilt of laughter, a soupçon of malice at the back of his voice, as if we were relishing some private joke all his own. Serge was tall and very thin. He was blond and his tow-colored hair usually fell in a lock over his left eye. He suffered from a serious speech impediment, a terrible stutter. Help would only confuse him, so one had to wait until he could say what was on his mind, and it was usually worth hearing. He was, among other things, a connoisseur of poetry, theater, and particularly ballet, and an asset in any salon or gathering. Usually he attended all the Diaghileff premiers wearing a flowing black theatre cape and carrying a pommeled cane.[51]

In contrast to Vladimir's compulsive documentation of Sergey's deficiencies, the accounts of Nicolas Nabokov and Lucie Leon Noel present Sergey as a refined young man taking full advantage of interwar Europe's cultural offerings. Unlike Vladimir, who maintained throughout his life a narrative of blissful isolation in exile, Sergey was keen on opening himself up to his new urban environments. Yet both brothers shared a profound dislike of Berlin, where they moved after finishing their studies in England. Their father's assassination in Berlin in spring 1922 added more reasons to want to leave the city. Much as Vladimir disparaged Berlin, he left only in 1937, when the Nazis appointed one of his father's assassins the deputy director of Russian émigré affairs. Later in life he claimed that he stayed in Berlin for nearly fifteen years to preserve the purity of his Russian; as he was fluent in French, his "precious layer of Russian" would have been lost in Paris.[52] Sergey had no such reservations.

I recently discovered a small cache of Sergey's letters to a young Russian émigré aristocrat like himself, Prince Dmitry Shakhovskoy.[53] These letters provide some much-needed details about Sergey's position regarding exile and sexuality. About living in Berlin, Sergey wrote to Shakhovskoy in 1922, "I work in a repugnant city, in a repugnant bank, wherefrom I write to you about my dreams. Any contact with those around me strains my heart with such depressing disgust, like when you touch something very sticky with your hands." A few months later he ended another letter with a request:

> Dmitry dear, I have a big favor to ask of you. You are more or less a resident of Paris, you know the conditions of life there, etc. So, could you write to me approximately how much would a day of modest living cost? What is it like to rent a room, somewhere in Montmartre? Aside from that, it would be good to know whether one can find some kind of work there. You know that I graduated first in my class, bachelor in letters with honors. I was even asked to stay and continue my studies in the department of French literature.[54]

Although Shakhovskoy's response was not terribly encouraging, informing him that "our émigré values are not rated all that highly," meaning that their credentials are not worth much, Sergey moved to Paris in 1923.[55] What Sergey neglects to mention in his letters is that despite Weimar Berlin's growing reputation as a hub for pleasure that offered its visitors a "masquerade of perversions," homosexuality was still a criminal offense in Germany, whereas in France all such laws were struck down during the French Revolution.[56]

Nevertheless, Sergey corresponded with Shakhovskoy not only about poetry, theater, and music, but also about his sexuality as he was trying to come to terms with it. In fact, in one of the letters, Sergey came out to Shakhovskoy in an elaborate and highly metaphoric style, writing:

> It's such a pity that during your visit here, I was doing mad things and picked from the tree of life its rotten fruit. Like a stone, thrown into the water, I reached the bottom, collided with it, but now find myself on the surface again with an "experienced" revulsion to the "bottom" and with cleared eyes, with the eyes ready and eager to take in any manifestation of beauty. And I think that only one hand, the hand of my beloved there, in Cambridge, could once again throw me like a stone to the "bottom." This is, of course, all rhetoric, since how can he and his love leave?—Well then: I accidentally opened to you the gates to my soul. You may enter. If you wish.

There are only rough, and often inscrutable, drafts of Shakhovskoy's responses to Sergey's letters. But from what I have been able to understand, it seems as though Shakhovskoy was far from sympathetic to Sergey's emotional travails and did not rush to walk through the gates to his soul. He reprimanded Sergey for his weakness and recommended that he become simpler (uprostit'sia). Having found a confidant in him, however, Sergey continued to seek Shakhovskoy's advice. On one occasion, he disclosed that he was having thoughts of committing suicide and that the only thing preventing him from taking his life was his fierce faith. On another occasion, he wrote about his search for a "guiding hand" and revealed that his psychotherapist had diagnosed him with neurasthenia. With uncompromising firmness, Shakhovskoy informed him that "there are many hands in this world, Sergey. Psychiatrist—the right hand; cocaine—the left." Then, in an attempt to lend a divine hand, Shakhovskoy, who was on the verge of entering the Orthodox priesthood, enclosed a copy of an Orthodox prayer. None of this deterred Sergey from confiding in Shakhovskoy; he likely suspected that Shakhovskoy was a kindred queer spirit who would eventually come out to him. But there is no indication that Shakhovskoy ever did. In 1926 he was ordained an Orthodox priest, and at around the same time Sergey converted to Catholicism.

Until then, Shakhovskoy wrote poetry and apparently valued Sergey's opinion about it. Indeed, the bulk of their correspondence is about literature. Sergey gave detailed comments on Shakhovskoy's creative pursuits but also used literary topics to convey certain details about himself, sometimes by invoking the names of his favorite writers. Explaining his sexual difference by crossing the boundaries between the aesthetic and the everyday, he wrote, "At times it seems to me that I was born under the same star as the great recluses of the heart: Flaubert, Gautier, Suarès, Huysmans." His imagined affinity with these influential French writers was based on his perception of their rejection of conventional family values. In the same letter, he reported that one of his favorite books was *À rebours* by Joris-Karl Huysmans and urged Shakhovskoy to read the novel: "If you haven't read it [*À rebours*] yet, do read it. It was misunderstood and undervalued. It went unnoticed after being declared immoral and shaky. It's amazing how people love justifying the absence of aesthetic taste by labeling books moral or immoral. The same fate befell *Madame Bovary* and—not many people know this—*Les Fleurs du Mal*!!! Meanwhile, Zola was read over and over again, and no one saw that he was as a god of the petty bourgeois heaven, and at times just a bad writer."

Sergey's rant against bourgeois moral values seems to target not so much the conservative public as the very logic of judging something—or someone—by the measure of arbitrary morality. His appeal to the ultimate universal success of Flaubert's prose and Baudelaire's poetry underscores his belief in contingency of moral standards and their irrelevance from a historical perspective. He invoked French literary precedent to overcome the normative pressures of his day. Contemporary French literature offered him further models for self-identification. When two years later, in 1925, Shakhovskoy asked Sergey to contribute some writing for a new literary journal he had established, Sergey responded:

> Would critical articles do? About the French, for example, Valéry, Gide, or Cocteau? In character, these articles would be not "informational" but rather "experiential" [zhiznennye], connected to the collapse of the pre-revolutionary and pre-war sense of the world.... I have an acute live love for thought and the likes of Valéry and Gide reveal entire worlds to me and prompt sweet visions. Since it's easier for you as the editor to decide whether such "visions" are of interest, I would only say that they extend beyond the line of criticism of, say, Valéry as Valéry. He represents, so to speak, a stimulant, a 'conduit' for thought.

The proposed article never materialized, but Sergey's description of it reveals a lot: asked to write a literary piece, presumably on any contemporary topic, he chose to pitch an essay on experimental and queer French authors, underscoring that his writing would reflect his personal beliefs and experiences.[57] As Shakhovskoy's response did not survive, it is unclear what happened next. Perhaps he declined the offer of Sergey's "sweet visions"; perhaps Sergey did not manage to write his article. Regardless, in comparison to his earlier angst-riddled notes, here Sergey appears to be attuned to the latest developments in the arts and content with living in exile.

Yet the most extraordinary aspect of this letter, which is also the last letter from Sergey in Shakhovskoy's archive, is that it was severely censored. A section of one of the pages was cut off and a substantial part of the remaining text was blotted out and crossed out in red ink (fig. 22). The censored text, most of which I was able to restore, conceals a description of Sergey's happy news:

> I work and I *live*. I don't languish. My entire day is busy: lessons, translations, reading. I consider the visits to the superfluous "bohemian" café to be idle and tedious. I look differently at young men, because my heart is full with one (he is a big friend of the Merezhkovskys, a Pole, Count Czapski). So, my dear, the little feather in my cap is an entire panache. I *gathered* these plumes there, in the depths, in the quiet, because I found that for which I searched for ten years. You must understand me and not smile, and not think that it's one of my old tricks. . . . My life has become simpler and deeper.

It is unclear who attempted to erase this part of Sergey's message or why. It is clear, however, that someone found it compromising.[58] Perhaps Sergey's tone seemed so friendly, it implied Shakhovskoy's approval of his lifestyle. Perhaps the mention of Sergey's lover Josef Czapski by name was too damning for the émigré community. Czapski was born into the Polish nobility of the Russian Empire and educated in prerevolutionary St. Petersburg. When the Bolsheviks came to power, his family lost their fortune. Once Poland gained independence, he moved to Paris to become a painter. During World War II he was captured by the Soviets but survived the massacre of Polish officers at Katyń in 1940 and was sent to Central Asia, where he met the poet Anna Akhmatova. After the war, Czapski spent the rest of his life in emigration in Paris, unwilling to return to Poland, now under Soviet control.[59] The presence of a romantic affair with Sergey in Czapski's biography makes it all the more extraordinary, but it also reveals the rarely acknowledged richness, complexity, and interconnectedness of the narratives of culture in exile—

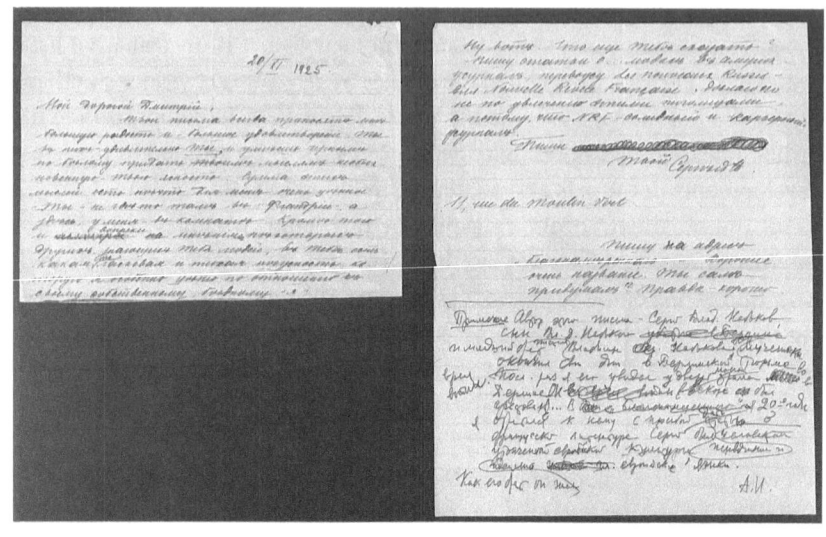
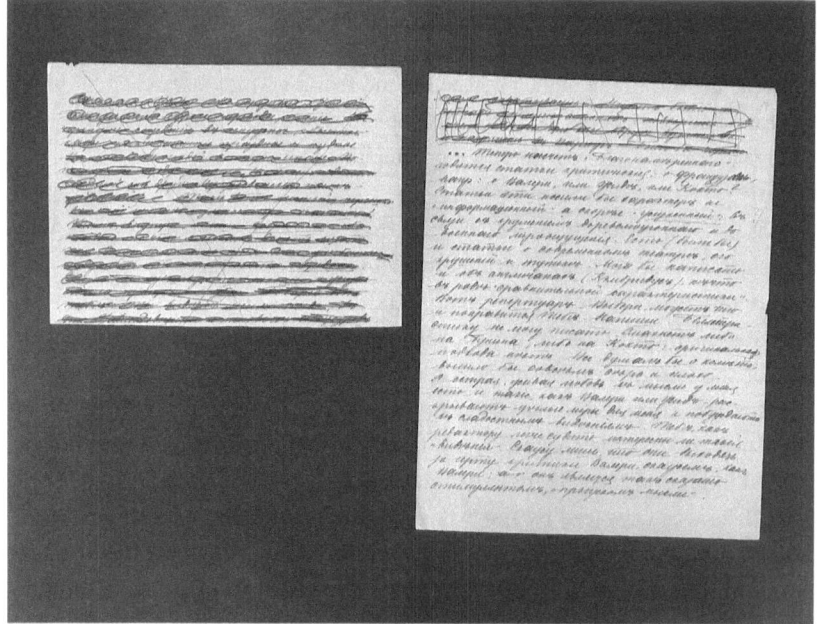

Figure 22. Sergey Nabokov's censored letter of November 20, 1925, to Dmitry Shakhovskoy. Amherst Center for Russian Culture.

and perhaps that is precisely why Sergey's candid letter was censored. The manipulation of this letter demonstrates the forces of systemic oblivion at work and thus raises the stakes of interrogating received historiographies.

For his part, Sergey attempted to be as open about his sexuality as he could. He repeatedly came out to his friends and family, looking for someone who would listen and take him seriously. When he and Czapski broke up in 1926, he experienced a profound crisis and considered transforming himself by becoming more religious, following Czapski's example. He wrote to his mother, "the man I've linked my life with, the man I love more than anything else in the world—had gone back to church.... Those were terrible days. I am becoming *Catholic* in full awareness of the inescapability of this step and with absolute belief in its necessity." He added, "This is not easy for me, it's very hard. I cannot cut off a huge part of my self with one blow. This part must change, and make way for something new and not sinful."[60] His mother forwarded this letter to Vladimir, who copied it for Véra, inserting its contents between reports of doing gymnastics and having veal cutlet for lunch. Amused more than anything else, Vladimir commented, "I think, overall, this is good for Sergey. It is true—Catholicism is a feminine, arrow-arched faith—the sweetness of painted glass, the suffering tenderness of young Sebastians..."[61]

Sergey's religious fervor subsided within a couple of years, and by 1932 he appears to have fully embraced his sexual difference, as another letter Vladimir wrote to Véra during a visit to Paris suggests: "[Sergey] said that he wanted to talk about the essential, to find out, apparently, my attitude to his life, and for that he'll call on me tomorrow, on Wednesday, at 3 p.m."[62] Sergey's sustained insistence on transparency, if not on acceptance, is remarkable. Life in exile seems to have been precarious enough to add the pressure of secrecy to it. By the time Sergey asked Vladimir for a meeting, he had already met Hermann Thieme, the man who would become his lifelong partner and whom Sergey introduced to his relatives.[63]

The remaining narrative of Sergey's life is fragmented into bits of more and less reliable information leading to his return to Berlin in 1942, imprisonment in the concentration camp in 1944, and death in 1945. It is worth noting that Sergey was imprisoned on political grounds, and not for being gay, as Dieter Zimmer has established. He was, however, under heightened surveillance for his prior conviction for "homosexual offenses" and as a stateless resident. According to Zimmer's archival findings, once in 1940 the Nazis took control of Paris, where Sergey and Hermann had been living, the couple decided to move to Austria, to Hermann's family estate at Schloss Weissenstein in Marei, East Tyrol. They both were arrested there in July 1941 and charged under Paragraph 129, the Austrian version of the infamous Paragraph 175 of the German Penal Code; the law prohibited all same-sex sexual contacts. As a result, Hermann was sent to a penal colony in North Africa under the German expeditionary force Afrikakorps. Sergey was sentenced to four months in prison and served his sentence in Austria until December 1942.

Sergey's decision to return to Berlin, the heart of the Nazi state, in 1942 is puzzling. Zimmer suggests that he would have had very few options for traveling because of the need of the hard-to-get visas, especially for someone with a prior conviction and a politically dubious status of a stateless émigré. Besides, Sergey would have had to go to Berlin to get necessary identification and travel documents. Once in Berlin, it appears that he lodged with his cousin Sophia (Onia) Fasolt in Wilmersdorf.[64] Before his arrest on December 15, 1944, Sergey worked as a translator at the Propaganda Ministry's Ostraum offices. It remains unclear exactly what provoked his arrest and transfer to KZ Neuengamme, but he likely was not a model employee. His file with the Nazi criminal police (Kripo) states only that he made "remarks hostile to the state" (staatsfeindliche Äusserungen).[65]

To Sergey's last (censored) letter, Shakhovskoy appended the following explanatory note: "The author of this letter is Sergey Vladimirovich Nabokov, the son of Vladimir Dmitrievich Nabokov and the brother of the writer Vladimir Nabokov. He ended his days martyr-like in a Berlin prison during the war. The last time I saw him was at the steps of my church in Berlin. He was arrested soon thereafter.... Sergey was a translator and a man of refined European culture. Like his brother, he knew the main European languages to perfection."

As this note suggests, Sergey makes it into the archive because of his prominent brother and father. Even in posterity he is situated in Vladimir's shadow. In fact, my own research on Sergey was conducted in the context of Vladimir's life. Vladimir himself ended his autobiographical vignette on Sergey by concluding that "It is one of those lives that hopelessly claim a belated something—compassion, understanding, no matter what—which the mere recognition of such a want can neither replace nor redeem."[66] However, this convenient and familiar narrative of doomed existence is countered by the record of Sergey's life as someone who insisted on equality and recognition, not tolerance and pity. In spite of normative hierarchies and structures of exclusion, through his letters Sergey helps us chart the origins of modern sexual identities that emerged in the time and place of exile.

LETTERS TO YOU

Sergey's life opens up an illuminating perspective onto queer exile, but his is also a story of an outsider who perseveres in spite of cultural and social norms of the day. If there is one cultural figure who helps to unite the strands of gender, ethnicity, sexuality, and nationality in Russian Berlin throughout the twentieth century, a figure who actively participated in creating a diasporic culture, it may be the poet Vera Lourié. A glance at Lourié's life and oeuvre deserves fuller exploration separately, but it also offers a profitable way to conclude this chapter and touch on the role of Russian exiles in shaping modern queer culture as they engaged with Berlin's urban space during the continuous negotiation of Russian cultural identity outside Russia.

Born in St. Petersburg in 1901, Vera Lourié arrived in Berlin with her family in 1921. She would never again leave and would die in Berlin in 1998. Lourié witnessed and survived Charlottengrad in all its glory and indignity—the hyperinflation, interrogations by the Gestapo, all of World War II in Berlin, the takeover of the city by the Red Army, life in the carved-up postwar city, and German unification. Brought up in a wealthy Russian Jewish family, she died in penury, renting out the only two bedrooms in her Wilmersdorf apartment while sleeping in its hallway.[67] The many contradictions in Lourié's biography pose a challenge to any neatly overarching narrative. Still, she was a living thread connecting the so-called Silver Age of Russian culture and the post-Soviet world.

Lourié was seemingly invisible, isolated, and frail later in her life, and her literary legacy was brought to light thanks to the efforts of American academics and German journalists.[68] Her only book of poems appeared in 1987.[69] Around that time she also worked on a book of her memoirs, published in 2014 as *Letters to You: Reminiscences of Russian Berlin*. Originally titled *The Diary of a Soul*, the memoir marked Lourié's return to writing, something she had not done since the postwar period. But in the mid-1980s, she chose to write in German. As she put it, "storytelling is difficult for me insofar as I do not speak German well enough to express myself freely. But I have no more desire for writing in Russian."[70] Her German is grammatically correct but unmistakably that of a nonnative speaker. Her sentences are short and plainly informative. The chapters, styled as private letters, are likewise brief, raising far more questions than they answer. Frequently, she complains of exhaustion, melancholia, and outright depression. She opens one of the final letters by reporting, "I have so little desire to write, but I must do it!"[71]

In more than one way, Lourié's *Letters to You* reference Shklovsky's *Zoo, or Letters Not about Love*. Both address their letters to a beloved woman. From the editor of *Letters to You*, Doris Liebermann, we know that Lourié frames every one of her letters as a message to her doctor's wife, one Reinhild H., who served as a visiting nurse.[72] Lourié herself conceals the name of Reinhild but opts for the familiar second person singular pronoun "you" ("Du"). In the poem called "It was. It is," which prefaces the memoir, Lourié identifies her love interest as a "fairy" ("die Fee"): "Gefallen die Schranken, / Die Leere genommen. / Dem Himmel ich danke, / Die Fee ist gekommen. / Nur Du!" (The barriers have fallen, / taking the emptiness with them. / I thank the heavens, / the fairy has arrived. Only you!)[73] Sadly, just like Alia in Shklovsky's *Zoo*, the unnamed addressee of Lourié's letters remains indifferent to the author's affections, as Lourié's laments make clear. Memoir writing becomes a way to soothe the pain of romantic rejection: "You called. You spoke so offensively, so harshly. It was too much for me. Then a regular dose of pills did not help. . . . I wonder why a worthy, kind person can be cruel to someone who loves them, has difficulty walking and is in pain. I am not a good person myself, but I don't think I could hit someone when they are down. Forgive these words. It would be good if I didn't have to wait for your calls, but I don't have the strength for that. I'd better wander back into the distant past."[74] The prohibition against writing about love is the premise of Shklovsky's narrative that he playfully circumvents by writing about (Russian) Berlin. Lourié writes about love, about being unloved, and about (Russian) Berlin.

Shklovsky also appears on the pages of *Letters to You*. Lourié recalls an incident in which he storms into the editorial offices of the newspaper where she worked and causes a scene, upset about a critical review of one of his books that Lourié had written with Alexander Bakhrakh. Furious that "children" were allowed to review books in print, Shklovsky apparently screamed and threw furniture around. Although Lourié mentions this scandal as but one episode in the tapestry of Charlottengrad's cultural life, her memoir can be read as a belated response to Shklovsky, who also lived a long life after leaving for Moscow—two epistolary narratives, bookends to Russian Berlin, one published in 1923, another in 2014.[75]

Unlike Shklovsky and so many others who left, Lourié made the largely circumstantial decision to remain in Berlin. Like Shklovsky and so many others, she welcomed the end of monarchy in Russia and was sympathetic to leftist political parties. Indeed, the newspaper offices where Shklovsky threw his temper tantrum and where Lourié was employed housed the operations of the Socialist Revolutionary daily *Dni*, edited by the ousted head of Russia's short-lived Provisional Government, Alexander Kerensky. Lourié also socialized with pro-Soviet writers and artists, as well as visitors from the Soviet Union. When the Leningrad-based critic Yuri Tynianov and writer Vera Inber visited Berlin in the late 1920s from Moscow, Lourié was their guide to the city.

There are no ruminations about life in exile and being an émigré in *Letters to You*. The decision to emigrate was her father's, and although Lourié describes in detail his procurement of counterfeited Latvian passports so that the family could enter Germany, she has surprisingly little to say about the emotional trauma of leaving Russia—a commonplace in narratives of exile. One need only think of Nabokov's *Speak, Memory* to access a depiction of precious and luminous old Russia, forever lost. On several occasions, Lourié mentions the murder of the elder Nabokov in Berlin's Philharmonic Hall, but she says nothing about the writer. And while it is unknown whether she was familiar with *Speak, Memory*, Lourié offers her own account of a pampered childhood in St. Petersburg.

Lourié's childhood in the imperial capital was that of a girl from a converted Jewish family. Her descriptions of domestic arrangements, governesses, dinners, and parties are as sharp as her awareness that most of her Jewish relatives were barred from that life unless they converted to Christianity. Yet in the memoir she also consistently obscures her Jewish background, referring to herself as half-Jewish and a "Mischling," ostensibly because her father converted to Protestantism. In detailing daily life in Charlottengrad, she includes a memory of shabbat dinners at her friends', where the night began with lighting candles and prayer and quickly progressed to "Two-Step, One-Step, Tango. It was fun."[76] Writing her memoir after having spent the entirety of World War II in Berlin as a single Jewish woman, she prioritized shaping the perception of her ethnic and cultural background—perhaps as a habitual way of managing visibility on which her life depended.

Lourié conveys information about Berlin's Russian community in a diligent, almost dry manner. But her tone grows effusive when she addresses the woman to whom she writes these letters, opening invariably with "Liebste," or "Meine Liebste" (dearest, my dearest). She acknowledges that she "could and can be artistically creative only when [her] feeling of love for another person is so strong that it leads to energy, which then culminates in a poem or in a memory brought to life."[77] She reiterates this point in the prefatory poem, "Da plötzlich das Wunder, das Wunder zu lieben! / Vergessen das Alter, nicht denken an Schmerzen!" (There suddenly was the miracle, the miracle of loving! / To forget old age, not think about the aches!)[78] And yet Lourié's memoir presents a certain paradox of discretion: she exercises great restraint in ensuring she does not disclose her addressee's gender more than necessary (as in the cordial, feminine "Liebste"), but the intensity of this avoidance only reinforces the fact that she repeatedly proclaims her love to a woman. It should be noted, too, that Lourié's ostensible concern about writing openly of her same-sex love was warranted. Ten years after her death, an incomplete version of her memoir was published in the Russian translation in an émigré literary journal in Berlin. It was scrubbed clean of all references to the woman Vera loved and who motivated her to write her memoir.[79]

Hardly a lesbian manifesto, at times *Letters to You* employs euphemism. At others, Lourié casually outs her fellow Russian Berliners: "the cubist Ivan Puni [Jean Pougny] was a handsome man but had little interest in women, though he was married. . . . His wife, the Ukrainian painter Ksana Boguslavskaia, who loved women for her part, was in a friendship with the lesser-known poetess Jelena Ferrari."[80] Lourié proceeds to describe a party at which Boguslavskaia suggested they spend the night together. When Vera refused, Ksana reportedly screamed, "You witch! With [Liuba] Ehrenburg you can, but with me you don't want to!"[81] There is no moral outrage on Lourié's part, but she is quick to clarify that her and Liubov Ehrenburg's "very loving relationship" was "purely platonic in nature. But anyone who saw us in Prager Diele feeding each other coffee cream, could have completely taken us for a couple in love."[82] Boguslavskaia was apparently one of those observers.

Let us pause at this scene of Vera Lourié and Liubov Ehrenburg sitting opposite each other in a café, feeding each other spoonfuls of cream, aware that their private actions in a public space can be read a certain way. The scene is a subtle reminder of the limits of what we can know, of what parts of the past can be reconstructed and ever understood. For the essence of this is the ephemeral connection between two people, which incidentally cannot be readily quantified, collected, or archived. The lives of these two women will take very different directions. Ehrenburg will continue her career as a painter and, alongside her husband Ilya Ehrenburg, join the ranks of the Soviet cultural elite, adapting to and surviving the twentieth century's harsh political winds. Lourié will remain single and will continue writing poems and reviews, never achieving either popularity or recognition. She will turn down an opportunity to move to England at the start of the war, during which she will miraculously avoid arrest and deportation.[83] Her decision to stay in Berlin will define her life as an immigrant.

In writing her memoir, however, she presents staying in Berlin merely as a fact of her life in a long string of mentioned and omitted biographical events. She avoids nostalgic spins on exile or using memoir writing as an opportunity to settle scores or set the record straight. Instead, she frames *Letters to You* as half-intimate, half-public notes that present the range of possibilities and temporalities of an immigrant's life in Berlin, a city that simultaneously welcomes and rejects difference, tradition, and any sense of certainty. Lourié's book can likewise be read as an epilogue to Charlottengrad, written by its last inhabitant, a prologue to an entirely new tradition of immigrant writing in German.

Importantly, *Letters to You* is also an explicitly queer text, one that searches for the language to express its queerness—a belated text, perhaps, but one that foregrounds the shimmering queerness—difference and awkwardness, shame and rejection, but also excitement and novelty—of making refugee life in Berlin. Lourié's letters to her nurse, Sergey's letters to Shakhovskoy, and Yuritsyn's letters to Tchelitchew offer a powerful record of living in a time that was much richer, more interconnected, and nonnormative than any master narrative of Russian émigré culture can account for. Their perspectives on exile, and on being queer in exile, prompt us to shift our thinking about the structures of émigré culture—its development, social hierarchies, enmeshment with the local, ways of losing and remembering, and, crucially, its queer potential.

Conclusion

As a cultural phenomenon, Charlottengrad unsettles neat accounts and defies sharply focused identities. It can be said that Charlottengrad anticipated a decentered perspective on postrevolutionary culture created by the former subjects of the Russian Empire who overlapped in Berlin and grappled with fitting into an upended world while pursuing distinct projects. Much like the terms "Soviet" and "émigré," which were in the process of becoming, the idea of "Russianness" was continuously renegotiated. Among those who eventually embraced the label "émigré," not all fashioned themselves as representatives of a pure national culture.[1] That is, being "Russian" legally or otherwise did not erase their other identities. For instance, Wasyl Masjutyn, a Riga-born, Moscow-educated Ukrainian painter who lived most of his life in Berlin, left behind a remarkable body of work that includes illustrations of Russian literary classics, a series of commemorative medals depicting Ukrainian military heroes, and a monumental sculpture adorning the facade of the former Soviet embassy by the Brandenburg Gate.[2] Roman Vishniac's Berlin photography is Russian in that this exceptional Jewish photographer grew up in St. Petersburg, trained in Moscow, arrived in Germany as a Latvian citizen, and shared a cultural heritage with many other Petersburgers in Berlin, such as the painter Magda Nachman Acharya. As the Nazi threat grew, Nachman Acharya relocated to Mumbai, where she tutored a generation of Indian painters.[3] Another Jewish native of St. Petersburg, Alisa Rozenbaum, better known as Ayn Rand, spent only a month in Berlin in 1926 before journeying to Hollywood to start her career as a screenwriter. But she, too, was a part of Charlottengrad.

Questions of identity were deeply linked with cultural production, whether they emerged in Vladimir Mayakovsky's desire for a denationalized metropolis or Vladimir Nabokov's vision of a hyper-national Germany. And these questions drove Russian cultural (and political) activity in Berlin well beyond the end of the Weimar Republic. Charlottengrad in the 1930s was much more modest in its literary output than it had been in the 1920s, and more exilic in tonality. The print run of the three poetry chapbooks published by Berlin's Russian Poets Club—*Housewarming* (*Novosel'e*, 1931), *A Grove* (*Roshcha*, 1932), and *A Dragnet* (*Nevod*, 1933)—never exceeded 400 copies each. Containing only lyrical poems, these chapbooks offer a record of displacement and countryless-ness. Although such themes seem pessimistic, the Berlin poets gave them a nuanced treatment, infusing the reality of exile with fortuitous encounters, linguistic inventiveness, and humor.

In these poems Berlin is repeatedly compared with Petersburg, which comes to signal Russian cultural achievement. Even poets who had never visited the city, or lacked personal connections to it, used the imagery associated with Petersburg to underscore their Russianness. Anna Akhmatova, who famously chose to stay in Russia and not emigrate, commented on the expatriates' obsession with Petersburg: "Have you noticed what happens to all of them in emigration? While Sasha Chiorny lived in Petersburg, there was no worse city in the world. Petersburg was but vulgarity, petty bourgeoisie, and miasma. He left, and it turned out that Petersburg is in fact a paradise. There is no Paris, no Mediterranean Sea—only Petersburg is perfect."[4]

The poet Vladimir Korvin-Piotrovsky, a native of Kyiv, offers a notable variation on this theme. He envisions Alexander Pushkin as one of his late-night guests in Berlin. In "Verses to Pushkin," the two poets share a bohemian chat about the hardships of being a poet: "Берлин? Еще бы, так и в старину, / Российской музе странствовать не внове" (Berlin? Of course, just like in the old days, / the Russian muse is used to wandering).[5] By depicting Pushkin stationed in "Charlottenburg, Kurfürstendamm" amidst the glossy asphalt and shop windows, Korvin-Piotrovsky grants Pushkin an opportunity Pushkin never had: to travel abroad to Europe. In doing so, Korvin-Piotrovsky also legitimizes himself as a Russian poet, in Berlin. Although he eventually left Berlin for Paris in 1939, Korvin-Piotrovsky and the coterie of poets to which he belonged show that Charlottengrad remained an active center of Russian expatriate writing until the war.

The rise of Nazism opened a new chapter in Charlottengrad's development and laid bare divisions within the community along nationalist lines. As historians have documented, some Russian émigrés welcomed Nazism enthusiastically, embracing the opportunity to justify antisemitism, which was always rampant among supporters of the monarchy, and seeing in Hitler a way to reclaim Russia.[6] Others, like Vladimir Nabokov and his family, fled the country. Yet others, such as Sergey Nabokov, were forced to translate for the Nazis and ultimately ended their days in concentration camps. After the war, Russian culture acquired an entirely new meaning in a defeated and divided Berlin.

Nina Berberova, one of the illustrious residents of Charlottengrad in its early 1920s heyday, wrote a sort of epilogue to the interwar chapter in the city's history in her 1977 poetry cycle *Berlin Zoo*. Like Lourié in her *Letters to You*, Berberova followed Shklovsky's influential example and turned to the image of the zoo as a symbol and metaphor. However, for Berberova the zoo is the spatiotemporal embodiment not just of exile but of the entire postwar European world. This is particularly visible in the cycle's second poem:

В зоологическом
Трагическом саду
Каждый второй—хромает с палкой,
Каждый пятый—сидит в колясочке,
Напевает немецкую песенку:

«Вы катитесь, колесики, по дороженькам,
Я давно сказал прости-прощай своим ноженькам,
С той поры, как лежал под Орлом
В сугробе голубом,
Тому тридцать лет и три года.

А зовут меня Илья Муромец,
Протезы у меня американские,
Челюсти—швейцарские,
Слуховой аппарат—французский,
А стеклянный глаз—английский.

Но память у меня русская:
Голубой сугроб,
Да чужой сапог,
Но милостив Бог:
Не в висок, а в лоб».

Берлин, 1977[7]

In the zoological
Tragical garden
Every second person walks with a cane, limping,
Every fifth person is in the wheelchair sitting,
Singing a little German song:

"Roll, o little wheels, along the little roads,
I long ago bid farewell to my little legs,
From the time when I lay near Orel
In the blue snowdrift,
Thirty and three years ago.

And my name is Ilya of Murom,
My prosthetics are American,
My jaws are—Swiss,
My hearing aids—French,
My glass eye—English.

But my memory is Russian:
The blue snowdrift
And someone's boot,
But God is merciful,
Not in the temple, but in the forehead."

    Berlin, 1977

Blending folklore and the documentary, Berberova imagines the Berlin Zoo populated by disabled war veterans. The poem's key figure is a modern version of the bogatyr, or knight-errant, Ilya of Murom. In the oral epic poem, a *bylina*, Ilya of Murom is paralyzed until age thirty-three, when he miraculously gains fantastic strength and goes on to engage in many heroic adventures. In Berberova's poem he is defeated and deformed, though he avoids execution, as the final line suggests. He now resembles Frankenstein's monster in its transnational iteration, his body consisting of American, Swiss, French, and English prosthetic devices. Yet his memory remains Russian. Berberova is soberly ruthless in her depiction of postwar life among the ruins and wartime atrocities. She offers no forward-looking hope for regeneration, reconstruction, or revitalization. But memory redeems the bleak present and, as the passage of time testifies, some wounds heal.

Conclusion

Like the histories of all major cities and especially capitals, Berlin's history is one of overlap, multiplicity, and messiness. In sketching a panoramic overview of Russophone culture in Berlin between the wars, I envisioned this study as a contribution, however limited, to the ever-growing scholarship on the city of Berlin, on postrevolutionary Russian literature, and on global cultures in Russian. And perhaps one of the more important tasks of this project has been to maintain the memory of how many roads led to and through Berlin for authors and intellectuals fleeing Russia, thinking of moving to Soviet Russia, and pondering their relationship to the changing country. To paraphrase Shklovsky's description of Gleisdreieck in *Zoo*, Berlin is a place where a multitude of roads and lives intersect, much as "the threads of a shawl drawn through a ring intersect." A site of loss and displacement, Charlottengrad was also a site of encounter, serving to remind us how proximate, implicated, and intertwined these stories of exile and return are.

APPENDIX

The Russian Poets Club Meeting Minutes, Berlin, 1928

The below meeting minutes from Berlin's Russian Poets Club are included in the Vladimir Korvin-Piotrovsky Papers at Yale University's Beinecke Rare Book and Manuscript Library. The minutes are part of the club's journal, a large-format scrapbook ("Notebook 31") filled with drawings, photographs, newspaper clippings, scribbled-on napkins, and other such ephemera. The minutes represent an inserted notebook handwritten by the poet Mikhail Gorlin from February 10 until July 26, 1928. I have used angled brackets to indicate words I was unable to transcribe (i.e., <illegible>) and square brackets for informed guesses. Gorlin's style is performatively bureaucratic, and I have striven to preserve his deliberately run-on syntax in translation.

Club members are identified as "poet," "poetess," or "prose poet" (prozopoet). Informative and witty, the minutes reveal noteworthy aspects of the poets' "literary everyday," such as their intellectual concerns (see the list of proposed presentations announced in the First Meeting), the range of their collective reading (from Zoshchenko to Goethe), and the need to articulate the club's political platform (expressed humorously in the Twelfth Meeting). It is also curious to see Vladimir Nabokov (Sirin) as but one among many contemporary writers, though he is distinguished with the title of "maître," as is Vladimir Korvin-Piotrovsky.[1] Several times, Gorlin records the group's awareness of their own historicity, which is sometimes expressed in a hopeful, if provocatively funny, way—as when it is proposed that the club celebrate "October 19, the day of Pushkin's graduation from the lyceum so as to underscore the internal connection of the Berlin poets with the epoch of Russian poetry's flourishing."

MEMBERS OF THE POETS CLUB

Prose Poet Essad-Bey[2]	Fasanenstr. 72 b/Pruszak	
Poetess Bloch	Jenaerstr. 4 b/Steinbock	PFALZBURG 42-58
Poet P. S. Volf	Pariserstr. 19	OLIVA 15-51
Poet Gorlin, Club Secretary	Sächsischestr. 72	OLIVA 27-66
Prose Poet Gofman	Schönstedtstr. 1 N20	
Poet Dzhanumov	Vorbergstr. 8 b/Aschl Schöneberg	
Prose Poetess Zalkind	Pariserstr. 1	OLIVIA 15-04
Prose Poet Kaplun	Motzstr. 24	NOLLENDORF 5846
Poet Kumming \<Komnin\>	Hildegardstr. 2	Schöneberg
Poetess Levina	Martin Lutherstr. 89/b v. Barby W307	
Poet Ofrosimov	use the newspaper "Rul'" address Friedrichstr. 76, Aufg6 SW48	
Poet Pavlovich	Regensburgerstr. 24	BAVARIA 85-72
Poet Piotrovsky	Rückerstr. 3 b/Reich Charl	
Poet Polishchuk	Tile-Wardenbergstr. 25 NW	
Poet Rabinovich	Regensburgerstr. 9III W50	NOLLEND.54-35
Poet Sirin	Passauerstr. 12	BAVARIA 13-81
Poetess Tal	Pension Pragerplatz	PFALZBURG 20-94
Poet Eliashov	Hohenzollerndamm 27 b/Magat	UHLAND 66-73
Prose Poet Brodsky	Nettelbergstr. 17	KURFÜRST 10-12
Poet Rozen	Pariserstr. 3	OLIVIA 55-73
Guest Poet Rakita	Augsburgerstr. 37 b/Bernstein	BISMARK 40-24
Prose Poetess Veksler	Gossowstr. 4I b/Hass	
Prose Poet Shteinberg	[Kalkreuthstr.] 18 b/Haffer	
Poetess Levina	Würzburgerstr. 19II b/ v. Wedel W50 BAVARIA 60-46	
Poetess Tal	Nassausischerstr. 56 b/Scherk	PFALZBURG 14-44
	Nürnbergerstr. 23 b/Wallnig	

FIRST MEETING OF THE POETS CLUB

Minutes

The first meeting of the Poets Club took place on Friday, February 10 at Poet [honoris causa] Volf's apartment.

Present: Essad-Bey, Bloch, Volf, Gorlin, Dzhanumov, Kumming, Ofrosimov, Pavlovich, Piotrovsky, Polishchuk, Rab, Eliashov.

The Club's program was set forth: the Poets Club sets forth the goal of concentrating all the young poets and poetesses of (Russian) Berlin within its ranks.

Only poets may be members of the Club.

Meetings of the Club will be devoted to the reading of works by its members and reports on general literary subjects.

Meetings of the Club will take place once every 2 weeks, on Mondays.

Poet Rabinovich and Poet Pavlovich read their poetry.

Poet Bloch read a translation of Jacopone da Todi.

Poets Essad-Bey, Bloch, Gorlin, Dzhanumov, Ofrosimov, Pavlovich, Piotrovsky, Rabinovich and Eliashov promised to deliver reports on the following subjects in the near future:

Essad-Bey	Representation of the Orient in Russian literature
Bloch	On vertical versification
Gorlin	The problem of prosaism in contemporary poetry
Dzhanumov	Contemporary humorous language (mainly in Western literature, mainly Zoshchenko)
Ofrosimov	On poetry in Russia and abroad
Pavlovich	Classical meters and stanzas in contemporary poetry
Piotrovsky	Development of poetic language from the Symbolists to today
Rabinovich	On the revolution in poetry and poetry in the revolution
Eliashov	Theater in Russian lyric

SECOND MEETING OF THE POETS CLUB

Minutes

The second meeting of the Poets Club took place on Monday, February 20 at Poet Gorlin's apartment.

Present: Essad-Bey, Bloch, Volf, Gorlin, Gofman, Dzhanumov, Zalkind, Kumming, Levina, Pavlovich, Piotrovsky, Polishchuk, Rabinovich, Eliashov.

Poet Gorlin, Poet Kumming, Poet Piotrovsky, Poet Dzhanumov and Poetess Levina read their poetry.

After the official program, a discussion of a journal suggested for publication by the In the Attic Club (Na cherdake) took place.

The discussion was heated and unpleasant.

THIRD MEETING OF THE POETS CLUB

Minutes

The third meeting of the Poets Club took place on Monday, March 5 at Poet Gorlin's apartment.

Present: Essad-Bey, Bloch, Gorlin, Gofman, Dzhanumov, Zalkind, Kumming, Levina, Ofrosimov, Pavlovich, Piotrovsky, Rabinovich, Tal, Eliashov.

All those present, as well as the absent Volf and Polishchuk, were automatically made members of the Poets Club with the titles Poet, Prose Poet, Poet [honoris causa].

It was decreed that a Chairman should be chosen for each meeting.

Rabinovich was elected Chairman.

Poet Gorlin was named Permanent Secretary.

Poet Piotrovsky read a dramatic poem, "The King."

Poet Eliashov read 4 poems: "Over the illuminated forestage," "The window looked out on the field," "A Petersburg dreamer," and "Jazz Band."

FOURTH MEETING OF THE POETS CLUB

Minutes

The fourth meeting of the Poets Club took place on Monday, March 19 at Poet [honoris causa] Volf's apartment.

Present: Essad-Bey, Bloch, Volf, Gorlin, Gofman, Dzhanumov, Zalkind, Kaplun, Levina, Rabinovich, Sirin, Eliashov.

Prose Poet Kaplun and Poet Sirin were made members of the Club.

It was decreed to inform all members in writing of Club meetings going forward.

Prose Poet Essad-Bey read 4 tales: "Al-Hazani," "The Dervish and the Sultan" (from Saadi), "The Tale of the Talkative Prince," [and "How beautiful women began making themselves up"].

Poet Sirin read "Conversation" (a poetic dialog) and the poem "Islands."

Poet Dzhanumov read two poems: "It must be so" and "All that is earthly in <illegible>."

Poetess Bloch read three poems: "Sparrow," "How easy it is to remember this," and <illegible>.

After the official program, Poet Eliashov recited parodies from *Parnassus on End* to the poets' considerable amusement.

FIFTH MEETING OF THE POETS CLUB

Minutes

The fifth meeting of the Poets Club took place on Monday, April 2 at Poetess Zalkind's apartment.

Present: Essad-Bey, Brodsky, Gorlin, Dzhanumov, Zalkind, Kaplun, Levina, Ofrosimov, Piotrovsky, Rabinovich, Rakita, Rozen, Sirin, Eliashov. Ofrosimov presided.

Prose Poet Brodsky and Poet Rozen were made members of the Club.

As an exemption for valid reason, Poet Rakita was named Guest of the Club with the title Guest Poet.

All minutes of the previous meetings were read and adopted.

It was decreed to begin the reading of reports promised by the Poets in the near future. Gorlin, Essad-Bey and Rabinovich promised to read the first three reports.

Poet Sirin read "A University Poem."

Prose Poetess Zalkind read the short story "Silence" and the poem "To trade away..."

Poet Eliashov read three poems: "Duel," "A Terrifying Theater," and "There are half-musings."

Poet Dzhanumov read the poem "To sit in the café."

Poet Piotrovsky read two poems: "In the Bay" and "Iambs."

As an exception, the next meeting was set for Tuesday, April 17.

The program was outlined: M. Gorlin's report, "Problems of prosaism in contemporary poetry" and the reading of works by those poets who have yet to read within the Club.

SIXTH MEETING OF THE POETS CLUB

Minutes

The sixth meeting of the Poets Club took place on Tuesday, April 17 at Poet Gorlin's apartment.

Present: Essad-Bey, Bloch, Brodsky, Veksler, Volf, Gorlin, Dzhanumov, Zalkind, Kaplun, Kumming, Levina, Pavlovich, Piotrovsky, Rabinovich, Rakita, Rozen, Shteinberg, Eliashov.

Poet Rabinovich presided.

Prose Poetess [illegible] Veksler and Prose Poet Shteinberg were made members of the Club.

In light of the fact that the list of proposed Club members has been exhausted with the addition of these two individuals, those present decreed after discussing the question of accepting new members: the Club member proposing a new member is suggested to acquaint the collective with the poetic character and works of the candidate, after which the collective will resolve to accept the member by secret ballot.

Poet Gorlin read his report, "The problem of prosaism in contemporary poetry." Poets Essad-Bey, Brodsky, Kumming, Pavlovich, Piotrovsky, Rabinovich and Rozen took part in the debate regarding the report.

In light of the fact that Prose Poet Brodsky's teeth began to hurt, Poet Gorlin read him an Ancient Babylonian spell against tooth pain (in German translation), which quickly helped the matter and is recommended to all poets (not recommended to mere mortals).

Prose Poet Kaplun read "Story Without a Title."

Poet Rozen read 2 poems: [*titles not included*]

Prose Poet Brodsky delivered a report on his work with the journal commission.

Due to the late hour, Poets Bloch, Kaplun, Levin and Shteinberg had to retire.

Under Rembrandtian lighting, Poet Kumming read his mystical pamphlet, "Hammer and Sickle" to those who remained, vigorously exciting all [presil'no vsekh vzbudorazhivshii].

The next meeting was set for Monday, April 30.

The program was proposed: Poet Kumming's novel, prose works by Essad-Bey and Gofman, poetry by Poets Rabinovich and Rakita.

SEVENTH MEETING OF THE POETS CLUB

Minutes

The seventh meeting of the Poets Club took place on Monday, April 30 at Prose Poetess Zalkind's apartment.

Present: Essad-Bey, Bloch, Brodsky, Veksler, Gorlin, Gofman, Dzhanumov, Zalkind, Kaplun, Levina, Pavlovich, Piotrovsky, Rabinovich, Sirin, Eliashov.

It was decreed: the Chairman of a given meeting will be named by the Chairman of the previous meeting.

The Chairman of the sixth meeting, Poet Rabinovich named Poet Eliashov as Chairman of the seventh meeting.

Based on Poet Gorlin's suggestion, it was decided to invite Mrs. Berta Shiratskaia to the next meeting as a guest.

The absence of the meeting's marquee attraction, Poet Kumming, was noted with deep sorrow, given that he had promised his novel.

Prose Poet Essad-Bey read the Eastern legend, "Ashkar-Abat."

Prose Poet Gofman read the prose symphony "Eolna: In the Evening on Suicides."

The prose symphony gave rise to lively debates about the possibility and internal justification of such art. Poet Piotrovsky distinguished himself in these debates.

Poet Rabinovich read 3 poems: "Siena," "Orvieto," and "I remember you, murals and <illegible>," as well as a free rendering of Odysseus's story on the themes of Dante's *Inferno*.

Guest Poet Rakita read a German translation of Gumilev's "The Captains," recognized by all as marvelous, and two poems: "You are far, my piece of the steppe" and <blank>.

Toward the end of the meeting, Poet Pavlovich offered a suggestion to celebrate the two-hundred-twenty-fifth anniversary of St. Petersburg's founding.

The next meeting was set for Tuesday, May 15.

The program was set: poetry by Poetess Bloch and Poet Gorlin, Rabinovich's translation from *Faust*, prose works by Poets Gorlin and Gofman, and Kumming's novel once again.

On the way home, Prose Poet Brodsky read his companions a brief presentation about the eroticism of thin silk stockings in Poet Rabinovich's writings and the eroticism of "magical girls" in Poet Essad-Bey's writings. This was done in a manner entirely unflattering to the latter.

EIGHTH MEETING

Minutes

The eighth meeting of the Poets Club took place on Tuesday, May 15 at Poet S. Volf's apartment.

Present: Essad-Bey, Bloch, Brodsky, Volf, Gorlin, Dzhanumov, Zalkind, Levina, Ofrosimov, Pavlovich, Piotrovsky, Rabinovich, Rakita, Rozen, Sirin, Eliashov.

Mrs. Berta Shiratskaia did not come.

In light of yet another absence by Poet Kumming, whose novel was once again featured in the program, it was decided to declare said novel fictitious and Poet Kumming a mythmaker.

Poet Rabinovich read a translation from *Faust* ("Prelude in the Theater," "Suicide Scene"). The translations gave rise to spirited debate. Poet Piotrovsky declared the following theses: "Either Goethe's bad and the translation is good. Or Goethe is good, and the translation's bad." He personally believes the latter hypothesis to be more likely, though he was not so bold as to insist on this due to his lacking knowledge of German. Poet Sirin supported Poet Piotrovsky and also confessed to his insufficient knowledge of German. In light of the fact that the two aforementioned poets spoke of their ignorance of German not with a respectable, shameful self-deprecation, but with a kind of boastful superiority, it was decreed to grant them the title of Obscurantist Poets (titul Poetov Mrakobesov).

Poetess Bloch read 3 poems: "At the Heavy Hour of Daybreak Prayers," "Since I've Learned."

Poet Eliashov read two poems: [Vatek] and "Fragment from a Poem." In "Vatek," the following line was unanimously declared the best: "Hearts burn under dense crystal." To general confusion, however, it was discovered that Poet Eliashov's [line] <illegible> and the Obscurantist Poet Sirin, having devoted particular attention to this line, had composed it himself.

Poet Gorlin read "Triptych" and the poems "Expectation" ("Ozhidanie"), "LF" <illegible>. The reading of Poet Gorlin's poetry was distinguished by an important event. Poet Ofrosimov, emerging from many weeks of silence for the first time, expressed his opinion on "Triptych."

After the official program, Poet Piotrovsky delighted a considerable number of those present with his sharp and deep impromptu poem in German on the utility of [Veroner], after whose reading Poet Piotrovsky was deprived of his title of Obscurantist in light of his service to German literature, leaving only Poet Sirin with such a title.

It was decided to celebrate the next, ninth meeting with a ceremonial feast. Poets Ofrosimov and Piotrovsky were tasked with purchasing wine, while Prose Poetess Zalkind was to prepare sandwiches.

NINTH MEETING

In lieu of minutes

The ninth, ceremonial meeting of the Poets Club took place on Monday, May 28 at Poet Gorlin's apartment.

Present: Essad-Bey, Bloch, Brodsky, Veksler, Volf, Gorlin, Dzhanumov, Zalkind, Kaplun, Levina, Ofrosimov, Piotrovsky, Rakita, Sirin, Eliashov and guests O. Brodsky, Golberts and <illegible>.

The recording of minutes for this meeting was extraordinarily complicated by the not-entirely sober state of Secretary Poet Gorlin during the feast. Due to the lack of exact written records, such a work is [outside] the capacity of a single person in any event. Since this meeting is, however, extremely important to the history of Russian culture, I propose forming a special historical commission to this end, headed by Prose Poetess Zalkind, a specialist in Russian history. On my part, I will readily inform this commission of my recollections and reminiscences, as well as provide a small amount of existing written documentation.

Tenth Meeting

Minutes

The tenth meeting of the Club took place on Monday, June 11 at Poetess Zalkind's apartment.

Present: Essad-Bey, Gorlin, Gofman, Dzhanumov, Zalkind, Kaplun, Levina, Rabinovich, Rakita, Eliashov.

The question of inviting Poetesses Pasternak and [Shats] (a Jewish Poetess) to the Club was reviewed. It was decided to invite Poetess Pasternak as a permanent member and Poetess [Shats] as a guest, given that she is a poetess of foreign "exoticism," to the next meeting.

The "Alphabet of the Club," sent in by Poet Brodsky, was unveiled.

Poet Essad-Bey read his novella "An Educational and Curious Tale of the Great King, Noble Count Esperanto and the Beautiful Marquise Eugenia."

Poet Gorlin read the story "Aver the Engineer."

The debates inspired by both works were lengthy and lively, but unlike the usual debates, they led to an almost unanimous appreciation. Poet Essad-Bey's work was recognized as quite comical and skillful, though not especially unique, and superior to his previous works in cleverness and taste.

Poet Gorlin's work was recognized as unique and interesting [though overloaded at times] [in essence] but quite weakly thought-through and developed with regard to its subject.

Poetess Levina read poems whose names were not included in the minutes, as she ungraciously refused to announce them.

ELEVENTH MEETING

Minutes

The eleventh meeting of the Club took place on Monday, June 25 at [Poet] Volf's apartment.

Present: Essad-Bey, Bloch, Brodsky, Volf, Gorlin, Gofman, Dzhanumov, Zalkind, Levina, Ofrosimov, Pavlovich, Piotrovsky, Rakita, Sirin, Eliashov and guests. The absence of <illegible> Essad-Bey, Poet Kumming, who informed the secretary of his new novel by telephone, resulted in laughter and chaotic general displeasure. It was decided to censure Poet Kumming in writing for cruelly leading all those present around by the nose, a task which was entrusted to the Secretary.

It was decreed to no longer consider any poet who fails to appear at meetings 4 times in a row without appropriate apologies a member. This decree takes effect beginning July 9, meaning that missed meetings before July 9 are not to be counted.

All available humorous works related to the ceremonial meeting of May 28 were read, to the great enjoyment of all: Brodsky's "Alphabet of the Club"; "Parodies," a joint work by Eliashov and Gorlin; Dzhanumov's "A Hardly Unsentimental Journey to the Land of Tall Tales," and "Couplets," a joint work by Zalkind and <illegible>.

Prose Poet Gofman read a prose symphony, "<illegible>," recognized as a far more successful attempt than his first, "<illegible>."

Poet Dzhanumov read two poems, "The Cripple" and "The Burghers" [Meshchane]. While the latter poem earned general praise, the former led to a difficult, deep and not quite intelligible by others dispute between Poets Rabinovich and Piotrovsky on clarity in art.

Poet Sirin read 2 poems, "The Hornet" and "To Russia."

Poet Pavlovich read 2 poems, "Let my prayer be righted" and "<illegible>."

TWELFTH MEETING

Minutes

The twelfth meeting of the Club took place on Monday, July 9 at Poet Gorlin's apartment.

Present: Essad-Bey, Bloch, Brodsky, Gorlin, Gofman, Zalkind, Kumming, Piotrovsky, Rakita, Sirin, Pavlovich.

Since all manner of misfortune comes from the number 13, it was decided upon Poet Gorlin's suggestion to pass over the thirteenth meeting in the following way: the meetings of the Poets Club would be divided into *dodecades* (groups of twelve meetings). The third meeting of each *dodecade* will be an open meeting, at which guests would be permitted in large numbers; such a meeting can also take place in some public place, for example at the In the Attic Club. The ninth meeting of each *dodecade* will be dedicated to feasting. The third meeting of the third *dodecade*, the ninth meeting of the ninth and the twelfth meeting of the twelfth must be celebrated with special pomp as follows: a procession on elephants and camels along the Kurfürstendamm, a toast to the health of all members of the Poets Club on Wittenbergplatz with President Hindenburg, Minister of People's Education Becker, Iuzi Levin, and other notable guests in attendance.

In addition to this, celebrations are to take place on February 10 (the day of the Club's founding); on June 28 (July 15 Old Style), the Name Day of both maîtres, Vladimir Piotrovsky and Vladimir Sirin; and on October 19, the day of Pushkin's graduation from the lyceum so as to underscore the internal connection of the Berlin poets with the epoch of Russian poetry's flourishing.

The number of celebrations is naturally not limited to this.

The Club's political program, proposed by Poet Gorlin, was unanimously approved:

"The political platform of the Poets Club is determined exclusively by its relationship to the Maharaja of Benares. This relationship is a negative one. The Maharaja of Benares (see the photograph in [Berliner] Illustrierte [sic] [Zeitung]), with his mustache à la Wilhelm II and egglike and, we would say, trickstery eyes, looks more like a provincial dentist than a Maharaja. The Poets Club therefore considers him unworthy of his title, hallowed in its fabulousness, and refuses to enter into diplomatic relations with him."

A member of the Poets Club who enters into diplomatic or any other relations with the Maharaja of Benares will be swiftly excluded from the Club.

Only a gift by the Maharaja of Benares of a considerable sum of money for the Club's journal can lead to a revision of this decree.

NOTE: In light of the ancient friendship of the Essad-Bey clan with the clan of the Maharaja of Benares, Essad-Bey is permitted in extraordinary cases to enter into private relations with the Maharaja.

It was decreed, in recognition of extraordinary deeds, to name poets "Honorary Vladimir" (in honor of the two maîtres) and to name Poetesses "Honorary Anna."

An historical and archival commission under the Poets Club was established to collect and preserve all materials related to the Club. Elected to membership in the commission were: Poet Brodsky, Poetess Bloch, Poet Gorlin, Poetess Zalkind and the famous Artist and Archivist Zaretsky, who graciously offered his service.

Poet Kumming's appearance made a deep impression, after which he managed to read a short, but unique in its conceit and execution, iambic poem, "I will come next time." He then immediately disappeared.

Poet Eliashov read 3 poems: "Fehrbelliner [Platz]," "Over the spine of the iron bridge" and "Stanzas" and fragments from a poem of his youth, which <illegible> promised to read next time.

Poet Gorlin recited a recently discovered rough draft by Pushkin: a continuation of "At the beginning of my life, I remember school . . ." For this recitation, gratitude was expressed to Poet Gorlin upon Poet Sirin's suggestion.

Poet Piotrovsky read his rough and still-unfinished tragedy, "Francesca da Rimini," which made quite a strong impression, even stronger than that of the appearance and disappearance of Poet Kumming.

SECOND DODECADE: FIRST MEETING

Minutes

The first meeting of the second *dodecade* took place on Thursday, July 26 at Poetess E. Zalkind's apartment.

Present: Essad-Bey, Brodsky, Volf, Gofman, Zalkind, Kaplun, Piotrovsky, Eliashov and guests: Alekin, Zaretsky and <illegible>.

In connection with the departure of many members of the Poets Club, it was decreed to set a summer holiday for the entire month of August. The second meeting of the second *dodecade* was set for September 3 or 10, depending on the Secretary's return.

It was decided not to celebrate Vladimir Day on July 28, but to move this celebration to the second meeting. To prepare this celebration, a special commission was established; it includes Poets Brodsky, Gorlin, Zalkind, and Ofrosimov.

Poet and Secretary Gorlin, who is to depart for France, was given by the Club unlimited power to enter into various contracts, [conduct] various official receptions, and so on.

Since all meetings of the Poets Club will be taking place on Pariserstr[aße], on the corner of Sächsische[straße], it was decided to submit a request to rename the location as the Street of Russian Culture, Die Straße der russischen Kultur.

Poet Eliashov read 2 poems: "Romance" and "Petersburg Verses." Both poems were met with general approval. Poet Piotrovsky told Poet Eliashov that he did well (nazval molodtsom). The last two lines of "Petersburg Verses"—"The magnificent and simple Admiralty spire"—led to long debates about the possibility of combined usage of two epithets as vastly different as those, brilliantly resolved by Poet Brodsky, who called Eliashov a magnificent and simple fellow. After that, Poet Eliashov read a poem in jest: "To a beautiful woman who cannot" and a poem of his youth, "Petersburg-Petrograd-Leningrad-Berlin."

Poet Gorlin read 10 new poems in one fell swoop: "Murderers," <illegible>, "A Pitiful Song of a Traveling Lord," "Kandidat Wedekind," "Her Portrait," "Song of a Dreaming Law Student," "Elegy," "Rise, My Soul," "To Myself," and "A dreamer remembers his life."

The objectivity characteristic of Poet Gorlin as Secretary must overcome the modesty characteristic of him as a person and add to these minutes that these poems were quite a success.

NOTES

Introduction

1. Hans-Erich Volkmann, *Die russische Emigration in Deutschland, 1919–1929* (Würzburg: Holzner Verlag, 1966), 6–7; Robert C. Williams, *Culture in Exile: Russian Émigrés in Germany, 1881–1941* (Ithaca, NY: Cornell University Press, 1972), 111–13. Estimating the population figures is very difficult as record keeping was often influenced by political concerns and is inconsistent across the archives of the American Red Cross, Russian émigré organizations, and the German Foreign Office. See Sergei Ippolitov, Vladimir Nedbaevskii, and Iuliia Rudentsova, *Tri stolitsy izgnaniia: Konstantinopol', Berlin, Parizh* (Moscow: Spas, 1999), 62–69.

2. Andrei Belyi, *Odna iz obitelei tsarstva tenei* (Leningrad: Gosudarstvennoe izdatel'stvo, 1924), 26. Many Russians also lived in the neighboring southwestern boroughs of Schöneberg, Friedenau, and Wilmersdorf. The former imperial embassy was in Berlin Mitte. See Robert C. Williams, *Culture in Exile*, 113–15.

3. William Chapin Huntington, *The Homesick Million: Russia-out-of-Russia* (Boston, MA: Stratford Co., 1933); Marc Raeff, *Russia Abroad: A Cultural History of the Russian Emigration, 1919–1939* (Oxford, UK: Oxford University Press, 1990).

4. Raeff, *Russia Abroad*, 3.

5. Maria Rubins, "Conceptual Territories of 'Diaspora': Introduction. The Unbearable Lightness of Being a Diasporian: Modes of Writing and Reading Narratives of Displacement," in *Redefining Russian Literary Diaspora, 1920–2020*, ed. Maria Rubins (London: UCL Press, 2021), 15. See also Raeff, *Russia Abroad*, 95.

6. For instance, Leonid Livak and Maria Rubins have explored the complexities of Russia Abroad by focusing on Paris. See Livak, *How It Was Done in Paris: Russian Émigré Literature and French Modernism* (Madison: University of Wisconsin Press, 2003); and Rubins, *Russian Montparnasse: Transnational Writing in Interwar Paris* (London: Palgrave Macmillan, 2015). See also Mark Gamsa, *Harbin: A Cross-Cultural Biography* (Toronto: University of Toronto Press, 2020).

7. Vladislav Khodasevich, "Vse kamennoe, v kamennyi prolet . . . ," in *Sobranie sochinenii v chetyrekh tomakh*, ed. I. P. Andreeva et al., vol. 1 (Moscow: Soglasie, 1997),

266. The writer Boris Pilniak's short story "Tret'ia stolitsa," written upon the author's return from Berlin in 1923, was first published under the title "Mat'-machekha," meaning "coltsfoot flower" but also translating literally as "mother-stepmother."

8. V. P. Adrianova-Peretts, ed., *Povest' vremennykh let: Chast' pervaia. Tekst i perevod* (Moscow: Izdatel'stvo Akademii nauk SSSR, 1950), 20.

9. Iaroslava Ananko, *Kanikuly Kaina: Poetika promezhutka v berlinskikh stikhakh V. F. Khodasevicha* (Moscow: Novoe literaturnoe obozrenie, 2020), 153.

10. Viktor Shklovsky, *Zoo, or Letters Not about Love*, trans. and ed. Richard Sheldon (Ithaca, NY: Cornell University Press, 1971), 136.

11. Vadim Andreev, *Istoriia odnogo puteshestviia* (Moscow: Sovetskii pisatel', 1974), 281.

12. See Oleg Budnitskii and Aleksandra Polian, *Russko-evreiskii Berlin, 1920–1941* (Moscow: Novoe literaturnoe obozrenie, 2013); Gennady Estraikh and Mikhail Krutikov, eds., *Yiddish in Weimar Berlin: At the Crossroads of Diaspora Politics and Culture* (London: Legenda, 2010); Verena Dohrn and Gertrud Pickhan, eds., *Transit und Transformation: Osteuropäisch-jüdische Migranten in Berlin, 1918–1939* (Göttingen: Wallstein Verlag, 2010); Verena Dohrn and Gertrud Pickhan, eds., *Berlin Transit: Jüdische Migranten aus Osteuropa in den 1920er Jahren* (Göttingen: Wallstein Verlag, 2012); Rachel Seelig, *Strangers in Berlin: Modern Jewish Literature between East and West, 1919–1933* (Ann Arbor: University of Michigan Press, 2016); Shachar M. Pinsker, *Literary Passports: The Making of Modernist Hebrew Fiction in Europe* (Stanford, CA: Stanford University Press, 2011), 105–45; Allison Schachter, *Diasporic Modernisms: Hebrew and Yiddish Literature in the Twentieth Century* (London: Oxford University Press, 2012), 84–119; Małgorzata Stolarska-Fronia, ed., *Polish Avant-Garde in Berlin* (Berlin: Peter Lang, 2019); Marc Caplan, *Yiddish Writers in Weimar Berlin: A Fugitive Modernism* (Bloomington: Indiana University Press, 2021).

13. Leonid Livak, *In Search of Russian Modernism* (Baltimore, MD: Johns Hopkins University Press, 2018), 114–17.

14. A landmark 1978 conference in Geneva was devoted to a single question: "One or Two Russian Literatures?" The volume of conference proceedings, which includes transcripts of debates, shows how contentious it was at the time to talk about Russian literature in the USSR and abroad as one. See Georges Nivat, ed., *Odna ili dve russkikh literatury? Mezhdunarodnyi simpozium, sozvannyi fakul'tetom slovesnosti Zhenevskogo universiteta i Shveitsarskoi akademiei slavistiki. Zheneva, 13-14-15 aprelia 1978* (Lausanne: L'Age D'Homme, 1978).

15. Gleb Struve, *Russkaia literatura v izgnanii: Opyt istoricheskogo obzora zarubezhnoi literatury*, 3rd ed. (Paris: YMCA-Press; Moscow: Russkii put', 1996), 32–35. Frank Boldt, Dmitry Segal, and Lazar Fleishman proposed viewing twentieth-century Russian literature as a master system subdivided into two subsystems—Soviet and émigré—though they acknowledge that this division was not definitive in Berlin in 1921–23; see Frank Bol'dt, Dmitrii Segal, and Lazar' Fleishman, "Problemy izucheniia russkoi literatury pervoi treti XX veka," *Slavica Hierosolymitana* 3 (1978): 75–88.

16. Quoted in Donald A. Lowrie, *Rebellious Prophet: A Life of Nicolai Berdyaev* (New York: Harper & Brothers, 1960), 167.

17. See Pasternak's 1923 poem "Gleisdreieck"; Tsvetaeva's 1922 poem "Berlinu" ("To Berlin"); Shklovsky's 1923 novel *Zoo, or Letters Not about Love*; Chagall's interview with Edouard Roditi; and Nabokov's 1928 novel *King, Queen, Knave*; as well as Khodasevich's Berlin poems from his *European Night*.

18. Raymond Williams, "When Was Modernism?," in *The Politics of Modernism: Against the New Conformists*, ed. Tony Pinkney (London: Verso, 1989), 34.

19. Shklovsky, *Zoo*, 63.

20. Compare Shklovsky's text and Ivan Bunin's 1924 Parisian speech "The Mission of Russian Emigration," in which Bunin drew on Biblical imagery to emphasize the historical righteousness of (Orthodox Christian) émigrés, whose purpose in exile was to preserve the spirit of genuine Russianness. See Ivan Bunin, "Missiia russkoi emigratsii: Rech', proiznesennaia v Parizhe 16 fevralia," *Rul'*, April 3, 1924, 5–6. Maria Rubins notes that, in general, "exile (*izgnanie*) was a preferred definition that circulated in extraterritorial Russian publications practically throughout the entire Soviet period (along with Russia Abroad (*Russkoe Zarubezh'e*), emigration and scattering (*rasseianie*)), while diaspora has been used very infrequently, perhaps because of its lack of romantic pathos." Rubins, *Redefining Russian Literary Diaspora*, 11.

21. For an account of radical political émigrés before 1917, see Faith Hillis, *Utopia's Discontents: Russian Émigrés and the Quest for Freedom, 1830s–1930s* (Oxford, UK: Oxford University Press, 2021).

22. For the uses of the word "émigré," see S. I. Levin, "Polozhenie russkikh emigrantov v Germanii," *Rul'*, August 2, 1922; O. Färber, "Die russischen Emigranten und wir," *Allgemeine Rundschau*, April 8, 1922, 162; "Emigranten-Cabarett," *Das Kulturblatt*, no. 12 (1922): 539; and Ernst Drahn, "Russische Emigration: Eine kulturstatistische Studie," *Zeitschrift für die gesamte Staatswissenschaft* 89, no. 1 (1930): 124–30.

23. The difference between exiles and émigrés is not unlike the difference between refugees and migrants. As with most binaries, the refugee/migrant opposition can be problematic as it does not capture the complexity of circumstances necessitating one's move abroad. Rebecca Hamlin has proposed rethinking this binary and using the term "border crosser" instead. See Hamlin, *Crossing: How We Label and React to People on the Move* (Stanford, CA: Stanford University Press, 2021).

24. In her *The Origins of Totalitarianism* (1951), Arendt included the Armenian and Assyro-Chaldean refugees in the "aristocracy" category as well. See Mira L. Siegelberg, *Statelessness: A Modern History* (Cambridge, MA: Harvard University Press, 2019), 259n65.

25. See Fritz Mierau, ed., *Russen in Berlin: Literatur, Malerei, Theater, Film, 1918–1933* (Leipzig: Reclam, 1987), v; Karl Schlögel, *Das russische Berlin*, new and expanded edition (Berlin: Suhrkamp, 2019), 149.

26. According to Thomas Beyer's calculations, 471 Russian books appeared in Berlin in 1922 and 667 the following year. See his "Russkii Berlin. Ekspatriatsiia? Izgnanie? Emigratsiia?," *Diapazon* 1 (1993): 65. See also Thomas R. Beyer et al., *Russische Autoren und Verlage in Berlin nach dem Ersten Weltkrieg* (Berlin: Verlag Arno Spitz, 1987); Sergei Ippolitov and Almaziia Kataeva, *Ne mogu otorvat'sia ot Rossii: Russkie knigoizdateli v Germanii v 1920-kh gg.* (Moscow: Izdatel'stvo Ippolitova, 2000); Schlögel, *Das russische*

Berlin, 182–87; and Nadezhda A. Egorova, ed., *Zolotoi vek rossiiskogo knigoizdaniia v Germanii* (Moscow: Dom russkogo zarubezh'ia im. A. S. Solzhenitsyna, 2013).

27. Nicolas Nabokov, *Bagázh: Memoirs of a Russian Cosmopolitan* (New York: Atheneum, 1975), 124–32. On Esenin and Duncan in Berlin in 1922, see also Natal'ia Krandievskaia-Tolstaia, *Vospominaniia* (Leningrad: Lenizdat, 1977), 195–203.

28. See the interview with Lourié in *Spurensicherung: Rußland an der Spree*, dir. Doris Liebermann and Dennis Weiler (1987; Berlin: Rundfunk Berlin-Brandenburg), Persönlicher Archivbestand Doris Liebermann, Robert Havemann Gesellschaft, Berlin.

29. On Tsvetaeva and Vishniak, see Mina Polianskaia, *Florentiiskie nochi v Berline: Tsvetaeva, Leto 1922* (Moscow, Berlin: Golos-Press, Gelikon), 135–74.

30. On Berlin's café culture, see Shachar M. Pinsker, *A Rich Brew: How Cafés Created Modern Jewish Culture* (New York: New York University Press, 2018), 142–85.

31. Edouard Roditi, "Entretien avec Marc Chagall," *Preuves: Cahiers mensuels du Congrès pour la liberté de la culture* 84 (1958): 27.

32. Roditi, "Entretien avec Marc Chagall," 27.

33. Dovid Bergelson, "Among Refugees," in *The Shadows of Berlin*, trans. Joachim Neugroschel (San Francisco: City Lights Books, 2005), 21–43.

34. Leonid L. Škarenkov, "Eine Chronik der russischen Emigration in Deutschland: Die Materialien des Generals Aleksej A. von Lampe," in *Russische Emigration in Deutschland, 1918 bis 1941: Leben im europäischen Bürgerkrieg*, ed. Karl Schlögel (Berlin: Akademie Verlag, 1995), 70. Quoted in Lesley Chamberlain, *The Philosophy Steamer: Lenin and the Exile of the Intelligentsia* (London: Atlantic Books, 2006), 204–5.

35. Pavel Tchelitchew Collection, box 2, folder 228, Yale Collection of American Literature, Beinecke Rare Book and Manuscript Library.

36. Robert Harold Johnston, *New Mecca, New Babylon: Paris and the Russian Exiles, 1920–1945* (Montreal: McGill-Queen's University Press, 1988); Livak, *How It Was Done in Paris*; Greta Slobin, *Russians Abroad: Literary and Cultural Politics of Diaspora, 1919–1939*, ed. Dan Isaac Slobin et al. (Boston: Academic Studies Press, 2013); Leonid Livak and Andrei Ustinov, eds., *Literaturnyi avangard russkogo Parizha: Istoriia, khronika, antologiia, dokumenty, 1920–1926* (Moscow: OGI, 2014); and Rubins, *Russian Montparnasse*.

37. Raymond Williams, *The Politics of Modernism*, 44–45.

38. Peter Gay, *Weimar Culture: The Outsider as Insider* (New York: Harper & Row, 1968), 1.

39. Roman Gul', *Zhizn' na fuksa* (Moscow: Gosizdat, 1927), 133–34. UFA, or Universum-Film Aktiengesellschaft, was a major German motion-picture production company based in Berlin.

40. See Chamberlain, *The Philosophy Steamer*.

41. See Lazar' Fleishman, "Vysylka intelligentsii i Russkii Berlin v 1922 g.," in *Russkii Berlin, 1920–1945: Mezhdunarodnaia konferentsiia, 16–18 dekabria 2002 g.*, ed. Lazar' Fleishman (Moscow: Russkii put', 2006), 98, 104.

42. Hilde Hardeman, *Coming to Terms with the Soviet Regime: The "Changing Landmarks" Movement among Russian Émigrés in the Early 1920s* (DeKalb: Northern Illinois University Press, 1994), 137–75.

43. The Change of Landmarks originated as a genuine initiative among younger émigrés but was ultimately subsumed by Soviet interests. For an example of the Soviet secret police's nefarious operations abroad, see Lazar' Fleishman, *V tiskakh provokatsii: Operatsiia "Trest" i russkaia zarubezhnaia pechat'* (Moscow: Novoe literaturnoe obozrenie, 2003).

44. Tolstoy infamously published a private letter from Korney Chukovsky in *On the Eve*—without Chukovsky's consent—that exposed the many tensions building among writers inside and outside Russia. See Lazar Fleishman, Robert Hughes, and Olga Raevsky-Hughes, eds., *Russkii Berlin, 1921–1923* (Paris: YMCA-Press, 1983), 31–46.

45. Quoted in Robert C. Williams, "'Changing Landmarks' in Russian Berlin, 1922–1924," *Slavic Review* 27, no. 4 (1968): 592.

46. Particularly scandalous was the publisher Evgeny Lundberg's decision to burn in 1921 the entire print run of the short book *What Is Russian Bolshevism* because he disagreed with its contents. That the book's author was his friend and mentor Lev Shestov made the book burning all the more symbolic of Russian Berlin's paradoxical nature. See Fleishman, Hughes, and Raevsky-Hughes, *Russkii Berlin, 1921–1923*, 28–30.

47. Ewa Berard, "The 'First Exhibition of Russian Art' in Berlin: The Transnational Origins of Bolshevik Cultural Diplomacy, 1921–1922," *Contemporary European History* 30 (2021): 164–80; and Horst Richter, "Erste Russische Kunstausstellung: Berlin 1922," in *Die Russen in Berlin, 1910–1930* (Berlin: Galerie Stolz, 1995), 52–61.

48. Anatolii Lunacharskii, "Russkaia vystavka v Berline," *Izvestiia VTsIK*, December 2, 1922.

49. Gul', *Zhizn' na fuksa*, 267.

50. See Roman Gul', *Ia unes Rossiiu: Apologiia emigratsii*, vol. 1, *Rossiia v Germanii* (New York: Most, 1984). Volumes 2 and 3 are devoted to Gul's life in France and the United States, respectively.

51. By convention, "Russian" emigration is divided into four waves, though such a division is imprecise and neglects prerevolutionary migration out of the Russian Empire. According to the four-wave schema, the first wave occurs after the 1917 revolutions; the second wave consists mainly of persons displaced by World War II; the third wave takes place in the 1970s and late 1980s as Soviet Jews and some other ethnic minorities leave the country; and the fourth wave follows the collapse of the Soviet Union in 1991. See Maria Rubins, "A Century of Russian Culture(s) 'Abroad': The Unfolding of Literary Geography," in *Global Russian Cultures*, ed. Kevin M. F. Platt (Madison: University of Wisconsin Press, 2019), 21–47; and Oleg Budnitskii, *Drugaia Rossiia: Issledovaniia po istorii russkoi emigratsii* (Moscow: Novoe literaturnoe obozrenie, 2021), 12–45.

52. See Elena Liessner-Blomberg et al., eds., *Elena Liessner-Blomberg, oder die Geschichte vom Blauen Vogel* (Berlin: Buchverlag Der Morgen, 1978).

53. The Blue Bird's programs and advertisement catalogs, for example, were printed on expensive paper and in full color—only in German. See also Alexandre Vassiliev, *Beauty in Exile: The Artists, Models, and Nobility Who Fled the Russian Revolution and Influenced the World of Fashion*, trans. Antonina W. Bouis and Anya Kucharev (New York: Harry N. Abrams, 2000).

54. Gottfried Benn, *Doppelleben* (Munich: Deutscher Taschenbuch Verlag, 1967), 40; Hans Richter, *Köpfe und Hinterköpfe* (Zürich: Arche, 1967). Relatedly, Vladimir Nabokov wrote that his British peers at Cambridge were captivated by the Great Experiment taking place in young Soviet Russia. See his *Speak, Memory: An Autobiography Revisited* (New York: Knopf, 1999), 261–64. Nevertheless, one of the first scholarly discussions of "fugitive Russian authors" is found in a 1924 German history of Russian literature. See Arthur Luther, *Geschichte der russischen Literatur* (Leipzig: Bibliographisches Institut, 1924). See also Alexander Eliasberg, *Russische Literaturgeschichte in Einzelporträts* (Munich: Oskar Beck, 1922). It should also be noted that Berlin stage and screen stars like Olga Chekhova (Tschechowa), Elsa Krueger, and Tatjana Gsovsky remained popular with German audiences.

55. See Zenzinov Papers, "Postcards and Letters to A. Fondaminsky," Amherst Center for Russian Culture.

56. See Sergei Tretiakov, *Liudi odnogo kostra: Literaturnye portrety* (Moscow: Khudozhestvennaia literatura, 1936).

57. The post-Soviet art exhibition *Berlin/Moskau Moskva/ Berlin, 1900–1950*, co-organized by the Berlinische Galerie and the Pushkin State Museum of Fine Arts, left the impression that the Russian community in Berlin consisted of Soviet cultural producers temporarily residing in Germany. See Irina Antonova and Jörn Merkert, eds., *Berlin/Moskau Moskva/Berlin, 1900–1950* (Munich: Prestel, 1995). The monumental 2012 show *Russians and Germans: 1000 Years of History, Art, and Culture* avoided altogether using words like "exile" and "emigration" and, with the exception of one drawing by Alexey Remizov, highlighted the work of several writers who chose to return from Berlin to the Soviet Union: Alexey Tolstoy, Ivan Sokolov-Mikitov, Nikolai Nikitin, and Andrei Bely. See Aleksandr Lavrent'ev and Heino Neumayer, eds., *Russkie i nemtsy: 1000 let istorii, iskusstva i kul'tury* (Moscow, Berlin: Michael Imhof Verlag, 2012). A catalog of a related exhibition edited by Olga Medvedko, *Nikolai Zagrekov i Russkii Berlin* (Moscow: M-Skanrus, 2013), opens with a greeting from the Minister of Culture, Vladimir Medinsky, who chooses to use the word "compatriots" (sootechestvenniki) instead of "émigrés." The catalog closes with a reproduction of the last chapter of Shklovsky's novel *Zoo*—Letter to the All-Russian Central Committee—in which the author emphatically begs the authorities to allow him to return because he cannot bear living in Berlin, away from Russia.

58. Z. S. Pyshnovskaia and U. Kukhirt, eds., *Vzaimosviazi russkogo i sovetskogo iskusstva i nemetskoi khudozhestvennoi kul'tury* (Moscow: Nauka, 1980).

59. Simon Karlinsky, "Foreword: Who Are the Émigré Writers?," *TriQuarterly* 27 (1973): 5–9. *TriQuarterly* volumes 27 and 28 were subtitled "Russian Literature and Culture in the West, 1922–1972" and later republished as *The Bitter Air of Exile: Russian Writers and the West, 1922–1972*, ed. Simon Karlinsky and Alfred Appel Jr. (Berkeley: University of California Press, 1977).

60. Contemporary Russian studies of Russian Berlin include Artem Lysenko, *Golos izgnaniia: Stanovlenie gazet russkogo Berlina i ikh evoliutsiia v 1919–1922 gg.* (Moscow: Russkaia kniga, 2000); Vera Sorokina, *Literaturnaia kritika russkogo Berlina 20-kh godov XX veka* (Moscow: Izdatel'stvo Moskovskogo universiteta, 2010); and Galina

Time, *Puteshestvie Moskva-Berlin-Moskva: Russkii vzgliad Drugogo, 1919–1939* (Moscow: Rosspen, 2011).

61. Klaus Kändler, Helga Karolewski, and Ilse Siebert, eds., *Berliner Begegnungen: Ausländische Künstler in Berlin 1918 bis 1933* (Berlin: Dietz Verlag, 1987).

62. Eberhard Steneberg, *Russische Kunst Berlin 1919–1932* (Berlin: Gebr. Mann Verlag, 1969).

63. The first edition of Schlögel's book was titled *Berlin, Ostbahnhof Europas: Russen und Deutsche in ihrem Jahrhundert* (Berlin: Siedler Verlag, 1998), but the title of the 2019 expanded edition was changed to *Das russische Berlin*. See also Michaela Böhmig, *Das russische Theater in Berlin, 1919–1931* (Munich: Verlag Otto Sagner in Kommission, 1990); Amory Burchard and Ljudmila Duwidowitsch, eds., *Das russische Berlin* (Berlin: Die Ausländerbeauftragte des Senats, 1994); Karl Schlögel, ed., *Russische Emigration in Deutschland, 1918 bis 1941*; Amory Burchard, *Klubs der russischen Dichter in Berlin, 1920–1941: Institutionen des literarischen Lebens im Exil* (Munich: Verlag Otto Sagner in Kommission, 2001); and Thomas Urban, *Russische Schriftsteller in Berlin der zwanziger Jahre* (Berlin: Nicolai, 2003).

64. Boris Pasternak, *Polnoe sobranie sochinenii s prilozheniiami v odinnadtsati tomakh*, ed. E. V. Pasternak and M. A. Rashkovskaia, vol. 7 (Moscow: Slovo, 2005), 444; Il'ia Erenburg, *Viza vremeni* (Berlin: Petropolis, 1930), 7.

65. Belyi, *Odna iz obitelei tsarstva tenei*, 33.

66. Nina Berberova, *The Italics Are Mine*, trans. Philippe Radley (New York: Knopf, 1992), 165.

67. Vladimir Nabokov, *Mashen'ka* (Berlin: Knigoizdatel'stvo Slovo, 1926); Nabokov, *Speak, Memory*, 276. Vadim Andreev wrote, "the two cities, one German and one Russian, like water and oil poured into the same container did not mix with each other." "Vozvrashchenie v zhizn'," *Zvezda* 5 (1969): 121.

68. Luke Parker, "The Shop Window Quality of Things: 1920s Weimar Surface Culture in Nabokov's *Korol', dama, valet*," *Slavic Review* 77, no. 2 (2018): 390–416; and his *Nabokov Noir: Cinematic Culture and the Art of Exile* (Ithaca, NY: Cornell University Press, 2022).

69. Raymond Williams, *Visions and Blueprints: Avant-garde Culture and Radical Politics in Early Twentieth-Century Europe*, ed. Edward Timms and Peter Collier (Manchester: Manchester University Press, 1988), 59.

70. Alexander Betts and Will Jones, *Mobilising the Diaspora: How Refugees Challenge Authoritarianism* (Cambridge: Cambridge University Press, 2016), 8; Zainab Saleh, *Return to Ruin: Iraqi Narratives of Exile and Nostalgia* (Stanford, CA: Stanford University Press, 2020).

71. Brent Hayes Edwards, "The Uses of Diaspora," *Social Text* 19, no. 1 (Spring 2001): 64.

CHAPTER 1. UNSENTIMENTAL JOURNEYS

1. Il'ia Erenburg and El Lissitzky, "Blokada Rossii konchaetsia," *Veshch'/Gegenstand/Objet: Mezhdunarodnoe obozrenie sovremennogo iskusstva*, no. 1–2 (1922): 1–4.

2. The original "window onto Europe" being St. Petersburg.

3. See Bol'dt, Segal, and Fleishman, "Problemy izucheniia russkoi literatury pervoi treti XX veka," 84.

4. See Ben Dhooge, "Constructive Art à la Ehrenburg: Vesc-Gegenstand-Objet," *Neohelicon* 42, no. 2 (2015): 493–527; Christina Lodder, "El Lissitzky and the Export of Constructivism," in *Situating El Lissitzky: Vitebsk, Berlin, Moscow*, ed. Nancy Perloff and Brian Reed (Los Angeles, CA: Getty Research Institute, 2003), 27–46; and Kristin Romberg, *Gan's Constructivism: Aesthetic Theory for an Embedded Modernism* (Berkeley: University of California Press, 2018), 124–25.

5. In Berlin Ehrenburg and Lissitzky also collaborated on Ehrenburg's book *Six Tales of Easy Endings*, which was illustrated by Lissitzky. See Il'ia Erenburg, *Shest' povestei o legkikh kontsakh* (Berlin: Gelikon, 1922).

6. Susanne Marten-Finnis has observed that while the Berlin publishing house that produced *Firebird*, Russkoe iskusstvo, relied on the labor and expertise of émigré Russian artists and art historians, functionally it was a Soviet publisher. Moreover, *Firebird* was meant to generate income "to boost Soviet book production." See Marten-Finnis, *Der Feuervogel als Kunstzeitschrift: Žar Ptica. Russische Bildwelten in Berlin, 1921–1926* (Vienna: Böhlau Verlag, 2012), 46, 57, 160–61.

7. See Schlögel, *Russische Emigration in Deutschland 1918–1945*; Fleishman, Hughes, and Raevsky-Hughes, *Russkii Berlin, 1921–1923*, 9–67; Struve, *Russkaia literatura v izgnanii*.

8. Berlin offered an unmediated experience of life in a similarly post-imperial democratic republic. Like Soviet Russia, the Weimar Republic was the result of a socialist revolution, albeit a failed one.

9. Fedor Ivanov, *Krasnyi Parnas: Literaturno-kriticheskie ocherki* (Berlin: Russkoe universal'noe izdatel'stvo, 1922), 7.

10. Yuri Tynianov, "Interlude," in *Permanent Evolution: Selected Essays on Literature, Theory, and Film*, trans. and ed. Ainsley Morse and Philip Redko (Boston, MA: Academic Studies Press, 2019), 175.

11. See, for example, such accounts of Russian cultural history as W. Bruce Lincoln, *Between Heaven and Hell: The Story of a Thousand Years of Artistic Life in Russia* (New York: Viking, 1998), 361–89; and Orlando Figes, *Natasha's Dance: A Cultural History of Russia* (New York: Metropolitan Books, 2002), 523–86.

12. Tynianov, *Permanent Evolution*, 216.

13. Ananko, *Kanikuly Kaina*, 15. Ananko applies Tynianov's concept to her examination of Khodasevich's poetry from Berlin. Ananko and I developed our approaches to this period through the prism of Tynianov's "Interlude" independently of each other.

14. This moment could also be understood in terms of the opposition of avant-garde time and vanguard time as conceptualized by Susan Buck-Morss in her *Dreamworld and Catastrophe: The Passing of Mass Utopia in East and West* (Cambridge, MA: MIT Press, 2000), 42–69.

15. Evgenii B. Pasternak, *Boris Pasternak: Biografiia* (Moscow: Tsitadel', 1997), 345–63.

16. These poems are "Babochka-buria" ("The Butterfly-Tempest"), "Otplyt'e" ("Sailing Away"), "Nastuplenie zimy" ("Arrival of Winter"), "Sed'moi etazh" ("The

Seventh Floor"), "Petukhi" ("Roosters"), "Osen'" ("Autumn"), "Bodrost'" ("Vigor"), "Perelet" ("Flying Across"), "Morskoi shtil'" ("Calm Sea"), "Stikhotvoren'e" ("A Poem"), and "Gleisdreieck." Valentin Belentschikow, who has dedicated a short monograph to Pasternak's Berlin poems, argues that they can be read as a cycle. See his *Zur Poetik Boris Pasternaks: Der Berliner Gedichtzyklus, 1922–1923* (Frankfurt am Main: Peter Lang, 1998), 47–52. Belentschikow's study is mainly concerned with formal characteristics of the poems on the levels of vocabulary, phonetics, and syntax; he provides interpretative remarks on two poems, "Stikhotvoren'e" and "Bodrost'."

17. For commentary on these debates, see Vladimir Markov, *Russian Futurism: A History* (Berkeley: University of California Press, 1968), 231, 382; Raeff, *Russia Abroad*, 73–117; Sorokina, *Literaturnaia kritika Russkogo Berlina*, 109–85; and John E. Malmstad, "Edinstvo protivopolozhnostei: Istoriia vzaimootnoshenii Khodasevicha i Pasternaka," *Literaturnoe obozrenie* 2 (1990): 51–59.

18. Lazar' Fleishman, *Boris Pasternak v dvadtsatye gody* (Munich: Wilhelm Fink Verlag, 1980), 14. Pasternak's poems appeared in such Berlin publications as *Poetry of the Bolshevik Days* and *Poetry of Revolutionary Moscow*, as well as in *Veshch'*—all thanks to Ehrenburg's efforts to promote Pasternak as the leading poet of his generation. Ehrenburg also included a selection of Pasternak's poems and a brief introductory essay about him in the popular anthology *Portrety russkikh poetov*, ed. Il'ia Erenburg (Berlin: Argonavty, 1922), 127–36.

19. On Pasternak and state-sponsored ideology, see Olga R. Hughes, *The Poetic World of Boris Pasternak* (Princeton, NJ: Princeton University Press, 1974), 128–67; and Catherine Ciepiela, *The Same Solitude: Boris Pasternak and Marina Tsvetaeva* (Ithaca, NY: Cornell University Press, 2007), 131–77. Molly Thomasy Blasing offers an illuminating account of Pasternak's transition from acute lyricism to the historical epic by focusing on his engagement with the photographic. See her *Snapshots of the Soul: Photo-Poetic Encounters in Modern Russian Culture* (Ithaca, NY: Cornell University Press, 2021), 68–78.

20. Fleishman, *Pasternak v dvadtsatye gody*, 25.

21. Fleishman, *Pasternak v dvadtsatye gody*, 26.

22. Boris Pasternak, *Polnoe sobranie sochinenii*, vol. 7, 418.

23. Josephine Pasternak, *Tightrope Walking: A Memoir*, ed. Helen Ramsay and Rimgailia Salys (Bloomington, IN: Slavica Publishers, 2005), 167.

24. Josephine Pasternak, *Tightrope Walking*, 169. A number of Pasternak's contemporaries, Boris Zaitsev, Zinovy Arbatov, and Elena Kannak among them, also suggested that in Berlin he was trying to decide whether to return to Russia or not. Zinovii Arbatov, "'Nollendorfplatskafe': Literaturnaia mozaika," in *Russkii Berlin*, ed. Vera V. Sorokina (Moscow: Izdatel'stvo Moskovskogo universiteta, 2003), 162; Kannak, *Vernost': Vospominaniia, rasskazy, ocherki* (Paris: YMCA-Press, 1992), 233; Boris K. Zaitsev, *Sochineniia v trekh tomakh*, ed. E. Voropaeva and A. Tarkhov, vol. 3 (Moscow: Khudozhestvennaia literatura—Terra, 1993), 414–22.

25. Boris Pasternak, *Polnoe sobranie sochinenii*, vol. 7, 438. The critic Boris Zaitsev wrote about Pasternak's "highly artistic and genuinely cubist unintelligibility." Boris Pasternak, *Polnoe sobranie sochinenii*, vol. 7, 438. The major exception to negative criticism is Tsvetaeva's famous essay "Svetovoi liven'."

26. In a letter to Sergey Bobrov he complained about one newspaper in which reviews of his poetry were printed under the heading "Explorations," right next to the rubric "Achievements" with responses to Khodasevich's books. Boris Pasternak, *Polnoe sobranie sochinenii*, vol. 7, 438. The review itself can be found in Kirill Kirillov and Vera Lur'e, "Puti poezii: Iskaniia. Dostizheniia," *Dni* January 14, 1923, 15.

27. The only exception to this rule is Pasternak's poem "Matros v Moskve" ("A Sailor in Moscow"), which appeared in the journal *Strugi* in 1923. See Fleishman, *Pasternak v dvadtsatye gody*, 17.

28. For example, in a letter to his brother Alexander of November 24, 1923, he writes, "We like living here and I am satisfied with Berlin insofar as it's a place where I can again spend time in *such a way*, and maybe I'll become myself again here." In a letter to V. P. Polonsky of January 10, 1923, he writes: "Recently I feel like the sparkles have returned to my eyes after five years of absence. Until this recent joy I wanted to go home more than once. But now I'll wait." Boris Pasternak, *Polnoe sobranie sochinenii*, vol. 7, 418, 430. But then Pasternak dubs Berlin an "impersonal Babylon" in a postcard to Sergey Bobrov from Marburg on February 11, 1923. M. A. Rashkovskaia, ed., *Boris Pasternak i Sergei Bobrov: Pis'ma chetyrekh desiatiletii* (Stanford, CA: Department of Slavic Languages and Literatures, Stanford University, 1996), 135. However, in his letters to Bobrov of December 15, January 17, and February 27, 1923, he writes about Berlin's economic and technological achievements and advantages.

29. I analyze these poems in their original Berlin versions.

30. Ivanov examined the poem in his "Razyskaniia o poetike Pasternaka: Ot buri k babochke," in Viacheslav Vsevolodovich Ivanov, *Izbrannye trudy po semiotike i istorii kul'tury*, vol. 1 (Moscow: Iazyki russkoi kul'tury, 1999), 15–141.

31. See "Tak nachinaiut. Goda v dva" ("They so begin. At around age two," 1921), "Opredelenie poezii" ("The Definition of Poetry"), "Poeziia" ("Poetry"), and "Kosykh kartnin, letiashchikh livmia" ("Slanted pictures, flying pouring," all in 1922). See also *The Marsh of Gold: Pasternak's Writings on Inspiration and Creation*, ed. Angela Livingstone (Boston, MA: Academic Studies Press, 2008).

32. Ivanov discusses many aspects of this poem, from Pasternak's allusions to Goethe, Innokenty Annensky, and Diego Velasquez to the peculiarities of insect metamorphosis, telegraphic communication, and the use of nominalized verbs. But he centers his analysis on the theme of a girl becoming a woman (as in a cocoon becoming a butterfly).

33. Incidentally, in a 1921 poem Mayakovsky turns to this street to criticize the Soviet ambition of transforming the world by describing the sad reality of dilapidated Miasnitskaia. The street also appears in Pushkin's poem "Dorozhnye zhaloby" ("Travel Complaints," 1824), in which the poet laments being far away from his friends who live there.

34. Ivanov, "Ot buri k babochke," 30.

35. Boris Pasternak, *Polnoe sobranie sochinenii*, vol. 1, 220.

36. See Katherine Tiernan O'Connor, *Boris Pasternak's "My Sister—Life": The Illusion of Narrative* (Ann Arbor, MI: Ardis Publishers, 1988). On the topoi of the road, see Olga R. Hughes, *The Poetic World*, 7–41; and Iurii Lotman, "Stikhotvoreniia rannego Pasternaka: Nekotorye voprosy strukturnogo izucheniia teksta," in *O poetakh i poezii* (St. Petersburg: Isskustvo SPb, 1996), 713–17.

37. Compare to Gumilev's poem: "Сердце—улей, полный сотами, / Золотыми, несравненными! / Я борюсь с водоворотами / И клокочущими пенами" (The heart is a beehive full of honeycomb, / golden and incomparable! / I battle the maelstroms / and seething foam). Nikolai Gumilev, *Stikhotvoreniia i poemy* (Leningrad: Sovetskii pisatel', 1988), 149. The meter of Gumilev's poem also reads as a reversal of Alexander Blok's "The Unknown Woman" (1906).

38. See Aleksandr Zholkovskii, "Ekstaticheskie motivy Pasternaka v svete ego lichnoi mifologii," in *Boris Pasternak 1890–1990*, ed. Lev Losev (Northfield, VT: Russian School of Norwich University, 1991), 52–74; and Jerzy Faryno, *Poetika Pasternaka: "Putevye zapiski" i "Okhrannaia gramota"* (Vienna: Gesellschaft für Förderung slawistischer Studien, 1989).

39. In a 1929 edition of *Poverkh bar'erov*, Pasternak changes the "sea" to "sky."

40. Boris Pasternak, *Polnoe sobranie sochinenii*, vol. 1, 221.

41. See Vladimir Nabokov, "A Guide to Berlin," in *Details of a Sunset and Other Stories* (New York: McGraw-Hill, 1976), 96; Vladislav Khodasevich, "Atlantida," in his *Sobranie sochinenii v chetyrekh tomakh*, vol. 3, 116–18; Vladimir Korvin-Piotrovskii, *Atlantida pod vodoi* (Berlin: Polyglotte, 1928); Georgii Golokhvastov, *Gibel' Atlantidy: Stikhotvoreniia. Poema* (Moscow: Vodolei Publishers, 2008).

42. See Katerina Clark, *Petersburg: The Crucible of Cultural Revolution* (Cambridge, MA: Harvard University Press, 1995), 183–84.

43. Il'ia Erenburg, *Liudi, gody, zhizn': Knigi pervaia, vtoraia, tret'ia*, ed. Boris Frezinskii (Moscow: Tekst, 2005), 424.

44. "Потоп кончается. Звери выходят из своих ковчегов . . ." Viktor Shklovskii, "Pis'mo k Romanu Iakobsonu," *Veshch'/Gegenstand/Objet*, no. 1–2 (1922): 5.

45. His acquaintance Shklovsky wrote in *Zoo, or Letters Not about Love* (1923) that Pasternak appeared anxious (trevozhnyi) on the streets of Berlin, adding, "he feels the lack of propulsion among us [émigrés]." Shklovsky, *Zoo*, 63.

46. See, for example, the lines in the poem "Klevetnikam" ("To the Slanderers," 1917): "О детство! Ковш душевной глуби!" (O childhood! A dipper of soul's depth!). Boris Pasternak, *Polnoe sobranie sochinenii*, vol. 1, 186.

47. Kannak, *Vernost'*, 232. See also Shklovsky, *Zoo*, 67–68; Joseph Roth, *What I Saw: Reports from Berlin, 1920–1933*, trans. Michael Hofmann (New York: Norton, 2003), 105–8.

48. Boris Pasternak, *Polnoe sobranie sochinenii*, vol. 2, 232. On Pasternak's use of montage in poetry, see Kirill Taranovskii, "O poetike Borisa Pasternaka," in *O poetakh i poezii* (Moscow: Iazyki russkoi kultury, 2000), 213.

49. Kannak, *Vernost'*, 232.

50. Aleksandr Dolinin, "'The Stepmother of Russian Cities': Berlin of the 1920s through the Eyes of Russian Writers," in *Cold Fusion: Aspects of the German Cultural Presence in Russia*, ed. Gennady Barabtarlo (New York: Berghahn, 2000), 234.

51. Matthias Freise and Britta Korkowsky, "Drei Gleisdreiecke: Boris Pasternak, Viktor Shklovskii, and Joseph Roth sehen Berlin," *Germanoslavica: Zeitschrift für germano-slawische Studien* 1 (2011): 1–8.

52. Pasternak was intimately familiar with old-world Germany, epitomized in the kitschy comfort of the Biedermeier style, because before the Great War he studied at the University of Marburg. See Valentin Belentschikow, "Boris Pasternak i Germaniia,

1906–1924: Berlin, Marburg i rannie nemetskie ekspressionisty v tvorchestve B. Pasternaka," *Zeitschrift für Slawistik* 32, no. 5 (1987): 728–43.

53. Freise and Korkowsky, "Drei Gleisdreiecke," 18.

54. Alexander Zholkovsky, "The Window in the Poetic World of Boris Pasternak," *New Literary History* 9 no. 2 (1978): 290–93.

55. Vadim Serov, *Entsiklopedicheskii slovar' krylatykh slov i vyrazhenii* (Moscow: Lokid-Press, 2003).

56. Timothy D. Sergay, "Boris Pasternak's 'Christmas Myth': Fedorov, Berdiaev, Dickens, Blok" (PhD diss., Yale University, 2008), 111–29.

57. Boris Pasternak, *Polnoe sobranie sochinenii*, vol. 2, 236–37.

58. Bengt Jangfeldt, *Stavka—zhizn': Vladimir Maiakovskii i ego krug*, trans. Asia Lavrusha and the author (Moscow: Kolibri, 2009), 181.

59. Jangfeldt, *Stavka—zhizn'*, 205.

60. The poetry contributions in the joint first and second issue of *Veshch'* were arranged in the following order: Mayakovsky, Pasternak, Charles Vildrac, Iwan [sic] Goll, Sergey Esenin, Jules Romains. The third and final issue featured poems by Mayakovsky, André Salmon, Nikolai Aseev, and Sergey Esenin. Poems by Blaise Cendrars, Marina Tsvetaeva, and Osip Mandelshtam were announced but never published.

61. In 1923, the poem was edited, named "Decree No. 2 of the Armies of the Arts," and included in Mayakovsky's *For the Voice* designed by Lissitzky, published in Berlin.

62. Vladimir Maiakovskii, *Dlia golosa* (Berlin: Lutze & Vogt, 1923), 39.

63. Robert C. Williams, *Culture in Exile*, 159–241.

64. Mayakovsky loathed the free market, and the introduction of NEP had a big impact on his ideological conflict with the state. In her memoirs, Lilia Brik commented on the leftists' market-phobia by saying that they were genuinely concerned about the prospect of bourgeois lifestyle returning along with white bread. See Lilia Brik, *Pristrastnye rasskazy*, ed. Ia. I. Groisman and I. Iu. Gens (Nizhnii Novgorod: Dekom, 2003), 75. On the avant-garde and anti-capitalism in the Soviet Union, see Clark, *Petersburg*, 1–53; 143–61. As one of Mayakovsky's contemporaries noted, "In Germany he acted as though he were on a propaganda tour in the USSR. No matter where he was invited he always presented his propaganda verses." See Charles Moser, "Mayakovsky's Unsentimental Journeys," *American Slavic and East European Review* 19, no. 1 (1960): 88.

65. In the 1918 version of the play, Mayakovsky's target was Paris, not Berlin.

66. Vladimir Maiakovskii, *Polnoe sobranie sochinenii v trinadtsati tomakh*, vol. 2 (Moscow: Gosudarstvennoe izdatel'stvo khudozhestvennoi literatury, 1956), 252.

67. Mayakovsky demonstratively does not pursue the Berlin/Sodom parallel that captivated the minds of so many other itinerant Berliners. See, for example, Ivan Goll's 1929 novel, *Sodom et Berlin: Roman* (Paris: Éditions Émile-Paul Frères, 1929), and Christopher Isherwood's 1976 memoir, *Christopher and His Kind: A Memoir 1929–1939* (New York: Farrar, Straus and Giroux, 2015).

68. Maiakovskii, *Polnoe sobranie sochinenii*, vol. 2, 251.

69. See, for example, his famous proclamation in *Oblako v shtanakh* (*A Cloud in Trousers*, 1914): "Я над всем, что сделано, / ставлю nihil" (upon everything that has gone before / I stamp *nihil*).

70. See Edward J. Brown, *Mayakovsky: A Poet in the Revolution* (Princeton, NJ: Princeton University Press, 1973), 190–204; Victor Erlich, *Modernism and Revolution: Russian Literature in Transition* (Cambridge, MA: Harvard University Press, 1994), 50–55; Aleksandr Fevral'skii, *Pervaia sovetskaia p'esa "Misteriia Buff"* (Moscow: Sovetskii pisatel', 1971); Roswitha Loew and Bella Tschistowa, eds., *Majakowski in Deutschland: Texte zur Rezeption, 1919–1930* (Berlin: Academie Verlag, 1986), 130–75; and Aleksandra Azarkh-Granovskaia, *Vospominaniia. Besedy s V. D. Duvakinym* (Moscow, Jerusalem: Mosty kul'tury, Gesharim, 2001), 38–47; and R. V. Ivanov-Razumnik, *Vladimir Maiakovskii ("misteriia" ili "buff")* (Berlin: Skify, 1922).

71. See J. Gumperz, "W. Majakowski: *Mysterium-Buff*: Zur Auffürung in deutscher Sprache in Moskau anläßlich des III. Kongresses," *Der Gegner: Blätter zur Kritik der Zeit* 2, no. 10/11 (1921): 404–5. Reprinted in Loew, *Majakowski in Deutschland*, 17–18.

72. In his comments on Mayakovsky's work of the early 1920s, Anatoly Lunacharsky writes, "the Party as such, the Communist Party, regards with hostility not only Mayakovsky's early works, but those in which he presents himself a trumpeter of Communism." Quoted in Jangfeldt, *Stavka—zhizn'*, 181. In the 1920s, Mayakovsky visited Latvia, Estonia, Germany, France (where he attended the funeral of Marcel Proust in 1922), Cuba, Mexico, and the USA. He visited Germany every year from 1922 to 1929, except for 1926. See Vasilii Katanian, *Maiakovskii: Literaturnaia khronika* (Moscow: Gosudarstvennoe izdatel'stvo khudozhestvennoi literatury, 1961).

73. Wieland Herzfelde, "Mit Majakowski durch Berlin," in *Berliner Begegnungen: Ausländische Künstler in Berlin 1918 bis 1933*, ed. Klaus Kändler, Helga Karolewski, and Ilse Siebert (Berlin: Dietz Verlag, 1987), 39. Lilia Brik recorded a sample of Mayakovsky's untranslatable spoken German at a Berlin restaurant: "Их фюнф порцьон мелоне и фюнф порцьон компот. Их бин эйн руссишер дихтер, бекант им руссишем ланд, мне меньше нельзя" (I five portions melons and five portions compote. I am a Russian poet, famous in the Russian land, I can't have any less). Brik, *Pristrastnye rasskazy*, 75.

74. Loew, *Majakowski in Deutschland*, 139.

75. In addition to "Germaniia," Mayakovsky wrote a poem titled "Moscow to Königsberg" in Berlin in 1922.

76. Maiakovskii, *Polnoe sobranie sochinenii*, vol. 4, 49.

77. For example, even in Tsvetaeva's sympathetic poem "Berlinu" ("To Berlin," 1922), the city is represented as one big army barrack.

78. Mayakovsky was much more explicit on the topic in his travel reports "Chto delaet Berlin?" ("What Is Berlin Up To?" 1922) and "Segodniashnii Berlin" ("Today's Berlin" 1923).

79. Maiakovskii, *Polnoe sobranie sochinenii*, vol. 4, 50.

80. Edward J. Brown writes that during the first two years of the Great War, Mayakovsky "was caught up in the mighty wave of patriotic and anti-German fever that infected all levels of Russian society in [1914]"; he wrote patriotic jingles that portrayed Austrians and Germans as "repellent cartoon characters impaled on the bayonets or pitchforks of brave Russian soldiers defending the Slavic lands." *Mayakovsky: A Poet in the Revolution*, 109–10.

81. Arguably, he achieved this status after his death in 1930. See, for instance, Gustav von Wangenheim's 1935 poem "Majakowski in Berlin 1924": "He, / Mayakovsky, / a Soviet poet / and a Tribune of the People / of the International." See also "Majakowski" by Johannes R. Becher in *Sieg der Zukunft: Die Sowjetunion im Werk deutscher Schriftsteller*, ed. Alexander Abusch (Berlin: Aufbau Verlag, 1952), 47–51.

82. Maiakovskii, *Polnoe sobranie sochinenii*, vol. 4, 51.

83. Nordend is the Pankow borough; there is a street there named in the poet's honor, Majakowskiring. Ironically, the street was originally populated with villas for GDR officials.

84. The idea of claiming the luxury hotels on Unter den Linden for the proletariat may have stemmed from Mayakovsky's biographical experience: during all his visits to Berlin he stayed at the fashionable Kurfürstenhotel. See Brik, *Pristrastnye rasskazy*, 75. According to Brik, during his first trip to Berlin Mayakovsky, a compulsive gambler, did not see much of the city because he spent most of his time in the hotel obsessively playing cards.

85. The KPD (die Kommunistische Partei Deutschlands) garnered the support of 3,693,280 German voters, or 12.61 percent—a remarkable result for a party hindered by the failed November Revolution of 1918.

86. Maiakovskii, *Polnoe sobranie sochinenii*, vol. 6, 46.

87. Moscow was hailed by some Orthodox Slavs as the Third Rome since the Middle Ages. Katerina Clark writes on Soviet Moscow as a center of secular enlightenment in her *Moscow, The Fourth Rome: Stalinism, Cosmopolitanism, and Evolution of Soviet Culture* (Cambridge, MA: Harvard University Press, 2011).

88. Mayakovsky realizes in his poetry what Walter Benjamin would observe in a 1935/39 essay: "the *Communist Manifesto* brings [bourgeois flâneurs'] political existence to an end." Walter Benjamin, "Paris, the Capital of the Nineteenth Century," in *The Work of Art in the Age of Its Technological Reproducibility, and Other Writings on Media*, ed. Michael W. Jennings et al. (Cambridge, MA: Belknap Press of Harvard University Press, 2008). Also see Walter Benjamin, *The Arcades Project*, ed. Rolf Tiedemann, trans. Howard Eiland and Kevin McLaughlin (Cambridge, MA: Belknap Press of Harvard University Press, 1999), 10.

89. Maiakovskii, *Polnoe sobranie sochinenii*, vol. 6, 45.

90. Maiakovskii, *Polnoe sobranie sochinenii*, vol. 6, 46.

91. This is reminiscent of what Michel de Certeau describes in "Walking in the City." See his *The Practice of Everyday Life*, trans. Steven Rendall (Berkeley: University of California Press, 1984), 97–110. In his 1926 essay "How to Make Poems?" Mayakovsky will connect the experience of walking in the city with composing a poem's rhythmic pattern. See his *Polnoe sobranie sochinenii*, vol. 12, 100.

92. Maiakovskii, *Polnoe sobranie sochinenii*, vol. 6, 46.

93. Trips to Berlin inspired Mayakovsky to write one of his best long poems, *Pro eto* (*About That*, 1923).

94. "As one drives into Berlin, one is impressed by the cemetery-like silence. (Relatively speaking.) . . . Then you are not surprised, of course, that the streets gradually get dimmer, darker, and shrouded in death; grass starts to grow from under the

train tracks and punctuality, regularity of life gets disorganized." Maiakovskii, *Polnoe sobranie sochinenii*, vol. 4, 257.

95. Maiakovskii, *Polnoe sobranie sochinenii*, vol. 12, 466–67.

96. The summary appeared in the newspaper *Nakanune*, November 18, 1922. Reprinted in Katanian, *Maiakovskii*, 172.

97. Ilya Ehrenburg had similar concerns. See his article "Torzhestvuiushchii oboz" ("A Triumphant Wagon"), *Veshch'/Gegenstand/Objet*, no. 3 (1922): 2–3.

98. Dolinin, "The Stepmother of Russian Cities," 225–40.

99. Robert P. Hughes, "Khodasevich: Irony and Dislocation. A Poet in Exile," in *The Bitter Air of Exile*, ed. by Simon Karlinsky and Alfred Appel Jr. (Berkeley: University of California Press, 1977), 63.

100. Gleb Struve wrote that life in exile led Khodasevich to a "spiritual and poetic cul de sac." See David Bethea, *Khodasevich: His Life and Art* (Princeton, NJ: Princeton University Press, 1983), 254. See also Vladimir Nabokov, "On Khodasevich," in Karlinsky, *The Bitter Air of Exile*, 83–87.

101. Adrianova-Peretts, *Povest' vremennykh let*, 20. See the introduction for the historical contingencies of translating this phrase from Old Church Slavonic as the "mother of Russian cities" versus the "mother of the towns of Rus'."

102. Bethea, *Khodasevich*, 254. See also Nikolai A. Bogomolov, "Kak Khodasevich stanovilsia emigrantom," in *Sopriazhenie dalekovatykh: O Viacheslave Ivanove i Vladislave Khodaseviche* (Moscow: Izdatel'stvo Kulaginoi Intrada, 2011), 208–17; Pavel Uspenskij, "Vladislav Khodasevich in the Emigration: Literature and the Search for Identity," *Russian Review* 77 (2018): 88–108; and his "Kompositsiia *Evropeiskoi nochi* Khodasevicha: Kak emigratsiia opredelila strukturu sbornika?," *Russian Literature* 83–84 (2016): 91–111.

103. Vladislav Khodasevich, *Kamer-fur'erskii zhurnal* (Moscow: Ellis Lak, 2002). See also Boris Orekhov, Pavel Uspenskii, and Veronika Fainberg, "Tsifrovye podkhody k 'Kamer-fur'erskomu zhurnalu' V. F. Khodasevicha," *Russkaia literatura* 3 (2018): 19–53; Robert Hughes, "Belyi i Khodasevich: K istorii otnoshenii," *Vestnik russkogo khristianskogo dvizheniia* 151 (1987): 144–65; and John Malmstad, "Chodasevič and Belyj: A Parody Revisited," *Russian Literature* 83–84 (2016): 249–58.

104. Bethea, *Khodasevich*, 256–58.

105. Valerii Shubinksii, *Vladislav Khodasevich: Chaiushchii i govoriashchii* (St. Petersburg: Vita Nova, 2011), 453–87, 544.

106. Khodasevich, *Sobranie sochinenii v chetyrekh tomakh*, vol. 4, 447.

107. In a brief autobiography written in Berlin in 1922, Khodasevich stated: "Authentic literature is in Petersburg: Sologub, Akhmatova, Zamiatin, Kuzmin, Bely, Gumilev, Blok. The wonderful, lovely literary youth: The Serapion Brothers and the poetic circle called the Resonating Seashell." Vladislav Khodasevich, *Belyi koridor: Vospominaniia. Izbrannaia proza v dvukh tomakh*, ed. Iosif Brodskii, vol. 1 (New York: Serebrianyi vek, 1982), 11.

108. Khodasevich, *Belyi koridor*, 11.

109. Britannica Academic, s.v. "Extraterritoriality," accessed December 13, 2022, https://academic-eb-com.eu1.proxy.openathens.net/levels/collegiate/article/extraterritoriality/33469. See also Giorgio Agamben, *State of Exception*, trans. Kevin Attell (Chicago: University of Chicago Press, 2003).

110. See Matthew Hart and Tania Lown-Hecht, "The Extraterritorial Poetics of W. G. Sebald," *Modern Fiction Studies* 58, no. 2 (Summer 2012): 214–38.

111. George Steiner, *Extraterritorial: Papers on Literature and the Language Revolution* (New York: Atheneum, 1976), 3–11; and Michael Seidel, *Exile and Narrative Imagination* (New Haven, CT: Yale University Press, 1986). See also Galin Tihanov, "Narratives of Exile: Cosmopolitanism beyond the Liberal Imagination," in *Whose Cosmopolitanism? Critical Perspectives, Relationalities and Discontents*, ed. Nina Glick Schiller and Andrew Irving (New York: Berghahn, 2014), 141–59.

112. Slobin, *Russians Abroad*, 74–92. It can be said that Pasternak's "The Butterfly-Tempest" uses a similar photographic device, though in a less explicit manner.

113. Berberova, *The Italics Are Mine*, 214.

114. Michael Wachtel, "Vladislav Khodasevich as Innovator," in *Living through Literature: Essays in Memory of Omry Ronen*, ed. Julie Hansen, Karen Evans-Romaine, and Herbert Eagle (Uppsala: Uppsala University, 2019), 64. See also Rubins, "A Century of Russian Culture(s) 'Abroad,'" 31; Ananko, *Kanikuly Kaina*.

115. Tynianov, "Promezhutok," 172–73; Nikolai Aseev, "Po moriu bumazhnomu," *Krasnaia nov'* 4 (1922): 236–49.

116. Pavel Uspenskii, "'Zhili vmeste dva tramvaia': 'Berlinskoe' V. F. Khodasevicha," *Russkaia filologiia: Sbornik nauchnykh rabot molodykh filologov* 23 (2016): 112–21. Wachtel has analyzed a number of Berlin poems to argue that Khodasevich consciously experimented with conventions of Russian versification and deserves to be recognized as the innovator that he is. See Wachtel, "Vladislav Khodasevich as Innovator," 63–77.

117. Khodasevich, *Sobranie sochinenii*, vol. 1, 266.

118. Bethea, *Khodasevich*, 294; Dolinin, "'The Stepmother of Russian Cities,'" 232–33.

119. Khodasevich, *Sobranie sochinenii*, vol. 1, 195.

120. Vladimir Veidle, *Poeziia Khodasevicha* (Paris: n.p., 1928), 19. The myth of Pushkin's nanny Arina Rodionovna Iakovleva is also important in this context.

121. The theme of an adopted motherland also appeared in his 1917 poem "I was born in Moscow," which he rewrote in 1923 in Saarow, near Berlin. In a revised version he stressed the notion that even though he is "Russia's stepson," he is uncertain about his relation to Poland; what he knows without a doubt is that his entire homeland can fit into an eight-volume edition of Pushkin. Having to choose between exile or a life of compromise in Soviet Russia, the poem's subject is unwilling to embrace either. Instead, he packs his Russia, in the form of books, into a travel sack and embarks on a journey. See also Ananko, *Kanikuly Kaina*, 256.

122. Khodasevich, "Literatura v izgnanii," *Sobranie sochinenii*, vol. 2, 256–67.

123. In a letter of November 28, 1924. See Andrei Shishkin, "Rossiia raskololas' popolam: Neizvestnoe pis'mo Vl. Khodasevicha," *Russica Romana* 9 (2002): 107–14.

124. Khodasevich, *Sobranie sochinenii*, vol. 1, 137. See also Bethea, *Khodasevich*, 103–85.

125. Bethea, *Khodasevich*, 294.

126. Bethea, *Khodasevich*, 292.

127. Bethea, *Khodasevich*, 293.

128. Sarah Clovis Bishop, "The Book of Poems in Twentieth-Century Russian Literature: Khodasevich, Gippius and Shvarts" (PhD diss., Princeton University, 2004), 13–14.

129. Bishop, "The Book of Poems," 14. *Grain's Way* appeared as part of Khodasevich's *Collection of Poems* that also included *European Night*.

130. Robert P. Hughes, "Irony and Dislocation," 63; Frank Göbler, *Vladislav F. Chodasevič: Dualität und Distanz als Grundzüge sener Lyrik* (Munich: Verlag Otto Sagner in Komission, 1988).

131. See Khodasevich's poems "Dachnoe" ("From the Dacha," 1923/24), "Slepoi" ("A Blind Man," 1922/23), a four-poem cycle "U moria" ("By the Sea," 1922/23), "S berlinskoi ulitsy" ("From a Berlin Street," 1922/23), "An Mariechen" (1923), and "Berlinskoe" ("A Berlin Poem," 1922).

132. John Malmstad, "Poeziia Vladislava Khodasevicha," in Khodasevich, *Sobranie sochinenii*, vol. 1, 20.

133. See Starr Figura, ed., *German Expressionism: The Graphic Impulse* (New York: Museum of Modern Art, 2011); and Uspenskii, "Berlinskoe," 112–21.

134. See Alexander Blok, "Na zheleznoi doroge" ("On the Railroad," 1910); and Maria Tatar, *Lustmord: Sexual Murder in Weimar Germany* (Princeton, NJ: Princeton University Press, 1995). "An Mariechen" was also inspired by Andrei Bely's frantic dancing in Berlin and his infatuation with a daughter of a pub owner. See Khodasevich, *Sobranie sochinenii*, vol. 1, 452.

135. For contextual analyses of Mayakovsky's and Lissitzky's *For the Voice* project, see Patricia Railing, ed., *For the Voice: Vladimir Mayakovsky and El Lissitzky* (Cambridge, MA: MIT Press, 2000).

CHAPTER 2. GUIDES TO BERLIN

1. The terrorists aimed at the leader of the Kadets Pavel Miliukov, who was shielded by Nabokov. See Brian Boyd, *Vladimir Nabokov: The Russian Years* (Princeton, NJ: Princeton University Press, 1990), 190; and Grigorii Arosev, *Vladimir Nabokov, otets Vladimira Nabokova* (Moscow: Al'pina Non-Fikshn, 2021), 249–55.

2. Rubins, "Conceptual Territories of 'Diaspora,'" 15. See also Raeff, *Russia Abroad*; and Robert C. Williams, *Culture in Exile*.

3. See Schlögel, *Das russische Berlin*, 110–13; and Fleishman, "Vysylka intelligentsii i russkii Berlin v 1922 g.," 94–106.

4. See Robert C. Williams, "'Changing Landmarks' in Russian Berlin, 1922–1924," 581–93; and Fleishman, Hughes, and Raevsky-Hughes, *Russkii Berlin, 1921–1923*, 9–69.

5. The title of Konstantin Fedin's enthusiastically received novel *Cities and Years* (*Goroda i gody*, 1924) indicates a productive formula of anchoring the historical moment as it unfolded in modern cities.

6. Shklovsky, *Zoo*, 66. Viktor Shklovskii, *Sobranie sochinenii*, vol. 2, *Biografiia*, ed. Il'ia Kalinin (Moscow: Novoe literaturnoe obozrenie, 2019), 303. All quotations from *Zoo* refer to these editions and will be cited parenthetically in the text; Sheldon's English translation is occasionally modified for clarity.

7. Belyi, *Odna iz obitelei tsarstva tenei*.

8. Il'ia Erenburg, *Belyi ugol' ili slezy Vertera* (Leningrad: Priboi, 1928), 119–49. "Letters from Cafés" were first published in 1923 in the literary journal *Rossiia*.

9. Vladimir Nabokov, "Putevoditel' po Berlinu" was originally published in the Berlin émigré daily *Rul'* on December 24, 1925. The English translation is quoted from Nabokov's *Details of a Sunset and Other Stories*, 90–98.

10. Larisa Reisner, "Berlin v oktiabre 1923g.," in *Gamburg na barrikadakh* (Moscow: Novaia Moskva, 1924), 71–94. Her other Berlin texts from this period were published in Larisa Reisner, *V strane Gindenburga: Ocherki sovremennoi Germanii* (Moscow: Pravda, 1926). A similarly partisan account of Berlin can be found in Nikolai Nikitin, *Seichas na Zapade: Berlin, Rur, London* (Leningrad-Moscow: Petrograd, 1924).

11. Cf. Mary Louise Pratt, *Imperial Eyes: Travel Writing and Transculturation*, 2nd ed. (New York: Routledge, 2008).

12. Originally published under the title "Literatura i literaturnyi byt" in *Na literaturnom postu* 9 (1927): 47–52. Carol Any translates this term as "the literary milieu" in *Boris Eikhenbaum: Voices of a Russian Formalist* (Stanford, CA: Stanford University Press, 1994). Victor Erlich translates it as the "literary mores" in *Russian Formalism: History-Doctrine* (The Hague: Mouton, 1969), 125. I. R. Titunik opts for the "literary environment." See his translation of Eikhenbaum's essay in *Readings in Russian Poetics: Formalist and Structuralist Views*, ed. Ladislav Matejka and Krystyna Pomorska (Cambridge, MA: MIT Press, 1971), 56–65. In her study of Soviet Constructivism, Kristin Romberg has identified "the aesthetic of embeddedness" as a major innovation of the Russian avant-garde. See *Gan's Constructivism*, 5–12.

13. D. Mirskii, "Molodye russkie prozaiki," in *O literature i iskusstve: Stat'i i retsenzii, 1922–1937*, ed. O. A. Korostelev and M. V. Efimov (Moscow: Novoe literaturnoe obozrenie, 2014), 103. See also Mirskii, "Vozrozhdenie russkoi prozy," 50–53.

14. Boris M. Eikhenbaum, "Literaturnyi byt," in *O literature* (Moscow: Sovetskii pisatel'*, 1987), 428–36. See Any, *Boris Eikhenbaum*, 105–6; and Erlich, *Russian Formalism*, 125–29.

15. Sergei Ushakin, "Odnorazovaia periodika Borisa Eikhenbauma," in Boris Eikhenbaum, *Moi vremennik: Slovesnost', nauka, kritika, smes'* (Ekaterinburg: Kabinetnyi uchenyi, 2020), 14.

16. Tapp, "Boris Eikhenbaum's Response to the Crisis of the Novel in the 1920s," *Slavonica* 15, no. 1 (2009): 33. See also Eikhenbaum's essay "V poiskakh zhanra," in *Literatura: Teoriia, kritika, polemika* (Leningrad: Priboi, 1927), 291–95.

17. Ushakin, "Odnorazovaia periodika," 13.

18. Ushakin, "Odnorazovaia periodika," 19; Tapp, "Boris Eikhenbaum's Response," 45.

19. D. Mirskii, *O literature i iskusstve*, 51, 389.

20. Iosif Gessen, *Gody izgnaniia: Zhiznennyi otchet* (Paris: YMCA-Press, 1979), 106.

21. Egorova, *Zolotoi vek rossiiskogo knigoizdaniia v Germanii*, 7–20. See also Efim Dinershtein, *Siniaia ptitsa Zinoviia Grzhebina* (Moscow: Novoe literaturnoe obozrenie, 2014), 293–376; and Raeff, *Russia Abroad*, 73–94.

22. For a brief history of Petropolis and its founder Abram Kagan's relationships with writers coming to Berlin from Soviet Russia, see Michael Atherton, ed., *In Exile*

from St Petersburg: The Life and Times of Abram Saulovich Kagan, Book Publisher, as Told by His Son Anatol Kagan (Blackheath, Australia: Brandl and Schlesinger, 2017).

23. Boris Frezinskii, *Ob Il'e Erenburge: Knigi, liudi, strany* (Moscow: Novoe literaturnoe obozrenie, 2013), 524–75; Vladimir Berezin, *Viktor Shklovskii* (Moscow: Molodaia gvardiia, 2014), 165–200; and Mina Polianskaia, *Foxtrot belogo rytsaria: Andrei Belyi v Berline* (St. Petersburg: Demetra, 2009), 19. Publishing Russian titles in Berlin also meant that the authors established their copyright under the Berne Convention, which Russia joined only in 1995. See Atherton, *In Exile from St Petersburg*, 135–36, 270.

24. Shklovsky's letter to Maxim Gorky of March 16, 1922, shows that Shklovsky brought to Berlin the print galleys for *Revolution and the Front* (published in Petrograd in 1921 and ultimately constituting the first part of *A Sentimental Journey*), its "continuation, 1918–1922" (which became the second part of *A Sentimental Journey*), and the manuscripts for *The Knight's Move* (Gelikon, 1923). Stressing his financial hardship, he asked Gorky to see if Grzhebin would be interested in publishing him. Shklovskii, *Sobranie sochinenii*, vol. 1, 184.

25. Joshua Rubenstein, *Tangled Loyalties: The Life and Times of Ilya Ehrenburg* (Tuscaloosa: University of Alabama Press, 1999), 102–3.

26. *Novaia russkaia kniga* 1 (1922): 21.

27. *Izvestiia*, October 1, 1923. Cited in Boris Frezinksii, *Ob Il'e Erenburge*, 103.

28. Gaik Adonts, "Predislovie," in Erenburg, *Bely ugol'*, 5.

29. Rubenstein, *Tangled Loyalties*, 88.

30. Erenburg, "Vmesto predisloviia," in *Belyi ugol'*, 10.

31. In a 1927 essay on Berlin, "Dlinnee zhizni," Ehrenburg would clarify that "during the first revolutionary years in Russia we lived in the twenty-first century." Presumably, since Soviet Russia jumped a century ahead, it found itself out of joint with the rest of Europe. See *Belyi ugol'*, 154.

32. Katerina Clark has suggested that in the 1930s Ehrenburg's international activity can be described in terms of "cosmopolitan patriotism." See *Moscow, the Fourth Rome*, 30–41.

33. As Alexander Galushkin, Ilya Kalinin, and Vladimir Nekhotin point out, some of Shklovsky's contemporaries believed him to be a Menshevik. See Shklovskii, *Sobranie sochinenii*, vol. 1, 960.

34. Omry Ronen has argued that Nabokov's "A Guide to Berlin" and especially its English translation were written against Shklovsky's defeatism and conformism in *Zoo*. See his "Viktor Shklovsky's Tracks in 'A Guide to Berlin,'" trans. Susanne Fusso, in *The Joy of Recognition: Selected Essays of Omry Ronen*, ed. Barry P. Sherr and Michael Wachtel, 202–31.

35. Undated letter of September 1923. Shklovskii, *Sobranie sochinenii*, vol. 1, 201.

36. For example, the First Preface to the novel's fourth edition (1964) included the following lines: "I wanted to live and make decisions honestly: I did not want to shun what was difficult, but I lost my way. At fault and off course, I found myself an émigré in Berlin." Shklovsky, *Zoo*, 111.

37. From a Postscript to *A Sentimental Journey* added in 1924. See Shklovsky, *Zoo*, 135, 161.

38. See I. Vainberg, "Zhizn' i gibel' berlinskogo zhurnala Gor'kogo 'Beseda': Po neizvestnym arkhivnym materialam i neizdannoi perepiske," *Novoe literaturnoe obozrenie* 21 (1996): 361–76; Barry P. Sherr, "A Curtailed Colloquy: Gorky, Khodasevich, and *Beseda*," in *Russian Literature and the West: A Tribute for David M. Bethea, Part II*, ed. Alexander Dolinin et al. (Stanford, CA: Department of Slavic Languages and Literatures, Stanford University, 2008), 129–46.

39. Sherr, "A Curtailed Colloquy," 134, 145.

40. See "Pis'ma Maksima Gor'kogo k V. F. Khodasevichu," *Novyi zhurnal* 29 (1952): 207; and Richard Sheldon's Introduction to his translation of *Zoo, or Letters Not about Love*, xxii.

41. Shklovskii, *Sobranie sochinenii*, vol. 1, 197.

42. J. D. Elsworth, *Andrey Bely* (Letchworth: Bradda Books, 1972), 94.

43. Elsworth, *Andrey Bely*, 99. See also Thomas R. Beyer, "Andrej Belyj: The Berlin Years, 1921–1923," *Zeitschrift für Slavische Philologie* 50, no. 1 (1990): 90–142.

44. Aleksandr Lavrov, John Malmstad, and Monika Spivak, eds., *Andrei Belyi: Avtobiograficheskie svody. Literaturnoe nasledstvo* (Moscow: Nauka, 2016), 470.

45. For example, he was curious to learn about the White émigrés' perspective on the Revolution and did so by way of reading the memoirs of White Guard generals. See Lavrov, Malmstad, and Spivak, *Andrei Belyi*, 471.

46. The news was reported in "Khronika," *Rul'*, November 24, 1921. Bely also spoke at a public meeting in support of Russian famine relief. See Lavrov, Malmstad, and Spivak, *Andrei Belyi*, 613. Roman Gul wrote in his memoir that in those days in Berlin, Bely gave several well-attended public talks, but whenever "Bely touched upon political questions, unimaginable cacophony commenced. He was ready to curse the Bolsheviks, as well as to praise them." See Gul', *Ia unes Rossiiu*, 81.

47. N. M. Minskii, A. M. Remizov, and S. G. Kaplun, eds., *Biulliuteni Doma iskusstv Berlin* 1–2 (February 17, 1922): 22. See also "Dom iskusstva," *Rul'*, December 2, 1922, 5.

48. The Soviet writer Vladimir Lidin wrote in his memoir that in Berlin, "Bely was an émigré one day, and the poet of the world revolution the next." See Lidin, *Liudi i vstrechi* (Moscow: Sovetskii pisatel', 1959), 144. In 1922 and 1923 Bely also published in the Paris-based émigré journal *Sovremennye zapiski*. See E. A. Takho-Godi and M. Shruba, "Ob Andree Belom, Fedore Stepune, Dmitrii Chizhevskom i odnoi nesostoiavsheisia publikatsii v 'Sovremennykh zapiskakh,'" in *Literatura russkogo zarubezh'ia (1920–1940-e gody): Vzgliad iz XXI veka*, ed. L. E. Iezuitova and S. D. Titarenko (St. Petersburg: St. Petersburg State University, 2008), 110–22.

49. Polianskaia, *Foxtrot belogo rytsaria*, 172–80; Lazar Fleishman, "Bely's Memoirs," in *Andrey Bely: Spirit of Symbolism*, ed. John Malmstad (Ithaca, NY: Cornell University Press, 219), 216–41.

50. He wrote in a letter to Nadezhda Shchupak, "маму хватил удар, а вернуться к ней в Россию нельзя: *путь отрезан*." See Boris Sapir, "An Unknown Correspondent of Andrey Bely (Andrey Bely in Berlin, 1921–1923)," *Slavonic and East European Review* 49, no. 116 (1971): 451. Moreover, as Lazar Fleishman, Robert Hughes, and Olga Raevsky-Hughes have observed, Bely was averse to the "Change of Landmarks" movement, which encouraged the émigrés to make peace with the Bolsheviks and return. See *Russkii Berlin*, 221.

51. The black and red color binary also implied an ideological distinction since black stood for fascists and red for communists.
52. Monika Spivak, *Andrei Belyi: Mistik i sovetskii pisatel'* (Moscow: Rossiiskii gosudarstvennyi gumanitarnyi universitet, 2006), 354. Compare *Kingdom of Shades* with Bely's much more balanced essay "O 'Rossii' v Rossii i o 'Rossii' v Berline," published in *Beseda* 1 (1923): 211–36.
53. See Chamberlain, *The Philosophy Steamer*.
54. Ian Levchenko, *Drugaia nauka: Russkie formalisty v poiskakh biografii* (Moscow: Izdatel'skii dom Vysshei shkoly ekonomiki, 2012), 94.
55. Iurii Tynianov, "Literaturnoe segodnia," *Russkii sovremennik* 1 (1924): 305.
56. Beyer, "Andrej Belyj," 140.
57. In the Russian literary tradition, travel writing in letters can be traced back to Nikolai Karamzin's *Letters of a Russian Traveler* (1789–90).
58. Linda Kauffman, *Special Delivery: Epistolary Modes in Modern Fiction* (Chicago: University of Chicago Press, 1992), xvii.
59. Asiya Bulatova, "'I'm Writing to You in This Magazine': The Mechanics of Modernist Dissemination in Shklovsky's Open Letter to Jakobson," *Comparative Critical Studies* 11, no. 2–3 (2014): 185. Naturally, it is also important that Shklovsky models his epistolary novel on such a canonical precedent as Rousseau's *Julie; or, The New Heloise* (1761).
60. Bulatova, "I'm Writing to You in This Magazine," 187, 197.
61. Kauffman, *Special Delivery*, xiv; Levchenko, *Drugaia nauka*, 94. Cf. Svetlana Boym, "Poetics and Politics of Estrangement: Victor Shklovsky and Hannah Arendt," *Poetics Today* 26, no. 4 (2005): 581–611.
62. Asiya Bulatova has argued that the inclusion of Khlebnikov's "Menagerie" in *Zoo*'s epigraph "not only sets the scene for the novel in which Russian immigrants are also restrained and removed from their habitat but also places Shklovsky's book in the canon of Russian modernist literature." See her "Displaced Modernism: Shklovsky's *Zoo, or Letters Not about Love* and the Borders of Literature," *Poetics Today* 37, no. 1 (2016): 34–35.
63. See Ivan Bunin's famous speech "Missiia russkoi emigratsii," 5–6.
64. See Anne Dwyer, "Standstill as Extinction: Viktor Shklovsky's Poetics and Politics of Movement in the 1920s and 1930s," *PMLA* 131, no. 2 (2016): 269–88; and Britta Korkowsky, *Selbstverortung ohne Ort: Russisch-jüdische Exilliteratur aus dem Berlin der Zwanziger Jahre* (Göttingen: Wallstein Verlag, 2013), 161–67.
65. See Rad Borislavov, "'I Know What Motivation Is': The Politics of Emotion and Viktor Shklovskii's Sentimental Rhetoric," *Slavic Review* 74, no. 4 (2015): 787–807.
66. Ehrenburg updated his German impressions five years later in a 1927 collection of essays, "Piat' let spustia." See his *Bely ugol' ili slezy Vertera*, 151–91.
67. Vkhutemas stands for Vysshie khudozhestvenno-tekhnicheskie masterskie, or the Higher Art and Technical Studios, which operated in Moscow from 1920 until 1926.
68. Il'ia Erenburg, *A vse-taki ona vertitsia* (Berlin: Gelikon, 1922).
69. Further complications include the fact that Slavophile thought was closely connected to German idealist philosophy, as opposed to the French philosophes championed by the Westernizers. Moreover, the Eurasianist movement, which originated

in émigré circles in the early 1920s, took on the mantle of Slavophilism, but Bely considered Eurasianism an "unusually bright and talentedly conceived madness and evil." See Spivak, *Andrei Belyi*, 107.

70. Aleksandr Dolinin, *"Gibel' Zapada" i drugie memy: Iz istorii raskhozhikh idei i slovesnykh formul* (Moscow: Novoe izdatel'stvo, 2020), 40–41.

71. David Bethea, *The Shape of Apocalypse in Modern Russian Fiction* (Princeton, NJ: Princeton University Press, 1989), 126–27.

72. Spivak, *Andrei Belyi*, 111, 255.

73. Bely refers to the book as *Zakat Zapada* and not *Zakat Evropy*, as it was translated into Russian. According to his diaries, he read it in the original German in 1921. Later that year he also participated in a public debate devoted to the book in Petrograd. See Belyi, *Avtobiograficheskie svody*, 464, 468.

74. See Andrei Belyi, "Osnovy moego mirovozzreniia," with preface by Larisa Sugai ("Andrei Belyi protiv Osval'da Shpenglera"), *Literaturnoe obozrenie* 4–5 (1995): 10–37.

75. Nikolai Aleksandrovich Berdiaev et al., *Osval'd Shpengler i Zakat Evropy* (Moscow: Bereg, 1922). The Soviet authorities expelled Berdyaev, Stepun, and Frank, along with scores of other intellectuals, to Berlin in 1922.

76. S. Chlenov, "Segodniashnii Berlin (Mimoletnye vpechatleniia)," *Krasnaia nov'* 1 (1923): 201–13. A forum on *The Decline of the West* was published in *Krasnaia nov'* 2 (1922). For an overview of Russian responses to Spengler's book, see Galina Time, "Zakat Evropy kak 'tsentral'naia mysl' russkoi filosofii': O mirovozzrencheskoi samoidentifikatsii Rossii v nachale 1920-kh gg.," in *XX vek. Dvadtsatye gody: Iz istorii mezhdunarodnykh sviazei russkoi literatury*, ed. Galina Time (St. Petersburg: Nauka, 2006), 62–88.

77. See Pavel Lyssakov and Stephen Norris, "The City in Russian Culture: Space, Culture, and the Russian City," in *The City in Russian Culture*, ed. Pavel Lyssakov and Stephen Norris (London: Routledge, 2018), 1–12. See also Robert Alter, *Imagined Cities: Urban Experience and the Language of the Novel* (New Haven, CT: Yale University Press, 2005); and Donald Fanger, "The City of Modern Russian Fiction," in *Modernism, 1890–1930*, ed. Malcolm Bradbury and James McFarlane (London: Penguin Books, 1986), 467–80.

78. Nikolai Antsiferov's book *Dusha Peterburga* (Petersburg: Brokgauz i Efron, 1922) pioneered the study of Petersburg's representation in the Russian literary imagination. See also V. N. Toporov, *Peterburgskii tekst russkoi literatury: Izbrannye trudy* (St. Petersburg: Iskusstvo-SPb, 2003).

79. Cf. Evgenii Ponomarev, "'Berlinskii ocherk' 1920-kh godov kak variant peterburgskogo teksta," *Voprosy literatury* 3 (2013): 42–67. See also Time, *Puteshestvie Moskva-Berlin-Moskva*.

80. Schlögel, *Das russische Berlin*, 295.

81. To use the term introduced by Michel de Certeau, walking through the city defines "spaces of enunciation" resulting in "pedestrian rhetorics." See *The Practice of Everyday Life*, 97–98.

82. "Night! Tauentzien [Street]! Cocaine! / That's Berlin"; "Boom-Boom." Notably, Bely's poem "Malen'kii balagan na malen'koi planete 'Zemlia,'" included in the book

of poems *Posle razluki: Berlinskii pesennik* (Berlin: Epokha, 1922), begins with the lines "One shrieks into the open window: Boom-Boom! It began!"

83. The use of the word "black" connotes both a reference to fascism and a racial marker. Bely extended the modernist fascination with African cultures to conceptualizing the urban bourgeoise. For instance, he maintained that the bowler hat and formal suit of an average Berliner concealed primal "African" instincts, which manifested themselves during nighttime dancing of the foxtrot and the shimmy. Bely's problematic invocation of race deserves to be explored in depth, but such an undertaking is beyond the scope of this study.

84. See Marina Tsvetaeva, "Plennyi dukh: Moia vstrecha s Andreem Belym," in *Izbrannaia proza v dvukh tomakh*, ed. Aleksandr Sumerkin, vol. 2 (New York: Russica Publishers, 1979), 80–121. See also Monika Spivak, "Koshmar v pissuare: K voprosu o genezise odnogo emigrantskogo vpechatleniia Andreiia Belogo," *Europa Orientalis* 22, no. 2 (2003): 51–70.

85. Andrei Belyi, *Avtobiograficheskie svody*, 474.

86. Gary Saul Morson, *The Boundaries of Genre: Dostoevsky's "Diary of a Writer" and the Traditions of Literary Utopia* (Austin: University of Texas Press, 1981), 53. See also Kauffman, *Special Delivery*, 3–51; and Bulatova, "Displaced Modernism," 29–53.

87. Cf. Carol Avins, *Border Crossings: The West and Russian Identity in Soviet Literature, 1917–1934* (Berkeley: University of California Press, 1983), 98.

88. Leon Trotsky, *Literature and Revolution*, trans. Rose Strunsky (Ann Arbor: University of Michigan Press, 1960), 55.

89. Shklovskii, "Pamiatnik nauchnoi oshibke," in *Sobranie sochinenii*, vol. 1, 871–78.

90. Fedor Raskol'nikov in the foreword to the 1933 edition of Erenburg's *Viza vremeni*. See Evgenii Ponomarev, "Putevoditel' po Evrope," *Neva* 11 (2008), https://magazines.gorky.media/neva/2008/11/putevoditel-po-evrope-glavy-iz-knigi-ili-eren-burga-viza-vremeni-1931.html.

Chapter 3. Performing Exile

1. Gessen, *Gody izgnaniia*, 85.
2. Gessen, *Gody izgnaniia*, 86.
3. Walter Schrenk, "'Der goldene Hahn.' Urauffürung in der Staatsoper," *Deutsche Allgemeine Zeitung*, June 19, 1923, 2; Edmund Kühn, "'Der goldene Hahn.' Märchenoper von N. Rimskij-Korsakoff," *Germania: Zeitung für das deutsche Volk*, June 20, 1923, 2; R. Engel, "'Zolotoi petushok' v Gos. Opere," *Dni*, June 21, 1923, 5; Iurii Ofrosimov, "K postanovke 'Zolotogo petushka,'" *Rul'*, June 17, 1923, 9. Ofrosimov's review, written after seeing a dress rehearsal, was largely positive and cautiously optimistic. See also *Berliner Illustrirte Zeitung*, July 1, 1923, 502.
4. See Julius Kapp, ed., *Die Staatsoper Berlin 1919 bis 1925: Ein Almanach* (Berlin: Deutsche Verlags-Anstalt, 1925).
5. Gessen, *Gody izgnaniia*, 86.
6. I will refrain from commenting on the musical aspects of this production or on Rimsky-Korsakov's score, which has been examined by musicologists. See V. V. Goriachikh, "*Zolotoi petushok* Rimskogo-Korsakova—'nebylitsa v litsakh' (problema zhanra

i stilia)," in *Pushkin v russkoi opere*, ed. E. Ruch'evskaia (St. Petersburg: Goskonservatoriia, 1998), 247–98; and Marina Frolova-Walker, ed., *Rimsky-Korsakov and His World* (Princeton, NJ: Princeton University Press, 2018).

7. The most comprehensive list of the remaining set and costume design sketches for this opera, to my knowledge, can be found in Richard Nathanson's *Pavel Tchelitchew: A Collection of Theatre Designs, 1919–1923* (London: Alpine Club, 1976). Several of those drawings are now in a private collection. I would like to thank the collector, Alexander Kuznetsov, for generously sharing the color copies of those drawings with me and allowing me to reproduce them.

8. Tat'iana Belova, "Skazochnye nameki: Ot skazki Pushkina k opere Rimskogo-Korsakova," in *Rimskii-Korsakov: Zhizn' i tvorchestvo russkogo kompozitora*, http://www.rimskykorsakov.ru/belova.html; Edward R. Reilly, "Rimsky-Korsakov's *The Golden Cockerel*: A Very Modern Fairy Tale," *Musical Newsletter* 6, no. 1 (1976): 9–16; Igor' Glebov [Boris Asaf'ev], *Simfonicheskie etiudy* (Petersburg: Gosfilarmoniia, 1922); Richard Taruskin, "Rimsky-Korsakov, Nikolay Andreyevich (opera)," *Oxford Music Online* (2002), https://www.oxfordmusiconline.com/grovemusic/view/10.1093/gmo/9781561592630.001.0001/omo-9781561592630-e-5000002126; and Natal'ia Zimianina, "Vozmozhna li politicheskaia opera," *Vremia MN*, April 8, 2003.

9. Aleksandr Pushkin, *Sobranie sochinenii v desiati tomakh*, ed. D. D. Blagoi, vol. 3 (Moscow: Gosudarstvennoe izdatel'stvo khudozhestvennoi literatury, 1960), 365.

10. Anna Akhmatova was first to disrupt the notion that Pushkin's *The Golden Cockerel* is a charming tale rooted in Russian folklore and pointed out that not only is the plot borrowed from foreign sources, but the fairy tale is imbued with dissent against Nicholas I. See her *O Pushkine* (Leningrad: Sovetskii pisatel', 1977), 8–38. Roman Jakobson developed Akhmatova's ideas in his famous article on the myth of the statue coming to life and linked *The Golden Cockerel* with *The Bronze Horseman*, arguably the most dissenting of Pushkin's works. See his *Pushkin and His Sculptural Myth*, trans. and ed. John Burbank (The Hague: Mouton, 1975). Mikhail Pashchenko has traced the influence of Slavic folklore, as well as Egyptian and Masonic symbolism, which were popular in the 1820s, on the fairy tale's conception. See his "'Skazka o zolotom petushke': Skazka-lozh' i skazka-pravda," *Voprosy literatury* 2 (2009): 202–34. Sona Hoisington and Boris Gasparov each have shown the text's intricate network of allusions to Pushkin's biography at the time of the fairy tale's writing and connected the Astrologer's belonging to the sect of the Skoptsy and the Cockerel's phallic connotations with the author's emasculation anxiety. See Hoisington, "Pushkin's 'Golden Cockerel': A Critical Re-Examination," in *The Golden Age of Russian Literature and Thought: Selected Papers from the Fourth World Congress for Soviet and East European Studies, Harrogate, 1990*, ed. Derek Offord (New York: St. Martin's, 1992), 24–33; and Gasparov, "Pushkin's Year of Frustration, or How 'The Golden Cockerel' Was Made," *Ulbandus Review* 12 (2009/10): 41–62. Alexander Etkind has argued that Pushkin's true hint and lesson here is a warning against tampering with one's sexuality. See *Sodom i Psikheia: Ocherki intellektual'noi istorii Serebrianogo veka* (Moscow: ITs-Garant, 1996), 140–213.

11. See Abram Gozenpud, *N. A. Rimsky-Korsakov: Temy i idei ego opernogo tvorchestva* (Moscow: Gosmuzizdat, 1957), 162–86; and Marina Frolova-Walker, "Staging

Defeat: *The Golden Cockerel* and the Russo-Japanese War," in *Rimsky-Korsakov and His World*, 197–219.

12. Simon Morrison, "*The Golden Cockerel*, Censored and Uncensored," in *Rimsky-Korsakov and His World*, 178–79. As Morrison details, *The Golden Cockerel* was beleaguered by censorship from its inception. The premiere was first cancelled and then allowed to proceed in a version that was a less obvious parody of the court of Nicholas II. Furthermore, after the 1917 Revolution, the critique of authority inherent in the opera was welcome only briefly. The Soviet Union's most visible stage, the Bolshoy, excluded *The Golden Cockerel* from its repertoire from 1933 until 1988. See http://archive.bolshoi.ru/entity/OPERA/103132. In 2011, the opera was revived at the Bolshoy and promptly closed after Vladimir Putin's third-term presidential (re)election, lest the grotesque version of Russia onstage become too apparent a reflection of real life.

13. Konstantin Stanislavsky envisioned the Tsarina as a harbinger of liberated humanity in his staging of the opera at Moscow's Opera Theater in 1932. See I. E. Grabar', ed., *K. S. Stanislavskii: Materialy, pis'ma, issledovaniia* (Moscow: Izdatel'stvo Akademii nauk SSSR, 1955), 327. See also Justin Weir, "*The Golden Cockerel* between Realism and Modernism," in *Intersections and Transpositions: Russian Music, Literature, and Society*, ed. Andrew Baruch Wachtel (Evanston, IL: Northwestern University Press, 1998), 73–89.

14. V. Berkov and V. Protopopov, *Zolotoi petushok, nebylitsa v litsakh: Opera N. A. Rimskogo-Korsakova, libretto V. I. Bel'skogo po skazke A. S. Pushkina* (Moscow: Muzgiz, 1937), 131.

15. Weir, "*The Golden Cockerel* between Realism and Modernism," 73–89.

16. Morson, *The Boundaries of Genre*, 48–51.

17. See Alexei Lalo, *Libertinage in Russian Culture and Literature: A Bio-History of Sexualities at the Threshold of Modernity* (Boston: Brill, 2011), 130–31.

18. Susan Sontag, "Notes on Camp," in *Camp: Queer Aesthetics and the Performing Subject: A Reader*, ed. Fabio Cleto (Ann Arbor: University of Michigan Press, 1999), 51–65.

19. Fabio Cleto, "The Spectacles of Camp," in *Camp: Notes on Fashion*, ed. Andrew Bolton (New York: Metropolitan Museum of Art, 2019), 17.

20. See Tavia Nyong'o, *Afro-Fabulations: The Queer Drama of Black Life* (New York: New York University Press, 2019), 1–21.

21. Madison Moore, *Fabulous: The Rise of the Beautiful Eccentric* (New Haven, CT: Yale University Press, 2018), vii.

22. Moore, *Fabulous*, 19.

23. See Donna Haraway, "SF: Science Fiction, Speculative Fabulation, String Figures, So Far," *Ada: A Journal of Gender, New Media, and Technology* 3 (2013), https://adanewmedia.org/2013/11/issue3-haraway/.

24. Cf. Mark Redhead, "Dissent (Political Theory)," *Encyclopedia Britannica*, https://www.britannica.com/topic/dissent-political.

25. For a similar framing of dissent, see Alfred Thomas, *Shakespeare, Dissent, and the Cold War* (New York: Palgrave Macmillan, 2004).

26. Mikhail Bakhtin, *Rabelais and His World*, trans. Helene Iswolsky (Cambridge, MA: MIT Press, 1968), 196–277.

27. Maria Tatar, *Off with Their Heads! Fairy Tales and the Culture of Childhood* (Princeton, NJ: Princeton University Press, 1993), xv–xxviii.
28. Michael Warner, *Publics and Counterpublics* (New York: Zone Books, 2002), 65–124.
29. Caryl Emerson, *Boris Godunov: Transpositions of a Russian Theme* (Bloomington: Indiana University Press, 1986), 3.
30. Emerson, *Boris Godunov*, 3.
31. Emerson, *Boris Godunov*, 8.
32. [Anonymous] "'Der goldene Hahn.' Märchenoper von Nikolaus Rimskij-Korsakoff. Zur deutschen Aufführung in der Berliner Staatsoper," *Germania: Zeitung für das deutsche Volk*, June 15, 1923, 2.
33. "Der goldene Hahn," *Germania*, 2.
34. See Kapp, *Die Staatsoper Berlin 1919 bis 1925*, as well as the special issue of *Blätter der Staatsoper* devoted to *The Golden Cockerel*, Heft 8, June 1923.
35. Marina Raku, *Muzykal'naia klassika v mifotvorchestve sovetskoi epokhi* (Moscow: Novoe literaturnoe obozrenie, 2014), 321–32.
36. Kühn, "Der goldene Hahn," 2. In the Ballets Russes production the singers are grouped together on elevated ramps on stage right and stage left, with the dancers in prime position at center stage, as is evident in Natalia Goncharova's set design for the 1937 revival of the original production and in the Metropolitan Opera's 1918 staging, which preserved Michel Fokine's choreography. Perhaps even more importantly, the Ballets Russes also made cuts to the music (and thus infuriated Rimsky-Korsakov's widow).
37. Heinrich Möller translated the libretto into German.
38. Schrenk, "Der goldene Hahn," 2.
39. Kühn, "Der goldene Hahn," 2.
40. Engel, "Zolotoi petushok," 5.
41. Engel, "Zolotoi petushok," 5.
42. Ofrosimov, "K postanovke 'Zolotogo petushka,'" 9.
43. Nicolas Nabokov, *Bagázh*, 123.
44. Antonova, *Berlin/Moskau Moskva/Berlin, 1900–1950*. For more on the role that the Russian expatriates played in the development of German dance, see Marion Kant, "Russians in Berlin, 1920–1945," in *Russian Movement Culture of the 1920s and 1930s*, ed. Lynn Garafola (New York: Columbia University Harriman Institute, 2015), 73–79, https://harriman.columbia.edu/files/harriman/newsletter/Russian%20Movement%20Culture%20Corrected%20July%202017pdf.pdf.
45. See *Deutscher Bühnenspielplan*, May 9, 1923, 159–60.
46. Georgii F. Kovalenko, *Pavel Chelishchev* (Moscow: Iskusstvo—XXI vek, 2021), 45–88.
47. Raeff, *Russia Abroad*, 95–117.
48. Laurence Senelick, "Émigré Cabaret and the Reinvention of Russia," *New Theatre Quarterly* 35, no. 1 (2019): 44–59.
49. Kovalenko, *Pavel Chelishchev*, 54.
50. See Jane A. Sharp, *Russian Modernism between East and West: Natal'ia Goncharova and the Moscow Avant-Garde* (Cambridge: Cambridge University Press, 2006).

51. In his unpublished notes on Tchelitchew's biography, Allen Tanner writes that in the early 1920s, Tchelitchew was fascinated by Rousseau, Braque, Léger, De Chirico, and Picasso. See Pavel Tchelitchew Collection, box 30, folder 514, Yale Collection of American Literature, Beinecke.

52. In an essay on the state of the arts in exile, Osip Brik labeled Tchelitchew's work Eurasianist hackwork (evraziiskaia khaltura). Osip Brik, "A lia rius," in *Foto i kino* (Moscow: Ad Marginem, 2015), 73.

53. See Sergey Glebov, *From Empire to Eurasia: Politics, Scholarship, and Ideology in Russian Eurasianism, 1920s–1930s* (DeKalb: Northern Illinois University Press, 2017).

54. See Michael Kunichika, *"Our Native Antiquity": Archeology and Aesthetics in the Culture of Russian Modernism* (Boston, MA: Academic Studies Press, 2016); and Irina Shevelenko, *Modernizm kak arkhaizm: Natsionalizm i poiski modernistskoi estetiki v Rossii* (Moscow: Novoe literaturnoe obozrenie, 2017).

55. Adalyat Issykieva, "Nikolai Rimsky-Korsakov and His Orient," in *Rimsky-Korsakov and His World*, ed. Marina Frolova-Walker (Princeton, NJ: Princeton University Press, 2018), 145–75.

56. Lincoln Kirstein, *Tchelitchew* (Santa Fe, NM: Twelvetrees Press, 1994), 30–31.

57. See her designs for *Les Noces* (1923) as well as Nicholas Roerich's designs for *The Rite of Spring* (1913).

58. Georgii F. Kovalenko, "Pavel Chelishchev: Rannie gody," in *Russkoe iskusstvo XX vek: Issledovaniia i publikatsii*, vol. 3 (Moscow: Nauka, 2007), 79.

59. Richard Nathanson, *Pavel Tchelitchew: A Collection of Theatre Designs*, 3; Kovalenko, *Pavel Chelishchev*, 85.

60. Kühn, "Der goldene Hahn," 2.

61. Maxim Gorky's play *Children of the Sun* (1905) is another intertextual possibility of this staging.

62. Tchelitchew could have been aware of Kruchenykh's text and Malevich's pre-Suprematist designs, and perhaps even Lissitzky's sketches for this avant-garde opera through Exter. Malevich, Lissitzky, and Exter also spent time in Berlin in the 1920s.

63. Donald Windham, "The Stage and Ballet Designs of Pavel Tchelitchew," *Dance Index* 1 (1944): 7.

64. Berkov and Protopopov, *Zolotoi petushok, nebylitsa v litsakh*, 108.

65. Berkov and Protopopov, *Zolotoi petushok, nebylitsa v litsakh*, 109.

66. Berkov and Protopopov, *Zolotoi petushok, nebylitsa v litsakh*, 117.

67. In this connection, see also Inna Naroditskaya, *Bewitching Russian Opera: The Tsarina from State to Stage* (New York: Oxford University Press, 2012).

68. Petra Dierkes-Thrun, *Salome's Modernity: Oscar Wilde and the Aesthetics of Transgression* (Ann Arbor: University of Michigan Press, 2011), 3.

69. See Rachel Morley, *Performing Femininity: Woman as Performer in Early Russian Cinema* (London: I.B. Tauris, 2017) 26.

70. Morley, *Performing Femininity*, 29. According to Tchelitchew's biographer Kovalenko, the artist loved dancing Salomé's Dance of the Seven Veils as a child. See Kovalenko, *Pavel Chelishchev*, 23.

71. Igor' Glebov, *Simfonicheskie etiudy*, 152.

72. Hoisington, "Pushkin's 'Golden Cockerel,'" 30–31. See also Etkind's discussion in *Sodom i Psikheia* of the prominence of the region of Shemakha (today's Shamakhi in Azerbaijan) as the place where the Skoptsy (the self-castrates) were exiled in the early nineteenth century.

CHAPTER 4. NABOKOV, BERLIN, AND THE
FUTURE OF RUSSIAN LITERATURE

The epigraph is quoted from Vladimir Nabokov, *Drugie berega* (New York: Izdatel'stvo im. Chekhova, 1954), 241. In *Speak, Memory* Nabokov rendered this sentence as: "I have sufficiently spoken of the gloom and glory of exile in my Russian novels, and especially in the best of them, *Dar*." Nabokov, *Speak, Memory*, 280.

1. The editorial in the first issue of the literary magazine *Novyi Dom* (New House) contained a sentence indicative of this generational divide: "While living abroad [na chuzhbine] and not forgetting about Russia, we, however, do not pine [ne toskuem] for its 'little birch trees' [berezkam] and 'brooklets' [rucheikam]." See *Novyi Dom* 1 (1926): 2. Naturally, this opposition was not static and continued to develop, with some authors changing their positions over time, but the divide as such remained in place. See Leonid Livak, *How It Was Done in Paris*, 14–44; and Maria Rubins, *Russian Montparnasse*, 3–4.

2. The transcript of Nina Berberova's presentation was published in *Novyi korabl'* 2 (1927): 42–43 as part of a broader debate. The handwritten and unabridged version of Berberova's text can be found among her papers (box 41, folder 992) at the Beinecke.

3. Berberova uses the phrase "spetsial'nyi zakaz," while the Soviet term was "sotsial'nyi zakaz" (social command), popularized by the Left Front of the Arts (LEF) in the late 1920s.

4. V. Sirin, "Iubilei," *Rul'*, November 18, 1927, 2. Translated as "Anniversary" in Vladimir Nabokov, *Think, Write, Speak: Uncollected Essays, Reviews, Interviews, and Letters to the Editor*, ed. Brian Boyd and Anastasia Tolstoy (New York: Knopf, 2019), 62.

5. Andrei Babikov and Manfred Schruba, "Pis'ma V. V. Nabokova k V. F. Khodasevichu i N. N. Berberovoi (1930–1939). Pis'mo N. Berberovoi k V. Nabokovu," *Wiener Slavistisches Jahrbuch* 5 (2017): 234.

6. Burchard, *Klubs der russischen Dichter in Berlin*, 232–75.

7. Vladimir Korvin-Piotrovskii Papers, box 12, folder 252, "Notebook 31" (Oversize), Beinecke Library. The following two stanzas of the poem read "Так что ж печалиться / Народ [раскается?] / Советы свалятся / Со всей чекой; В дни нашей [младости] / Не знали радости / Одни лишь гадости / Послал нам рок" (So why should we feel sorrow / The people will repent / The Soviets will collapse / with their entire Cheka; / In the days of our youth / We knew no joy. / The fate sent us / Nothing but vile misfortune).

8. See Iurii Mandel'shtam, "Berlinskie i prazhskie poety," *Vozrozhdenie*, June 1, 1933, 4; and Eugenie Salkind, "Die junge russische Literatur in der Emigration," *Osteuropa* 6, no. 10 (1931): 575–90.

9. Boyd, *The Russian Years*, 342–43. Among the young Berlin writers, Nabokov's rival was Vladimir Korvin-Piotrovskii (1891–1966), whose poetry Nabokov valued highly. See V. Sirin, "'Beatriche' V. L. Piotrovskogo," *Rossiia i slavianstvo*, October 11, 1930, reprinted in Vladimir Vladimirovich Nabokov, *Sobranie sochinenii russkogo*

perioda v piati tomakh, ed. N. I. Artemenko-Tolstaia and Aleksandr Dolinin, vol. 3 (St. Petersburg: Simpozium, 2000), 681–84.

10. On Nabokov's "un-Russianness," see Struve, *Russkaia literatura v izgnanii*, 189–96; Livak, *How It Was Done in Paris*, 17–19; and Aleksandr Dolinin, *Kommentarii k romanu Vladimira Nabokova "Dar"* (Moscow: Novoe izdatel'stvo, 2019), 504. On Nabokov's engagement with the literary canon, see Marijeta Bozovic, *Nabokov's Canon: From Onegin to Ada* (Evanston, IL: Northwestern University Press, 2016).

11. Struve, *Russkaia literatura v izgnanii*, 192; Iouri Mandelstamm, "Lettres russes. Wladimir Sirine," *La Revue de France* 23, December 1, 1934, 560–67. About Mandelstamm's review, Nabokov wrote to Khodasevich, "A few days ago I received the issue of R[evue] de France with an article by Mandelstamm; it is very interesting and flattering but I energetically protest suggestions of a 'German influence' and the 'influence of Zweig' as I don't know German and can't even read a newspaper. Meanwhile, judging by translations, [Stefan] Zweig seems to be a talentless *poshliak* [a vulgar person], but then again, so is the other Zweig." Note that Nabokov objects to suggestions of influence not least because he knows contemporary fiction in German well enough to distinguish between the Austrian writer Stefan Zweig and the German writer Arnold Zweig. See Babikov and Schruba, "Pis'ma V. V. Nabokova k V. F. Khodasevichu i N. N. Berberovoi," 235–36.

12. In a 1932 interview with Andrey Sedykh [Iakov Tswibak] for the Riga-based newspaper *Segodnia*, Nabokov stated that he was well aware of "accusations" of German influence in his novels and added, "I actually speak and read German rather poorly. It would be more appropriate to speak of a French influence: I love Flaubert and Proust. Curiously, I first felt the proximity to Western culture in Russia. But here, in the West, I didn't consciously learn anything new. Instead, I have begun feeling especially sharply the charm of Gogol and, closer to us, of Chekhov." See Andrei Sedykh, "Vstrecha s V. Sirinym. Ot parizhskogo korrespondenta 'Segodnia': An Interview with Nabokov," *Segodnia*, November 4, 1932, reprinted in Nabokov, *Sobranie sochinenii russkogo perioda*, vol. 5, 641–43.

13. See Irina Paperno, "How Nabokov's *Gift* is Made," in *Literature, Culture, and Society in the Modern Age: In Honor of Joseph Frank*, ed. Edward J. Brown, Lazar Fleishman, Gregory Freidin, and Richard D. Schupbach, vol. 2 (Stanford, CA: Department of Slavic Languages and Literatures, Stanford University, 1992), 295–322; and John Burt Foster, *Nabokov's Art of Memory and European Modernism* (Princeton, NJ: Princeton University Press, 1993).

14. When quoting from *The Gift*, I give the page numbers parenthetically, first to the English translation and then, when necessary, to the original Russian. I use the following editions: Vladimir Nabokov, *The Gift*, trans. Michael Scammell with the collaboration of the author (New York: Vintage International, 1991); and Nabokov, *Sobranie sochinenii russkogo perioda*, vol. 4.

15. Yuri Leving, *Keys to the Gift: A Guide to Nabokov's Novel* (Boston, MA: Academic Studies Press, 2011), 144. In Nabokov's estimation, the years 1925–27 comprise the best period of interwar émigré life. As he put it in an interview published upon his arrival to New York in 1940, "It seems to me that with the [defeat] of France, a certain period of the Russian emigration has ended. Now its life will assume some absolutely new forms. The period from 1925 to 1927 should be considered the best moment in

the life of that emigration. Though before the war it was also not bad." See Nikolai All, "V. V. Sirin-Nabokov v N'iu-Iorke chuvstvuet sebia 'svoim': Rabotaet srazu nad dvumia knigami—angliiskoi i russkoi," *Novoe russkoe slovo*, June 23, 1940, reprinted in Nabokov, *Sobranie sochinenii russkogo perioda*, vol. 5, 643–46.

16. Dolinin, *Kommentarii*, 566.

17. Boyd, *The Russian Years*, 447.

18. See Constantine Muravnik, "Nabokov's Philosophy of Art," *Nabokov Studies* 15 (2017), doi:10.1353/nab.2017.0002.

19. Simon Karlinsky, "Vladimir Nabokov's Novel *Dar* as a Work of Literary Criticism: A Structural Analysis," *Slavic and East European Journal* 7, no. 3 (1963): 284–90.

20. Karlinsky, "*Dar* as a Work of Literary Criticism," 285, 288.

21. Simon Karlinsky Papers, Bancroft Library, University of California, Berkeley.

22. Karlinsky, "*Dar* as a Work of Literary Criticism," 289.

23. The two German monographs on Nabokov and his German environment are concerned primarily with establishing biographical facts of Nabokov's presence in Berlin. See Thomas Urban, *Vladimir Nabokov: Blaue Abende in Berlin* (Berlin: Propyläen, 1999); and Dieter Zimmer, *Nabokovs Berlin* (Berlin: Nicolai, 2001). In his book-length study of the novel, Stephen Blackwell acknowledges Berlin's importance without examining the implications of the urban setting in depth. Blackwell sides with Nabokov's statement in the 1962 Foreword to the novel's English translation that the world of *The Gift* is "as much of a phantasm as most of my other worlds." Blackwell writes, "*The Gift*'s world is therefore best conceived as an artistic reprojection of a mass hallucination." See his *Zina's Paradox: The Figured Reader in Nabokov's "Gift"* (New York: Peter Lang, 2000), 12.

24. Stanislav Shvabrin, "Berlin," in *Vladimir Nabokov in Context*, ed. David Bethea and Siggy Frank (Cambridge: Cambridge University Press, 2018), 87.

25. Boyd, *The Russian Years*, 492–96.

26. Catherine Andreyev and Ivan Savicky, *Russia Abroad: Prague and the Russian Diaspora, 1918–1938* (New Haven, CT: Yale University Press, 2004), 164.

27. Boyd, *The Russian Years*, 241–69.

28. Vladimir Nabokov, *Strong Opinions* (New York: McGraw-Hill Book Company, 1973), 189.

29. Nicolas Nabokov, *Bagázh*, 112.

30. On Nabokov's engagement with the urban space of Berlin, see Annelore Engel-Braunschmidt, "Die Suggestion Berliner Realität bei Vladimir Nabokov," in Schlögel, *Russische Emigration in Deutschland 1918 bis 1941*, 367–78; Nassim Winnie Berdjis, *Imagery in Nabokov's Last Russian Novel ("Dar"), Its English Translation ("The Gift"), and Other Prose Works of the 1930s* (Frankfurt am Main: Peter Lang, 1995); Urban, *Blaue Abende*; Zimmer, *Nabokovs Berlin*; Emery, "Guides to Berlin," 275–90; Shvabrin, "Berlin," 87–93; Parker, "The Shop Window Quality of Things"; and, to an extent, Marina Turkevich Naumann, *Blue Evenings in Berlin: Nabokov's Short Stories of the 1920s* (New York: New York University Press, 1978); and Mariia Virolainen, *Rech' i molchanie: Siuzhety russkoi slovesnosti* (St. Petersburg: Amfora, 2003), 459–60.

31. Jerzy Skolimowski directed *King, Queen, Knave* in 1972, and Rainer Werner Fassbinder completed his adaptation of *Despair* in 1978.

32. Korvin-Piotrovskii Papers, "Notebook 31."

33. The metal facemask further complicates this image since it invokes the legend of the Man in the Iron Mask, elaborated in Alexandre Dumas's historical novel *Le Vicomte de Bragelonne* (1847–50). This story of the unjustly imprisoned twin brother of Louis XIV suits the proverbial image of the exiled author rather well: the adventurous narrative is laden with issues of visibility and invisibility and, most importantly, the problem of historical legitimacy. Additionally, compare Zalkind's verse to Nabokov's description of the poet Vladimirov in *The Gift*, "As a conversationalist Vladimirov was singularly unattractive. One blamed him for being derisive, supercilious, cold, incapable of thawing to friendly discussions—but that was also said about Koncheyev and about Fyodor himself, and about anyone whose thoughts lived in their own private house and not in a barrack-room or a pub" (321). In the Foreword to the novel's English translation Nabokov wrote, "I am not, and never was, Fyodor . . . it is rather in Koncheyev, as well as in . . . Vladimirov, that I distinguish odds and ends of myself as I was circa 1925" (i).

34. In reviewing the state of scholarship on Russian émigré literature in 1987, David Bethea remarked on the aptness of Nabokov's pen name Sirin as it stands for an "endangered bird . . . outside its native habitat." David Bethea, "Emigration and Heritage," *Slavic and East European Journal* 31 (1987): 141. Moreover, it's worth noting that while the allusion to Sirin-the-bird highlighted Nabokov's Slavic heritage, this image is consistent with the modernist preoccupation with primitivism and gender ambiguity.

35. Sedykh, "Vstrecha s V. Sirinym," 5.

36. Leland De La Durantaye, "Kafka's Reality and Nabokov's Fantasy: On Dwarves, Saints, Beetles, Symbolism, and Genius," *Comparative Literature* 59, no. 4 (2007): 315–31; Alexander Dolinin, "Nabokov as a Russian Writer," in *The Cambridge Companion to Nabokov*, ed. Julian W. Connolly (Cambridge: Cambridge University Press, 2005), 49–64; and Aleksandr Dolinin, *Istinnaia zhizn' pisatelia Sirina: Raboty o Nabokove* (St. Petersburg: Akademicheskii proekt, 2004), 25; Zimmer, *Nabokovs Berlin*, 140–41; Michael Maar, *The Two Lolitas*, trans. Perry Anderson (London: Verso, 2005); Michael Maar, *Speak, Nabokov*, trans. Ross Benjamin (London, Verso, 2009); and Stacy Schiff, *Véra (Mrs. Vladimir Nabokov)* (New York: Modern Library, 2000).

37. The translation corrections Nabokov made can be seen in the reproduction of the opening page of "The Metamorphosis" in his teaching copy. See Vladimir Nabokov, *Lectures on Literature*, ed. Fredson Bowers (New York: Harcourt, Brace, Jovanovich, 1980), 250. In *The Gift*, Fyodor says that he hates "working on translations into German" when speaking about translating legal documents (363).

38. Nabokov translated the "Dedication" to *Faust* ("Iz Gete. Posviashchenie k Faustu") in 1923 and published it nine years later in *Poslednie novosti*, December 15, 1932, 3. As Nabokov admitted in *Strong Opinions*, he translated Heinrich Heine while still living in Russia. See *Strong Opinions*, 189.

39. Robert Louis Jackson, "From the Other Shore: Nabokov's Translation into Russian of Goethe's 'Dedication' to *Faust*," in *Close Encounters: Essays on Russian Literature* (Boston, MA: Academic Studies Press, 2013), 360.

40. Dieter Zimmer has posited that *King, Queen, Knave* "contains more Berlin" than the best-selling Berlin novels of 1928 written by Germans: Vicki Baum's *Menschen im Hotel*, Leonhard Frank's *Bruder und Schwester*, and Erich Kästner's *Fabian*. Zimmer, *Nabokovs Berlin*, 12.

41. Parker, "The Shop Window Quality of Things," 392.

42. V. Sirin, "Berlinskaia vesna," *Rul'*, May 24, 1925; Vladimir Nabokov, *Stikhotvoreniia*, ed. M. E. Malikova (St. Petersburg: Akademicheskii proekt, 2002), 303–4. Nabokov's fascination with springtime Berlin continued into the 1930s. In a letter to Khodasevich of June 26, 1934, he wrote, "Berlin is now exceptionally fine, thanks to the spring which is especially succulent this year; and I lose my mind like a dog from various fascinating smells." See Babikov and Schruba, "Pis'ma V. V. Nabokova," 233.

43. In his memoir *Speak, Memory*, Nabokov will write of living in "material indigence and intellectual luxury" during his European exile (276).

44. See Walter Benjamin's interpretation of the classic flâneur figure in Charles Baudelaire's Paris poetry, "[The flâneur's] way of life still conceals behind a mitigating nimbus the coming desolation of the big-city dweller. The flâneur still stands on the threshold—of the metropolis as of the middle class. Neither has him in its power yet. In neither is he at home. He seeks refuge in the crowd." See Benjamin, "Paris, the Capital of the Nineteenth Century," 105.

45. For an overview of Tiutchev's reception by the Silver Age poets as recounted in exile, see Nikolai Otsup, "F. I. Tiutchev," *Chisla* 1 (1930): 150–61.

46. Dolinin, *Kommentarii*, 68.

47. *The Gift*'s opening has been interpreted extensively, albeit with different conclusions, by several scholars. See, for example, Vladimir Alexandrov, *Nabokov's Otherworld* (Princeton, NJ: Princeton University Press, 1991), 108–9; Blackwell, *Zina's Paradox*, 12–13; Livak, *How It Was Done in Paris*, 173; Leving, *Keys to "The Gift,"* 343–67; and Dolinin, *Kommentarii*, 66–70.

48. See Dolinin, *Kommentarii*, 255–56.

49. As Brian Ladd explains, the *Mietkaserne* (literally, "rental barracks") is "the preeminent symbol of Berlin as industrial metropolis . . . This kind of building was a distinct Berlin type, although it influenced tenement designs in other cities. Because of the depth of Berlin blocks and the large size of building parcels, the tenements were enormous. A single building typically had a hundred or more residents." See Brian Ladd, *The Ghosts of Berlin: Confronting German History in the Urban Landscape* (Chicago, IL: The University of Chicago Press, 1997), 100–1. The *Mietkaserne* are structurally and functionally comparable to residential buildings with narrow, well-like courts (dvory-kolodtsy) in St. Petersburg.

50. The story of Yasha Chernyshevsky—which Nabokov published independently as "Triangle within Circle" in the *New Yorker* (March 23, 1963, 37–41)—can be read as a biography as well. That would make it the novel's third biography in addition to Fyodor's own autobiography. In his study of the novel, Sergei Davydov has analyzed *The Gift*'s structure as the "Russian-nesting-doll texts." See *"Teksty-matreshki" Vladimira Nabokova* (Munich: Otto Sagner Verlag, 1982). Relatedly, Thomas Karshan has argued that the theme of play is an integral part of Nabokov's poetics in *Vladimir Nabokov and the Art of Play* (London: Oxford University Press, 2011).

51. In a scene at a tobacco shop very early in *The Gift*, for example, Fyodor is tricked into buying cigarettes he does not want. He loathes the shop, the advertising posters, and the marketplace generally. But in exchange for the unwanted cigarettes, Fyodor acquires the impression of a memorable Berliner type: a tobacconist in a

"speckled vest with mother-of-pearl buttons" and a "pumpkin-colored bald spot" (6). Victoria Ivleva has analyzed the many ways in which Nabokov recycled this "speckled vest" in the novel, and V. S. Kissel has explored the theme of monetary exchange in *The Gift*, including in this tobacco shop. See Victoria Ivleva, "A Vest Reinvested in *The Gift*," *Russian Review* 68, no. 2 (2009): 283–301; and V. S. Kissel, "O nemetskikh pfenningakh i russkom zolotom fonde: Tema deneg v romane V. Nabokova *Dar*," trans. Galina Time, *Russkaia literatura* 4 (2008): 23–36.

52. By including such a precisely numbered sequence ("at first seven and then three doors away"), Nabokov might be referring to syllabic verse, in which there must be a caesura (slovorazdel) after the seventh syllable, as in Antiokh Kantemir's poetry. In the Russian, "chtoby stat' cherez sem', a tam cherez tri" scans almost like an anapest or a dol'nik, depending on which versification system is used (syllabic, tonic, or syllabotonic). I am grateful to Nila Friedberg for sharing these observations with me. There are several comments on versification technique in *The Gift*—for example, about Yasha Chernyshevsky's dabbling in poetry (38–39) and Fyodor's Aunt Ksenya's "complete disregard for the subtleties of syllabic verse" (148).

53. See Sergei Davydov, "Weighing Nabokov's *Gift* on Pushkin's Scales," in *Cultural Mythologies of Russian Modernism: From the Golden Age to the Silver Age*, ed. Boris Gasparov, Robert Hughes, and Irina Paperno (Berkeley: University of California Press, 1992), 415–28; and Monika Greenleaf, "Fathers, Sons, and Imposters: Pushkin's Trace in *The Gift*," *Slavic Review* 53, no. 1 (1994): 140–58. Livak offers a corrective to the Pushkin-centric readings of Nabokov's novel by showing the many ways in which Nabokov engaged with André Gide's 1925 novel *The Counterfeiters*. See Livak's *How It Was Done in Paris*, 166. On Fyodor's place in the broader Russian literary tradition, see also Alexander Dolinin, "*The Gift*," in *The Garland Companion to Vladimir Nabokov*, ed. Vladimir E. Alexandrov (New York: Routledge, 1995), 144–45.

54. The bees are symbolically significant in Nabokov's oeuvre, even if not as prevalent as butterflies. For example, in the second half of the poem "Berlin Spring," the poet compares the process of artistic creation to the labor inside a beehive, which is also compared to a mailbox ("Ещё листов не развернули, / Ещё никто их не прочёл . . . / Гуди, гуди, железный улей / Почтовый ящик, полный пчёл").

55. Vladimir Alexandrov has observed that here Nabokov evokes Andrei Bely's novel *Kotik Letaev* (1918) in which the words "rhythm" and "swarm" merge into a leitmotif and suggest a link between the spiritual and material worlds. Vladimir Alexandrov, "Nabokov and Bely," in *The Garland Companion to Vladimir Nabokov*, ed. Vladimir E. Alexandrov (New York: Routledge, 1995), 363.

56. Nabokov frequently describes Berlin anthropomorphically: for example, the buds on linden trees on Tannenberg Street are portrayed as eyes ("tomorrow each drop would contain a green pupil"; 4); the streets have feelings ("He was walking along streets that had already long since insinuated themselves into his acquaintance—and if that were not enough, they expected affection"; 53); and residential buildings are animated ("beyond [a vacant lot] the continuous slaty-black backs of houses that seemed to have turned to leave, carried strange, attractive and seemingly completely autonomous whitish designs"; 163; and the "old houses [toast] their tattooed backs in the morning sunshine"; 328). For more context on Nabokov's urban poetics, see Iurii

Leving, *Vokzal-garazh-angar: Vladimir Nabokov i poetika russkogo urbanizma* (St. Petersburg: Ivan Limbakh, 2004), 17–20.

57. See Alexandrov, "Nabokov and Bely," 363–64; Ol'ga Skonechnaia, "Cherno-belyi kaleidoskop: Andrei Belyi v otrazheniiakh V. V. Nabokova," in *Nabokov: Pro et contra*, ed. Boris Averin, Mariia Malikova, and Aleksandr Dolinin (St. Petersburg: Izdatel'stvo Russkogo khristianskogo gumanitarnogo instituta, 1997), 686–87; and Joseph Schlegel, "The Shapes of Poetry: Andrei Bely's Poetics in Vladimir Nabokov's *The Gift*," *Slavic and East European Journal* 59, no. 4 (2015): 567–68. Nabokov included Bely's *Petersburg* in his personal pantheon of the four best twentieth-century prose works, next to James Joyce's *Ulysses*, Marcel Proust's *In Search of Lost Time*, and Franz Kafka's "Metamorphosis." See Vladimir Nabokov, *Strong Opinions*, 57.

58. One possible "film commercial" where letters find their places at the end is an animated short film, *Der Sieger*, made by Walther Ruttmann and Julius Pinschewer in 1922 to advertise Excelsior tires. See YouTube, uploaded by kenef3 on May 12, 2011, https://www.youtube.com/watch?v=X9q0igq61No. On Nabokov's use of advertisement as part of his argument against utilitarianism, see Sergei Davydov, "*The Gift*: Nabokov's Esthetic Exorcism of Chernyshevskii," *Canadian-American Slavic Studies* 19, no. 3 (1985): 364.

59. Viacheslav Kuritsyn has noted that the abundance of character names with the sibilants "ч," "ш," and "щ" in them (Cherdyntsev, Chernyshevsky, Shchegolev, etc.) can be read as Nabokov's challenge to his future German readers because those names look grotesquely difficult in German transliteration. For example, the nine letters of the Russian "Сухощоков" turn into sixteen in the German "Suchoschtschokow." See Viacheslav Kuritsyn, *Nabokov bez Lolity: Putevoditel' s kartami, kartinkami, i zadaniiami* (Moscow: Novoe izdatel'stvo, 2013), 209.

60. Constantine Muravnik has suggested that the title "Nabor" can be read as the author's personal signature: *Nabo*-kov, *nabo*-r. See "Choosing the Hero: Nabokov's Short Story 'Recruiting' as an Introduction to His Aesthetics," *Russian Literature* 64, no. 1 (2008): 77.

61. Dolinin, *Kommentarii*, 254–55.

62. In her analysis of a Shakespearian intertext in *The Gift*, Polina Barskova has argued that the word "be" here is an answer to Hamlet's famous question, "To be or not to be?" See "Filial Feelings and Paternal Patterns: Transformations of *Hamlet* in *The Gift*," *Nabokov Studies* 9 (2005): 205–6.

63. Dolinin, *Kommentarii*, 254–55. Blackwell has noted that the blackbird sitting on the "A" actually does makes an alphabetic vignette because blackbird is "Amsel" in German. See *Zina's Paradox*, 147.

64. Compare this episode to a similar passage in Nabokov's short story "Recruiting," where the narrator comments about "the impersonal Berlin crush of the tram" (v tramvae sredi chuzhoi berlinskoi tesnoty).

65. Mikhail Bakhtin, "Author and Hero in Aesthetic Activity (ca. 1920–1923)," in *Art and Answerability: Early Philosophical Essays*, ed. Michael Holquist and Vadim Liapunov (translator), Kenneth Brostrom (supplement translator) (Austin: University of Texas Press, 1990), 57–309. See also Blackwell, *Zina's Paradox*, 44–45.

66. Bakhtin, "Author and Hero," 212. Additionally, in his illuminating discussion of Nabokov's indebtedness to Yuly Aikhenvald's thought, Blackwell writes about Aikhenvald's and, by extension Nabokov's, conceptions of the codependent relationship between the writer and the reader. Aikhenvald's ideas would fortify the process of Bakhtinian "aesthetic empathizing" I describe. See Blackwell, *Zina's Paradox*, 29–30.

67. The narrator comments on the labor of memory and memory's pitfalls very early in chapter 1: "namely, the snow piled caplike on granite cones joined by a chain somewhere in the vicinity of the statue of Peter the Great. Somewhere! Alas, it is already difficult for me to gather all the parts of the past; already I am beginning to forget relationships and connections between objects that still thrive in my memory, objects I thereby condemn to extinction" (18).

68. Zina's name is included fully in the Russian: "Ты полу-Мнемозина, полумерцанье в имени твоем" (176; emphasis mine).

69. In his foreword to *The Gift*, Nabokov writes that chapter 3's "real hub is the love poem dedicated to Zina" (ii). For an analysis of this poem and its implications for understanding the interrelationship of art and love in the novel, see Blackwell, *Zina's Paradox*, 159–64. See also Paul D. Morris, "Nabokov's Poetic Gift: The Poetry in and of *Dar*," *Russian Literature* 48 (2000): 464.

70. At the end of the novel, Berlin's stately boulevard Unter den Linden is described as having a "pseudo-Parisian character" (359).

71. Livak interprets the differences between the ways the keys are handled in Paris and Berlin as Nabokov's nod to André Gide and contemporary French literary models. See *How It Was Done in Paris*, 186.

72. The other Russian texts include Viktor Shklovsky's novel *Zoo, or Letters Not about Love* (1923); Ilya Ehrenburg's travelogues "Letters from Cafés (Germany in 1923)" and "Five Years Later" (1928); and Roman Gul's book of essays about Germany *Zhizn' na fuksa* (1927). Wittenberg Square features prominently in Nabokov's *King, Queen, Knave* because of its proximity to the Kaufhaus des Westens department store.

73. Blackwell analyzes the significance of various boundaries in the novel in depth. See *Zina's Paradox*, 141–68.

74. V. N. Teliia, ed., *Bol'shoi frazeologicheskii slovar' russkogo iazyka: Znachenie, upotreblenie, kul'turologicheskii kommentarii* (Moscow: AST-Press Kniga, 2006), 492.

75. See Philip T. Sicker, "Shadows of Exile in Nabokov's Berlin," *Thought* 62, no. 246 (1987): 281–82.

76. Public book burnings by the Nazis begin in the early 1930s, and the infamous Degenerate Art Exhibition takes place in 1937 as Nabokov is finishing *The Gift*. Socialist Realism is enshrined as the only acceptable mode of artistic production in the Soviet Union in 1934.

77. Nabokov often alludes to mimicry in nature to underscore the importance of seeing clearly. See Alexandrov, *Nabokov's Otherworld*, 130–36, and his "A Note on Nabokov's Anti-Darwinism; or, Why Apes Feed on Butterflies in *The Gift*," in *Freedom and Responsibility in Russian Literature: Essays in Honor of Robert Louis Jackson*, ed. Elizabeth Cheresh Allen and Gary Saul Morson (Evanston, IL: Northwestern University Press, 1995), 239–44.

78. For an overview of the scholarly interpretations of *The Gift*'s formal structure as a Möbius strip (Omry and Irena Ronen); a Figure-Eight Pattern (Leona Toker); an Apple Peel (Leonid Livak); and other variations of the spiral, see Leving, *Keys to "The Gift,"* 208–12. See also Iurii Levin, "Ob osobennostiakh povestvovatel'noi struktury i obraznogo stroia romana V. Nabokova *Dar*," *Russian Literature* 9 (1981): 191–230; and Ekaterina Liapushkina, "'Karusel' istiny': Smysl epigrapha v romane V. V. Nabokova *Dar*," *Russkaia literatura* 1 (2020): 210.

79. Dolinin has documented a large number of these references in his *Kommentarii*. Regarding Fyodor's nudism and its relation to Nabokov's aesthetics and the contemporary Weimar context, see Igor' P. Smirnov, "Obnazhenie mastera, zasekrechivaiushchego priem: Istochniki grunewal'dskogo epizoda v romane Vladimira Nabokova *Dar*," in *A/Z: Essays in Honor of Alexander Zholkovsky*, ed. Dennis Ioffe, Marcus Levitt, Joe Peschio, and Igor Pilshchikov (Boston, MA: Academic Studies Press, 2018), 526–46.

80. In chapter 5, Fyodor undertakes four extensive routes across Berlin's central and western parts. Kuritsyn has described them in detail and reconstructed the maps of Fyodor's movement in Berlin in *Nabokov bez Lolity*, 180–213.

81. Kuritsyn, *Nabokov bez Lolity*, 210.

82. Dolinin interprets the image of the Brandenburg Gate's narrow passage in biblical terms (Matthew 7:13–14). In general, on the eastern side of the Brandenburg Gate, Fyodor sees the cityscape in "narrow" terms ("the narrowness of the commercial streets"; "that narrow slit" behind the rooftops, 359) and on the western side things get wider ("those old postcards of [the Potsdam square] where everything is so spacious," 358).

83. One famous example is the image of Fyodor's erection sublimated in the image of a cloud: "He imagined what he had constantly been imagining during the past two months—the beginning (tomorrow night!) of his full life with Zina—the release, the slaking—and meanwhile a sun-charged cloud, filling up, growing, with swollen, turquoise veins, with a fiery itch in its thunder-root, rose in all its turgid, unwieldy magnificence and embraced him" (345–46). Naiman has suggested that this passage is meant to be Nabokov's "example of how writing suffers aesthetically when the author is unduly under the influence of the demands of the flesh." See Nabokov, *Perversely* (Ithaca, NY: Cornell University Press, 2010), 173.

84. Arguably, the sexual, and especially masturbatory, imagery in *The Gift*, meticulously gathered and analyzed by Naiman in his *Nabokov, Perversely*, might be understood as Nabokov's provocation meant to remind the reader that texts can stimulate desire but they multiply by other means.

85. Priscilla Meyer, "The Hidden Nabokov," unpublished keynote address at the Hidden Nabokov Conference, June 15–19, 2022, Wellesley College.

86. Karlinsky, "*Dar* as a Work of Literary Criticism," 288.

87. Eric Naiman has suggested that Zina may be but a figment of Fyodor's imagination. See *Nabokov, Perversely*, 171. Cf. Blackwell, *Zina's Paradox*, 2–3. Alexandrov has proposed a more radical reading, arguing that in *The Gift* Russian literature itself "was neither specially privileged, nor of course an end in itself for [Nabokov]." See *Nabokov's Otherworld*, 136.

88. It's worth noting that in chapter 1, when remembering his childhood, Fyodor describes himself as "transparent as a cut-glass egg" (22), and in chapter 5, he is robbed of his clothes at the beach and returns home clothed in nothing but his trunks ("trusiki"; 346). He becomes a perfect vessel for absorbing and channeling external phenomena.

89. Fyodor also quotes an excerpt from Gogol's 1836 letter to Vasily Zhukovsky that is applicable to himself, "Longer, longer, and for as long as possible, shall I be in a strange country. And although my thoughts, my name, my works will belong to Russia, I myself, my mortal organism, will be removed from it" (180). See Dolinin, *Kommentarii*, 258.

90. Mark Lipovetsky has argued for reading *The Gift* as the "epilogue of Russian modernism" and a "metanovelistic summary [obobshchenie] of all of Nabokov's Russian prose." See Lipovetskii, "Epilog russkogo modernizma: Khudozhestvennaia filosofiia tvorchestva v *Dare* Nabokova," in *Nabokov: Pro et contra*, 645.

91. Irina Paperno, *Chernyshevsky and the Age of Realism: A Study in the Semiotics of Behavior* (Stanford, CA: Stanford University Press, 1988), 4. On Chernyshevsky in *The Gift*, see Boyd, *The Russian Years*, 456–62.

92. Dana Dragonoiu, *Vladimir Nabokov and the Poetics of Liberalism* (Evanston, IL: Northwestern University Press, 2011), 54.

93. The complete version of *Dar* appeared in 1952. For the novel's publication history, see Dolinin, *Kommentarii*, 23–28. As Dolinin notes, the editors at *Sovremennye zapiski* also required Nabokov to edit out a mocking reference to Vissarion Belinsky, another major figure of the Russian progressive intelligentsia. Dolinin, *Kommentarii*, 272.

94. On the homophobic origins of Nabokov's portrayal of Yasha, see Livak, *How It Was Done in Paris*, 192–203.

95. See Will Norman, *Nabokov, History and the Texture of Time* (New York: Routledge, 2012), 11–13. See also Duffield White, "Radical Aestheticism and Metaphysical Realism in Nabokov's *The Gift*," in *Russian Literature and American Critics: In Honor of Deming Brown*, ed. Kenneth N. Brostrom (Ann Arbor: University of Michigan Department of Slavic Languages and Literatures, 1984), 273–91.

96. Boyd, *The Russian Years*, 450.

97. See Blackwell, *Zina's Paradox*, 37–57; Boris Maslov, "Traditsii literaturnogo diletantizma i esteticheskaia ideologiia romana *Dar*," in *Imperiia N: Nabokov i nasledniki*, ed. Iurii Leving and Evgenii Soshkin (Moscow: Novoe literaturnoe obozrenie, 2006), 70; and Naiman, *Nabokov, Perversely*, 175.

98. Nikolai Chernyshevsky, *What Is to Be Done?*, trans. Michael R. Katz (Ithaca, NY: Cornell University Press, 1989), 41.

99. Lopukhov returns to St. Petersburg disguised as the American businessman Charles Beaumont. But he first reappears in the novel in chapter 4 by sending Vera Pavlovna a letter from Berlin, sharing his address, "Berlin, Friedrichstrasse 20, Agentur von H. Schweigler." Chernyshevsky, *What Is to Be Done?*, 322.

100. Davydov, "*The Gift*," 357–74.

101. Marina Kostalevsky, "The Young Godunov-Cherdyntsev, or How to Write a Literary Biography," *Russian Literature* 43 (1998): 283.

102. Nikolai Gavrilovich Chernyshevskii, *Chto delat'? Iz rasskazov o novykh liudiakh*, vol. 1 of *Sobranie sochinenii v piati tomakh* (Moscow: Pravda, 1974).

103. As Will Norman writes, "While *What Is to Be Done*? concludes with Vera Pavlovna's dream of the social future, it finds its true temporal destiny in the *literary* future, in the hands of an émigré novelist in flight from the historical attempt to realize that same utopia." See his *Nabokov, History and the Texture of Time*, 13.

104. Whereas Chernyshevsky was famously invested in creating a perpetual motion machine, Nabokov realizes the principle of a *perpetuum mobile* in *The Gift*'s narrative structure. See Justin Weir, *The Author as Hero: Self and Tradition in Bulgakov, Pasternak, and Nabokov* (Evanston, IL: Northwestern University Press, 2002), 98.

105. Maslov charts the development of "literary dilettantism" before and after the term acquired its negative meaning. Etymologically, the word "dilletante" has roots in the Latin "delectare" (to delight, pleasure, amuse). See Maslov, "Traditsii literaturnogo diletantizma," 42.

106. Maslov, "Traditsii literaturnogo diletantizma," 47.

107. Vladimir Nabokov, *Lectures on Literature*, 126. Quoted in Maslov, "Traditsii literaturnogo diletantizma," 47.

108. Maslov, "Traditsii literaturnogo diletantizma," 70.

109. In writing about Nabokov's autobiography *Speak, Memory*, Barbara Straumann has identified an ambivalence in Nabokov's poetics that can be applied to *The Gift* as well: "On the one hand, then, Nabokov fashions himself as an isolated figure who inhabits a purely textual world. On the other hand, he could not write his text unless he had lost an entire cultural world and several family members—unless 'the things and beings that I had most loved in the security of my childhood had been turned to ashes or shot through the heart' [*Speak, Memory*, 92]. Like so many others, his exilic trajectory is thus embedded in the very real exilic movements and cultural displacements of the time." See her *Figurations of Exile in Hitchcock and Nabokov* (Edinburgh: Edinburgh University Press, 2008), 9.

110. As Blackwell underscores, Fyodor "has unsocial living habits: he sleeps till noon, stays up most of the night, skips obligations, walks out on meetings, borrows money, and socializes badly; with Zina he tends to be self-centered (more precisely: art-centered) despite his love for her." *Zina's Paradox*, 40.

111. Davydov points out that Nabokov likely borrows the very device of "autocriticism" from Chernyshevsky. See "Nabokov's Exorcism of Chernyshevskii," 265. On the extent of Nabokov's engagement with contemporary writers in *The Gift*, see Livak, *How It Was Done in Paris*, 164–203; and Dolinin, "Literaturnyi fon," in *Kommentarii*, 38–56; as well as Kostalevsky, "The Young Godunov-Cherdyntsev," 283–95; Edward Brown, "Nabokov, Chernyshevsky, Olesha, and the Gift of Sight," in *Literature, Culture, and Society in the Modern Age*, 280–94; Henrietta Mondri, "O dvukh adresatakh literaturnoi parodii v *Dare* V. Nabokova (Iu. Tynianov i V. Rozanov)," *Rossiiskii literaturovedcheskii zhurnal* 4 (1994): 95–102; Olga Skonechnaia, "'People of the Moonlight': Silver Age Parodies in Nabokov's *The Eye* and *The Gift*," *Nabokov Studies* 3 (1996): 33–47; Anna Brodsky, "Homosexuality and the Aesthetic of Nabokov's *Dar*," *Nabokov Studies* 4 (1997): 95–115; and Anne Nesbet, "Suicide as Literary Fact in the 1920s," *Slavic Review* 50, no. 4 (1991): 827–35.

112. Weir, *The Author as Hero*, 95. Relatedly, Davydov has proposed reading "The Life of Chernyshevsky" as a variation on the genre of Menippean satire. See "Nabokov's Exorcism of Chernyshevskii," 373–74.

113. Stephen Blackwell, "Nabokov's *The Gift*, Dostoevsky, and the Tradition of Narratorial Ambiguity," *Slavic Review* 76, no. 1 (2017): 167.

114. Paperno, "How Nabokov's *Gift* Is Made," 295–322.

115. See Norman, *Nabokov, History and the Texture of Time*, 29.

116. For example, consider Alfred Döblin's novel *Berlin Alexanderplatz* (1929) and Dziga Vertov's documentary film *Man with a Movie Camera* (1929) in their attempts to convey the human experience of the city by radically experimental means. Vertov's film was screened in Berlin in 1929. Also, Yuri Levin has posited that *The Gift* "is a productionist [proizvodstvennyi] novel of sorts"—a central genre of Soviet literature of the 1920s and 1930s. See Levin, "Ob osobennostiakh povestvovatel'noi struktury," 201.

117. This statement echoes the ideas of Marina Tsvetaeva, his contemporary and an émigré poet until 1939. See her 1932 essay "Poet i vremia" (Poet and Time), in *Izbrannaia proza v dvukh tomakh*, ed. Aleksandr Sumerkin, vol. 1 (New York: Russica Publishers, 1979), 372. Nabokov's position on authorship in exile also corresponds to that of Thomas Mann, who famously declared in the wake of his own emigration in 1938, "Germany is where I am. I carry my German culture in me." See "Mann Finds U.S. Sole Peace Hope," *New York Times*, February 22, 1938, 13.

118. Vladimir Nabokov, "Definitions" in *Think, Write, Speak*, 141. First published as "Opredeleniia" in the New York émigré daily *Novoe russkoe slovo*. On the implications of this essay, see Dolinin, "Nabokov as a Russian Writer," 57; Andrei Babikov, "Opredeleiniia Nabokova," *Zvezda* 9 (2013): 112–16. Developing the idea of an artist as perpetually in exile, Nabokov would say later in his life, "The writer's art is his real passport." See *Strong Opinions*, 63.

Chapter 5. Queering the Russian Diaspora

1. Pavel Tchelitchew Collection, box 16, folder 297, Beinecke. All Yuritsyn quotations are from this collection.

2. As Georgy Adamovich told Yuri Ivask much later in 1960, "People gossip . . . without a complete understanding; there is no 'wholesome' knowledge [Сплетничают . . . а не [понимают] целого, нет 'целокупного' знания]." Adamovich then shared some of that sort of gossip with Ivask about Zinaida Gippius and Dmitry Merezhkovsky: "During their wedding night, Z[inaida] N[ikolaevna] [Gippius]: 'Dmitry, have mercy on me.' And the following night again the same . . . As though they both could, but she did not want to. In S[aint] P[etersburg], Z[inaida] N[ikolaevna] had the nickname 'white she-devil' (белая дьяволица)—she is wearing tights, and nearby *he* is breathing heavily (пыхтит, [дышит]), while I am inaccessible (а я недоступна). 'Intercourse is such a horror' (Половой акт—такой ужас). . . . With Z. N.'s permission, Merezhkovsky brought home boys. I don't believe this very much, just like everything that people say here. All Parisians are myth-makers (мифотворцы)." The Yurii [George] P. Ivask Papers, Box 1, Amherst.

3. Klaus Mann, *The Turning Point* (1942), cited in Robert Beachy, *Gay Berlin: Birthplace of a Modern Identity* (New York: Knopf, 2014), ix. For a concise summary

of queer emancipation in Berlin, see Ralf Dose, *Magnus Hirschfeld: The Origins of the Gay Liberation Movement*, trans. Edward H. Willis (New York: Monthly Review Press, 2014).

4. Mel Gordon, *Voluptuous Panic: The Erotic World of Weimar Berlin*, expanded edition (Los Angeles: Feral House, 2006), 1. Christopher Isherwood, who played a major role in mythologizing Weimar Berlin as a sexually liberated metropolis, suggested in his 1976 memoir that Weimar Berlin's reputation for the risqué was what attracted all manner of tourists to the city: "In the [wealthier] West End there were also dens of pseudo-vice catering to heterosexual tourists. Here screaming boys in drag and monocled, Eton-cropped girls in dinner jackets play-acted the high jinks of Sodom and Gomorrah, horrifying the onlookers and reassuring them that Berlin was still the most decadent city in Europe." Isherwood, *Christopher and His Kind*, 29.

5. George Mosse, *Nationalism and Sexuality: Respectability and Abnormal Sexuality in Modern Europe* (New York: Howard Fertig, 1985), 131–32.

6. Anna Hájková, "Den Holocaust queer erzählen," *Jahrbuch Sexualitäten* (2018): 109. See also Heather Love, *Feeling Backward: Loss and the Politics of Queer History* (Cambridge, MA: Harvard University Press, 2007).

7. Belyi, *Odna iz obitelei tsarstva tenei*, 32.

8. Erenburg, *Belyi ugol'*, 128–29. Ironically, Ehrenburg's early poetry is quoted in Isherwood's memoir. The British writer was likely unaware of the Russian author's less than flattering references to gay men in Berlin. See Isherwood, *Christopher and His Kind*, 10.

9. Shklovsky, *Zoo*, 136. Khodasevich expressed a similar sentiment in his 1923 Berlin poem "Pod zemlei." Ehrenburg did not fail to mention the bathrooms in Berlin's bohemian cafés where "young men languidly powder their faces and draw eyebrows." Erenburg, *Belyi ugol'*, 160.

10. Gregory Woods, *The Homintern: How Gay Culture Liberated the Modern World* (New Haven, CT: Yale University Press, 2016), xi. It remains unclear who coined the term "Homintern"—Cyril Connoly, W. H. Auden, or Harold Norse.

11. See Evgenii Bershtein, "Eisenstein's Letter to Magnus Hirschfeld: Text and Context," in *The Flying Carpet: Studies on Eisenstein and Russian Cinema in Honor of Naum Kleiman*, ed. Joan Neuberger and Antonio Somaini (Sesto San Giovani: Éditions Mimésis, 2017), 75–86. According to Nicolas Nabokov, Esenin insisted that they "go together to a pederast [*sic*] night club"—"I'm told it's close to here. Men get undressed there and bugger each other on the stage. I want to see it. Come with me and Dunkansha." Of course, it is difficult to say how truthful this account is, written as it was over fifty years after their meeting took place. See Nicolas Nabokov, *Bagázh*, 126. Nabokov also writes that this episode occurred in the presence of Harry Graf Kessler, a notable diplomat and a prominent queer intellectual of interwar Germany. On Graf Kessler's Russian connections, see Schlögel, *Das russische Berlin*, 114–40.

12. To my knowledge, the first book written in emigration that tackles openly the problem of homosexuality is Nina Berberova's biography of Tchaikovsky: *Chaikovskii: Istoriia odinokoi zhizni* (Berlin: Petropolis, 1936). Roman Gul's brochure about Andrei Bely's writings is a curious, though not entirely coherent, early attempt to theorize gender: *Pol v tvorchestve: Razbor proizvedenii Andreia Belogo* (Berlin: Manfred, 1923).

13. Daniel Marshall, Kevin Murphy, and Zeb Tortorici, "Editors' Introduction. Queering Archives: Intimate Tracings," *Radical History Review* 122 (May 2015): 1.

14. Raeff, *Russia Abroad*, 4.

15. Although less known, the poets Georgy Adamovich and Valery Pereleshin come to mind as well.

16. There are exceptions, however, such as Vitaly Chernetsky, "Displacement, Desire, Identity and the 'Diasporic Momentum': Two Slavic Writers in Latin America," *Intertexts* 7, no. 1 (Spring 2003): 49–70.

17. See Ethan Pollok, *Without the Banya We Would Perish: A History of the Russian Bathhouse* (Oxford, UK: Oxford University Press, 2019).

18. Wolfgang Theis and Andreas Sternweiler, "Alltag im Kaiserreich und in der Weimarer Republik," in *Eldorado: Homosexuelle Frauen und Männer in Berlin 1850–1950: Geschichte, Alltag und Kultur*, ed. Michael Bolle (Berlin: Frölich und Kaufmann, 1984), 55–56. See also David James Prickett, "Defining Identity via Homosexual Spaces: Locating the Male Homosexual in Weimar Berlin," *Women in German Yearbook: Feminist Studies in German Literature and Culture* 21 (2005): 134–62.

19. Gayatri Gopinath, "Archive, Affect, and the Everyday: Queer Diasporic Re-Visions," in *Political Emotions*, ed. Janet Staiger, Ann Cvetkovich, and Ann Reynolds (New York: Routledge), 171. In his study of queer modernism, Octavio González examines the case studies of travelers and expatriates advancing claims about exile. See *Misfit Modernism: Queer Forms of Double Exile in the Twentieth-Century Novel* (University Park: Pennsylvania State University Press, 2020).

20. Greta Slobin, *Russians Abroad*, 74–92. See also Svetlana Boym, *The Off-Modern* (London: Bloomsbury Academic, 2017), 79–89.

21. Livak, *How It Was Done in Paris*, 41.

22. Vladimir Nabokov, *Speak, Memory*, 257.

23. Arnaldo Cruz-Malavé and Martin F. Manalansan, eds., *Queer Globalizations: Citizenship and the Afterlife of Colonialism* (New York: New York University Press, 2002), 2.

24. Meg Wesling, "Why Queer Diaspora?," *Feminist Review* 90 (2008): 30–47. Cf. Jarrod Hayes, "Queering Roots, Queering Diaspora," in *Rites of Return: Diaspora Poetics and the Politics of Memory*, ed. Marianne Hirsch and Nancy K. Miller (New York: Columbia University Press, 2011), 72–87.

25. Marina Tsvetaeva, *Letter to the Amazon*, trans. A'Dora Phillips and Gaëlle Cogan, introduction by Catherine Ciepiela (Brooklyn: Ugly Duckling Presse, 2016). On Tsvetaeva and Barney, see Irina Shevelenko, *Literaturnyi put' Tsvetaevoi: Ideologiia—poetika—identichnost' avtora v kontekste epokhi* (Moscow: Novoe literaturnoe obozrenie, 2002), 375–78.

26. Brent Hayes Edwards, *The Practice of Diaspora: Literature, Translation, and the Rise of Black Internationalism* (Cambridge, MA: Harvard University Press, 2003), 13; and Edwards, "The Uses of Diaspora," 45–73.

27. For the uses of the term "queer" in contemporary Russian, see the thematic cluster of articles I edited, "Illegal Queerness: Russian Culture and Society in the Age of Anti-LGBTQ Censorship," *Russian Review* 80, no. 1 (2021): 7–99.

28. Although there were some exceptions—the poet Sofia Parnok presented herself as the Russian Sappho. Nabokov uses the phrase "sexual lefty" (seksual'nyi levsha) to denote queer sexuality in his novel *The Eye* (1930; 1965). On the turn-of-the century queer vocabularies, see Lindsay F. Watton, "Constructs of Sin and Sodom in Russian Modernism, 1906–1909," *Journal of the History of Sexuality* 4, no. 3 (January 1994): 369–94; Evgenii Bershtein, "The Discourse of Sexual Psychopathy in Russian Modernism," in *Reframing Russian Modernism*, ed. Irina Shevelenko (Madison: University of Wisconsin Press, 2018), 143–71; Diana Burgin, "Mother Nature versus the Amazons: Marina Tsvetaeva and Female Same-Sex Love," *Journal of the History of Sexuality* 6, no. 1 (1995): 62–88; Olga Matich, *Erotic Utopia: The Decadent Imagination in Russia's Fin de Siècle* (Madison: University of Wisconsin Press, 2004); and Brian James Baer, "Translating Sexology in Late-Tsarist and Early-Soviet Russia: Politics, Literature, and the Science of Sex," in *Sexology and Translation: Cultural and Scientific Encounters across the Modern World*, ed. Heike Bauer (Philadelphia, PA: Temple University Press, 2015), 115–34.

29. Heike Bauer, *The Hirschfeld Archives: Violence, Death, and Modern Queer Culture* (Philadelphia, PA: Temple University Press, 2017), 10.

30. Eric Naiman has attempted to answer the question "What is to be done with the homosexuals who inhabit Nabokov's novels?" in chapter 4 of his book *Nabokov, Perversely*, 105–31. See also Steven Bruhm, "Queer, Queer Vladimir," *American Imago* 53, no. 4 (Winter 1996): 281; Maar, *Speak, Nabokov*, 26–31; and Meghan Vicks, "Paranoid Reading, Reparative Reading, and Queering *The Real Life of Sebastian Knight*," in *Reimagining Nabokov: Pedagogies for the 21st Century*, ed. Sara Karpukhin and José Vergara (Amherst: Amherst College Press, 2022), 128–47. In a 1968 interview, Nabokov said that Oscar Wilde "got caught" for "flaunting a flamboyant perversion." See *Strong Opinions*, 119.

31. The case of Kinbote/Botkin in *The Real Life of Sebastian Knight* is one of the more complex instances of Nabokov's engagement with the theme. Furthermore, as Stephen Blackwell has determined, Nabokov began his imaginings of *Pale Fire* by thinking about the life of a gay college professor in "a puritanical country, where a handshake would be the only possible erotic contact." See Blackwell, *The Quill and the Scalpel: Nabokov's Art and the Worlds of Science* (Columbus: Ohio State University Press, 2009), 234.

32. Versions of the law criminalizing sexual relations between men were part of the Russian criminal code since the early eighteenth century. See Dan Healey, *Homosexual Desire in Revolutionary Russia: The Regulation of Sexual and Gender Dissent* (Chicago: University of Chicago Press, 2001).

33. Laura Engelstein, *The Keys to Happiness: Sex and the Search for Modernity in Revolutionary Russia* (Ithaca, NY: Cornell University Press, 1994), 66–70. See also Vladimir Nabokov, *Speak, Memory*, 178–79.

34. Vladimir D. Nabokoff, "Die Homosexualität im russischen Strafgesetzbuch," *Jahrbuch für sexuelle Zwischenstufen* 2 (1903): 1159–71.

35. See Beachy, *Gay Berlin*; and Laurie Marhoefer, *Sex and the Weimar Republic: German Homosexual Emancipation and the Rise of the Nazis* (Toronto: University of Toronto Press, 2015). Evidently, in Berlin there was interest in Russian sexual mores,

too. See Bernhardt Stern, *Geschichte der Öffentlichen Sittlichkeit in Russland: Kultur, Aberglaube, Sitten und Gebräuche* (Berlin: Verlag von Hermann Barsdorf, 1908), 556–70. Stern's two-volume study was published in multiple editions into the 1920s.

36. The fullest-to-date account of Sergey's biography in exile is offered in Dieter Zimmer's article "What Happened to Sergey Nabokov" (2017), http://www.d-e-zimmer.de/PDF/SergeyN.pdf.

37. Vladimir Nabokov, *Speak, Memory*, 257. Will Norman has offered a generous interpretation of Vladimir's portrayal of Sergey rooted in "Nabokov's historical anxiety." See *Nabokov, History, and the Texture of Time*, 70–71.

38. Vladimir Nabokov, *Speak, Memory*, 257–58.

39. Boyd, *The Russian Years*, 192.

40. Boyd, *The Russian Years*, 192.

41. Vladimir Nabokov, *Speak, Memory*, 214.

42. Robyn Jensen, "Authorizing the Image: Photography in Nabokov's *Speak, Memory*," *Slavic and East European Journal* 63, no. 2 (Summer 2019): 192–93.

43. Avery Gordon has argued that haunting is "one form by which something lost, or barely visible, or seemingly not there to our supposedly well-trained eyes, makes itself known or apparent to us." She investigates palpable absences of something or someone in the form of ghost-like traces, shadows, and rhetorical residues. In the case of the Nabokov brothers, we are presented with an inverted version of this process: Sergey is not a haunted presence but a haunted absence. See *Ghostly Matters: Haunting and the Sociological Imagination* (Minneapolis: University of Minnesota Press, 1997), 8.

44. Vladimir Nabokov, *Speak, Memory*, 258.

45. Simon Karlinsky, ed. and trans., *Dear Bunny, Dear Volodya: The Nabokov-Wilson Letters, 1940–1971*, revised and expanded edition (Berkeley: University of California Press, 2001), 173.

46. Vladimir Nabokov, *Letters to Véra*, ed. and trans. Olga Voronina and Brian Boyd (New York: Knopf, 2014), 208. The word "pederast" is misleading in translation. Taking into account the historical specificities of the term, the original Russian "совершенно не тип педераста" would be more accurately rendered as "absolutely not the homosexual type."

47. Vladimir Nabokov, *Letters to Véra*, 159.

48. Dieter Zimmer has suggested that it is possible there is important correspondence concerning Sergey among Vladimir's currently restricted papers in the Berg Collection of the New York Public Library. To counter the lack of archival materials, the novelist Paul Russell wrote a speculative biography, *The Unreal Life of Sergey Nabokov* (2011). The title alludes to Vladimir's first novel in English, *The Real Life of Sebastian Knight* (1939), in which the narrator searches for his elusive half brother.

49. Nicolas Nabokov, *Bagázh*, 110. Their "babushka" is Maria Ferdinandovna Nabokov, née von Korff.

50. Cited in Eric Karpeles, *Almost Nothing: The 20th-Century Art and Life of Józef Czapski* (New York: New York Review of Books, 2018), 59.

51. Lucie Léon Noel, "Playback," *TriQuarterly* 17 (Winter 1970): 212. Cited in Zimmer, "What Happened to Sergey Nabokov," 11–12. Vladimir Nabokov contested some of the details of Léon Noel's account, but not those concerning his brother or their

relationship. See his *Strong Opinions*, 292–93. A pommeled cane makes a memorable appearance in *Speak, Memory* in the description of Vladimir and Sergey's escape to Crimea by train: "The cane I carried, a collector's item that had belonged to my uncle Ruka, was of a light-colored, beautifully freckled wood, and the knob was a smooth pink globe of coral cupped in a gold coronet" (243).

52. Vladimir Nabokov, *Strong Opinions*, 189.

53. Dmitry Shakhovskoy (1902–89) is more commonly known as the Archbishop Ioann of San Francisco.

54. The Archbishop Ioann Shakhovskoy Papers, box 34, folder 11, Amherst. All further quotations are from this collection, except for the letter of November 20, 1925.

55. Shakhovskoy wrote: "I'm answering your question about Paris, though I don't know to what degree my 'more or less' Parisianness entitles me to do so. You can find a room in Quartier Latin for 3 francs a day, but that is, of course, a room in quotation marks. A modest and decent room should be considered for no less than 150–180 francs a month. That's in the cheap neighborhoods; though, perhaps, [they can be found] even in some corners of those velvet streets where the eye still discerns the traces of family crests above the gates. I don't know how 'difficult' you are with food. That's a big obstacle in determining the nutritional minimum. For five paper francs you won't die of hunger and, moreover, with some nervousness, you could feel satiated. If you budget 10 francs a day (if you manage to find a 'practical' situation, that is), and if you don't include in these 10 francs 3 francs for the tip, then this sum is normal. It remains to summarize the results: 150 + 300 = 450 without the metro, bus, and the books of [André] Suarès. Concerning employment, I think now the time is almost favorable. Many Russians got strewn into various French corners, though our émigré values are not rated all that highly. Write to me as soon as your decision is finalized and, if you wish, I will give you several addresses."

56. The phrase "masquerade of perversions" belongs to Isherwood, who wrote in his memoir, "Wasn't Berlin's famous 'decadence' largely a commercial 'line,' which the Berliners had instinctively developed in their competition with Paris? Paris had long since cornered the straight-girl market, so what was left for Berlin to offer its visitors but a masquerade of perversions?" See *Christopher and His Kind*, 29. On the intersection of sexual politics, art, and activism in Weimar Berlin, see James Steakley, "Cinema and Censorship in the Weimar Republic: The Case of *Anders als die Andern*," *Film History* 11, no. 2 (1999): 181–203.

57. In his travel writings from Berlin, Ehrenburg quipped that the young French writers "vacillate between academic Catholicism and compulsory homosexuality." Erenburg, *Belyi ugol'*, 167.

58. This letter of November 20, 1925, is part of the Shakhovskoy Family Archive, box 14, at the Amherst Center for Russian Culture. The Archbishop Ioann's papers were prepared for archiving by his sister, the émigré writer Zinaïda Shakhovskaia, the author of *In Search of Nabokov*, a biography based in large part on her correspondence with Vladimir. See her *V poiskakh Nabokova* (Paris: La Presse Libre, 1979).

59. See Karpeles, *Almost Nothing*, 189–229.

60. Vladimir Nabokov, *Letters to Véra*, 77–78.

61. Vladimir Nabokov, *Letters to Véra*, 78.

62. Vladimir Nabokov, *Letters to Véra*, 196.
63. See Sergey's letter in the Nicolas Nabokov Papers, box 2, folder 59, Beinecke Library.
64. Zimmer, "What Happened to Sergey Nabokov," 16–17.
65. See Zimmer, "What Happened to Sergey Nabokov," 17–25.
66. Vladimir Nabokov, *Speak, Memory*, 258.
67. Doris Liebermann, "Einleitung," in Vera Lourié, *Briefe an Dich: Erinnerungen an das russische Berlin*, ed. Doris Liebermann (Frankfurt on Main: Schöffling & Co., 2014), 10.
68. See Lieberman, "Einleitung," 7–20.
69. Vera Lur'e, *Stikhotvoreniia*, ed. Thomas R. Beyer Jr. (Berlin: Spitz, 1987).
70. Lourié, *Briefe an Dich*, 25.
71. Lourié, *Briefe an Dich*, 154.
72. Lourié, *Briefe an Dich*, 7. The name of the doctor's wife is disclosed in a review of Lourié's memoir. See "Vera Lourié und ihre 'Briefe an dich': Alles bleibt unendlich weit," *Tagesspiegel*, April 26, 2014, https://www.tagesspiegel.de/kultur/vera-lourie-und-ihre-briefe-an-dich-alles-bleibt-unendlich-weit/9809932.html.
73. Lourié, *Briefe an Dich*, 27.
74. Lourié, *Briefe an Dich*, 89–90.
75. In the late 1970s Nina Berberova wrote a cycle of poems called "The Berlin Zoo," as if responding to Shklovsky's *Zoo* and describing post–World War II Berlin. See *Stikhi: 1921–1983* (New York: Russica, 1984), 113–16.
76. Lourié, *Briefe an Dich*, 68.
77. Lourié, *Briefe an Dich*, 25.
78. Lourié, *Briefe an Dich*, 26.
79. The translation was published in *Studiia/Studio* in 2006, issues 9, 10, 11, and 12. It's possible the translation is based on an alternative archival version of Lourié's memoir.
80. Lourié, *Briefe an Dich*, 57.
81. Lourié, *Briefe an Dich*, 58.
82. Lourié, *Briefe an Dich*, 58.
83. In this regard, Vera's life was not atypical. See Marie Jalowicz Simon, *Underground in Berlin: A Young Woman's Extraordinary Tale of Survival in the Heart of Nazi Germany*, trans. Anthea Bell (London: Little, Brown, 2015).

Conclusion

1. Cf. Raeff, *Russia Abroad*, 95. Commenting on the difficulty of parsing what Russian culture means, particularly in a globally networked world, Kevin Platt has recently written that "Russian culture is fragmented and multiple, and everywhere it is the object of diverse and contradictory institutional, political, and economic forces that seek to define and constrain it." He adds that "it always exceeds any one location and presents a unity only in its perpetually renegotiated multiplicity." See "Introduction: Putting Russian Cultures in Place," in *Global Russian Cultures*, 6.
2. See Waltraud Werner, *1884 Wassili Masjutin 1955: Ein russischer Künstler 1922–1955 in Berlin* (Berlin: Verlag Willmuth Arenhövel, 2003).

3. See Lina Bernstein, *Magda Nachman: An Artist in Exile* (Boston, MA: Academic Studies Press, 2020).

4. Vladimir Khazan and Roman Timenchik, "Na zemle byla odna stolitsa," introduction to *Peterburg v poezii russkoi emigratsii: Pervaia i vtoraia volna*, ed. V. Khazan and R. Timenchik (St. Petersburg: Akademicheskii proekt, 2006), 10.

5. Vladimir Korvin-Piotrovskii, "Stikhi k Pushkinu," in *Novosel'e* (Berlin: Slovo, 1931), 38.

6. Robert C. Williams, *Culture in Exile*, 331–63.

7. Berberova, *Stikhi*, 114.

Appendix

1. See Elena Kannak, "Berlinskii kruzhok poetov (1928–1933)," in *Russkii Berlin*, ed. Vera V. Sorokina (Moscow: Izdatel'stvo Moskovskogo Universiteta, 2003), 280.

2. On Essad-Bey, see Tom Reiss, *The Orientalist: Solving the Mystery of a Strange and Dangerous Life* (New York: Random House, 2005).

BIBLIOGRAPHY

Archival Sources

Nina Berberova Papers. General Collection, Beinecke Rare Book and Manuscript Library, Yale University (Beinecke).
Yurii [George] P. Ivask Papers. Amherst Center for Russian Culture, Amherst College (ACRC).
Simon Karlinsky Papers. Bancroft Library, University of California, Berkeley.
Vladimir Korvin-Piotrovskii Papers. General Collection, Beinecke.
Nicolas Nabokov Papers. General Collection, Beinecke.
Archbishop Ioann Shakhovskoy Papers. ACRC.
The Shakhovskoy Family Papers. ACRC.
Pavel Tchelitchew Collection. Yale Collection of American Literature, Beinecke.
Vladimir Zenzinov Papers. ACRC.

Published Sources

Adrianova-Peretts, V. P., ed. *Povest' vremennykh let: Chast' pervaia. Tekst i perevod.* Moscow: Izdatel'stvo Akademii nauk SSSR, 1950.
Agamben, Giorgio. *State of Exception.* Translated by Kevin Attell. Chicago, IL: University of Chicago Press, 2003.
Akhmatova, Anna. *O Pushkine.* Leningrad: Sovetskii pisatel', 1977.
Alexandrov, Vladimir. "Nabokov and Bely." In *The Garland Companion to Vladimir Nabokov*, edited by Vladimir E. Alexandrov, 358–66. New York: Garland, 1995.
———. *Nabokov's Otherworld.* Princeton, NJ: Princeton University Press, 1991.
———. "A Note on Nabokov's Anti-Darwinism; or, Why Apes Feed on Butterflies in *The Gift.*" In *Freedom and Responsibility in Russian Literature: Essays in Honor of Robert Louis Jackson*, edited by Elizabeth Cheresh Allen and Gary Saul Morson, 239–44. Evanston, IL: Northwestern University Press, 1995.
All, Nikolai. "V. V. Sirin-Nabokov v N'iu-Iorke chuvstvuet sebia 'svoim': Rabotaet srazu nad dvumia knigami—angliiskoi i russkoi." In *Novoe russkoe slovo*, June 23, 1940. Reprinted in Vladimir Nabokov, *Sobranie sochinenii russkogo perioda v piati*

tomakh, vol. 5, edited by N. I. Artemenko-Tolstaia and Aleksandr Dolinin, 643–46. St. Petersburg: Simpozium, 2000.

Alter, Robert. *Imagined Cities: Urban Experience and the Language of the Novel*. New Haven, CT: Yale University Press, 2005.

Ananko, Iaroslava. *Kanikuly Kaina: Poetika promezhutka v berlinskikh stikhakh V. F. Khodasevicha*. Moscow: Novoe literaturnoe obozrenie, 2020.

Andreev, Vadim. *Istoriia odnogo puteshestviia*. Moscow: Sovetskii pisatel', 1974.

———. "Vozvrashchenie v zhizn'." *Zvezda* 5 (1969): 85–129.

Andreyev, Catherine, and Ivan Savicky. *Russia Abroad: Prague and the Russian Diaspora, 1918–1938*. New Haven, CT: Yale University Press, 2004.

Anonymous. "'Der goldene Hahn.' Märchenoper von Nikolaus Rimskij-Korsakoff. Zur deutschen Aufführung in der Berliner Staatsoper." *Germania: Zeitung für das deutsche Volk*, June 15, 1923, 2.

Antonova, Irina, and Jörn Merkert, eds. *Berlin/Moskau Moskva/Berlin, 1900–1950*. Munich: Prestel, 1995.

Antsiferov, Nikolai. *Dusha Peterburga*. Petersburg: Brokgauz i Efron, 1922.

Any, Carol. *Boris Eikhenbaum: Voices of a Russian Formalist*. Stanford, CA: Stanford University Press, 1994.

Arbatov, Zinovii. "'Nollendorfplatskafe': Literaturnaia mozaika." In *Russkii Berlin*, edited by Vera V. Sorokina, 160–83. Moscow: Izdatel'stvo Moskovskogo universiteta, 2003.

Arosev, Grigorii. *Vladimir Nabokov, otets Vladimira Nabokova*. Moscow: Al'pina Non-Fikshn, 2021.

Aseev, Nikolai. "Po moriu bumazhnomu." *Krasnaia nov'* 4 (1922): 236–49.

Atherton, Michael, ed. *In Exile from St Petersburg: The Life and Times of Abram Saulovich Kagan, Book Publisher, as Told by His Son Anatol Kagan*. Blackheath, Australia: Brandl and Schlesinger, 2017.

Avins, Carol. *Border Crossings: The West and Russian Identity in Soviet Literature, 1917–1934*. Berkeley: University of California Press, 1983.

Azarkh-Granovskaia, Aleksandra. *Vospominaniia. Besedy s V. D. Duvakinym*. Moscow: Mosty kul'tury, Gesharim, 2001.

Babikov, Andrei. "Opredeleniia Nabokova." *Zvezda* 9 (2013): 112–16.

Babikov, Andrei, and Manfred Schruba. "Pis'ma V. V. Nabokova k V. F. Khodasevichu i N. N. Berberovoi (1930–1939). Pis'mo N. Berberovoi k V. Nabokovu." *Wiener Slavistisches Jahrbuch* 5 (2017): 217–48.

Baer, Brian James. "Translating Sexology in Late-Tsarist and Early-Soviet Russia: Politics, Literature, and the Science of Sex." In *Sexology and Translation: Cultural and Scientific Encounters across the Modern World*, edited by Heike Bauer, 115–34. Philadelphia: Temple University Press, 2015.

Bakhtin, Mikhail. "Author and Hero in Aesthetic Activity (ca. 1920–1923)." In *Art and Answerability: Early Philosophical Essays*, edited by Michael Holquist and Vadim Liapunov (translator), Kenneth Brostrom (supplement translator), 57–309. Austin: University of Texas Press, 1990.

———. *Rabelais and His World*. Translated by Helene Iswolsky. Cambridge, MA: MIT Press, 1968.

Barskova, Polina. "Filial Feelings and Paternal Patterns: Transformations of *Hamlet* in *The Gift*." *Nabokov Studies*, no. 9 (2005): 191–208.
Bauer, Heike. *The Hirschfeld Archives: Violence, Death, and Modern Queer Culture*. Philadelphia, PA: Temple University Press, 2017.
Beachy, Robert. *Gay Berlin: Birthplace of a Modern Identity*. New York: Knopf, 2014.
Becher, Johannes R. "Majakowski." In *Sieg der Zukunft: Die Sowjetunion im Werk deutscher Schriftsteller*, edited by Alexander Abusch, 47–51. Berlin: Aufbau Verlag, 1952.
Belentschikow, Valentin. "Boris Pasternak i Germaniia, 1906–1924: Berlin, Marburg i rannie nemetskie ekspressionisty v tvorchestve B. Pasternaka." *Zeitschrift für Slawistik* 32, no. 5 (1987): 728–43.
———. *Zur Poetik Boris Pasternaks: Der Berliner Gedichtzyklus, 1922–1923*. Frankfurt am Main: Peter Lang, 1998.
Belova, Tat'iana. "Skazochnye nameki: Ot skazki Pushkina k opere Rimskogo-Korsakova." *Rimskii-Korsakov: Zhizn' i tvorchestvo russkogo kompozitora*. Accessed December 13, 2022. http://www.rimskykorsakov.ru/belova.html.
Belyi, Andrei. *Odna iz obitelei tsarstva tenei*. Leningrad: Gosudarstvennoe izdatel'stvo, 1924.
———. "O 'Rossii' v Rossii i o 'Rossii' v Berline." *Beseda* 1 (1923): 211–36.
———. "Osnovy moego mirovozzreniia." Preface by Larisa Sugai ("Andrei Belyi protiv Osval'da Shpenglera"). *Literaturnoe obozrenie* 4–5 (1995): 10–37.
———. *Posle razluki: Berlinskii pesennik*. Berlin: Epokha, 1922.
Benjamin, Walter. *The Arcades Project*. Edited by Rolf Tiedemann. Translated by Howard Eiland and Kevin McLaughlin. Cambridge, MA: Belknap Press of Harvard University Press, 1999.
———. "Paris, the Capital of the Nineteenth Century." In *The Work of Art in the Age of Its Technological Reproducibility, and Other Writings on Media*, edited by Michael W. Jennings, Brigid Doherty, and Thomas Y. Levin, 96–115. Cambridge, MA: Belknap Press of Harvard University Press, 2008.
Benn, Gottfried. *Doppelleben*. Munich: Deutscher Taschenbuch Verlag, 1967.
Berard, Ewa. "The 'First Exhibition of Russian Art' in Berlin: The Transnational Origins of Bolshevik Cultural Diplomacy, 1921–1922." *Contemporary European History* 30 (2021): 164–80.
Berberova, Nina. *Chaikovskii: Istoriia odinokoi zhizni*. Berlin: Petropolis, 1936.
———. ["Neskol'ko slov po povodu literaturnoi molodezhi v emigratsii."] *Novyi korabl'* 2 (1927): 42–43.
———. *The Italics Are Mine*. Translated by Philippe Radley. New York: Knopf, 1992.
———. *Stikhi: 1921–1983*. New York: Russica, 1984.
Berberova, Nina, Dovid Knut, Iurii Terapiano, Vsevolod Fokht. "Ot redaktsii." *Novyi Dom* 1 (1926): 2.
Berdiaev, Nikolai Aleksandrovich, Iakov Markovich Bukshpan, Fedor Stepun, and Semen Liudvigovich Frank. *Osval'd Shpengler i Zakat Evropy*. Moscow: Bereg, 1922.
Berdjis, Nassim Winnie. *Imagery in Nabokov's Last Russian Novel ("Dar"), Its English Translation ("The Gift"), and Other Prose Works of the 1930s*. Frankfurt am Main: Peter Lang, 1995.

Berezin, Vladimir. *Viktor Shklovskii*. Moscow: Molodaia gvardiia, 2014.
Bergelson, Dovid. "Among Refugees." In *The Shadows of Berlin*, translated by Joachim Neugroschel, 21–43. San Francisco, CA: City Lights Books, 2005.
Berkov, V., and V. Protopopov. *Zolotoi petushok, nebylitsa v litsakh: Opera N. A. Rimskogo-Korsakova, libretto V. I. Bel'skogo po skazke A. S. Pushkina*. Moscow: Muzgiz, 1937.
Bershtein, Evgenii. "The Discourse of Sexual Psychopathy in Russian Modernism." In *Reframing Russian Modernism*, edited by Irina Shevelenko, 143–71. Madison: University of Wisconsin Press, 2018.
———. "Eisenstein's Letter to Magnus Hirschfeld: Text and Context." In *The Flying Carpet: Studies on Eisenstein and Russian Cinema in Honor of Naum Kleiman*, edited by Joan Neuberger and Antonio Somaini, 75–86. Sesto San Giovani: Éditions Mimésis, 2017.
Bethea, David. "Emigration and Heritage." *Slavic and East European Journal* 31 (1987): 141–64.
———. *Khodasevich: His Life and Art*. Princeton, NJ: Princeton University Press, 1983.
———. *The Shape of Apocalypse in Modern Russian Fiction*. Princeton, NJ: Princeton University Press, 1989.
Betts, Alexander, and Will Jones. *Mobilising the Diaspora: How Refugees Challenge Authoritarianism*. Cambridge: Cambridge University Press, 2016.
Beyer, Thomas R. "Andrej Belyj: The Berlin Years, 1921–1923." *Zeitschrift für Slavische Philologie* 50, no. 1 (1990): 90–142.
———. "Russkii Berlin. Ekspatriatsiia? Izgnanie? Emigratsiia?" *Diapazon* 1 (1993): 64–67.
Beyer, Thomas R., Gottfried Kratz, Vasilij N. Masiutin, and Xenia Werner. *Russische Autoren und Verlage in Berlin nach dem Ersten Weltkrieg*. Berlin: Verlag Arno Spitz, 1987.
Bishop, Sarah Clovis. "The Book of Poems in Twentieth-Century Russian Literature: Khodasevich, Gippius and Shvarts." PhD diss., Princeton University, 2004.
Blackwell, Stephen. "Nabokov's *The Gift*, Dostoevsky, and the Tradition of Narratorial Ambiguity." *Slavic Review* 76, no. 1 (2017): 147–68.
———. *The Quill and the Scalpel: Nabokov's Art and the Worlds of Science*. Columbus: Ohio State University Press, 2009.
———. *Zina's Paradox: The Figured Reader in Nabokov's "Gift."* New York: Peter Lang, 2000.
Blasing, Molly Thomasy. *Snapshots of the Soul: Photo-Poetic Encounters in Modern Russian Culture*. Ithaca, NY: Cornell University Press, 2021.
Blätter der Staatsoper. Heft 8, June 1923.
Bogomolov, Nikolai A. "Kak Khodasevich stanovilsia emigrantom." In *Sopriazhenie dalekovatykh: O Viacheslave Ivanove i Vladislave Khodaseviche*, 208–17. Moscow: Izdatel'stvo Kulaginoi Intrada, 2011.
Böhmig, Michaela. *Das russische Theater in Berlin, 1919–1931*. Munich: Verlag Otto Sagner in Kommission, 1990.
Bol'dt, Frank, Dmitrii Segal, and Lazar' Fleishman. "Problemy izucheniia russkoi literatury pervoi treti XX veka." *Slavica Hierosolymitana* 3 (1978): 75–88.

Borislavov, Rad. "'I Know What Motivation Is': The Politics of Emotion and Viktor Shklovskii's Sentimental Rhetoric." *Slavic Review* 74, no. 4 (2015): 787–807.

Boyd, Brian. *Vladimir Nabokov: The Russian Years*. Princeton, NJ: Princeton University Press, 1990.

Boym, Svetlana. *The Off-Modern*. London: Bloomsbury Academic, 2017.

———. "Poetics and Politics of Estrangement: Victor Shklovsky and Hannah Arendt." *Poetics Today*, 26, no. 4 (2005): 581–611.

Bozovic, Marijeta. *Nabokov's Canon: From Onegin to Ada*. Evanston: Northwestern University Press, 2016.

Brik, Lilia. *Pristrastnye rasskazy*. Edited by Ia. I. Groisman and I. Iu. Gens. Nizhnii Novgorod: Dekom, 2003.

Brik, Osip. "A lia rius." In *Foto i kino*, 71–4. Moscow: Ad Marginem, 2015.

Brodsky, Anna. "Homosexuality and the Aesthetic of Nabokov's *Dar*." *Nabokov Studies* 4, no. 1 (1997): 95–115.

Brown, Edward J. *Mayakovsky: A Poet in the Revolution*. Princeton, NJ: Princeton University Press, 1973.

———. "Nabokov, Chernyshevsky, Olesha, and the Gift of Sight." In *Literature, Culture, and Society in the Modern Age: In Honor of Joseph Frank*, edited by Edward J. Brown, Lazar Fleishman, Gregory Freidin, and Richard D. Schupbach, vol. 2, 280–94. Stanford, CA: Department of Slavic Languages and Literatures, Stanford University, 1992.

Bruhm, Steven. "Queer, Queer Vladimir." *American Imago* 53, no. 4 (Winter 1996): 281–306.

Buck-Morss, Susan. *Dreamworld and Catastrophe: The Passing of Mass Utopia in East and West*. Cambridge, MA: MIT Press, 2000.

Budnitskii, Oleg. *Drugaia Rossiia: Issledovaniia po istorii russkoi emigratsii*. Moscow: Novoe literaturnoe obozrenie, 2021.

Budnitskii, Oleg, and Aleksandra Polian. *Russko-evreiskii Berlin, 1920–1941*. Moscow: Novoe literaturnoe obozrenie, 2013.

Bulatova, Asiya. "Displaced Modernism: Shklovsky's *Zoo, or Letters Not about Love* and the Borders of Literature." *Poetics Today* 37, no. 1 (2016): 29–53.

———. "'I'm Writing to You in This Magazine': The Mechanics of Modernist Dissemination in Shklovsky's Open Letter to Jakobson." *Comparative Critical Studies* 11, no. 2–3 (2014): 185–202.

Bunin, Ivan. "Missiia russkoi emigratsii: Rech', proiznesennaia v Parizhe 16 fevralia." *Rul'*, April 3, 1924, 5–6.

Burchard, Amory. *Klubs der russischen Dichter in Berlin, 1920–1941: Institutionen des literarischen Lebens im Exil*. Munich: Verlag Otto Sagner in Kommission, 2001.

Burchard, Amory, and Ljudmila Duwidowitsch, eds. *Das russische Berlin*. Berlin: Die Ausländerbeauftragte des Senats, 1994.

Burgin, Diana. "Mother Nature versus the Amazons: Marina Tsvetaeva and Female Same-Sex Love." *Journal of the History of Sexuality* 6, no. 1 (1995): 62–88.

Caplan, Marc. *Yiddish Writers in Weimar Berlin: A Fugitive Modernism*. Bloomington: Indiana University Press, 2021.

Certeau, Michel de. *The Practice of Everyday Life*. Translated by Steven Rendall. Berkeley: University of California Press, 1984.

Chamberlain, Lesley. *The Philosophy Steamer: Lenin and the Exile of the Intelligentsia*. London: Atlantic Books, 2006.

Chernetsky, Vitaly. "Displacement, Desire, Identity and the 'Diasporic Momentum': Two Slavic Writers in Latin America." *Intertexts* 7, no. 1 (Spring 2003): 49–70.

Chernyshevskii, Nikolai Gavrilovich [Nikolai Chernyshevsky]. *Chto delat'? Iz rasskazov o novykh liudiakh*. Vol. 1 of *Sobranie sochinenii v piati tomakh*. Moscow: Pravda, 1974.

——. *What Is to Be Done?* Translated by Michael R. Katz. Ithaca, NY: Cornell University Press, 1989.

Chlenov, S. "Segodniashnii Berlin (Mimoletnye vpechatleniia)." *Krasnaia nov'* 1 (1923): 201–13.

Ciepiela, Catherine. *The Same Solitude: Boris Pasternak and Marina Tsvetaeva*. Ithaca, NY: Cornell University Press, 2007.

Clark, Katerina. *Moscow, The Fourth Rome: Stalinism, Cosmopolitanism, and Evolution of Soviet Culture*. Cambridge, MA: Harvard University Press, 2011.

——. *Petersburg: The Crucible of Cultural Revolution*. Cambridge, MA: Harvard University Press, 1995.

Cleto, Fabio. "The Spectacles of Camp." In *Camp: Notes on Fashion*, edited by Andrew Bolton, 9–59. New York: Metropolitan Museum of Art, 2019.

Cruz-Malavé, Arnaldo, and Martin F. Manalansan, eds. *Queer Globalizations: Citizenship and the Afterlife of Colonialism*. New York: New York University Press, 2002.

Davydov, Sergei. "*The Gift*: Nabokov's Esthetic Exorcism of Chernyshevskii." *Canadian-American Slavic Studies* 19, no. 3 (1985): 357–74.

——. "*Teksty-matreshki*" *Vladimira Nabokova*. Munich: Otto Sagner Verlag, 1982.

——. "Weighing Nabokov's *Gift* on Pushkin's Scales." In *Cultural Mythologies of Russian Modernism: From the Golden Age to the Silver Age*, edited by Boris Gasparov, Robert Hughes, and Irina Paperno, 415–28. Berkeley: University of California Press, 1992.

Dhooge, Ben. "Constructive Art à la Ehrenburg: Vesc-Gegenstand-Objet." *Neohelicon* 42, no. 2 (2015): 493–527.

Dierkes-Thrun, Petra. *Salome's Modernity: Oscar Wilde and the Aesthetics of Transgression*. Ann Arbor: University of Michigan Press, 2011.

Dinershtein, Efim. *Siniaia ptitsa Zinoviia Grzhebina*. Moscow: Novoe literaturnoe obozrenie, 2014.

Dohrn, Verena, and Gertrud Pickhan, eds. *Berlin Transit: Jüdische Migranten aus Osteuropa in den 1920er Jahren*. Göttingen: Wallstein Verlag, 2012.

——, eds. *Transit und Transformation: Osteuropäisch-jüdische Migranten in Berlin, 1918–1939*. Göttingen: Wallstein Verlag, 2010.

Dolinin, Aleksandr [Alexander Dolinin]. *"Gibel' Zapada" i drugie memy: Iz istorii raskhozhikh idei i slovesnykh formul*. Moscow: Novoe izdatel'stvo, 2020.

——. "The Gift." In *The Garland Companion to Vladimir Nabokov*, edited by Vladimir E. Alexandrov, 135–69. New York: Garland, 1995.

——. *Istinnaia zhizn' pisatelia Sirina: Raboty o Nabokove*. St. Petersburg: Akademicheskii proekt, 2004.

———. *Kommentarii k romanu Vladimira Nabokova "Dar."* Moscow: Novoe izdatel'stvo, 2019.

———. "Nabokov as a Russian Writer." In *The Cambridge Companion to Nabokov*, edited by Julian W. Connolly, 49–64. Cambridge: Cambridge University Press, 2005.

———. "The Stepmother of Russian Cities: Berlin of the 1920s through the Eyes of Russian Writers." In *Cold Fusion: Aspects of the German Cultural Presence in Russia*, edited by Gennady Barabtarlo, 225–40. New York: Berghahn, 2000.

"Dom iskusstva." *Rul'*, December 2, 1922.

Dose, Ralf. *Magnus Hirschfeld: The Origins of the Gay Liberation Movement*. Translated by Edward H. Willis. New York: Monthly Review Press, 2014.

Dragonoiu, Dana. *Vladimir Nabokov and the Poetics of Liberalism*. Evanston, IL: Northwestern University Press, 2011.

Drahn, Ernst. "Russische Emigration. Eine kulturstatistische Studie." *Zeitschrift für die gesamte Staatswissenschaft* 89, no. 1 (1930): 124–30.

Durantaye, Leland De La. "Kafka's Reality and Nabokov's Fantasy: On Dwarves, Saints, Beetles, Symbolism, and Genius." *Comparative Literature* 59, no. 4 (2007): 315–31.

Dwyer, Anne. "Standstill as Extinction: Viktor Shklovsky's Poetics and Politics of Movement in the 1920s and 1930s." *PMLA* 131, no. 2 (2016): 269–88.

Edwards, Brent Hayes. *The Practice of Diaspora: Literature, Translation, and the Rise of Black Internationalism*. Cambridge, MA: Harvard University Press, 2003.

———. "The Uses of Diaspora." *Social Text* 19, no. 1 (Spring 2001): 45–73.

Egorova, Nadezhda A., ed. *Zolotoi vek rossiiskogo knigoizdaniia v Germanii*. Moscow: Dom russkogo zarubezh'ia im. A. S. Solzhenitsyna, 2013.

Eikhenbaum, Boris M. "Literary Environment." Translated by I. R. Titunik. In *Readings in Russian Poetics: Formalist and Structuralist Views*, edited by Ladislav Matejka and Krystyna Pomorska, 56–65. Cambridge, MA: MIT Press, 1971.

———. "Literatura i literaturnyi byt." *Na literaturnom postu* 9 (1927): 47–52.

———. "Literaturnyi byt." In *O literature*, 428–36. Moscow: Sovetskii pisatel', 1987.

———. "V poiskakh zhanra." In *Literatura: Teoriia, kritika, polemika*, 291–95. Leningrad: Priboi, 1927.

Eliasberg, Alexander. *Russische Literaturgeschichte in Einzelporträts*. Munich: Oskar Beck, 1922.

Elsworth, J. D. *Andrey Bely*. Letchworth: Bradda Books, 1972.

Emerson, Caryl. *Boris Godunov: Transpositions of a Russian Theme*. Bloomington: Indiana University Press, 1986.

Emery, Jacob. "Guides to Berlin." *Comparative Literature* 54, no. 4 (2002): 301.

"Emigranten-Cabarett." *Das Kulturblatt* 12 (1922): 539.

Engel, R. "'Zolotoi petushok' v Gos. Opere." *Dni*, June 21, 1923, 5.

Engel-Braunschmidt, Annelore. "Die Suggestion Berliner Realität bei Vladimir Nabokov." In *Russische Emigration in Deutschland, 1918 bis 1941: Leben im europäischen Bürgerkrieg*, edited by Karl Schlögel, 367–78. Berlin: Akademie Verlag, 1995.

Engelstein, Laura. *The Keys to Happiness: Sex and the Search for Modernity in Revolutionary Russia*. Ithaca, NY: Cornell University Press, 1994.

Erenburg, Il'ia. *A vse-taki ona vertitsia*. Berlin: Gelikon, 1922.
———. *Belyi ugol' ili slezy Vertera*. Leningrad: Priboi, 1928.
———. *Liudi, gody, zhizn': Knigi pervaia, vtoraia, tret'ia*. Edited by Boris Frezinskii. Moscow: Tekst, 2005.
———. "Boris Leonidovich Pasternak." In *Portrety russkikh poetov*, edited by Il'ia Erenburg, 127–36. Berlin: Argonavty, 1922.
———. *Shest' povestei o legkikh kontsakh*. Berlin: Gelikon, 1922.
———. "Torzhestvuiushchii oboz." *Veshch'/Gegenstand/Objet: Mezhdunarodnoe obozrenie sovremennogo iskusstva*, no. 3 (1922): 2–3.
———. *Viza vremeni*. Berlin: Petropolis, 1930.
Erenburg, Il'ia, and El Lissitzky. "Blokada Rossii konchaetsia." *Veshch'/Gegenstand/Objet*, no. 1–2 (1922): 1–4.
Erlich, Victor. *Modernism and Revolution: Russian Literature in Transition*. Cambridge, MA: Harvard University Press, 1994.
———. *Russian Formalism: History-Doctrine*. The Hague: Mouton, 1969.
Estraikh, Gennady, and Mikhail Krutikov, eds. *Yiddish in Weimar Berlin: At the Crossroads of Diaspora Politics and Culture*. London: Legenda, 2010.
Etkind, Aleksandr. *Sodom i Psikheia: Ocherki intellektual'noi istorii Serebrianogo veka*. Moscow: ITs-Garant, 1996.
Fanger, Donald. "The City of Modern Russian Fiction." In *Modernism, 1890–1930*, edited by Malcolm Bradbury and James McFarlane, 467–80. London: Penguin Books, 1986.
Färber, Otto. "Die russischen Emigranten und wir." *Allgemeine Rundschau*, April 8, 1922, 162.
Faryno, Jerzy. *Poetika Pasternaka: "Putevye zapiski" i "Okhrannaia gramota."* Vienna: Gesellschaft für Förderung slawistischer Studien, 1989.
Fevral'skii, Aleksandr. *Pervaia sovetskaia p'esa "Misteriia Buff."* Moscow: Sovetskii pisatel', 1971.
Figes, Orlando. *Natasha's Dance: A Cultural History of Russia*. New York: Metropolitan Books, 2002.
Figura, Starr, ed. *German Expressionism: The Graphic Impulse*. New York: Museum of Modern Art, 2011.
Fleishman, Lazar [Lazar' Fleishman]. "Bely's Memoirs." In *Andrey Bely: Spirit of Symbolism*, edited by John Malmstad, 216–41. Ithaca, NY: Cornell University Press, 2019.
———. *Boris Pasternak v dvadtsatye gody*. Munich: Wilhelm Fink Verlag, 1980.
———. *V tiskakh provokatsii: Operatsiia "Trest" i russkaia zarubezhnaia pechat'*. Moscow: Novoe literaturnoe obozrenie, 2003.
———. "Vysylka intelligentsii i Russkii Berlin v 1922 g." In *Russkii Berlin, 1920–1945: Mezhdunarodnaia konferentsiia, 16–18 dekabria 2002 g.*, edited by Lazar' Fleishman, 92–106. Moscow: Russkii put', 2006.
Fleishman, Lazar, Robert Hughes, and Olga Raevsky-Hughes, eds. *Russkii Berlin, 1921–1923*. Paris: YMCA-Press, 1983.
Foster, John Burt. *Nabokov's Art of Memory and European Modernism*. Princeton, NJ: Princeton University Press, 1993.

Freise, Matthias, and Britta Korkowsky. "Drei Gleisdreiecke: Boris Pasternak, Viktor Shklovskii, and Joseph Roth sehen Berlin." *Germanoslavica: Zeitschrift für germanoslawische Studien* 1 (2011): 1–8.

Frezinskii, Boris. *Ob Il'e Erenburge: Knigi, liudi, strany*. Moscow: Novoe literaturnoe obozrenie, 2013.

Frolova-Walker, Marina, ed. *Rimsky-Korsakov and His World*. Princeton, NJ: Princeton University Press, 2018.

———. "Staging Defeat: The Golden Cockerel and the Russo-Japanese War." In *Rimsky-Korsakov and His World*, edited by Marina Frolova-Walker, 197–219. Princeton, NJ: Princeton University Press, 2018.

Gamsa, Mark. *Harbin: A Cross-Cultural Biography*. Toronto: University of Toronto Press, 2020.

Gasparov, Boris. "Pushkin's Year of Frustration, or How 'The Golden Cockerel' Was Made." *Ulbandus Review* 12 (2009/2010): 41–62.

Gay, Peter. *Weimar Culture: The Outsider as Insider*. New York: Harper & Row, 1968.

Gessen, Iosif. *Gody izgnaniia: Zhiznennyi otchet*. Paris: YMCA-Press, 1979.

Glebov, Igor' [Boris Asaf'ev]. *Simfonicheskie etiudy*. Petersburg: Gosfilarmoniia, 1922.

Glebov, Sergey. *From Empire to Eurasia: Politics, Scholarship, and Ideology in Russia Eurasianism, 1920s–1930s*. DeKalb: Northern Illinois University Press, 2017.

Göbler, Frank. *Vladislav F. Chodasevič: Dualität und Distanz als Grundzüge seiner Lyrik*. Munich: Verlag Otto Sagner in Komission, 1988.

Goethe, Johann Wolfgang von. "Dedication." Translated by Vladimir Nabokov. *Poslednie novosti*, December 15, 1932, 3.

Goll, Ivan. *Sodom et Berlin: Roman*. Paris: Éditions Émile-Paul Frères, 1929.

Golokhvastov, Georgii. *Gibel' Atlantidy: Stikhotvoreniia. Poema*. Moscow: Vodolei Publishers, 2008.

González, Octavio. *Misfit Modernism: Queer Forms of Double Exile in the Twentieth-Century Novel*. University Park: Pennsylvania State University Press, 2020.

Gopinath, Gayatri. "Archive, Affect, and the Everyday: Queer Diasporic Re-Visions." In *Political Emotions*, edited by Janet Staiger, Ann Cvetkovich, and Ann Reynolds, 165–92. New York: Routledge, 2010.

Gordon, Avery. *Ghostly Matters: Haunting and the Sociological Imagination*. Minneapolis: University of Minnesota Press, 1997.

Gordon, Mel. *Voluptuous Panic: The Erotic World of Weimar Berlin*. Expanded edition. Los Angeles: Feral House, 2006.

Goriachikh, V. V. "Zolotoi petushok Rimskogo-Korsakova—'nebylitsa v litsakh' (problema zhanra i stilia)." In *Pushkin v russkoi opere*, edited by E. Ruch'evskaia, 247–98. St. Peterburg: Goskonservatoriia, 1998.

Gozenpud, Abram. *N. A. Rimsky-Korsakov: Temy i idei ego opernogo tvorchestva*. Moscow: Gosmuzizdat, 1957.

Grabar', I. E., ed. *K. S. Stanislavskii: Materialy, pis'ma, issledovaniia*. Moscow: Izdatel'stvo Akademii nauk SSSR, 1955.

Greenleaf, Monika. "Fathers, Sons, and Imposters: Pushkin's Trace in *The Gift*." *Slavic Review* 53, no. 1 (1994): 140–58.

Gul', Roman. *Ia unes Rossiiu: Apologiia emigratsii.* Vol. 1, *Rossiia v Germanii.* New York: Most, 1984.
——. *Pol v tvorchestve: Razbor proizvedenii Andreia Belogo.* Berlin: Manfred, 1923.
——. *Zhizn' na fuksa.* Moscow: Gosizdat, 1927.
Gumilev, Nikolai. *Stikhotvoreniia i poemy.* Leningrad: Sovetskii pisatel', 1988.
Gumperz, J. "W. Majakowski: Mysterium-Buff: Zur Auffürung in deutscher Sprache in Moskau anläßlich des III. Kongresses." *Der Gegner: Blätter zur Kritik der Zeit* 2, no. 10–11 (1921): 404–5.
Hájková, Anna. "Den Holocaust queer erzählen." *Jahrbuch Sexualitäten* (2018): 86–110.
Hamlin, Rebecca. *Crossing: How We Label and React to People on the Move.* Stanford, CA: Stanford University Press, 2021.
Haraway, Donna. "SF: Science Fiction, Speculative Fabulation, String Figures, So Far." *Ada: A Journal of Gender, New Media, and Technology* 3 (2013). https://adanewmedia.org/2013/11/issue3-haraway/.
Hardeman, Hilde. *Coming to Terms with the Soviet Regime: The "Changing Landmarks" Movement among Russian Émigrés in the Early 1920s.* DeKalb: Northern Illinois University Press, 1994.
Hart, Matthew, and Tania Lown-Hecht. "The Extraterritorial Poetics of W. G. Sebald." *Modern Fiction Studies* 58, no. 2 (Summer 2012): 214–38.
Hayes, Jarrod. "Queering Roots, Queering Diaspora." In *Rites of Return: Diaspora Poetics and the Politics of Memory*, edited by Marianne Hirsch and Nancy K. Miller, 72–87. New York: Columbia University Press, 2011.
Healey, Dan. *Homosexual Desire in Revolutionary Russia: The Regulation of Sexual and Gender Dissent.* Chicago: University of Chicago Press, 2001.
Herzfelde, Wieland. "Mit Majakowski durch Berlin." In *Berliner Begegnungen: Ausländische Künstler in Berlin 1918 bis 1933*, edited by Klaus Kändler, Helga Karolewski, and Ilse Siebert, 39. Berlin: Dietz Verlag, 1987.
Hillis, Faith. *Utopia's Discontents: Russian Émigrés and the Quest for Freedom, 1830s–1930s.* Oxford, UK: Oxford University Press, 2021.
Hoisington, Sona. "Pushkin's 'Golden Cockerel': A Critical Re-Examination." In *The Golden Age of Russian Literature and Thought: Selected Papers from the Fourth World Congress for Soviet and East European Studies, Harrogate, 1990*, edited by Derek Offord, 24–33. New York: St. Martin's, 1992.
Hughes, Olga R. *The Poetic World of Boris Pasternak.* Princeton, NJ: Princeton University Press, 1974.
Hughes, Robert. "Belyi i Khodasevich: K istorii otnoshenii." *Vestnik russkogo khristianskogo dvizheniia* 151 (1987): 144–65.
——. "Khodasevich: Irony and Dislocation. A Poet in Exile." In *The Bitter Air of Exile: Russian Writers and the West, 1922–1972*, edited by Simon Karlinsky and Alfred Appel Jr., 52–66. Berkeley: University of California Press, 1977.
Huntington, William Chapin. *The Homesick Million: Russia-out-of-Russia.* Boston, MA: Stratford Co., 1933.
Ippolitov, Sergei, and Almaziia Kataeva. *Ne mogu otorvat'sia ot Rossii: Russkie knigoizdateli v Germanii v 1920-kh gg.* Moscow: Izdatel'stvo Ippolitova, 2000.

Ippolitov, Sergei, Vladimir Nedbaevskii, and Iuliia Rudentsova. *Tri stolitsy izgnaniia: Konstantinopol', Berlin, Parizh*. Moscow: Spas, 1999.
Isherwood, Christopher. *Christopher and His Kind: A Memoir 1929–1939*. New York: Farrar, Straus and Giroux, 2015.
Issykieva, Adalyat. "Nikolai Rimsky-Korsakov and His Orient." In *Rimsky-Korsakov and His World*, edited by Marina Frolova-Walker, 145–75. Princeton, NJ: Princeton University Press, 2018.
Ivanov, Fedor. *Krasnyi Parnas: Literaturno-kriticheskie ocherki*. Berlin: Russkoe universal'noe izdatel'stvo, 1922.
Ivanov, Viacheslav Vsevolodovich. "Razyskaniia o poetike Pasternaka: Ot buri k babochke." In *Izbrannye trudy po semiotike i istorii kul'tury*, vol. 1, 15–141. Moscow: Iazyki russkoi kul'tury, 1999.
Ivanov-Razumnik, R. V. *Vladimir Maiakovskii ("misteriia" ili "buff")*. Berlin: Skify, 1922.
Ivleva, Victoria. "A Vest Reinvested in The Gift." *Russian Review* 68, no. 2 (2009): 283–301.
Jackson, Robert Louis. "From the Other Shore: Nabokov's Translation into Russian of Goethe's 'Dedication' to *Faust*." In *Close Encounters: Essays on Russian Literature*, 354–65. Boston, MA: Academic Studies Press, 2013.
Jakobson, Roman. *Pushkin and His Sculptural Myth*. Translated and edited by John Burbank. The Hague: Mouton, 1975.
Jangfeldt, Bengt. *Stavka—zhizn': Vladimir Maiakovskii i ego krug*. Translated by Asia Lavrusha and Bengt Jangfeldt. Moscow: Kolibri, 2009.
Jensen, Robyn. "Authorizing the Image: Photography in Nabokov's *Speak, Memory*." *Slavic and East European Journal* 63, no. 2 (Summer 2019): 179–205.
Johnston, Robert Harold. *New Mecca, New Babylon: Paris and the Russian Exiles, 1920–1945*. Montreal: McGill-Queen's University Press, 1988.
Kändler, Klaus, Helga Karolewski, and Ilse Siebert, eds. *Berliner Begegnungen: Ausländische Künstler in Berlin 1918 bis 1933*. Berlin: Dietz Verlag, 1987.
Kannak, Elena. "Berlinskii kruzhok poetov (1928–1933)." In *Russkii Berlin*, edited by Vera V. Sorokina, 279–82. Moscow: Izdatel'stvo Moskovskogo Universiteta, 2003.
———. *Vernost': Vospominaniia, rasskazy, ocherki*. Paris: YMCA-Press, 1992.
Kant, Marion. "Russians in Berlin, 1920–1945." In *Russian Movement Culture of the 1920s and 1930s*, edited by Lynn Garafola, 73–79. New York: Columbia University Harriman Institute, 2015. https://harriman.columbia.edu/files/harriman/newsletter/Russian%20Movement%20Culture%20Corrected%20July%202017pdf.pdf.
Kapp, Julius, ed. *Die Staatsoper Berlin 1919 bis 1925: Ein Almanach*. Berlin: Deutsche Verlags-Anstalt, 1925.
Karlinsky, Simon, ed. and trans. *Dear Bunny, Dear Volodya: The Nabokov-Wilson Letters, 1940–1971*. Revised and expanded edition. Berkeley: University of California Press, 2001.
———. "Foreword: Who Are the Émigré Writers?" *TriQuarterly* 27 (1973): 5–9.
———. "Vladimir Nabokov's Novel *Dar* as a Work of Literary Criticism: A Structural Analysis." *Slavic and East European Journal* 7, no. 3 (1963): 284–90.
Karlinsky, Simon, and Alfred Appel Jr., eds. *The Bitter Air of Exile: Russian Writers and the West, 1922–1972*. Berkeley: University of California Press, 1977.

Karpeles, Eric. *Almost Nothing: The 20th-Century Art and Life of Jósef Czapski*. New York: New York Review of Books, 2018.
Karshan, Thomas. *Vladimir Nabokov and the Art of Play*. London: Oxford University Press, 2011.
Katanian, Vasilii. *Maiakovskii: Literaturnaia khronika*. Moscow: Gosudarstvennoe izdatel'stvo khudozhestvennoi literatury, 1961.
Kauffman, Linda. *Special Delivery: Epistolary Modes in Modern Fiction*. Chicago, IL: University of Chicago Press, 1992.
Khazan, Vladimir, and Roman Timenchik, eds. *Peterburg v poezii russkoi emigratsii: Pervaia i vtoraia volna*. St. Petersburg: Akademicheskii proekt, 2006.
Khodasevich, Vladislav. *Belyi koridor: Vospominaniia. Izbrannaia proza v dvukh tomakh*. Edited by Iosif Brodskii. Vol. 1. New York: Serebrianyi vek, 1982.
———. *Kamer-fur'erskii zhurnal*. Moscow: Ellis Lak, 2002.
———. *Sobranie sochinenii v chetyrekh tomakh*. Edited by I. P. Andreeva, S. G. Bocharov, N. A. Bogomolov, V. P. Kochetov. Moscow: Soglasie, 1997.
Kirillov, Kirill, and Vera Lur'e [Vera Lourié]. "Puti poezii: Iskaniia. Dostizheniia." *Dni*, January 14, 1923.
Kirstein, Lincoln. *Tchelitchew*. Santa Fe, NM: Twelvetrees Press, 1994.
Kissel, V. S. "O nemetskikh pfenningakh i russkom zolotom fonde: Tema deneg v romane V. Nabokova *Dar*." Translated by Galina Time. *Russkaia literatura* 4 (2008): 23–36.
Korkowsky, Britta. *Selbstverortung ohne Ort: Russisch-jüdische Exilliteratur aus dem Berlin der Zwanziger Jahre*. Göttingen: Wallstein Verlag, 2013.
Korvin-Piotrovskii, Vladimir. *Atlantida pod vodoi*. Berlin: Polyglotte, 1928.
———. "Stikhi k Pushkinu." In *Novosel'e*, 37–43. Berlin: Slovo, 1931.
Kostalevsky, Marina. "The Young Godunov-Cherdyntsev, or How to Write a Literary Biography." *Russian Literature* 43 (1998): 283–95.
Kovalenko, Georgii F. *Pavel Chelishchev*. Moscow: Iskusstvo—XXI vek, 2021.
———. "Pavel Chelishchev: Rannie gody," 68–122. *Russkoe iskusstvo XX vek: Issledovaniia i publikatsii*. Vol. 3. Moskva: Nauka, 2007.
Krandievskaia-Tolstaia, Natal'ia. *Vospominaniia*. Leningrad: Lenizdat, 1977.
Kühn, Edmund. "'Der goldene Hahn.' Märchenoper von N. Rimskij-Korsakoff." *Germania: Zeitung für das deutsche Volk*, June 20, 1923.
Kunichika, Michael. *"Our Native Antiquity": Archeology and Aesthetics in the Culture of Russian Modernism*. Boston, MA: Academic Studies Press, 2016.
Kuritsyn, Viacheslav. *Nabokov bez Lolity: Putevoditel' s kartami, kartinkami, i zadaniiami*. Moscow: Novoe izdatel'stvo, 2013.
Ladd, Brian. *The Ghosts of Berlin: Confronting German History in the Urban Landscape*. Chicago, IL: The University of Chicago Press, 1997.
Lalo, Alexei. *Libertinage in Russian Culture and Literature: A Bio-History of Sexualities at the Threshold of Modernity*. Boston, MA: Brill, 2011.
Lavrent'ev, Aleksandr, and Heino Neumayer, eds. *Russkie i nemtsy: 1000 let istorii, iskusstva i kul'tury*. Moscow, Berlin: Michael Imhof Verlag, 2012.
Lavrov, Aleksandr, John Malmstad, and Monika Spivak, eds. *Andrei Belyi: Avtobiograficheskie svody. Literaturnoe nasledstvo*. Moscow: Nauka, 2016.

Léon Noel, Lucie. "Playback." *TriQuarterly* 17 (Winter 1970): 209–19.
Levchenko, Ian. *Drugaia nauka: Russkie formalisty v poiskakh biografii*. Moscow: Izdatel'skii dom Vysshei shkoly ekonomiki, 2012.
Levin, Iurii. "Ob osobennostiakh povestvovatel'noi struktury i obraznogo stroia romana V. Nabokova *Dar*." *Russian Literature* 9 (1981): 191–230.
Levin, S. I. "Polozhenie russkikh emigrantov v Germanii." *Rul'*, August 2, 1922.
Leving, Yuri [Iurii Leving]. *Keys to the Gift: A Guide to Nabokov's Novel*. Boston, MA: Academic Studies Press, 2011.
———. *Vokzal-garazh-angar: Vladimir Nabokov i poetika russkogo urbanizma*. St. Petersburg: Ivan Limbakh, 2004.
Liapushkina, Ekaterina. "'Karusel' istiny': Smysl epigrapha v romane V. V. Nabokova *Dar*." *Russkaia literatura* 1 (2020): 210.
Lidin, Vladimir. *Liudi i vstrechi*. Moscow: Sovetskii pisatel', 1959.
Liebermann, Doris. "Einleitung." In Vera Lourié, *Briefe an Dich: Erinnerungen an das russische Berlin*, edited by Doris Liebermann, 7–18. Frankfurt am Main: Schöffling & Co., 2014.
Liessner-Blomberg, Elena, Gerhard Wolf, Jürgen Rennert, and Werner Schmidt, eds. *Elena Liessner-Blomberg, oder die Geschichte vom Blauen Vogel*. Berlin: Buchverlag Der Morgen, 1978.
Lincoln, Bruce W. *Between Heaven and Hell: The Story of a Thousand Years of Artistic Life in Russia*. New York: Viking, 1998.
Lipovetskii, Mark. "Epilog russkogo modernizma: Khudozhestvennaia filosofiia tvorchestva v *Dare* Nabokova." In *Nabokov: Pro et Contra: Lichnost' i tvorchestvo V. Nabokova v otsenke russkikh i zarubezhnykh myslitelei i issledovatelei. Antologiia*, edited by D. K. Burlaka, 643–66. St. Petersburg: Izdatel'stvo Russkogo khristianskogo gumanitarnogo instituta, 1997.
Livak, Leonid. *How It Was Done in Paris: Russian Émigré Literature and French Modernism*. Madison: University of Wisconsin Press, 2003.
———. *In Search of Russian Modernism*. Baltimore, MD: Johns Hopkins University Press, 2018.
Livak, Leonid, and Andrei Ustinov, eds. *Literaturnyi avangard russkogo Parizha: Istoriia, khronika, antologiia, dokumenty, 1920–1926*. Moscow: OGI, 2014.
Lodder, Christina. "El Lissitzky and the Export of Constructivism." In *Situating El Lissitzky: Vitebsk, Berlin, Moscow*, edited by Nancy Perloff and Brian Reed, 27–46. Los Angeles: Getty Research Institute, 2003.
Loew, Roswitha, and Bella Tschistowa, eds. *Majakowski in Deutschland: Texte zur Rezeption, 1919–1930*. Berlin: Academie Verlag, 1986.
Lotman, Iurii. "Stikhotvoreniia rannego Pasternaka: Nekotorye voprosy strukturnogo izucheniia teksta." In *O poetakh i poezii*, 713–17. St. Petersburg: Isskustvo SPb, 1996.
Lourié, Vera [Vera Lur'e]. *Briefe an Dich: Erinnerungen an das russische Berlin*. Edited by Doris Liebermann. Frankfurt on Main: Schöffling & Co., 2014.
———. *Stikhotvoreniia*. Edited by Thomas R. Beyer Jr. Berlin: Spitz, 1987.
Love, Heather. *Feeling Backward: Loss and the Politics of Queer History*. Cambridge, MA: Harvard University Press, 2007.

Lowrie, Donald A. *Rebellious Prophet: A Life of Nicolai Berdyaev.* New York: Harper & Brothers, 1960.
Lunacharskii, Anatolii. "Russkaia vystavka v Berline." *Izvestiia VTsIK,* December 2, 1922.
Luther, Arthur. *Geschichte der russischen Literatur.* Leipzig: Bibliographisches Institut, 1924.
Lysenko, Artem. *Golos izgnaniia: Stanovlenie gazet russkogo Berlina i ikh evoliutsiia v 1919–1922 gg.* Moscow: Russkaia kniga, 2000.
Lyssakov, Pavel, and Stephen Norris. "The City in Russian Culture: Space, Culture, and the Russian City." In *The City in Russian Culture,* edited by Pavel Lyssakov and Stephen Norris, 1–12. London: Routledge, 2018.
Maar, Michael. *Speak, Nabokov.* Translated by Ross Benjamin. London, Verso, 2009.
———. *The Two Lolitas.* Translated by Perry Anderson. London: Verso, 2005.
Maiakovskii, Vladimir. *Polnoe sobranie sochinenii v trinadtsati tomakh.* Moscow: Gosudarstvennoe izdatel'stvo khudozhestvennoi literatury, 1956.
Malmstad, John. "Chodasevič and Belyj: A Parody Revisited." *Russian Literature* 83–84 (2016): 249–58.
———. "Edinstvo protivopolozhnostei: Istoriia vzaimootnoshenii Khodasevicha i Pasternaka." *Literaturnoe obozrenie* 2 (1990): 51–59.
Mandel'shtam, Iurii [Iouri Mandelstamm]. "Berlinskie i prazhskie poety." *Vozrozhdenie,* June 1, 1933.
———. "Lettres russes. Wladimir Sirine." *La Revue de France* 23, December 1, 1934, 560–67.
"Mann Finds U.S. Sole Peace Hope." *New York Times,* February 22, 1938, 13.
Marhoeffer, Laurie. *Sex and the Weimar Republic: German Homosexual Emancipation and the Rise of the Nazis.* Toronto: University of Toronto Press, 2015.
Markov, Vladimir. *Russian Futurism: A History.* Berkeley: University of California Press, 1968.
Marshall, Daniel, Kevin Murphy, and Zeb Tortorici. "Editors' Introduction. Queering Archives: Intimate Tracings." *Radical History Review* 122 (May 2015): 1–10.
Marten-Finnis, Susanne. *Der Feuervogel als Kunstzeitschrift: Žar Ptica. Russische Bildwelten in Berlin, 1921–1926.* Vienna: Böhlau Verlag, 2012.
Maslov, Boris. "Traditsii literaturnogo diletantizma i esteticheskaia ideologiia romana *Dar.*" In *Imperiia N: Nabokov i nasledniki,* edited by Iurii Leving and Evgenii Soshkin, 37–73. Moscow: Novoe literaturnoe obozrenie, 2006.
Matich, Olga. *Erotic Utopia: The Decadent Imagination in Russia's Fin de Siècle.* Madison: University of Wisconsin Press, 2004.
Medvedko, Ol'ga, ed. *Nikolai Zagrekov i Russkii Berlin.* Moscow: M-Skanrus, 2013.
Mierau, Fritz, ed. *Russen in Berlin: Literatur, Malerei, Theater, Film, 1918–1933.* Leipzig: Reclam, 1987.
Minskii, N. M., A. M. Remizov, and S. G. Kaplun, eds. *Biulliuteni Doma iskusstv Berlin* 1–2, February 17, 1922.
Mirskii, D. "Molodye russkie prozaiki." In *O literature i iskusstve: Stat'i i retsenzii, 1922–1937,* edited by O. A. Korostelev and M. V. Efimov, 103–6. Moscow: Novoe literaturnoe obozrenie, 2014.
Mondri, Henrietta. "O dvukh adresatakh literaturnoi parodii v *Dare* V. Nabokova (Iu. Tynianov i V. Rozanov)." *Rossiiskii literaturovedcheskii zhurnal* 4 (1994): 95–102.

Moore, Madison. *Fabulous: The Rise of the Beautiful Eccentric*. New Haven, CT: Yale University Press, 2018.
Morley, Rachel. *Performing Femininity: Woman as Performer in Early Russian Cinema*. London: I.B. Tauris, 2017.
Morris, Paul D. "Nabokov's Poetic Gift: The Poetry in and of *Dar*." *Russian Literature* 48 (2000): 457–69.
Morrison, Simon. "*The Golden Cockerel*, Censored and Uncensored." In *Rimsky-Korsakov and His World*, edited by Marina Frolova-Walker, 178–79. Princeton, NJ: Princeton University Press, 2018.
Morson, Gary Saul. *The Boundaries of Genre: Dostoevsky's Diary of a Writer and the Traditions of Literary Utopia*. Austin: The University of Texas Press, 1981.
Moser, Charles. "Mayakovsky's Unsentimental Journeys." *American Slavic and East European Review* 19, no. 1 (1960): 85–100.
Mosse, George. *Nationalism and Sexuality: Respectability and Abnormal Sexuality in Modern Europe*. New York: Howard Fertig, 1985.
Muravnik, Constantine. "Choosing the Hero: Nabokov's Short Story 'Recruiting' as an Introduction to His Aesthetics." *Russian Literature* 64, no. 1 (2008): 61–84.
———. "Nabokov's Philosophy of Art." *Nabokov Studies* 15 (2017), doi:10.1353/nab.2017.0002.
Nabokoff, Vladimir D. "Die Homosexualität im russischen Strafgesetzbuch." *Jahrbuch für sexuelle Zwischenstufen* 2 (1903): 1159–71.
Nabokov, Nicolas. *Bagázh: Memoirs of a Russian Cosmopolitan*. New York: Atheneum, 1975.
Nabokov, Vladimir Vladimirovich [Vladimir Nabokov]. *Drugie berega*. New York: Izdatel'stvo im. Chekhova, 1954.
———. *The Gift*. Translated by Michael Scammell with the collaboration of the author. New York: Vintage International, 1991.
———. "A Guide to Berlin." In *Details of a Sunset and Other Stories*, 89–98. New York: McGraw-Hill, 1976.
———. *Lectures on Literature*. Edited by Fredson Bowers. New York: Harcourt, Brace, Jovanovich, 1980.
———. *Letters to Véra*. Edited and translated by Olga Voronina and Brian Boyd. New York: Knopf, 2014.
———. *Mashen'ka*. Berlin: Knigoizdatel'stvo Slovo, 1926.
———. *Sobranie sochinenii russkogo perioda v piati tomakh*. Edited by N. I. Artemenko-Tolstaia and Aleksandr Dolinin. St. Petersburg: Simpozium, 2000.
———. *Speak, Memory: An Autobiography Revisited*. New York: Vintage International, 1989.
———. *Stikhotvoreniia*. Edited by M. E. Malikova. St. Petersburg: Akademicheskii proekt, 2002.
———. *Strong Opinions*. New York: McGraw-Hill, 1973.
———. *Think, Write, Speak: Uncollected Essays, Reviews, Interviews, and Letters to the Editor*. Edited by Brian Boyd and Anastasia Tolstoy. New York: Knopf, 2019.
———. "Triangle within Circle." *New Yorker*, March 23, 1963, 37–41.
Naiman, Eric. *Nabokov, Perversely*. Ithaca, NY: Cornell University Press, 2010.

Naroditskaya, Inna. *Bewitching Russian Opera: The Tsarina from State to Stage*. New York: Oxford University Press, 2012.
Nathanson, Richard. *Pavel Tchelitchew: A Collection of Theatre Designs, 1919–1923*. London: Alpine Club, 1976.
Naumann, Marina Turkevich. *Blue Evenings in Berlin: Nabokov's Short Stories of the 1920s*. New York: New York University Press, 1978.
Nesbet, Anne. "Suicide as Literary Fact in the 1920s." *Slavic Review* 50, no. 4 (1991): 827–35.
Nikitin, Nikolai. *Seichas na Zapade: Berlin, Rur, London*. Leningrad-Moscow: Petrograd, 1924.
Nivat, Georges, ed. *Odna ili dve russkikh literatury? Mezhdunarodnyi simpozium, sozvannyi fakul'tetom slovesnosti Zhenevskogo universiteta i Shveitsarskoi akademiei slavistiki. Zheneva, 13-14-15 aprelia 1978*. Lausanne: L'Age D'Homme, 1978.
Norman, Will. *Nabokov, History and the Texture of Time*. New York: Routledge, 2012.
Nyong'o, Tavia. *Afro-Fabulations: The Queer Drama of Black Life*. New York: New York University Press, 2019.
O'Connor, Katherine Tiernan. *Boris Pasternak's "My Sister—Life": The Illusion of Narrative*. Ann Arbor, MI: Ardis Publishers, 1988.
Ofrosimov, Iurii. "K postanovke 'Zolotogo petushka.'" *Rul'*, June 17, 1923, 9.
Orekhov, Boris, Pavel Uspenskii, and Veronika Fainberg. "Tsifrovye podkhody k 'Kamer-fur'erskomu zhurnalu' V. F. Khodasevicha." *Russkaia literatura* 3 (2018): 19–53.
Otsup, Nikolai. "F. I. Tiutchev." *Chisla* 1 (1930): 150–61.
Paperno, Irina. *Chernyshevsky and the Age of Realism: A Study in the Semiotics of Behavior*. Stanford, CA: Stanford University Press, 1988.
———. "How Nabokov's Gift Is Made." In *Literature, Culture, and Society in the Modern Age: In Honor of Joseph Frank*, edited by Edward J. Brown, Lazar Fleishman, Gregory Freidin, and Richard D. Schupbach, vol. 2, 295–322. Stanford, CA: Department of Slavic Languages and Literatures, Stanford University, 1992.
Parker, Luke. "The Shop Window Quality of Things: 1920s Weimar Surface Culture in Nabokov's *Korol', dama, valet*." *Slavic Review* 77, no. 2 (2018): 390–416.
———. *Nabokov Noir: Cinematic Culture and the Art of Exile*. Ithaca, NY: Cornell University Press, 2022.
Pashchenko, Mikhail. "'Skazka o zolotom petushke': Skazka-lozh' i skazka-pravda." *Voprosy literatury* 2 (2009): 202–34.
Pasternak, Boris. *The Marsh of Gold: Pasternak's Writings on Inspiration and Creation*. Edited by Angela Livingstone. Boston, MA: Academic Studies Press, 2008.
———. *Polnoe sobranie sochinenii s prilozheniiami v odinnadtsati tomakh*. 11 vols. Edited by E. B. Pasternak, E. V. Pasternak, et al. Moscow: Slovo, 2005–7.
Pasternak, Evgenii B. *Boris Pasternak: Biografiia*. Moscow: Tsitadel', 1997.
Pasternak, Josephine. *Tightrope Walking: A Memoir*, ed. Helen Ramsay and Rimgailia Salys. Bloomington, IN: Slavica Publishers, 2005.
Pinsker, Shachar M. *Literary Passports: The Making of Modernist Hebrew Fiction in Europe*. Stanford, CA: Stanford University Press, 2011.

———. *A Rich Brew: How Cafés Created Modern Jewish Culture*. New York: New York University Press, 2018.
"Pis'ma Maksima Gor'kogo k V. F. Khodasevichu." *Novyi zhurnal* 29 (1952): 207.
Platt, Kevin M. F. "Putting Russian Cultures in Place." Introduction to *Global Russian Cultures*, edited by Kevin M. F. Platt, 3–17. Madison: University of Wisconsin Press, 2019.
Polianskaia, Mina. *Florentiiskie nochi v Berline: Tsvetaeva, Leto 1922*. Moscow, Berlin: Golos-Press, Gelikon, 2009.
———. *Foxtrot belogo rytsaria: Andrei Belyi v Berline*. St. Petersburg: Demetra, 2009.
Pollok, Ethan. *Without the Banya We Would Perish: A History of the Russian Bathhouse*. Oxford, UK: Oxford University Press, 2019.
Ponomarev, Evgenii. "'Berlinskii ocherk' 1920-kh godov kak variant peterburgskogo teksta." *Voprosy literatury* 3 (2013): 42–67.
———. "Putevoditel' po Evrope." *Neva* 11 (2008).
Pratt, Mary Louise. *Imperial Eyes: Travel Writing and Transculturation*. 2nd ed. New York: Routledge, 2008.
Prickett, David James. "Defining Identity via Homosexual Spaces: Locating the Male Homosexual in Weimar Berlin." *Women in German Yearbook: Feminist Studies in German Literature and Culture* 21 (2005): 134–62.
Pushkin, Aleksandr. *Sobranie sochinenii v desiati tomakh*. Edited by D. D. Blagoi. Moscow: Gosudarstvennoe izdatel'stvo khudozhestvennoi literatury, 1960.
Pyshnovskaia, Z. S., and U. Kukhirt, eds. *Vzaimosviazi russkogo i sovetskogo iskusstva i nemetskoi khudozhestvennoi kul'tury*. Moscow: Nauka, 1980.
Raeff, Marc. *Russia Abroad: A Cultural History of the Russian Emigration, 1919–1939*. Oxford, UK: Oxford University Press, 1990.
Railing, Patricia, ed. *For the Voice: Vladimir Mayakovsky and El Lissitzky*. Cambridge, MA: MIT Press, 2000.
Raku, Marina. *Muzykal'naia klassika v mifotvorchestve sovetskoi epokhi*. Moscow: Novoe literaturnoe obozrenie, 2014.
Rashkovskaia, M. A., ed. *Boris Pasternak i Sergei Bobrov: Pis'ma chetyrekh desiatiletii*. Stanford, CA: Department of Slavic Languages and Literatures, Stanford University, 1996.
Redhead, Mark. "Dissent (Political Theory)." *Encyclopedia Britannica*. https://www.britannica.com/topic/dissent-political.
Reilly, Edward R. "Rimsky-Korsakov's *The Golden Cockerel*: A Very Modern Fairy Tale." *Musical Newsletter* 6, no. 1 (1976): 9–16.
Reisner, Larisa. "Berlin v oktiabre 1923 g[oda]." In *Gamburg na barrikadakh*, 73–94. Moscow: Novaia Moskva, 1924.
———. *V strane Gindenburga: Ocherki sovremennoi Germanii*. Moscow: Pravda, 1926.
Reiss, Tom. *The Orientalist: Solving the Mystery of a Strange and Dangerous Life*. New York: Random House, 2005.
Richter, Hans. *Köpfe und Hinterköpfe*. Zürich: Arche, 1967.
Richter, Horst. "Erste Russische Kunstausstellung: Berlin 1922." In *Die Russen in Berlin, 1910–1930*, 52–61. Berlin: Galerie Stolz, 1995.
Roditi, Edouard. "Entretien avec Marc Chagall." *Preuves: Cahiers mensuels du Congrès pour la liberté de la culture* 84 (1958): 17–28.

Romberg, Kristin. *Gan's Constructivism: Aesthetic Theory for an Embedded Modernism*. Berkeley: University of California Press, 2018.

Ronen, Omry. "Viktor Shklovsky's Tracks in 'A Guide to Berlin.'" Translated by Susanne Fusso. In *The Joy of Recognition: Selected Essays of Omry Ronen*, edited by Barry P. Sherr and Michael Wachtel, 202–31. Ann Arbor: Michigan Slavic Publications.

Roth, Joseph. *What I Saw: Reports from Berlin, 1920–1933*. Translated by Michael Hofmann. New York: Norton, 2003.

Rubenstein, Joshua. *Tangled Loyalties: The Life and Times of Ilya Ehrenburg*. Tuscaloosa: University of Alabama Press, 1999.

Rubins, Maria. "A Century of Russian Culture(s) 'Abroad': The Unfolding of Literary Geography." In *Global Russian Cultures*, edited by Kevin M. F. Platt, 21–47. Madison: University of Wisconsin Press, 2019.

———. "Conceptual Territories of 'Diaspora': Introduction. The Unbearable Lightness of Being a Diasporian: Modes of Writing and Reading Narratives of Displacement." In *Redefining Russian Literary Diaspora, 1920–2020*, edited by Maria Rubins. London: UCL Press, 2021.

———. *Russian Montparnasse: Transnational Writing in Interwar Paris*. London: Palgrave Macmillan, 2015.

Saleh, Zainab. *Return to Ruin: Iraqi Narratives of Exile and Nostalgia*. Stanford, CA: Stanford University Press, 2020.

Salkind, Eugenie. "Die junge russische Literatur in der Emigration." *Osteuropa* 6, no. 10 (1931): 575–90.

Sapir, Boris. "An Unknown Correspondent of Andrey Bely (Andrey Bely in Berlin, 1921–1923)." *Slavonic and East European Review* 49, no. 116 (1971): 450–52.

Schachter, Allison. *Diasporic Modernisms: Hebrew and Yiddish Literature in the Twentieth Century*. London: Oxford University Press, 2012.

Schiff, Stacy. *Véra (Mrs. Vladimir Nabokov)*. New York: Modern Library, 2000.

Schlegel, Joseph. "The Shapes of Poetry: Andrei Bely's Poetics in Vladimir Nabokov's *The Gift*." *Slavic and East European Journal* 59, no. 4 (2015): 567–68.

Schlögel, Karl. *Das russische Berlin*. New expanded edition. Berlin: Suhrkamp, 2019.

———, ed. *Russische Emigration in Deutschland 1918–1945: Leben im europäischen Bürgerkrieg*. Berlin: Akademie Verlag, 1995.

Schrenk, Walter. "'Der goldene Hahn.' Uraufführung in der Staatsoper." *Deutsche Allgemeine Zeitung*, June 19, 1923.

Sedykh, Andrei. "Vstrecha s V. Sirinym. Ot parizhskogo korrespondenta 'Segodnia': An Interview with Nabokov." *Segodnia*, November 4, 1932. Reprinted in Nabokov, *Sobranie sochinenii russkogo perioda, v piati tomakh*, vol. 5, edited by N. I. Artemenko-Tolstaia and Aleksandr Dolinin, 641–43. St. Petersburg: Simpozium, 2000.

Seelig, Rachel. *Strangers in Berlin: Modern Jewish Literature between East and West, 1919–1933*. Ann Arbor: University of Michigan Press, 2016.

Seidel, Michael. *Exile and Narrative Imagination*. New Haven, CT: Yale University Press, 1986.

Senelick, Laurence. "Émigré Cabaret and the Reinvention of Russia." *New Theatre Quarterly* 35, no. 1 (2019): 44–59.

Sergay, Timothy D. "Boris Pasternak's 'Christmas Myth': Fedorov, Berdiaev, Dickens, Blok." PhD diss., Yale University, 2008.
Serov, Vadim. *Entsiklopedicheskii slovar' krylatykh slov i vyrazhenii*. Moscow: Lokid-Press, 2003.
Shakhovskaia, Zinaïda. *V poiskakh Nabokova*. Paris: La Presse Libre, 1979.
Sharp, Jane A. *Russian Modernism between East and West: Natal'ia Goncharova and the Moscow Avant-Garde*. Cambridge: Cambridge University Press, 2006.
Sherr, Barry P. "A Curtailed Colloquy: Gorky, Khodasevich, and *Beseda*." In *Russian Literature and the West: A Tribute for David M. Bethea, Part II*, edited by Alexander Dolinin, Lazar Fleishman, and Leonid Livak, 129–46. Stanford, CA: Department of Slavic Languages and Literatures, Stanford University, 2008.
Shevelenko, Irina. *Literaturnyi put' Tsvetaevoi: Ideologiia—poetika—identichnost' avtora v kontekste epokhi*. Moscow: Novoe literaturnoe obozrenie, 2002.
———. *Modernizm kak arkhaizm: Natsionalizm i poiski modernistskoi estetiki v Rossii*. Moscow: Novoe literaturnoe obozrenie, 2017.
Shishkin, Andrei. "Rossiia raskololas' popolam: Neizvestnoe pis'mo Vl. Khodasevicha." *Russica Romana* 9 (2002): 107–14.
Shklovskii, Viktor [Viktor Shklovsky]. *Sobranie sochinenii*. Vol. 1, *Revoliutsiia*. Edited by Il'ia Kalinin. Moscow: Novoe literaturnoe obozrenie, 2018.
———. *Sobranie sochinenii*. Vol. 2, *Biograpfiia*. Edited by Il'ia Kalinin. Moscow: Novoe literaturnoe obozrenie, 2019.
———. *Zoo, or Letters Not about Love*. Translated and edited by Richard Sheldon. Ithaca, NY: Cornell University Press, 1971.
Shrayer, Maxim D. *The World of Nabokov's Stories*. Austin: University of Texas Press, 1999.
Shubinksii, Valerii. *Vladislav Khodasevich: Chaiushchii i govoriashchii*. St. Petersburg: Vita Nova, 2011.
Shvabrin, Stanislav. "Berlin." In *Vladimir Nabokov in Context*, edited by David Bethea and Siggy Frank, 87–93. Cambridge: Cambridge University Press, 2018.
Sicker, Philip T. "Shadows of Exile in Nabokov's Berlin." *Thought* 62, no. 3 (1987): 281–82.
Siegelberg, Mira L. *Statelessness: A Modern History*. Cambridge, MA: Harvard University Press, 2019.
Simon, Marie Jalowicz. *Underground in Berlin: A Young Woman's Extraordinary Tale of Survival in the Heart of Nazi Germany*. Translated by Anthea Bell. London: Little, Brown, 2015.
Škarenkov, Leonid L. "Eine Chronik der russischen Emigration in Deutschland: Die Materialien des Generals Aleksej A. von Lampe." In *Russische Emigration in Deutschland, 1918 bis 1941: Leben im europäischen Bürgerkrieg*, edited by Karl Schlögel, 39–75. Berlin: Akademie Verlag, 1995.
Skonechnaia, Ol'ga [Olga Skonechnaia]. "Cherno-belyi kaleidoskop: Andrei Belyi v otrazheniiakh V. V. Nabokova." In *Nabokov: Pro et contra*, edited by Boris Averin, Mariia Malikova, and Aleksandr Dolinin, 667–96. St. Petersburg: Izdatel'stvo Russkogo khristianskogo gumanitarnogo instituta, 1997.

———. "'People of the Moonlight': Silver Age Parodies in Nabokov's *The Eye* and *The Gift*." *Nabokov Studies* 3 (1996): 33–52.

Slobin, Greta. *Russians Abroad: Literary and Cultural Politics of Diaspora, 1919–1939*. Edited by Dan Isaac Slobin, Katerina Clark, Mark Slobin, and Nancy Condee. Boston, MA: Academic Studies Press, 2013.

Smirnov, Igor' P. "Obnazhenie mastera, zasekrechivaiushchego priem: Istochniki grunewal'dskogo epizoda v romane Vladimira Nabokova *Dar*." In *Essays in Honor of Alexander Zholkovsky*, edited by Dinnis Ioffe, Marcus Levitt, Joe Peschio, and Igor' Pilshchikov, 526–46. Boston, MA: Academic Studies Press, 2018.

Sontag, Susan. "Notes on Camp." In *Camp: Queer Aesthetics and the Performing Subject: A Reader*, edited by Fabio Cleto, 51–65. Ann Arbor: University of Michigan Press, 1999.

Sorokina, Vera. *Literaturnaia kritika Russkogo Berlina 20-kh godov XX veka*. Moscow: Izdatel'stvo Moskovskogo universiteta, 2010.

Spivak, Monika. *Andrei Belyi: Mistik i sovetskii pisatel'*. Moscow: Rossiiskii gosudarstvennyi gumanitarnyi universitet, 2006.

———. "Koshmar v pissuare: K voprosu o genezise odnogo emigrantskogo vpechatleniia Andreiia Belogo." *Europa Orientalis* 22, no. 2 (2003): 51–70.

Steakley, James. "Cinema and Censorship in the Weimar Republic: The Case of *Anders als die Andern*." *Film History* 11, no. 2 (1999): 181–203.

Steiner, George. *Extraterritorial: Papers on Literature and the Language Revolution*. New York: Atheneum, 1976.

Steneberg, Eberhard. *Russische Kunst Berlin 1919–1932*. Berlin: Gebr. Mann Verlag, 1969.

Stern, Bernhardt. *Geschichte der Öffentlichen Sittlichkeit in Russland: Kultur, Aberglaube, Sitten und Gebräuche*. Berlin: Verlag von Hermann Barsdorf, 1908.

Stolarska-Fronia, Małgorzata, ed. *Polish Avant-Garde in Berlin*. Berlin: Peter Lang, 2019.

Straumann, Barbara. *Figurations of Exile in Hitchcock and Nabokov*. Edinburgh: Edinburgh University Press, 2008.

Struve, Gleb. *Russkaia literatura v izgnanii. Opyt istoricheskogo obzora zarubezhnoi literatury*. 3rd ed. Paris: YMCA-Press; Moscow: Russkii put', 1996.

Takho-Godi. E. A. and M. Shruba. "Ob Andree Belom, Fedore Stepune, Dmitrii Chizhevskom i odnoi nesostoiavsheisia publikatsii v 'Sovremennykh zapiskakh'." In *Literatura russkogo zarubezh'ia (1920–1940-e gody): Vzgliad iz XXI veka*, edited by L. E. Iezuitova and S. D. Titarenko, 110–22. St. Petersburg: St. Petersburg State University, 2008.

Tapp, Alyson. "Boris Eikhenbaum's Response to the Crisis of the Novel in the 1920s." *Slavonica* 15, no. 1 (2009): 32–47.

Taranovskii, Kirill. "O poetike Borisa Pasternaka." In *O poetakh i poezii*, 213. Moscow: Iazyki russkoi kultury, 2000.

Taruskin, Richard. "Rimsky-Korsakov, Nikolay Andreyevich (opera)." Oxford Music Online, 2002. https://www.oxfordmusiconline.com/grovemusic/view/10.1093/gmo/9781561592630.001.0001/omo-9781561592630-e-5000002126.

Tatar, Maria. *Lustmord: Sexual Murder in Weimar Germany*. Princeton, NJ: Princeton University Press, 1995.

———. *Off with Their Heads! Fairy Tales and the Culture of Childhood*. Princeton, NJ: Princeton University Press, 1993.
Teliia, V. N., ed. *Bol'shoi frazeologicheskii slovar' russkogo iazyka: Znachenie, upotreblenie, kul'turologicheskii kommentarii*. Moscow: AST-Press Kniga, 2006.
Theis, Wolfgang, and Andreas Sternweiler. "Alltag im Kaiserreich und in der Weimarer Republik." In *Eldorado: Homosexuelle Frauen und Männer in Berlin 1850–1950: Geschichte, Alltag und Kultur*, edited by Michael Bolle, 55–56. Berlin: Frölich und Kaufmann, 1984.
Thomas, Alfred. *Shakespeare, Dissent, and the Cold War*. New York: Palgrave Macmillan, 2004.
Tihanov, Galin. "Narratives of Exile: Cosmopolitanism beyond the Liberal Imagination." In *Whose Cosmopolitanism? Critical Perspectives, Relationalities and Discontents*, edited by Nina Glick Schiller and Andrew Irving, 141–59. New York: Berghahn, 2014.
Time, Galina. *Puteshestvie Moskva-Berlin-Moskva: Russkii vzgliad Drugogo, 1919–1939*. Moscow: Rosspen, 2011.
———. "Zakat Evropy kak 'tsentral'naia mysl' russkoi filosofii': O mirovozzrencheskoi samoidentifikatsii Rossii v nachale 1920-kh gg." In *XX vek. Dvadtsatye gody: Iz istorii mezhdunarodnykh sviazei russkoi literatury*, edited by Galina Time, 62–88. St. Petersburg: Nauka, 2006.
Toporov, V. N. *Peterburgskii tekst russkoi literatury: Izbrannye trudy*. St. Petersburg: Iskusstvo-SPb, 2003.
Tretiakov, Sergei. *Liudi odnogo kostra: Literaturnye portrety*. Moscow: Khudozhestvennaia literatura, 1936.
Trotsky, Leon. *Literature and Revolution*. Translated by Rose Strunsky. Ann Arbor: University of Michigan Press, 1960.
Tsvetaeva, Marina. *Letter to the Amazon*. Translated by A'Dora Phillips and Gaëlle Cogan, introduction by Catherine Ciepiela. Brooklyn: Ugly Duckling Presse, 2016.
———. "Plennyi dukh: Moia vstrecha s Andreem Belym." In *Izbrannaia proza v dvukh tomakh*, edited by Aleksandr Sumerkin, vol. 2, 80–121. New York: Russica Publishers, 1979.
———. "Poet i vremia." In *Izbrannaia proza v dvukh tomakh*, edited by Aleksandr Sumerkin, vol. 1, 367–80. New York: Russica Publishers, 1979.
Tynianov, Yuri [Iurii Tynianov]. "Literaturnoe segodnia." *Russkii sovremennik* 1 (1924): 305.
———. *Permanent Evolution: Selected Essays on Literature, Theory and Film*. Translated by Ainsley Morse and Philip Redko, with an introduction by Daria Khitrova. Boston, MA: Academic Studies Press, 2019.
———. "Promezhutok." In *Poetika. Istoriia literatury. Kino*, edited by E. A. Toddes, A. P. Chudakov, and M. O. Chudakova, 169. Moscow: Nauka, 1977.
Urban, Thomas. *Russische Schriftsteller in Berlin der zwanziger Jahre*. Berlin: Nicolai, 2003.
———. *Vladimir Nabokov: Blaue Abende in Berlin*. Berlin: Propyläen, 1999.
Ushakin, Sergei. "Odnorazovaia periodika Borisa Eikhenbauma." In *Boris Eikhenbaum, Moi vremennik: Slovesnost', nauka, kritika, smes'*, 5–22. Ekaterinburg: Kabinetnyi uchenyi, 2020.

Uspenskii, Pavel [Pavel Uspenskii]. "Kompozitsiia Evropeiskoi nochi Khodasevicha: Kak emigratsiia opredelila strukturu sbornika?" *Russian Literature* 83-84 (2016): 91-111.

———. "Vladislav Khodasevich in the Emigration: Literature and the Search for Identity." *Russian Review* 77, no. 1 (2018): 88-108.

———. "'Zhili vmeste dva tramvaia:' 'Berlinskoe' V. F. Khodasevicha." *Russkaia filologiia: Sbornik nauchnykh rabot molodykh filologov* 23 (2016): 112-21.

Utkin, Roman, ed. "Illegal Queerness: Russian Culture and Society in the Age of Anti-LGBTQ Censorship." *Russian Review* 80, no. 1 (2021): 7-99.

Vainberg, I. "Zhizn' i gibel' berlinskogo zhurnala Gor'kogo 'Beseda': Po neizvestnym arkhivnym materialam i neizdannoi perepiske." *Novoe literaturnoe obozrenie* 21 (1996): 361-76.

Vassiliev, Alexandre. *Beauty in Exile: The Artists, Models, and Nobility Who Fled the Russian Revolution and Influenced the World of Fashion*. Translated by Antonina W. Bouis and Anya Kucharev. New York: Harry N. Abrams, 2000.

Veidle, Vladimir. *Poeziia Khodasevicha*. Paris: [n.p.], 1928.

Vicks, Meghan. "Paranoid Reading, Reparative Reading, and Queering *The Real Life of Sebastian Knight*." In *Reimagining Nabokov: Pedagogies for the 21st Century*, edited by Sara Karpukhin and José Vergara, 128-47. Amherst: Amherst College Press.

Virolainen, Mariia. *Rech' i molchanie: Siuzhety russkoi slovesnosti*. St. Petersburg: Amfora, 2003.

Volkmann, Hans-Erich. *Die russische Emigration in Deutschland, 1919-1929*. Würzburg: Holzner Verlag, 1966.

Wachtel, Michael. "Vladislav Khodasevich as Innovator." In *Living through Literature: Essays in Memory of Omry Ronen*, edited by Julie Hansen, Karen Evans-Romaine, and Herbert Eagle, 63-78. Uppsala: Uppsala University, 2019.

Warner, Michael. *Publics and Counterpublics*. New York: Zone Books, 2002.

Watton, Lindsay F. "Constructs of Sin and Sodom in Russian Modernism, 1906-1909." *Journal of the History of Sexuality* 4, no. 3 (January 1994): 369-94.

Weir, Justin. *The Author as Hero: Self and Tradition in Bulgakov, Pasternak, and Nabokov*. Evanston, IL: Northwestern University Press, 2002.

———. "*The Golden Cockerel* between Realism and Modernism." In *Intersections and Transpositions: Russian Music, Literature, and Society*, edited by Andrew Baruch Wachtel, 78-86. Evanston, IL: Northwestern University Press, 1998.

Wesling, Meg. "Why Queer Diaspora?" *Feminist Review* 90 (2008): 30-47.

White, Duffield. "Radical Aestheticism and Metaphysical Realism in Nabokov's *The Gift*." In *Russian Literature and American Critics: In Honor of Deming Brown*, edited by Kenneth N. Brostrom, 273-91. Ann Arbor: University of Michigan Department of Slavic Languages and Literatures, 1984.

Williams, Raymond. *Visions and Blueprints: Avant-garde Culture and Radical Politics in Early Twentieth-Century Europe*. Edited by Edward Timms and Peter Collier. Manchester: Manchester University Press, 1988.

———. "When Was Modernism?" In *The Politics of Modernism: Against the New Conformists*, edited by Tony Pinkney, 31-36. London: Verso, 1989.

Williams, Robert C. "Boris Trödtl: A Russian Fascist and Nazi Germany." In *Russia Imagined: Art, Culture, and National Identity, 1840–1995*, 177–83. New York: Peter Lang, 1997.

———. "'Changing Landmarks' in Russian Berlin, 1922–1924." *Slavic Review* 27, no. 4 (1968): 581–93.

———. *Culture in Exile: Russian Émigrés in Germany, 1881–1941*. Ithaca, NY: Cornell University Press, 1972.

Windham, Donald. "The Stage and Ballet Designs of Pavel Tchelitchew." *Dance Index* 1 (1944): 7.

Woods, Gregory. *The Homintern: How Gay Culture Liberated the Modern World*. New Haven, CT: Yale University Press, 2016.

Zaitsev, Boris K. *Sochineniia v trekh tomakh*. Edited by E. Voropaeva and A. Tarkhov. Moscow: Khudozhestvennaia literatura—Terra, 1993.

Zholkovskii, Aleksandr [A. K. Zholkovsky]. "Ekstaticheskie motivy Pasternaka v svete ego lichnoi mifologii." In *Boris Pasternak 1890–1990*, edited by Lev Losev, 52–74. Northfield, VT: Russian School of Norwich University, 1991.

———. "The Window in the Poetic World of Boris Pasternak." *New Literary History* 9, no. 2 (1978): 290–93.

Zimianina, Natal'ia. "Vozmozhna li politicheskaia opera." *Vremia MN*, April 8, 2003.

Zimmer, Dieter. *Nabokov's Berlin*. Berlin: Nicolai, 2001.

———. "What Happened to Sergey Nabokov." Unpublished article, 2017. http://www.d-e-zimmer.de/PDF/SergeyN.pdf.

INDEX

Page numbers in italics refer to illustrations.

"About These Verses" (Pasternak), 41
Acharya, Magda Nachman, 176
Adamovich, Georgy, 233n2
aesthetic empathizing, 132–33
Aikhenvald, Alexander, 9
Aikhenvald, Yuly, 9, 229n66
Aikhenvald-Tatarinov Circle, 117
Akhmatova, Anna, 168, 177, 218n10
Alexandrov, Vladimir, 227n55, 230n87
Alexandrovka, 15
alienation, 54, 65, 118, 132, 137, 156
"All is Stony. Into a Stony Passage"
   (Khodasevich), 3–4, 55–57, 61–62,
   134
Ananko, Yaroslava, 29, 202n13
"And Could You?" (Mayakovsky),
   61–62
Andreev, Vadim, 5, 201n67
Andreyev, Catherine, 119
And Yet It Spins (Ehrenburg), 81
anthroposophy, 73, 82
apocalypse. *See* Western civilization (the
   decay of)
Á rebours (Huysmans), 167
Arendt, Hannah, 8
artistic freedom, 4
Aseev, Nikolay, 55
"Author and Hero in Aesthetic Activity"
   (Bakhtin), 132

avant-garde art, 18, 23, 29–30, 43, 46–47,
   51–52, 62, 81, 92, 101–2, 108. *See also*
   modernism; primitivism

Bagázh (Nabokov, N.), 163
Bakhtin, Mikhail, 92, 97–98, 132
Balanchine, George, 154
Balieff, Nikita, 101
Ballets Russes, 98–99, 106, 154, 220n36
Barncy, Natalie Clifford, 157
Barskova, Polina, 228n59
Batalin, R.G., 136
Bauer, Heike, 158
Bauhaus, 81
Beckmann, Max, 60
Belentschikow, Valentin, 202n16
Belgrade, 8
Belsky, Vladimir, 93, 95, 112, 115
Bely, Andrei, 10, 17, 19, 21–22, 64–77,
   81–90, 129–30, 150, 214n46, 214n50,
   217n83. *See also specific works*
Bend Sinister (Nabokov), 158
Benjamin, Walter, 208n88, 226n44
Berberova, Nina, 19, 54, 116, 178–79,
   222nn2–3, 234n12
Berdyaev, Nikolay, 6, 13, 83
Bergelson, Dovid, 10–11
Berlin. *See* Charlottengrad (background
   on); communal living; cultural

Index

Berlin (*continued*)
  diversity; cultural identity; cultural isolation; literary maps; political diversity; population numbers (of Russians in Berlin); publishing; queer life; Red Berlin; Soviet Union; stepmother of Russian cities (Berlin); transitional space; wandering; Western civilization (the decay of)
Berlin, Europe's Eastern Station (Schlögel), 18
"Berlin in October of 1923" (Reisner), 65–66
Berlin/Moskau Moskva/Berlin, 200n57
"A Berlin Poem" (Khodasevich), 60
"Berlin Spring" (Nabokov), 123–24, 227n54
Berlin State Opera, 91–92, 98–100, 105
"Berlin Today" (Mayakovsky), 51
Berlin Zoo, 66, 85, 178–79
Berlin Zoo (Berberova), 178–79
Beseda, 9, 72–74
Bethea, David, 52, 58, 82, 225n34
Beyer, Thomas, 197n26
Bilibin, Ivan, 106, 108, *114*, 115
Bishop, Sarah, 59
Blackwell, Stephen, 146, 224n23, 228n63, 229n66, 232n110, 236n31
Blasing, Molly Thomasy, 203n19
Blok, Alexander, 60, 73
Bobrov, Sergey, 204n26
Boguslavskaia, Ksenia, 14
Boldt, Frank, 196n15
border crosser, 197n23
The Boyar's Wedding Feast (Tchelitchew), 102, *104*
Boyd, Brian, 118, 142
Brik, Lili, 206n64, 207n73, 208n84
Brik, Osip, 221n52
Brown, Edward J., 207n80
Bruegel, Pieter, 108
Buck-Morss, Susan, 202n14
Bukshpan, Yakov, 83
Bulatova, Asiya, 77–78, 215n62
Bunin, Ivan, 197n20

Burliuk, David, 14
"The Butterfly-Tempest" (Pasternak), 31–35, 37, 41–42, 204n32
"By the Shore" (Gumilev), 36
"By the winter's magic" (Tiutchev), 124

Cairo, 8
camp, 95–96
Candide (Voltaire), 88–89
carnivalesque, 97
causality, 29
censorship, 73, 95, 98, 142, 154, 167, *168*, 169–70, 219n12, 238n58
Chagall, Marc, 6, 10, 12, 14, 154
Change of Landmarks, 13, 199n43, 214n50
Charlottengrad (background on), 3–4, 6, 14–16, 176–78
Chernyshevsky, Nikolay, 141–45, 232n104
Chiorny, Sasha, 177
Chlenov, S., 83
"A Christmas Carol" (Dickens), 41
chronology, 29, 95
chronotope, 98
Chukovsky, Korney, 199n44
Cities and Years (Fedin), 211n5
city guides, 65–67, 77, 81, 84. *See also* literary maps
Clark, Katerina, 208n87
Cleto, Fabio, 95–96
Cold War, 18
Colloquy (Gorky), 9, 72–74
communal living, 10–11, 31
Communist International (Comintern), 17–18, 46
Communist Party of Germany, 49, 51
constructivism, 81, 102, 212n12
Copenhagen, 8
"Cozy Corner Berlin" (Eisenstein), *152–53*
Cruz-Malavé, Arnaldo, 157
cultural diversity, 5, 10–12, 16–17, 23, 26, 28, 63–64, 83, 149. *See also* queer life
cultural identity, 19, 26
cultural isolation, 19, 21
cultural studies, 54
Czapski, Josef, 168–69

"Declaration to the All-Russian Central Executive Committee" (Shklovsky), 79
Decline of the West (Spengler), 40, 83
de Gabineau, Arthur, 102
Der Sturm, 81
Despair (Nabokov), 120
Diaghilev, Sergey, 98–99, 154, 163
diaspora, 20, 22, 63–64, 68–69, 82, 116, 135, 157–58, 197n20. *See also* exile
Dickens, Charles, 41
Dix, Otto, 47, 60
"Dlinnee zhizni" (Ehrenburg), 213n31
Dni, 99–100, 173
Doctor Zhivago (Pasternak), 39
Dolinin, Alexander, 40–41, 82, 118, 131, 146, 230n79, 230n82, 231n93
Dostoevsky, Fyodor, 146
Dragonoiu, Dana, 141
Dreamworld and Catastrophe (Buck-Morss), 202n14
Drugie berega (Nabokov), 116
Duncan, Isadora, 9, 151

economy (of Berlin), 11–12, 44, 119
ecumenicalism, 73–74
Edwards, Brent, 20, 157–58
Ehrenburg, Ilya, 9–10, 19, 21–23, 31, 37–38, 65–71, 75, 80–90, 150, 203n18, 213n31. See also *Veshch'/Gegenstand/Objet*; specific works
Ehrenburg, Liubov, 174
Eikhenbaum, Boris, 67–68
Eisenstein, Sergey, 17, 22, 151, 152–53
"The Elements of My Worldview" (Bely), 83
Eliot, T.S., 138
Emerson, Caryl, 97–98
emigrant (as a term), 7, 15
emigration, 7, 26, 27–29, 52–53, 79, 199n51. *See also* immigration; trial emigration
émigré (as a term), 7, 14, 151, 154, 176, 197, 200n57. *See also* exile; trial emigration
epistolary modes. *See* letter writing
Epopeia, 74

Esenin, Sergey, 9, 22, 151, 234n11
Eugene Onegin (Pushkin), 139
Eurasianist movement, 104–5, 215n69, 221n52
European Night (Khodasevich), 52, 60–61
exile: and the 1917 Revolution, 3, 7; allegories of, 78; and an émigré literature, 140–47; and art, 21–23, 29, 37, 52, 54–58, 61, 65, 70; culture in, 30, 116–17, 120, 124–25, 136, 167, 171; definition of, 8, 197n20, 197n23; within exile, 157; and extraterritoriality, 54, 57, 59–60; and identity, 63; and isolation, 19, 21; and normativity, 157; and opera, 91–92, 100, 106–8; political, 47–48, 72; queer, 19, 96, 148–51, 154, 156–61, 164, 167, 169–71, 237n43; and Russian intellectuals, 12–13; and Russian Oriental exotica, 105, 112; self, 7. *See also* alienation; diaspora; Nabokov, Vladimir; *specific authors and works*
Exodus to the East, 104
Exter, Alexandra, 102
The Extraordinary Adventures of Julio Jurenito (Ehrenburg), 70
extraterritorial, 53–54, 57–60

fabulation, 96–97, 162
Fabulous (Moore), 96
fabulous dissent, 92, 95–97, 112, 115
The Fairy Tale of the Golden Cockerel (Pushkin), 93, 105–6, 108, 113, 115, 218n10
Faust (Goethe), 121–22
Fedin, Konstantin, 15, 211n5
Firebird, 25, 26, 202n6
First Exhibition of Russian Art, 14–15, 46
"The First of May" (Pasternak), 42–43
Fleishman, Lazar, 30, 196n15
Fokine, Michel, 220n36
Fondaminskaia, Amalia, 17
For the Voice (Mayakovsky), 61
Frank, Semyon, 83
Freise, Mattias, 40–41
futurism, 30, 43–46, 51, 60, 73

Gasparov, Boris, 218n10
gay liberation, 158–59
Gedächtniskirche, 74, 84
Gelikon, 69, 72
gender. *See* women
genre, 67–68, 75–84, 118. *See also* camp; carnivalesque; city guides; letter writing; literary maps; opera; poetry
geography. *See* literary maps
German Foreign Office, 14
"Germany" (Mayakovsky), 47–49, 51
Gessen, Iosif, 69, 91
The Gift (Nabokov), 21–22, 117–19, 125–47, 158, 224n23, 225n33, 226nn50–51, 227nn52–56, 228n59, 228nn62–64, 229nn66–72, 230n87, 230nn78–80, 230nn82–84, 231nn88–90, 232nn109–11
Glavlit, 73
Glebov, Igor, 114
"Gleisdreieck" (Pasternak), 32, 38–42, 88
Glory (Nabokov), 120, 158
Gobineau, Arthur de, 102
Goethe, 121–22
Gogol, 147
The Golden Cockerel (Rimsky-Korsakov), 21, 91–100, 105–15, 219n12, 220n36
Goncharova, Natalia, 106, 108, 220n36
Gopinath, Gayatri, 156
Gordon, Avery, 237n43
Gordon, Mel, 149
Gorky, Maxim, 9, 13, 53, 72, 213n24
"Grain's Way" (Khodasevich), 57–59
Grosz, George, 47, 60
the grotesque, 91–92
"A Guide to Berlin" (Nabokov), 21, 65, 84–85, 90, 120, 123, 213n34
Gul, Roman, 12, 15, 17
Gumilev, Nikolay, 22, 36, 205n37

Hájková, Anna, 149
Hamlin, Rebecca, 197n23
Harbin, 8
Heartfield, John, 47
The Heavy Lyre (Khodasevich), 59

Herzfelde, Wieland, 46
heteronormativity, 154, 156–57, 171. *See also* queer life
Hirschfeld, Magnus, 151, 159
historical citizenship, 149
historical narratives, 28, 149. *See also* interlude
Hoisington, Sona, 115, 218n10
Homintern, 151
homophobia, 22, 150, 158. *See also* queer life
homosexuality. *See* queer life
House of the Arts, 10, 17, 74
"How to Make Poems?" (Mayakovsky), 208n91
Hughes, Robert, 59
Huysmans, Joris-Karl, 167

I Carried Russia Away (Gul), 15
Ilyin, Ivan, 13
immigration, 7. *See also* emigration
Inber, Vera, 173
Institute for Sexual Science, 151, 159
interlude, 27–30, 64
"Interlude" (Tynianov), 54–55
Irving, Washington, 93
Isherwood, Christopher, 22, 234n4, 234n8, 238n56
isolationism, 116
Istanbul, 8
The Italics Are Mine (Berberova), 54
Ivanov, Fyodor, 26, 27, 34, 204n32
Ivanov, Viacheslav V., 32, 57
Ivanov, Vsevolod, 68–69
Ivask, Yuri, 233n2
"I Was Born in Moscow" (Khodasevich), 210n121

Jackson, Robert Louis, 122
Jakobson, Roman, 77–78, 218n10
Jangfeldt, Bengt, 43

Kadet Gessen, 73–74
Kammerfurier's Journal (Khodasevich), 52–53

Kandinsky, Vasily, 14
Karlinsky, Simon, 118–19, 140
Karshan, Thomas, 226n50
Kashchei the Deathless (Rimsky-Korsakov), 93
Kauffman, Linda, 77
Kerensky, Alexander, 47–48, 173
Khlebnikov, Velimir, 78–79, 215n62
Khodasevich, Vladislav: background on, 12, 27, 53; and Berlin literature, 53; the Berlin poetry of, 3–5, 52, 54–62, 210n116; and *Beseda*, 72; criticisms of, 54–55, 204n26; and duality, 59; and the House of the Arts, 10; and the language of poetry, 56–57; mythmaking about, 20–21; and Nabokov, 134–35; and surrogate motherhood, 56; and trial emigration, 20–21, 27, 29, 52–59. *See also specific works*
King, Queen, Knave (Nabokov), 120, 122–23, 225n40, 229n72
kinship, 5, 157, 161
Korkowsky, Britta, 40–41
Korovin, Konstantin, 106, 108
Korvin-Piotrovsky, Vladimir, 177, 222n9
Kostalevsky, Marina, 143
Kotik Letaev (Bely), 227n55
Kramer, Lawrence, 113
Kruchenykh, Alexey, 109
Kühn, Edmund, 99
Kuritsyn, Viacheslav, 228n59
Kusikov, Alexander, 23
Kuzina, Elena, 56*La Chauve-souris* (Balieff), 101

Ladd, Brian, 226n49
Lampe, Alexey von, 10
Landmarks (*Vekhi*), 13
The Land of Cockaigne (Bruegel), 108
language, 5–7, 28, 49, 57, 86, 130–31, 158. *See also* poetry; translation
Laughter in the Dark (Nabokov), 120, 158
League of Nations, 8
Left Front of the Arts (LEF), 42
"Left March" (Mayakovsky), 49

"The Legend of the Arabian Astrologer" (Irving), 93
Léger, Fernand, 102
Lermontov, Mikhail, 36
"Letters from Cafés" (Ehrenburg), 65, 67, 70–71, 75, 77, 80–81, 83–84, 89–90
Letters to You (Lourié), 22, 171–75, 178
Letter to the Amazon (Tsvetaeva), 157
letter writing, 75, 77–78, 80–82, 84, 90, 172–75
Levchenko, Yan, 77
Liebermann, Doris, 172
Lifar, Serge, 154
Lissitzky, El, 9–10, 17, 23, 61–62, 71. *See also Veshch'/Gegenstand/Objet*
literary criticism, 118
literary dilettantism, 144–45, 232n105
literary everyday, 67–68, 73
"The Literary Everyday" (Eikhenbaum), 67–68
literary maps, 21, 84–90, 139, 230n80. *See also* city guides
literature, 26, 27. *See also specific authors and works*
Literature and Revolution (Trotsky), 89
"Literature in Exile" (Khodasevich), 57
Livak, Leonid, 6, 156, 227n53, 229n71
Lolita (Nabokov), 158
London, 8
Lossky, Nikolay, 13
the Lost Generation (in Paris), 7
Lourié, Vera, 9–10, 22, 171–75, 178
Lunacharsky, Anatoly, 14–15, 207n72
Lundberg, Evgeny, 199n46
Lunts, Lev, 68–69
Lustmord (sexual murder), 60

"Majakowski in Berlin 1924" (Wangenheim), 208n81
Malevich, Kazimir, 46
Malmstad, John, 60
Manalansan, Martin, 157
Mandelstamm, Iouri, 223n11
Mann, Klaus, 149
Mann, Thomas, 17, 233n117

"An Mariechen" (Khodasevich), 60
Marshall, Daniel, 151
Marten-Finnis, Susanne, 202n6
Mary (Nabokov), 22, 120, 158
Masjutyn, Wasyl, 113, 176
Maslov, Boris, 144, 232n105
Matiushin, Mikhail, 109
"Matros v Moskve" (Pasternak), 204n26
Mayakovsky, Vladimir: background on, 27, 46–47; and Berlin, 17, 44, 47–51, 206n67, 208n94; the Berlin texts of, 43–51, 57, 61–62, 208n88; and the free market, 206n64; and futurism, 44–46; and the House of the Arts, 10; and identity, 176–77; mythmaking about, 20–21; the reputation of, 208n81; and the Russian Revolution, 37–38, 43–44, 46, 48, 207n72, 207n80; and trial emigration, 20, 27, 29, 47–52; and *Veshch'/Gegenstand/Objet*, 23. *See also specific works*
Medinsky, Vladimir, 200n57
Meidner, Ludwig, 60
"Menagerie" (Khlebnikov), 78–79, 215n62
Meyer, Priscilla, 139
Meyerhold, Vsevolod, 46
Miliukov, Pavel, 13
Mirsky, D.S., 67–68
"The Mission of Russian Emigration" (Bunin), 197n20
modernism, 81; German, 7, 12, 71; Hebrew, 5; as a keyword, 20; and nationalism, 102, 104; and Paris, 12; and queer life, 22; from realism to, 94; Russian, 6–7, 18, 71, 104; and Russian culture, 27–28; and Salomé, 113–14; traits of, 7; and the tram, 133; and urban imagery, 45–46; and the urban railroad, 38–40; and vocabulary, 106–8; Yiddish, 5. *See also* avant-garde art; poetry; primitivism: criticisms of
Moore, Madison, 96
morality, 149, 159, 167
Morley, Rachel, 113–14

Morrison, Simon, 94, 219n12
Morson, Gary Saul, 88, 94–95
Moscow, 49–52, 75, 81, 83, 208n87
Mosse, George, 149
Murphy, Kevin, 151
My Periodical (Eikhenbaum), 68
My Sister—Life (Pasternak), 9, 36
Mystery-Bouffe (Mayakovsky), 38, 44–46, 48–49, 51
myth, 5, 20–21, 82

Nabokov, Ivan, 163
Nabokov, Nicolas, 9, 100, 120, 163–64, 234n11
Nabokov, Sergey, 22, 159–71, 178, 237n48
Nabokov, Véra, 119, 162, 169
Nabokov, Vladimir: as aloof, 120–21, 127–28; background on, 117, 119–20, 159, 225n34; and Berlin, 6, 19, 21, 122–23, 128–36, 138–39, 223n15, 223nn11–12, 224n23, 226n42, 227n56; and censorship, 142; criticisms of, 117; and crossword puzzles, 125–28; descriptions of, 163–64, 225n33; and the erotic, 139, 230nn83–84; and exile, 17, 21–22, 65, 117–25, 132, 135–38, 140, 145, 147, 154, 156–57, 233n117; the gay characters of, 158–59; and golden poverty, 123–24, 145; and happiness, 142–43, 145–46; and homophobia, 22; and identity, 177; and insider/outsider, 132–33, 139; and liberalism, 142; and literary futurity, 140–41; and the multistable narrator, 146; the political views of, 71; and publishers, 69; and Sergey Nabokov, 159–64, 169–70, 237n51; the style of, 84, 90; and translation, 121–22, 136–37. *See also specific works*
Nabokov, Vladimir D., 63, 158–60
Naiman, Eric, 230n87, 230nn83–84
Nakanune, 31
Nansen Passport, 8
Narkompros, 14
narrative theory, 95–96
Nathanson, Richard, 218n7

Nazimova, Alla, 154
Nazism, 177–78, 229n76
The New Middle Ages (Berdyaev), 6
The New Russian Book (Yashchenko), 9
New York, 10
Nietzsche, 53
Nijinsky, Vaclav, 154
Noel, Lucie Leon, 163–64, 237n51
Norman, Will, 232n103
"Notes on Camp" (Sontag), 95

Ofrosimov, Yuri, 99
Onegin, Eugene (Tchaikovsky), 100
One of the Mansions of the Kingdom of Shades (Bely), 64–65, 67, 70, 74–75, 76, 77, 81–84, 89–90, 136, 150
"On LEF, White Paris, Gray Berlin, and Red Moscow" (Mayakovsky), 51
On the Eve (*Nakanune*), 13
opera, 91–115
orthography, 71
Oushakine, Serguei, 68

Pale Fire (Nabokov), 236n31
Paperno, Irina, 141, 146
Paris, 8, 10, 12, 51, 117, 135, 157, 164
Parker, Luke, 122–23
Parnok, Sofia, 236n28
Pashchenko, Mikhail, 218n10
Pasternak, Boris: background on, 23, 27, 30, 44; the Berlin poems of, 29–43, 50, 57, 202n16, 203n25, 203nn18–19; describing Berlin, 6, 19, 31, 204n28, 205n52; and futurism, 30, 41; myth-making about, 20–21; and the odd fellow, 41–42; and trains, 39–41; and trial emigration, 9, 27, 29–31, 42–43. *See also specific poems*
Pasternak, Elena, 36
Pasternak, Evgeny, 36
Pasternak, Josephine, 30–31
patriarchy, 113–15, 154
patriotism, 86
performance theory, 97–98
Petersburg, 84, 177

Petersburg (Bely), 70, 74–75, 82, 84, 129–30, 228n57
Petersburg on Wittenburg Square (Batalin), 136
Philosophy Steamer, 13
Pilniak, Boris, 15, 68–69, 195n7
Platt, Kevin, 239n1
poetry: and cafés, 10; and the demise of Western civilization, 40–41; and imagery, 37–39, 41, 45–46, 50, 56–61, 178–79; and interlude, 27–29, 202n13; and Nabokov, 129, 133–36, 227n52, 227n56. *See also* Aikhenvald-Tatarinov Circle; modernism; Russian Poets Club; *specific poets and poems*
pogroms, 10
political diversity, 63–64
population numbers (of Russians in Berlin), 3, 5, 195n1
Prague, 8
primitivism, 99, 102, 106, 108. *See also* avant-garde art
propaganda, 14, 30, 75, 108
"Prophet" (Pushkin), 139
Proust, 117
publishing, 9, 15, 23, 31, 47, 68–70, 74, 76, 78, 202n6, 213n23
Puni, Ivan, 14
Pushkin, Alexander, 36, 56, 58, 93, 105–9, 112–13, 115, 129, 139, 147, 177, 218n10. *See also specific works*

queer (as a term), 158
queer life, 9–10, 18–19, 22, 148–51, 154, 155, 156–59, 164–75, 234n11, 234nn8–9. *See also* cultural diversity; heteronormativity; homophobia; Lourié, Vera; Nabokov, Sergey
queer theory, 92, 96–97. *See also* fabulous dissent

racism, 217n83
radical coexistence, 19
Radical History Review, 151
Raeff, Marc, 4, 101

Rand, Ayn, 176
Rasputin, 95
The Real Life of Sebastian Knight (Nabokov), 236n31
"Recalcitrance" (Vishniac), 154, 155, 156
"Recruiting" (Nabokov), 130
Red Berlin, 49–51
Reisner, Larisa, 17, 21, 65–66
Remizov, Alexey, 200n57
The Return of the Odysseus (Gumilev), 36
Revolution (1905), 13, 63, 105
Revolution (1917): effects of the, 5, 23, 63, 100; and Moscow, 49–50; and Russia Abroad, 3, 8, 26; views on the, 6, 64, 70, 73, 79, 108
Revolution and the Front (Shklovsky), 213n24
Rimsky-Korsakov, Nikolay, 91–95, 98, 100, 105, 112–13, 115
Romberg, Kristin, 212n12
Ronen, Omry, 213n34
Rozenbaum, Alisa, 176
Rubenstein, Joshua, 71
Rubins, Maria, 197n20
Rubinstein, Ida, 154
Rul', 99–100
Russell, Paul, 237n48
Russia Abroad: and the 1970s, 15; and autobiography, 64, 77; background on, 3–4; and Berlin, 12–14, 16–17, 52, 66; and cultural diversity, 149; cultural figures of, 154; definition of, 4–5; depictions of, 154; and identity, 66; and Paris, 12; and poetry, 27; and public spheres, 78–80; and the Soviet Union, 6, 14; and two literatures, 5–7, 196nn14–15
Russian (as a descriptor), 14, 101, 176
"Russian Artists' Ball" (photograph), 9–10
Russian Berlin, 1921–1923 (volume of letters), 18
"Russian Berlin" (*Ulk*), 15, 16, 17
The Russian Book (Yashchenko), 9
Russian civil war, 8, 27, 63, 108
Russian Formalists, 146

Russian Literature in Exile (Struve), 6
Russian Poets Club, 22, 117, 120, 177
Russians and Germans (art show), 200n57
Russia-out-of-Russia. *See* Russia Abroad
Russo-Japanese War, 93–94, 105

"The Sail" (Lermontov), 36
"Sailing Away" (Pasternak), 31–32, 35–38, 41–42
Savicky, Ivan, 119
Savonarola (de Gabineau), 102–3
Scheidemannizing, 46
Schlögel, Karl, 18, 64, 85, 201n63
scholarship, 5, 8, 18, 22, 26, 63, 97, 154
Schrenk, Walter, 99
Sedykh, Andrey, 121
Segal, Dmitry, 196n15
Seifullina, Lydia, 68–69
Senelick, Laurence, 101
A Sentimental Journey (Shklovsky), 70, 77
Sergay, Timothy, 41
Shakhovskoy, Dmitry, 164–68, 170, 238n55, 238n58
Shestov, Lev, 199n46
Shklovsky, Viktor, 5–7, 21–23, 37–38, 64–80, 84–90, 150, 172–73, 180, 213n24. *See also specific works*
Shvabrin, Stanislav, 119
Six Stories about Easy Endings (Ehrenburg), 70–71
Slavophiles, 82, 215n69
Slobin, Greta, 54
The Snow Maiden (Rimsky-Korsakov), 100
social class, 71–73, 75, 85–87, 89–90, 144
social commentary, 65–66
social conservatism, 4
Social Democratic Party of Germany, 66
Sofia, 8
Somov, Konstantin, 154
Sontag, Susan, 95
Sorokin, Pitirim, 13
"Sorrento Photographs" (Khodasevich), 54

Soviet (as a term), 14, 176
Soviet Union: and the avant-garde, 23, 30, 43, 51–52, 105; and censorship, 73, 154; criticisms of the, 92; and diplomacy with Berlin, 11–12, 17–18, 23, 44; and historiography, 18; and literature, 5–7, 23, 26–27, 70, 72; and monarchy, 105; and the New Economic Policy, 13; as a pariah state, 44; and propaganda, 14, 30
Sovremennye zapiski, 142
spatial patriotism, 71
Speak, Memory (Nabokov), 156, 158–63, 173, 200n54, 222n, 232n109, 237n51
Spengler, Oswald, 40, 83–84
Spivak, Monika, 75, 82
squatters, 7, 79
Stanislavsky, Konstantin, 219n13
statelessness, 8
Stein, Gertrude, 157
stepmother of Russian cities (Berlin), 4–6, 52, 56, 61, 134–35
Stepun, Fyodor, 13, 83
Straumann, Barbara, 232n109
Stravinsky, Igor, 154
Struve, Gleb, 6
Suvchinsky, Pyotr, 102, 104
"Svetovoi liven'" (Tsvetaeva), 203n25

The Tale of Tsar Saltan (Rimsky-Korsakov), 93
Tanner, Allen, 221n51
Tapp, Alyson, 68
Taut, Bruno, 81
Tchaikovsky, 100
Tchelitchew, Pavel, 11, 21, 91–92, 96–97, 99–115, 148–51, 154, 157, 218n7, 221nn51–52. *See also specific works*
temporality, 28–29, 34, 71, 84, 88, 122
Thieme, Hermann, 162, 169–70
"This Is to You" (Mayakovsky), 43–44
threshold art, 94–95
Tiutchev, Fyodor, 124
"Today's Berlin" (Chlenov), 83
Toller, Ernst, 47

Tolstoy, Alexey N., 13, 15, 199n44
Tolstoy, Leo, 147
topography. *See* literary maps
Tortorici, Zeb, 151
"To the Sea" (Pushkin), 36
transitional space, 8, 26, 39
translation, 4, 46, 59, 92, 95, 121–22, 136–37, 159, 237n46. *See also* language
transposition, 97–98, 107, 110, 112, 114–15
Treaty of Brest-Litovsk, 11
Treaty of Rapallo, 11–12, 64
Treaty of Versailles, 11, 47, 87
"Tret'ia stolitsa" (Pilniak), 195n7
trial emigration, 9, 20–62
"Triangle within Circle" (Nabokov), 226n50
Triolet, Elsa, 78–79
Trotsky, 89
The Tsar's Bride (Rimsky-Korsakov), 100
Tsvetaeva, Marina, 6, 9, 17, 154, 157, 203n25
"Two Berlins" (Mayakovsky), 49–51
Tynianov, Yuri, 27–29, 34, 54–55, 77, 173, 202n13

Ulk, 15–17
"Underground" (Khodasevich), 58–59
The Unreal Life of Sergey Nabokov (Russell), 237n48
utilitarianism, 48, 65, 81, 120, 142–45

"Verses to Pushkin" (Korvin-Piotrovsky), 177
Veshch'/Gegenstand/Objet, 9, 23, 24, 26, 43, 81, 206n60
Victory over the Sun (Matiushin and Kruchenykh), 109
Vishniac, Roman, 154, 155, 156, 176
Vishniak, Abram, 9–10
Vkhutemas, 81
Voltaire, 88–89

Wachtel, Michael, 54, 210n116
wandering, 68, 84, 124
Weidle, Vladimir, 56

Weimar Republic, 11–12, 44, 105
Weir, Justin, 94, 145–46
Wesling, Meg, 157
Western civilization (the decay of), 40–41, 82–83
Westernizers, 82
What Is Russian Bolshevism (Shestov), 199n46
What Is to Be Done? (Chernyshevsky), 141–44
White Guard, 10–11, 14, 101
Williams, Raymond, 12, 19
Wilson, Edmund, 162
women, 66, 69, 112–15
"The Workers' Song" (Mayakovsky), 47–49
working class. *See* social class
World of Art, 106

Yashchenko, Alexander, 9
Yearbook of the Intermediate Sexual Types, 159
Yuritsyn, Pyotr, 148–51

Zaitsev, Boris, 203n25
Zalkind, Evgenia, 120–21, 225n33
Zamiatin, Evgeny, 68–69
Zenzinov, Vladimir, 17
Zhar-Ptitsa, 25, 26, 202n6
Zimmer, Dieter, 163, 169–70, 225n40, 237n48
Zoo (Shklovsky), 21–22, 64, 67, 70–80, 87–89, 150, 172, 180, 213n36, 215n62
Zoshchenko, Mikhail, 68–69

www.ingramcontent.com/pod-product-compliance
Lightning Source LLC
Chambersburg PA
CBHW032104230426
43672CB00009B/1635